Essential Strategies for Financial Services Compliance

Essential Strategies for Financial Services Compliance

Annie Mills

John Wiley & Sons, Ltd

Copyright © 2008   John Wiley & Sons Ltd, The Atrium, Southern Gate, Chichester,
West Sussex PO19 8SQ, England

Telephone   (+44) 1243 779777

Email (for orders and customer service enquiries): cs-books@wiley.co.uk
Visit our Home Page on www.wiley.com

Reprinted October 2009, September 2010, April 2011

Other Wiley Editorial Offices

John Wiley & Sons Inc., 111 River Street, Hoboken, NJ 07030, USA

Jossey-Bass, 989 Market Street, San Francisco, CA 94103-1741, USA

Wiley-VCH Verlag GmbH, Boschstr. 12, D-69469 Weinheim, Germany

John Wiley & Sons Australia Ltd, 42 McDougall Street, Milton, Queensland 4064, Australia

John Wiley & Sons (Asia) Pte Ltd, 2 Clementi Loop #02-01, Jin Xing Distripark, Singapore 129809

John Wiley & Sons Canada Ltd, 6045 Freemont Blvd. Mississauga, Ontario, L5R 4J3, Canada

Wiley also publishes its books in a variety of electronic formats. Some content that appears in print may not be available in electronic books.

Library of Congress Cataloging in Publication Data

Mills, Annie.
   Essential strategies for financial services compliance / Annie Mills.
     p. cm.
   Includes bibliographical references and index.
   ISBN 978-0-470-51904-2 (cloth : alk. paper)
   1. Financial services industry—Law and legislation—Great Britain.   2. Corporate governance—Law and legislation—Great Britain.   3. Ethics and compliance officers—Great Britain—Handbooks, manuals, etc. I. Title.
   KD1715.M55 2008
   346.41′082—dc22

                       2008019030

British Library Cataloguing in Publication Data

A catalogue record for this book is available from the British Library

ISBN 978-0-470-51904-2 (H/B)

Typeset in 10/12pt Times by Integra Software Services Pvt. Ltd, Pondicherry, India
Printed and bound in Great Britain by CPI Antony Rowe, Chippenham, Wiltshire

To my mother, Nicholas, Krista, Luke, Jenny,
Georgie, Sally and David

Contents

Acknowledgements   xi

List of Abbreviations   xiii

Preface (Or, How Not to be an Execution Officer)   xix

Foreword   xxiii

PART I   COMMENTARY AND CONTEXT   1

1   The UK Regulatory Environment   3
         1.1   Regulation in the UK   3
         1.2   Different regulatory regimes in the UK   5
         1.3   The FSMA regime for investment business   5
         1.4   The UK's anti-money laundering regime   11
         1.5   The UK's takeover regime   12
         1.6   Other UK regulatory regimes   13

2   The Compliance Function   15
         2.1   Compliance as a concept   16
                2.1.1   What is Compliance?   16
                2.1.2   Who is responsible for Compliance?   18
                2.1.3   Different Compliance models   20
         2.2   The Compliance Officer   21
                2.2.1   Key responsibilities of the Compliance Officer   21
                2.2.2   What are the characteristics of a good
                        Compliance Officer?   22
         2.3   Compliance: good and bad   24
                2.3.1   What are the characteristics of a good Compliance regime?   24
                2.3.2   What are the characteristics of a bad Compliance regime?   28
                2.3.3   Danger signals   29
         2.4   The argument for Compliance   30
                2.4.1   What are the benefits of Compliance, regulation and the
                        Compliance Officer?   30
                2.4.2   What are the costs of Compliance?   37
         2.5   Compliance as a profession   38

3	**The Compliance Contract**	**41**
	3.1 The Compliance Mission Statement	42
	3.2 The Compliance Charter	43
	3.2.1 Contents of a Compliance Charter	43
4	**Mapping Your Compliance Universe**	**49**
5	**Mapping Your Corporate Universe**	**53**
	5.1 Operating entities	53
	5.2 Business units	56
	5.3 External Service Providers	60
6	**Regulators and Other Industry Bodies**	**63**
	6.1 Exchanges	64
	6.2 Clearing houses	70
7	**The Legislative Environment and Rules Mapping**	**71**
	7.1 Rules mapping	73
	7.2 Detailed rules mapping for your own firm	73
	7.3 Rules mapping for an overseas jurisdiction	77
8	**Financial Products, Services and Documentation**	**79**
	8.1 Products and services	79
	8.2 Understanding products and services in context	80
	8.3 Documentation	82
9	**Compliance Outside the Compliance Department**	**83**
	9.1 The Front office	84
	9.2 The Back office and other support functions	84
10	**Key Compliance Department Activities**	**87**
	10.1 Routine activities	87
	10.2 Off Piste Compliance: advisory work	88
	10.2.1 Understanding what it is all about	89
	10.2.2 What are the regulatory implications?	91
	10.2.3 Your plan of attack	96
	10.3 Compliance conundrums	99
	10.4 Dealing with a lack of cooperation	99
11	**Comply or Die – When Things go Wrong**	**103**
	11.1 Someone's watching you	104
	11.2 The FSA has 'hot buttons'	109
	11.3 What the FSA can do to find out more	111
	11.4 What to do if you are being investigated or are subject to disciplinary action	112
	11.5 Consequences of rule breaches and other regulatory misdemeanours	115

APPENDICES

A   Routine Compliance Activities   121
B   Routine Anti-Money Laundering Activities   195
C   Compliance in the Front Office   209
D   Compliance for Senior Management, the Back Office and Other Support
    Departments   253
E   Compliance Conundrums – What Would You Do?   277

The following appendices can be found on the companion website
www.wiley.com/go/millsessential

 1   Regulators and Other Industry Bodies
 2   Exchanges and Clearing Houses
 3   Financial Services Legislation
 4   Anti-Money Laundering and Counter-Terrorist Financing
 5   EU Legislation Relevant to Financial Services in the UK
 6   US Legislation Relevant to Financial Services in the UK
 7   Equities, Bonds and Loans – Summary Differences
 8   Equities
 9   Bonds
10   Loans
11   Derivatives
12   Collective Investment
13   Foreign Exchange
14   The Money Market
15   Islamic Finance
16   Trade Finance
17   Trusts
18   National Savings and Investments
19   Customer Documents
20   Trade Documents
21   Regulatory Documents
22   UK Tax Documents
23   Sample Enforcement Actions
24   Sources and Resources

PART II   COMPLIANCE PERSPECTIVES   **315**

Box 1: Acting on Principle   317
Box 2: ARROW   320
Box 3: Basel II and CRD   321
Box 4: Extradition   323
Box 5: Financial Services Action Plan   324
Box 6: Going Global?   326
Box 7: Industry Guidance   328
Box 8: L&G v. the FSA – Who are the real winners and losers?   330
Box 9: Markets in Financial Instruments Directive   331

Box 10: Money Laundering Statistics   333
Box 11: Prudential Regulation of Capital Adequacy   334
Box 12: The Enforcement Process – Getting on the wrong side of the FSA   336
Box 13: The Lamfalussy Process   337
Box 14: The Laundering Process   339
Box 15: Treating Customers Fairly   340

Index   **343**

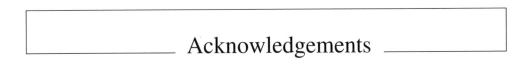

Acknowledgements

First and foremost, my most grateful thanks must go to Gordon McLean whose dedicated and tireless assistance played a major role in the successful completion of this text.

A man should choose a friend who is better than himself.
There are plenty of acquaintances in the world; but very few real friends.
Chinese proverb

I would also like to thank Alexander Davidson, Andrew Hall, Anita Bhaskar, Anthony Saint, Colin Harrison, David Symes, Estia Papadopoulos, Geoff Stoker, Graham Jelf, Ijeoma Aghanya, Isaac Sefchovich, James Tombazis, Jeffery Orenstein, Jenny McCall, Jonathan Eadie, Jonathan Falconer, Kenton Hartwell, Kevin Whyte, Larissa Duguid, Liam Crellin, Máire Gibson, Marcia Jayesuria, Mark Batts, Melanie Troop, Michael Callow, Mike Crabb, Pauline Lawton, Peter Redelinghuys, Seorus Simpson, Simon Gough, Stuart Pallant, Thys Terblanche and Vickie Guerreiro.

List of Abbreviations

The following provides a list of the main abbreviations used in this book

3ML	Third Money Laundering Directive 2005
ABFA	Asset Based Finance Association
ACD	Authorized corporate director
ADR	American Depositary Receipt
AIC	Association of Investment Companies.
AIM	Alternative Investment Market
AML	Anti-Money Laundering
APER	The FSA's Approved Persons Sourcebook
ARA	Asset Recovery Agency
ARROW	Advanced Risk Response Operating Framework
ATCSA	Anti Terrorism, Crime and Security Act
ATS	Alternative Trading System
Basel I	BCBS Capital Accord 1988
Basel II	BCBS Revised Capital Adequacy Framework 2004
BBA	British Bankers Association
BCBS	Basel Committee on Banking Supervision
BCD	Banking Consolidation Directive
BCSB	Banking Code Standard Board
BIMBO	Combination of a management buy-in and buy-out
BIS	Bank for International Settlements
BOE	Bank of England
BVCA	British Venture Capital Association
CA 06	Companies Act 2006
CARD	Consolidated Admissions and Reporting Directive 2001
CASS	The FSA's Client Assets Sourcebook
CC	Competition Commission
CCA	Consumer Credit Act 1974 or 2006
CCARs	Consumer Credit (Advertisements) Regulations 2004
CD	Certificate of deposit
CDS	Credit default swap
CEBS	Committee of European Banking Supervisors
CEO	Chief Executive Officer
CESR	Committee of European Securities Regulators

CFO	Chief Financial Officer
CI	Compliance Institute
CJA	Criminal Justice Act 1993
COAF	The FSA Sourcebook for complaints against the FSA
COBS	The FSA's Conduct of Business Sourcebook
COLL	The FSA's Collective Investment Scheme Sourcebook
COND	The FSA's Threshold Conditions Sourcebook
CP	Commercial paper
CPD	Continuing professional development
CRD	Capital Requirements Directive 2006
CTF	Counter terrorist financing
CTF	Child trust fund
DBERR	Department for Business, Enterprise and Regulatory Reform
DEPP	The FSA's Decision Procedure and Penalties Manual
DGS	Deposit Guarantee Schemes Directive
DIE	Designated Investment Exchange
DISP	The FSA's Dispute Resolution: Complaints Sourcebook
DMD	Distance Marketing Directive
DMO	Debt Management Office
DPA	Data Protection Act 1998
DTR	The FSA's Disclosure and Transparency Rules Sourcebook
EA	Enterprise Act 2002
EAW	European Arrest Warrant
EBRD	European Bank of Reconstruction and Development
ECAs	Export credit agencies
ECD	E Commerce Directive 2000
ECHR	European Convention on Human Rights
ECN	Electronic Communication Network
EEA	European Economic Area
EFP	International Uniform Exchange for Physical Transaction Agreement
EG	The FSA's Enforcement Guide
ERA	Employment Rights Act 1996
ESC	European Securities Committee
ESD	European Savings Tax Directive
ETFs	Exchange traded funds
EU	European Union
Euronext LIFFE	London International Financial Futures Exchange
FAIFs	Fund of alternative investment funds
FATF	Financial Action Taskforce
FCD	Financial Collateral Directive 2002
FCPA	Foreign Corrupt Practices Act 1977
FEOMA	Foreign Exchange and Options Master Agreement
FIA	Freedom of Information Act 2000
FINRA	US Financial Industry Regulatory Authority
FIT	The FSA Sourcebook containing the Fit and Proper Test for Approved Persons
FIU	Financial Intelligence Unit

FOA	Futures and Options Association
FOIA	Freedom of Information Act 2000
FOS	Financial Ombudsman Service
FOTRA	Free Of Tax to Residents Abroad (relating to securities)
FRNs	Floating rate notes
FSA	Financial Services Authority
FSAP	Financial Services Action Plan
FSCS	Financial Services Compensation Scheme
FSMA	Financial Services and Markets Act 2000
FSSC	Financial Services Skills Council
FTSE	Financial Times Stock Exchange
FX	Foreign Exchange
FXJSC	Foreign Exchange Joint Standing Committee
GDR	Global Depositary Receipt
GEN	The FSA's General Provisions Sourcebook
GMRA	Global Master Repurchase Agreement
GMSLA	Global Master Securities Lending Agreement
GP	General partner (in a limited partnership)
GTMA	Grid Trade Master Agreement
HMRC	Her Majesty's Revenue and Customs
HR	Human Resources
HRA	Human Rights Act 2000
ICA	International Compliance Association
ICC	International Chamber of Commerce
ICD	Investor Compensation Directive 1997
ICMA	International Capital Market Association
ICO	Information Commissioner's Office
ICOM	International Currency Options Master Agreement
ICVC	Investment Company with Variable Capital
IEC Act	Investment Exchanges and Clearing Houses Act 2006
IEEPA	International Emergency Economic Powers Act
IFEMA	International Foreign Exchange Master Agreement
IFXCO	International FX and Currency Option Master Agreement
ILSA	Iran and Libya Sanctions Act
IMLPO	Institute of Money Laundering Prevention Officers
IOSCO	International Organisation of Securities Commissions
IPO	Initial public offering
ISA	Individual Savings Account
ISD	Investment Services Directive 1993
ISDA	International Swaps and Derivatives Association
ISMA	International Securities Markets Association (now ICMA)
ISP 98	International Standby Practices issued by the ICC and the Institute of International Banking Law and Practice
IT	Information Technology
JMLSG	Joint Money Laundering Steering Group
KPI	Key Performance Indicator
KYC	Know Your Customer

L/C	Letter of Credit
LBMA	London Bullion Market Association
LIBOR	London Interbank Offered Rate
LMA	Loan Market Association
LME	London Metal Exchange
LP	Limited partner (in a limited partnership arrangement)
LSE	London Stock Exchange
MAD	Market Abuse Directive 2003
MAR	The FSA's Market Conduct Sourcebook
MBIs	Management buy-ins
MBOs	Management buy-outs
MEFISLA	Master Equity and Fixed Interest Stock Lending Agreement
MiFID	Markets in Financial Instruments Directive 2004
ML	The FSA's Money Laundering Sourcebook (no longer in force)
ML Regs	UK Money Laundering Regulations, as updated from time to time
MLA	Mandated Lead Arranger
MLRO	Money Laundering Reporting Officer
MPBR	More Principles Based Regulation
MTF	Multilateral Trading Facility
MTNs	Medium term notes
N2	The date the FSA became the UK's 'single financial services regulator' and the date on which FSMA took effect (1 December 2001)
NASD	US National Association of Securities Dealers (now merged into FINRA)
NASDAQ	National Association of Securities Dealers Automated Quotations
NCIS	National Criminal Intelligence Service (replaced by SOCA)
NDF	Non-Deliverable Forward
NIPs	Non-Investment Products Code
NPL	Non-performing loan
NUR	Non-UCITS retail scheme
OEIC	Open-Ended Investment Company (also known as an ICVC)
OFAC	Office of Foreign Assets Control in the US
OFT	Office of Fair Trading
OSLA	Overseas Securities Lending Agreement
OTC	Over the Counter
PA dealing	Personal Account Dealing
PACE	Police and Criminal Evidence Act 1984
PEP	Personal Equity Plan
PIBS	Permanent interest bearing shares
PIDA	Public Interest Disclosure Act 1998
POCA	Proceeds of Crime Act 2002
PRIN	The FSA's Principles for Businesses Sourcebook
QIS	Qualified Investor Schemes
RAO	Regulatory Activities Order
RDC	Regulatory Decisions Committee
REITs	Real estate investment trusts
RIE	Recognized Investment Exchange

RIPA	Regulation of Investigatory Powers Act 2000
Sarbox	Public Company Accounting Reform and Investor Protection Act of 2002, also known as the Sarbanes – Oxley Act
SFO	Serious Fraud Office
SHCOG	Securities Houses Compliance Officers Group
SIFMA	Securities Industry and Financial Markets Association
SII	Securities and Investment Institute
SMMLG	Sterling Money Markets Liaison Group
SOCA	Serious Organised Crime Agency
SOCAP	Serious Organised Crime and Police Act 2005
SRO	Self-Regulatory Organisation
SUP	The FSA's Supervision Sourcebook
SYSC	The FSA's Senior Management Arrangements, Systems and Controls Sourcebook
TACT	Terrorism Act (2000 or 2006)
T-Bills	Treasury Bills
TBMA	The Bond Market Association (now part of SIFMA)
T&C	Training and Competence
TCF	Treating Customers Fairly
TRUP	Transaction reporting user pack
UCITS	Undertakings for Collective Investment of Transferable Securities
UCP 600	ICC's Uniform Customs and Practices for Documentary Credits
UCPD	Unfair Commercial Practices Directive
UCR rules	ICC uniform rules for documentary collections
UNCITRAL	United Nations Commission on International Trade Law
URC 522	ICC's Uniform Rules for Collections
UTCCRs	Unfair Terms in Consumer Contracts Regulations 1999
VAT	Value Added Tax
VCTs	Venture capital trusts

Preface
(Or, How Not to be an Execution Officer)

Long ago, when the finance world appeared as weird and as unfamiliar to me as life on another planet, I applied for my first job in banking. I didn't know anything about broking or investments and found the interview a little daunting to say the least. Amidst all the confusion, what really stuck in my mind that day was my interviewer – someone with the curious job title of 'Compliance Officer'. In my bewilderment I found that by the time I returned home, with quite uncanny perception many might still say, the personage of 'Compliance Officer' had become in my mind the 'Execution Officer'. And a very sinister sounding person this seemed to be.

Fast forward a couple of months . . .

Amazingly I got the job (I wasn't even quite sure what it was at that first interview!) and started work as a junior on a team of stockbrokers. But some higher power had plans for me and, a few months further down the line the firm was restructured. The broking team that I worked for was 'demerged' and became an entity in its own right. As that was a time when both regulator and regulated had a rather more cavalier attitude towards Compliance than they do today, I, as a financial services fresher, was informed that I was to be the new entity's very own 'Execution Officer'.

By now, I had more of an idea of what Compliance was all about and I must admit that I was not too thrilled to have landed this role – it was not an area that sent even the faintest shiver of excitement down my spine. The idea of having a job that involved learning lots of rules simply to 'get people into trouble' for not obeying the regulator's every command did not seem like my idea of fun. But, being young and somewhat ambitious, I was not immune to the career potential of having what I considered to be such an important sounding job title embossed on my business cards. So I went for it and suddenly . . . I was a real, live Compliance Officer! Or to be correct, I was a very confused and bewildered individual, *masquerading* as a Compliance Officer, who at intervals of scary regularity was required to sign off as such on official documents that were despatched to the regulator of the day, the Securities and Futures Authority.

I was armed with my fantastic new business cards and my shiny new rule book, but what was I actually meant to do with them? I was aware that a rule breach was bad, and I knew that there were many, many rules out there that could be breached. But I was not very familiar with these rules or the legislation that had given rise to them; nor, being a relatively new recruit, did I know my firm very well, and I certainly wasn't very familiar with the finance industry.

I was simply not well placed to apply the few rules I did know to the business activities in which my firm engaged, and I regret to say that I was guilty of making more than a few of the classic mistakes:

- I'd select a rule, jump out from the rulebook behind which I had laid my ambush, and tell some poor, unsuspecting sales person that he was doing it all wrong, and that he'd better stop it pretty sharpish, with all sorts of threats of what would happen if he didn't. I don't think it occurred to me to propose an alternative approach to the one I was banning.
- I spent too much time with my head buried in rule books and regulatory notices, but I did not share my knowledge by providing training. How could I complain about someone doing something he did not know he should not have done because I had not given him proper guidance?
- I told the business what not to do without giving a reason why, or the consequences if they continued to do it.
- I worried more about keeping the regulator happy than I did about practical business solutions to regulatory problems.

Not surprisingly, my efforts were about as welcome as the news that we all had the Black Death! It simply seemed that, at every move I took, I was going to prevent some sort of business initiative or other. I'd be met with the resentful cries of my colleagues that things weren't done that way where their pals worked, or the rule I was quoting simply did not apply to their type of business. I was completely at a loss. Were *they* right? Was *I* right? I didn't know and, equally, I didn't know how to find out.

I felt that someone's head was going to roll; either mine, my colleagues' (or the regulator's!) and I began to be haunted by my old visions of the Execution Officer. In fact that's very much what I must have been perceived as being. I was scary. The whole thing was scary, and what was most scary was that my name was on that all-important dotted line that led straight to the regulator's door.

In desperation I headed to the City Business Library to find a reference book to help me, but unfortunately, when I reached the section that should have been marked 'Handy and User-Friendly Guidebooks for Compliance Officers', the shelf was bare. My kindly and more seasoned Compliance industry colleagues had omitted to provide me with any guidance about what I was meant to be doing or how I was meant to be doing it.

To be fair to them, however, I'm sure they had neither the time nor the energy to consider writing about what they were doing: most of them were too busy fire fighting, like me. Back then, there were far fewer Compliance professionals than there are today, and from the dealings I had with my peers it seemed that I was not the only scary member of the fraternity. Everyone seemed to be faced with much the same problem: Compliance had zero 'street cred!' The profession was new and suffered from an extreme lack of respect. It was often deemed worthy only of staff who had failed in all other areas. Or it was used as a cosy final resting place for elderly grandees of the firm who were gently being eased into retirement.

Many Compliance Officers had inadequate resources and undeveloped Compliance infrastructures. And so many of the new Compliance initiatives that they did take were met with such resentment and resistance that the easiest option was often to scare people into submission by threatening them with the regulator, who, in those days, seemed much less focused on what was good for business than it is today. It's not surprising that we earned the nickname of 'Business Prevention Officers'.

But all that was a few years ago. Today the regulator would never (we hope!) allow that type of worst case scenario in which a totally novice Compliance Officer is left in charge of a regulated firm. Both the Compliance profession and the regulator have moved on since then, and so have I. I soon realised that 'being scary' was not what it was all about. I began to wake up to the fact that . . .

COMPLIANCE OFFICERS ARE GREAT!!!

In fact, far from being their worst nightmare, we deserve to be every financial services practitioner's best friends! This view may not sound particularly familiar but it's true. Think about it. There are massive benefits to be gained from a Compliance function that is operating to its full potential and is properly aligned with the business. Just stop for a second and remind yourself of all the many benefits you bestow on your colleagues. If you need a little help thinking of why you should be the very light of their life, then just turn to Chapter 2, Section 2.4.1 ('What are the Benefits of Compliance, Regulation and the Compliance Officer?') to get some ideas.

Luckily many business managers are also beginning to wake up to all the benefits that a good Compliance department can bring to a firm. Of course the regulator and we Compliance professionals realized this quite some time ago and have done everything we can to move things forward. But there's still a lot of bad reputation to cut through – which is not surprising considering that there are still a few rogue Compliance Officers engaging in all the no-nos that I referred to earlier. The shadow of the dreaded 'Execution Officer' still looms large.

So, how can we ensure that we practise 'successful Compliance', execute the 'Execution Officer' and become the type of asset to the business that any chief executive would be pleased to have on board?

Well, it's no mystery, we simply have to equip ourselves to do the job. What is more complex is the equipping process itself. Unless you are a very unusual person indeed, you were not born with the skills or knowledge that will enable you to apply regulatory requirements and best practice in any meaningful or useful way to the firm you work for. And that's where this text comes in.

I've attempted to provide a straightforward, easy to read, and above all practical guide to the work of a Compliance Officer. This text is not simply about summarizing legislation or regurgitating regulations. If that's what you need, then there are already plenty of books on the shelves. Instead, this text is about what to do once you have your source material and you're not quite sure what to do next. It's the sort of guide that shows you how to roll your sleeves up, get stuck in and start to deliver 'successful Compliance'.

The text covers the basic areas of knowledge and competence with which Compliance Officers should feel comfortable if they are even to dream about gaining the respect of their colleagues by giving constructive advice, steering their firms away from regulatory pitfalls or proposing ways in which processes and procedures can be streamlined.

Scope, Coverage and Readership

Jurisdictional Focus

In this world of globalization and international conglomerates, much of the text is of relevance irrespective of the jurisdiction in which you work: after all, a bank is a bank and a loan is a loan no matter whether you are based in Peru or Kazakhstan. Where more detail is required, the focus is generally on the regulatory system in place in the UK but to a certain extent, detailed rule references are irrelevant: what is important is to get to grips with the issues at the heart of a particular regulatory concept. It does not matter how that concept is translated into rules from one jurisdiction to the next, what does matter is whether we are following the spirit of the requirement, delivering good value to our firms, protecting customer interest and working to maintain the integrity of the financial system. These concepts do not know national boundaries.

Industry Coverage

The scope of the financial services industry is too large to cover every aspect of each sector in one book. Much of the information and most of the guidance contained herein relate to a general regulatory framework that is of relevance to all sectors, but where there is a degree of specialization, the focus is on investment banking activity.

Readership

This text is targeted primarily at Compliance Officers but will also be of relevance to anyone who needs to find their way around some of the key concepts in financial regulation. This includes senior managers who need to get to grips with their Compliance responsibilities, regulators trying to find out how it really works in the firms they supervise, and students who have a regulatory component to their studies.

In short, this is the book I wish I had had on my desk when I first started out in Compliance and I hope you find it useful.

Foreword

Anti-money laundering and counter-terrorist financing programmes operating inside UK financial institutions today must rely upon the skills of their in-house compliance officers. These individuals are the gatekeepers of our financial world, and they must have the tools to allow them to properly discharge their duties and responsibilities. They must also promote an ethical compliance culture that seeks solutions.

Unfortunately, most compliance manuals in the marketplace today are outdated upon publication, and are generally uninspiring, as well as difficult, especially to the novice compliance trainee. This book seeks to demystify the complex world of anti-money laundering compliance by detailing for the reader the procedures and skills one must master, as well as to offer practical business solutions for regulatory problems. It is the reference guide we always wanted to have when the tough questions arose.

The first-person stories demonstrate that the author has clearly been a front-line compliance professional, and her positive approach to coping with the day-to-day tactical problems of compliance should be an example to the readers.

Keep this book handy, for there will be times when, at 4:30 on a Friday afternoon, you require the right answer, on a real-time basis, to a major compliance problem; Depend on it.

Kenneth Rijock
Financial Crime Consultant for World-Check

Part I
Commentary and Context

1
The UK Regulatory Environment

Although many of the concepts and practices described in this text are products of a growing Compliance discipline that does not proceed directly from any regulatory rule or guidance, regulation is undoubtedly the founding spark and ultimate justification of all Compliance activity in the financial services industry. It is almost certainly true that there would be no Compliance function, Compliance Officers or Compliance anything else if there had not first been a regulatory system in which to put them. It therefore follows that to get to grips with Compliance one should have a sound understanding of the regulatory environment that gave rise to it.

This is not to say that Compliance does not justify itself on its own terms, but no business ever volunteered for it; no one wants to be 'fettered' by a framework of 'restrictions'. Financial services regulations are there because the industry has purposes to serve beyond the enrichment of those it employs directly, but has a patchy record when it comes to making itself fit for the pursuit of any other ends. Compliance is there because it is too risky and too complicated to try to navigate the regulatory terrain without it.

Therefore, while I dedicate this text to making arguments for the positives that a business can take from effective Compliance, there is no question that it began and, to a large degree, remains an agent of regulation and can only be properly understood with the regulatory regime, in the UK as elsewhere, as a starting point.

Before looking in detail at the constituent parts of the Compliance Officer's world this chapter fills in the essential background with a brief description of the regulatory environment in the UK. Compliance Officers working in other jurisdictions should know at least as much about their own regulatory environment as that described here for the United Kingdom.

1.1 REGULATION IN THE UK

There is currently a myth in the UK that we have a single financial regulator (the FSA) and a single piece of regulatory legislation (the Financial Services and Markets Act 2000 (FSMA)). If you have bought into this story, then you need to think again. In the UK alone there are numerous regulatory bodies other than the FSA that cover financial services activities – the Pensions Regulator, for example, and the Takeover Panel. There are also a number of laws and regulatory-type bodies that govern the national anti-money laundering effort. And, looking further afield, it's impossible to deny that overseas legislation and regulators affect financial services activity carried on within the UK. (See Box 6, 'Going Global' on page 326 for further explanation on this point.)

Most, but it must be stressed *not* all, of the UK regulatory framework is based on UK and EU law.

Financial services legislation in the UK

UK Law

- UK law can be divided into two main types:
  - statute law – law created through acts of parliament.
  - case law or common law – law established through legal precedent developed over hundreds of years from custom, tradition and cases coming to court.
- Statute law is of most relevance to financial services although common law also has an impact through, for example, contract law in relation to loan agreements.
- A piece of statute law cannot become final until it has been agreed by both Houses of Parliament and has subsequently received Royal Assent from the Queen.
- Acts of Parliament cannot possibly contain every single detail relating to the area they govern. Consequently, secondary or delegated legislation is used to update and amend statute law without having to go through the full legislative process. This secondary legislation, referred to as *statutory instruments* or *regulations*, has the full force of law.

The EU Dimension

- As we are members of the European Union the UK government must implement EU legislation.
- The main way in which EU law impacts UK regulation is through the implementation of the directives and regulations issued as part of the EU's Financial Services Action Plan (see Box 5 on page 324) and the Lamfalussy Process (see Box 13 on page 337).
- Directives and regulations are pieces of EU legislation that are binding on its member states[1] and on non-member states within the European Economic Area (EEA).[2] Directives allow national governments certain flexibility in terms of how the end result is achieved and need to be transposed into the law of each member state (further details of key financial services directives are available in Appendix 5) whereas regulations do not require such transposition and thus apply directly to individual member states without being separately implemented in each country.
- EU law is aimed at harmonizing standards across the EEA in order to support the single market objective and the relevant directives and regulations apply across the EEA in the same way that they apply to the UK, although the extent to which they have really been implemented in letter and spirit across each member state is a matter of debate.

---

[1] At the time of writing there are 27 EU member states: Austria, Belgium, Bulgaria, Cyprus, the Czech Republic, Denmark, Estonia, Finland, France, Germany, Greece, Hungary, Ireland, Italy, Latvia, Lithuania, Luxemburg, Malta, the Netherlands, Poland, Portugal, Romania, Slovakia, Slovenia, Spain, Sweden and the UK.

[2] At the time of writing these are Norway, Iceland and Liechtenstein.

Overseas Legislation

- Some pieces of legislation enacted in other jurisdictions are applied on an extraterritorial basis.
- For the financial services industry, the main pieces of relevant legislation falling into this category come from the US – see Appendix 6.

Sitting underneath and alongside the legislation are the requirements that stem from sets of rules, guidelines and industry best practice that underpin the law.

1.2   DIFFERENT REGULATORY REGIMES IN THE UK

It is possible to group pieces of legislation, sets of requirements, etc., together into various subject areas and thus the UK regulatory framework can be divided into various distinct areas (although there is a certain degree of overlap). These include

- the FSMA regime for investment business;
- the anti-money laundering regime; and
- the takeover regime.

The key features of these are described below.

1.3   THE FSMA REGIME FOR INVESTMENT BUSINESS

The Financial Services and Markets Act 2000 (FSMA) came into effect on 30 November 2001, a date also referred to as N2 (more detailed guidance about the contents of FSMA is set out in Appendix 3). Under FSMA, the FSA (see Appendix 1) was established as the UK's regulator for a large proportion of financial services activity (see below), replacing the nine existing regulators that were previously responsible for supervising the UK's financial markets.

What does the FSA regulate?

FSMA and FSA requirements apply to 'specified activities' that are undertaken in relation to 'specified investments' (as defined by the Regulated Activities Order (RAO) – see Appendix 1) made under FSMA.

Examples of specified activities

- Dealing
- Managing investments
- Safeguarding and administering investments
- Establishing a collective investment scheme.

(Continued)

Examples of Specified Investments

- Shares
- Bonds
- Futures
- Options
- Contracts for differences
- Units in collective investment schemes.
  The term 'investment business' is commonly used to refer to the carrying out of specified activities in relation to specified investments.

Examples of Activities and Financial Instruments not Specified by the FSA

- Arranging credit
- Cash
- Premium bonds
- Spot FX
- Commodity derivative transactions undertaken for commercial rather than investment purposes
- Letters of credit
- Bills of exchange
- Promissory notes.

There is a further distinction between designated and non-designated investment business (see table on page 8).

Of course the above is summary information only. Full information is available in the RAO, which is an extremely useful document when determining what is and is not subject to FSA rules. This is not always clear cut, and there can be a few surprises. I will never forget the look of total astonishment on an overseas colleague's face when I told her that the FSA regulated funeral plans. We should not, get carried away in terms of the FSA's extensive reach though, as one of my non-Compliance friends did. She announced to me, perplexed that the FSA seemed to be involved in all sorts of things that you would not have expected – like milk production! My friend was thinking of the *other* FSA – the Food Standards Agency!

The merging of the regulators was implemented in order to reflect the fact that there is no longer a clear enough distinction between different types of firm to merit different types of regulator – banks are also providing stockbroking services, etc. Additionally, there was a degree of overlap in the responsibilities of some regulators, whereas other activities risked falling between two supervision regimes or not being reviewed at all; and there was always the possibility that inadequate information-sharing between regulators would contribute to a financial failing. Finally, there was a perception that the previous regime had not been a success (in part because it did give rise to some of the above weaknesses) and there was a desire to draw a line under past failures in order to start afresh.

The FSA is responsible to the Treasury and must also account to a consumer panel and a practitioner panel on the extent to which it is meeting the regulatory objectives that have been set out for it in FSMA. The FSA has translated requirements from FSMA and various EU laws into a comprehensive handbook of rules and guidance covering a wide range of topics including

- listings;
- conduct of business;
- enforcement;
- collective investment;
- financial resources; and
- senior management controls.

Both FSMA and the FSA Handbook must be amended on an ongoing basis to take account of new requirements stemming from EU law. The key EU legislative initiatives that are of relevance to financial services are the Financial Services Action Plan (see Box 5 on page 324) and the Lamfalussy Process (see Box 13 on page 337). The piece of EU legislation that has the greatest impact on the FSA Handbook is probably the Markets in Financial Instruments Directive (MiFID) (see Appendix 5 and Box 9 on page 331), so it is unfortunate that its scope does not entirely tally with that of the FSA/FSMA and gives rise to a situation in which different rules apply, dependent on whether an activity is regulated only under FSMA, or is also covered by MiFID. The table on page 8 gives further details on this.

Some of the other key elements of the FSMA regime are described below.

- The FSA must comply with the four statutory objectives imposed on it under FSMA (see Appendix 3).
- It is an offence to conduct a regulated activity in the UK unless you are authorized under FSMA or exempt from its requirements. This is known as 'the General Prohibition'.
- There are various ways of gaining authorization:

  – obtaining permission to carry out regulated activities under part IV of FSMA;
  – exercising passporting rights under a relevant EU directive (EEA Passport rights); or
  – exercising rights under the Treaty of Rome (Treaty rights).

- There are various categories of person subject to regulation:

  – regulated firms;
  – individuals working for regulated firms;
  – recognized professional bodies;
  – exchanges and clearing houses; and
  – collective investment schemes.

- Although FSMA requirements have been translated into the FSA's Handbook of Rules and Guidance, the FSA is now adopting a much more principles-based approach to regulation and the industry has yet to decide whether this is a good thing or not – see Box 1 on page 317 ('Acting on Principle').
- Although all business specified in the RAO is subject to FSA regulation, the FSA has further 'designated' certain types of investments and investment business to which it applies particular sets of rules, such as those in the Training and Competence and Conduct of Business Sourcebooks. Further detail is available in the table on page 8.
- The FSA is the competent authority for UK stock exchange listings.
- The FSA does not directly regulate takeovers and mergers, although it does endorse the Takeover Code and imposes a number of requirements that are relevant in such situations.

The FSA is often heavily criticized both by the Compliance fraternity and by our colleagues in other areas of finance, but much as it can be cathartic after a long day in the office to denigrate the regulator, there is also much to be said for giving credit where credit is due. Compared with a number of comparable overseas regulatory bodies, believe me, the FSA is not that bad. Some of its plus points are that it

- has a transparent and active enforcement process;
- consults widely on new requirements and has even been known to take account of the responses to these consultations when formulating new regulation;
- provides substantial guidance on its rules;
- has a comprehensive website for regulated firms;
- offers important consumer guidance in the form of brochures and leaflets, as well as via the dedicated sections of its website – Money Made Clear;
- has clear statutory and regulatory objectives which provide a valuable yardstick for assessing its performance and setting its priorities;
- cooperates with many other regulators in the UK and internationally, and does its best to protect us from the worst excesses of the EU regulatory machine;
- does not change its rules on a whim, and on an almost daily basis, as some regulators are wont to do;
- is manifestly accountable in its activities through a number of mechanisms including

  - the office of fair trading (which can scrutinize FSA rules and practices);
  - the financial services and Markets Tribunal;
  - the consumer panel;
  - the practitioner panel; and
  - the complaints commissioner.

And, in any case, London continues as a major financial centre with no prospect on the horizon of that changing. It would seem churlish to refuse the FSA at least some small part of the credit for establishing and maintaining a regulatory environment in which firms are happy to do business.

Types of business under FSMA/MiFID

Type	Source	Explanation
Investment services and activities	The FSA and MiFID	Services relating to financial instruments, including
		<ul><li>executing client orders;</li><li>operating an MTF;</li><li>portfolio management;</li><li>dealing on own account;</li><li>making a personal recommendation.</li></ul>

Financial instrument	The FSA and MiFID	<ul><li>Transferable securities, e.g. shares and bonds.</li><li>Money market instruments, e.g. treasury bills, certificates of deposit and commercial paper.</li><li>Units in collective investment undertakings.</li><li>Futures, options, swaps and forward rate agreements on a number of instruments including – securities; – currencies; – interest rates; – financial indices; – commodities that can be physically settled as long as they are traded on a regulated market and/or an MTF; – climatic variables; – freight rates; – telecommunications bandwidth.</li></ul>
Specified investment	RAO	Specified investments are those which have been listed as such in Part III of RAO, and to which FSMA requirements apply.
Specified activity	RAO	Specified activities are those which have been listed as such in Part II of RAO, and to which FSMA requirements apply.
Designated investment	The FSA	<ul><li>Designated investments are a subset of specified investments to which detailed FSA requirements apply, such as those in COBS and TC.</li><li>Examples of investments 'Specified' under RAO but not 'Designated' by the FSA include Lloyd's syndicate membership, rights under a funeral plan contract, deposits and electronic money, and certain mortgage contracts.</li><li>A number of designated investments are not defined as 'financial instruments' under MiFID.</li></ul>
Designated investment business	The FSA	<ul><li>Includes the following, where they are carried on by way of business: – dealing in investments as principal; – dealing in investments as agent; – arranging deals in designated investments; – managing designated investments; – operating an MTF; – safeguarding and administering designated investments;</li></ul>

(Continued)

Type	Source	Explanation
		– safeguarding and administering designated investments; – establishing, operating or winding up a collective investment scheme; – providing advice on designated investments; • Certain FSA rules (such as those in TC) are applicable to designated investment business whereas they do not apply to other activities. • Examples of investment activities 'specified' under RAO but not 'designated' by the FSA include accepting deposits, advising on Lloyd's syndicate participation and mortgage lending.
MiFID business	MiFID and the FSA	Investment services and activities, and where relevant ancillary services, carried on by a MiFID investment firm.
Non-MiFID business		Designated investment business that is not within the MiFID definition of investment services and activities. Examples include • Lloyd's business; • some investment research; • sports and leisure spread betting; • operators of collective investment schemes; • provision of insurance; • managers of investment trusts; and • provision of occupational pension scheme services, such as fund management.
Ancillary services	MiFID and the FSA	Includes • safekeeping and administration of financial instruments belonging to clients; • corporate finance advice; • providing margin trading services; • investment research; • underwriting services.
MiFID investment firm	MiFID and the FSA	An investment firm, or credit institution providing investment services, to which MiFID applies, and a firm providing services under Article 5(3) of UCITS (see Appendix 5).

| Equivalent business of a third country investment firm | MiFID and the FSA | The business of an investment firm operating in the UK but based in a non-EEA state, that would be MiFID business if the firm were a MiFID investment firm. |
| Common platform firm | The FSA | A firm to which both MiFID and CRD (the Capital Requirements Directive) apply. |

1.4   THE UK's ANTI-MONEY LAUNDERING REGIME

Money laundering is the process by which criminals hide the illicit origins of their cash or other assets (see Box 14 on page 339, 'The Laundering Process') and integrate them into the legitimate financial system. The term was traditionally used in relation to the spoils of drug trafficking but it now covers the proceeds of any sort of criminal activity, from petty crime and 'minor' tax fiddles to full-scale organized crime such as people smuggling and VAT fraud.

Another major area that comes under the banner of money laundering is terrorist financing which takes place when terrorists use the financial markets to

- carry on otherwise legitimate businesses of which the profits will be used to promote terrorism;
- finance bogus charities used to promote terrorist beliefs and causes;
- buy arms; and
- fund terrorist action.

Given the massive scale of the problem (some statistics are provided on page 333) how realistic is it to believe that not a single dirty dollar has ever passed through your firm? It is no wonder that one of the FSA's four statutory objectives is to reduce financial crime and that a range of other regulatory organizations also make this a priority. At the very highest level, the approach to anti-money laundering and counter-terrorist financing controls is set by the United Nations, which is behind a number of international conventions in this area, such as the 1988 Vienna Convention Against Drug Trafficking and the UN Convention for the Suppression of Terrorist Financing. The EU has also been an enthusiastic legislator against money laundering with its latest major initiative being the Third Money Laundering Directive (see Appendix 5).

Based to a large extent on the above, the UK has implemented its own anti-money laundering and counter-terrorist financing legislation and, in addition, we have a copious amount of industry guidance, some of which is voluntary, such as that from the Basel Committee of Banking Supervision, and some of which has quasi-regulatory status. The most significant entry in the latter category is the JMLSG Guidance Notes (see Appendix 1). These notes provide comprehensive 'guidance' on two levels:

- The internal anti-money laundering infrastructure that financial services firms should implement (staff training, identifying and reporting suspicions of money laundering etc).
- The actual 'know your customer/KYC' vetting that firms should carry out in respect of particular types of customer and transaction (see Appendix B for further information).

Although the JMLSG Guidance Notes are just what they say on the box – *guidance* – you would be rather foolish to ignore them without a good reason. This is because the FSA has stated very clearly that it regards observance of the JMLSG Guidance Notes as an indicator that a firm complies with the FSA's anti-money laundering requirements, and non-observance as an indicator of the opposite.[3] You should also be aware that the anti-money laundering requirements apply much more broadly than the FSMA regime, so you must comply with requirements in this area whether or not you are undertaking investment business as defined by the FSA. (Indeed, legislation also applies to a number of other sectors, including casinos, estate agents and dealers in high-value items.)

With the weight of this heavy legislative regime hanging over us if we get things wrong, Compliance Officers can truly be classed as the government's unpaid foot soldiers in the fight against global crime and terrorism, leading some to complain that if they had wanted to work in law enforcement they would have chosen a different career. They argue that, given the importance of controls in this area, it is not appropriate for so much responsibility to be placed on the private sector, which has at least a short-term vested interest in not identifying any money laundering at all.

Think of the massive costs incurred by firms implementing anti-money laundering regimes of the type envisaged by today's regulations – it is similar to being charged a tax for the privilege of being able to help the government to catch criminals, and we have to question just how effective the controls we are being asked to implement really are: for instance, it is hard to believe that an international syndicate of criminals who have almost unlimited funds and resources at their disposal will allow themselves to be tripped up by not being able to produce a phone bill. Indeed such is the sophistication of these organizations that they will probably employ lawyers who know the KYC rules as well as the firm itself, and will present themselves with a pristine set of KYC documents with which no fault can be found.

And despite the fact that we make all this effort and try to get things right we cannot even guarantee that this is enough: consider the case of Mr Judge for example, the poor MLRO who did everything by the book but still found himself being taken to court.

Regardless of the criticisms of the regime, however, the authorities argue that it is logical for financial services firms to take the lead in identifying suspicious activity as they know their customers and their normal patterns of activity, whereas the police do not. This, admittedly, is true and it does not look like we will be relieved of our front line duties in this area anytime soon.

1.5   THE UK's TAKEOVER REGIME

UK takeovers and mergers are regulated by the Panel on Takeovers and Mergers (see Appendix 1) which was established in 1968. Its key requirements are set out in the City Code on Takeovers and Mergers ('the Takeover Code'). Although the Code is not a piece of legislation, statutory weight is lent to the regime by means of

- the Companies Act 2006, part 28;
- the EU Takeover Directive; and
- endorsement by the FSA.

---

[3] See *The FSA Handbook* – SYSC 3.2.6E.

Even though the Takeover Panel is entirely separate from the FSA, the two regulators collaborate where necessary, especially in relation to market abuse, which is one of the main areas where there is likely to be an overlap in respect of their fields of responsibility.

Competition is another matter that must be considered at the time of a takeover or merger, and this area is governed by the Enterprise Act 2002 and a number of authorities including

- the Competition Commission;
- the Office of Fair Trading;
- the Competition Appeal Tribunal; and
- the EU's Directorate General for Competition.

1.6   OTHER UK REGULATORY REGIMES

In addition to the three regimes summarized above, other regulatory frameworks are in place for different aspects of the UK financial services industry, including those relating to

- consumer credit and hire purchase;
- personal and business banking; and
- company pensions.

2
The Compliance Function

Compliance is still a young profession: the odds are that if you tell the person sitting next to you at a dinner party that you are a Compliance Officer he or she will give you a blank look. But it is not just the general public that feels uncertain of what Compliance is all about. Many people reading this text will be 'Compliance Officers' working in a 'Compliance department', and will be conscious that these are components of a larger and more abstract phenomenon called the 'Compliance function', which is somehow an agent and sponsor of a 'Compliance culture'. As such, you will know that all of these terms are in wide circulation, particularly in regulatory circles, but can be extremely slippery when you try to define them. There is no universally accepted definition of the term 'Compliance Officer', nor is there a definitive list of what a Compliance Officer does or does not do, or of what the Compliance function comprises. And 'Compliance culture' is at once transparently obvious as an idea and frustratingly woolly as a practical proposition.

This chapter aims to establish satisfactory working definitions of all of these terms, but also attempts to untangle them. It is split into five sections, which give guidance on the main aspects of the Compliance Officer's world and explore various elements of Compliance as a financial services discipline. What I hope will emerge from these is a feeling for the underlying concept that all of our professional terminology overlays: the answer to the question 'What is compliance and why is it there?'.

The areas covered are as follows:

2.1 Compliance as a concept.
- What is Compliance?
- Who is responsible for Compliance?
- Different Compliance models.

2.2 The Compliance Officer
- Key tasks of the Compliance Officer.
- What are the characteristics of a good Compliance Officer?

2.3 Compliance good and bad
- What does a good Compliance function look like?
- What does a bad Compliance function look like?
- Danger signals.

2.4 The argument for Compliance
- What are the benefits of Compliance, regulation and the Compliance Officer?
- The costs of Compliance.

2.5 Compliance as a profession.

2.1   COMPLIANCE AS A CONCEPT

2.1.1   What Is Compliance?

To get to grips with the world of Compliance we have to start with a clear vision of what Compliance is and the part it plays in the financial services industry. As we saw above, our regulators have framed the 'what is Compliance?' question within a number of terms and concepts, which should be familiar and comprehensible to us in themselves. However, for want of a concrete definition, we can also distil these terms to arrive at a concept of what Compliance is 'in its essence', but in order to do this we need to explore the key regulatory concepts that 'comprise' Compliance:

- Compliance risk;
- The Compliance function;
- The Compliance department;
- The Compliance Officer;
- Compliance culture.

If you look up the word 'Compliance' in any standard dictionary you are unlikely to find a definition that is of any significance in the context of financial services. In all likelihood you will find something along the lines of 'obedience to a rule', which is certainly the first thing that people tend to grasp when they think of Compliance as a form of in-house police force. But when looking at various national and international guidelines which lay down a Compliance 'standard' of one form or another, we find them describing something more akin to a company-wide framework of procedures and controls and an aspect of business culture. Perhaps the most representative definition is from the Basel Committee on Banking Supervision (see Appendix 1), which in 2005 described Compliance risk as

> the risk of legal or regulatory sanctions, material financial loss, or loss to reputation a
> bank may suffer as a result of its failure to comply with laws, regulations, rules, related
> self-regulatory organization standards, and codes of conduct applicable to its banking
> activities (together, 'compliance laws, rules and standards').

From this undoubtedly considered and authoritative pronouncement we can infer, in a somewhat roundabout way, that the business of 'Compliance', as a function, office or profession, is to find ways of identifying, managing and mitigating these 'Compliance risks'. It must clearly be more than a matter of obedience, for banks and other financial firms do not earn their living merely by following rules: they must somehow find a *modus vivendi* between the business of making money and the rules and regulations that restrict or channel their means of doing so. The Compliance function must be instrumental in bridging these two seemingly incompatible concepts.

The Compliance department cannot by itself bridge this gap: it is a matter for the firm's culture and organization as a whole. This is where the concepts of the Compliance function and Compliance culture become important, in describing a firm's overall regulatory control framework and the means by which this has been infused into its philosophy and style, as opposed to subsisting in one (Compliance) department alone.

As noted above, there is no universally accepted definition of the term 'Compliance function' or 'Compliance culture', but various bodies consider it important enough as a concept to comment on what it means and what it entails, and I strongly recommend that you read the documents noted below.

Basel Committee on Banking Supervision (see Appendix 1)

Report issued in April 2005 on Compliance and the Compliance Function in Banks.[1] The report provides a definition of Compliance risk (as used above) and lists 10 principles which it recommends should be adhered to for the successful operation of a firm's Compliance function.

International Organization of Securities Commissions (IOSCO) (see Appendix 1)

Report issued in March 2006 on the Compliance Function at Market Intermediaries. The report recommends 8 topics to consider when assessing the adequacy of the Compliance function (although one of these relates to regulators rather than to regulated firms).

The European Union's Market in Financial Instruments Implementing Directive (see Appendix 5)

Article 6 stipulates that investment firms must establish and maintain a Compliance function. It also sets out the responsibilities of the Compliance function and describes certain conditions that must be satisfied to enable the Compliance function to carry out its duties satisfactorily.

The UK's Regulator – the Financial Services Authority (the FSA) (see Appendix 1)

- Two sections of the FSA *Handbook* provide rules and guidance on the Compliance function within UK firms:
  - The Senior Management Arrangements, Systems and Controls Manual (sections 3.2.6–3.2.9 and 6); and
  - The Supervision Manual, (sections 10.7.8–10.7.13 cover the Compliance oversight function and sections 10.7.13–10.7.16 cover the money laundering reporting function).

- The FSA also published a 'Dear CEO' letter in July 2007 called 'Managing Compliance risk in major investment banks – good practices' that gives clear guidelines about how the regulator expects us to organize our compliance activities.

Frustratingly for the Compliance Officer and other members of the Compliance department, the regulators and other industry bodies seem less concerned with defining or even referring

---

[1] Although the paper refers specifically to banks it is made clear that the issues it raises are relevant to any other financial services entity.

to our specific roles. Much less guidance is available on our job specification than on what the Compliance function represents as a whole, even though we are surely in some way vital components of that function. Neither 'Compliance Officer' nor 'Compliance department' has an official, internationally accepted definition. It is generally agreed, however, that the term 'Compliance department' refers to the team that is charged with implementing, operating and championing the Compliance function on a day-to-day basis (note therefore that the terms 'Compliance function' and 'Compliance department' are *not* synonymous). And the Compliance Officer is the person in charge of the Compliance department.

As for the initial question What is compliance?, if we take all of the above and draw it together we can we can devise a working definition that is at least more useful than that found in the dictionary:

> *In a financial services firm, Compliance is the function of identifying*
> *relevant legislative, regulatory and best practice requirements and*
> *implementing the necessary arrangements, systems and controls so as to*
> *facilitate adherence to these obligations.*

Even more succinctly put, we could also say that:

> *Compliance Officers are there to help stop things going wrong from a*
> *regulatory perspective, and to help to deal with them if they do.*

These definitions are flexible enough for each firm to be able to decide what such 'relevant requirements' are, and how to handle them; but they are precise enough to give us a reasonable understanding of what Compliance is there to achieve. In the remainder of this text we shall use these two definitions as the basis for expanding on the operation of Compliance within the financial services firm.

2.1.2   Who Is Responsible for Compliance?

Now we have considered the meaning of the term 'Compliance' we need to spend a little time considering who is responsible for what; a question to which there is no ready answer. If the IT department is responsible for IT and the HR department is responsible for HR, then surely the Compliance department, or more specifically the Compliance Officer, is responsible for Compliance? Life is not so simple, however, as the international consensus among regulatory bodies seems to be that *senior management* is responsible for Compliance. The following sample quotes make this perfectly clear:

Source	What it says
The FSA Principles of Good Regulation	'A firm's *senior management* is responsible for . . . ensuring that its business complies with regulatory requirements.'
The FSA's Enforcement Guide 8.2	'The FSA will proceed on the basis that a firm (together with its directors and *senior management*) is primarily responsible for ensuring the firm conducts its business in compliance with the Act[2] and the [FSA] Principles and the rules.'

---

[2]   Reference to the Financial Services and Markets Act 2000 – see Appendix 3.

IOSCO report on the Compliance function at market intermediaries, March 2006	'It is the role of *senior management* to establish and maintain a Compliance function, and Compliance policies and procedures designed to achieve compliance with securities regulatory requirements.'
Quote from Andrew Procter, head of FSA enforcement, 15/12/04	'. . . we will have to take very direct action against the senior management who are responsible for the failure to put in place a proper compliance culture . . .'
Basel Committee on Banking Supervision paper on Compliance and the Compliance function in Banks, April 2005	'The bank's *senior management* is responsible for establishing and communicating a Compliance policy, for ensuring that it is observed, and for reporting to the board of directors on the management of the bank's Compliance risk.'

Nowhere does it say that the Compliance Officer or the Compliance department are responsible for Compliance and you will in fact be hard pressed to find any official regulatory references to anyone called the Compliance Officer. So where does that leave us? It is somewhat paradoxical that so ill-defined a role should have given rise to such a well-populated profession as that which now comprises the Compliance industry. The reasons for this are twofold:

1. In the context of the FSA, for example, guidance on what Compliance comprises is deceptively simple as there is only a requirement to oversee three areas of the rulebook (Conduct of Business, Client Assets and Collective Investment Schemes) or four if you include anti-money laundering. This is easier said than done, as the legislation and regulation covering each of these areas is extremely lengthy and complex and you cannot apply it without having knowledge and experience of a whole host of matters, other than what a particular rule says.
2. Most firms will also add to the above FSA shortlist just about every other area of the rulebook. The majority of senior managers you will meet seem to have one particular character trait in common, and that is a congenital hatred of handling regulatory matters. This means that senior management is generally desperate to delegate as much practical responsibility as possible for anything that seems even vaguely to relate to Compliance to anyone who will have it, and generally the only person who *will* have it is the Compliance Officer.

(On that front, let us be truly grateful for the fact that senior management has been so good at exercising its collective delegation muscle when it comes to Compliance matters; after all, that is what has given birth to our profession and kept us in gainful employment for the last few years!)

So the model that has been provided by the FSA and its cohorts is based on the premise that senior management is responsible for Compliance, whereas the model that we actually find across most of the industry is that wholesale delegation has taken place: even though senior management (should) know that ultimately it carries the Compliance can, responsibility for day-to-day Compliance activities has been delegated to the Compliance department. As ever, when there are two distinct lines of responsibility for a single area there is some jockeying for position and a working balance needs to be set as to who does what in practice.

It may sometimes seem like a handy excuse to feel that, ultimately, matters can be 'palmed off' on senior management and that you do not need to go into battle with them if they make a bad regulatory decision, as it is all their responsibility in any case. But this is a double-edged sword. If management become frustrated with Compliance arrangements and complain that things are taking too long and are too cumbersome, you don't want them to override your decisions or bypass you altogether.

If your firm starts moving in that direction then you probably want to rein things back sharply, unless you have total confidence in the regulatory decision-making capabilities of your senior management . . . which you probably do not. And even if you did give senior management responsibility for day-to-day Compliance decision making in the areas in which their frustrations lie (KYC perhaps, or financial promotions approvals) you would probably find that they would want to delegate it back to you as quickly as they could. Once you have gone through the process of spelling out to them what their liabilities are if they make a wrong decision, and making them aware of all the detailed points they would have to check to be sure they were getting it right (JMLSG Guidance Notes, COBS etc.), they would quickly decide that they had much more important things to attend to and bounce all this 'administration' back in your direction. (Note: this absolutely does not mean that you should not examine your processes and try to rectify what is causing the frustration!)

You will probably find that the division of responsibilities between Compliance and senior management works best if it looks something like this:

Compliance Officer	Senior management
• Detailed involvement with day-to-day compliance activities (see Chapter 10 and Appendices A and B). • Owner of relationship with regulators. • Development of the firm's regulatory infrastructure. • Provision of regulatory advice and guidance.	• Ensuring that the Compliance culture is embedded into corporate infrastructure from the highest levels down. • Little hands-on involvement with the implementation of the Compliance infrastructure. • Assessing the activities of the Compliance department for adequacy and appropriateness.

You may wish to formalize the arrangement in the Compliance Charter – see Chapter 3.

2.1.3   Different Compliance Models

Quite apart from the division of responsibilities between the Compliance Officer and senior management there is another area of debate as to who does what in the world of Compliance. Broadly speaking, there are two models that can be adopted:

- *Model 1: Centralized* – The Compliance department undertakes the majority of ongoing Compliance tasks – approving gifts and benefits for example, or dealing with complaints.
- *Model 2: Decentralized* – The Compliance department exercises its own delegation muscle and gives much of the day-to-day responsibility for regulatory matters to the business. Compliance staff are then responsible for monitoring what the business has done, assessing its effectiveness and initiating remediation.

Neither of these models is 'correct' – you just have to work out what will work best for your firm. To help you to think about this, the characteristics of each model are explored below.

Centralized Model	Decentralized Model
Can lead to more regular confrontation with the business if they are constantly seeking Compliance department approval in areas where you are reluctant to give it.	On the face of it, less trying for the Compliance Officer – you tell the business what in your expert opinion you consider necessary but leave the business to decide whether they comply with what you say or not.
May be considered safer by the Compliance department as the Compliance Officer retains greater control over day-to-day operations.	More risky for the Compliance Officer though – is the regulatory judgement of your head of trading, for example, really as sound as your own?
More likely that responsibility for Compliance will be seen as something that rests with the Compliance department.	More likely that each employee will take ownership of Compliance matters within the scope of their own responsibilities and activities.
Important sources of management information are captured 'in real time' by Compliance such as trends in new account opening or the fact that there has recently been a surge in the offering of gifts by a particular department.	Business heads more in touch with the regulatory aspects of their departments. As a result of their regulatory responsibilities they are more likely to know of a questionable new account that someone wants to take on, or the fact that someone else is spending far too much time on personal trading.
Compliance heavily involved in administrative matters. Unless adequate staffing resources are available, this may detract from the department's ability to undertake strategic work.	Compliance is less involved with day-to-day administrative matters so more time is freed up to engage in strategic work on regulatory and corporate developments. Many people find this more interesting than processing administrative Compliance tasks.

More guidance in relation to defining responsibility for Compliance can be found on page 43, the Compliance Charter (Chapter 3).

2.2   THE COMPLIANCE OFFICER

2.2.1   Key Responsibilities of the Compliance Officer

We saw in Section 2.1 that the role of the Compliance Officer is defined to some extent by the type of Compliance model your firm chooses to adopt. Irrespective of the model, there are a number of common responsibilities that all Compliance Officers need to assume to meet our brief to 'stop things going wrong from a regulatory perspective, and to help to deal with them if they do'. These responsibilities are summarized below.

1. Developing a thorough understanding of the firm they work for.
2. Working out which legislative and regulatory requirements apply to their firm, and the impact of these requirements.
3. Determining which best practice standards they wish to apply over and above the basic regulatory and legislative requirements.
4. Determining how, in the context of their own firm, they can apply the requirements and best practice standards they have identified in a way that is workable for both Compliance and the business (indeed the Compliance regime should not only be workable for the business, but should also facilitate its growth and success).

(Continued)

---

5. Documenting the ways in which they intend their firm to achieve Compliance with all the applicable requirements and best practice standards they have identified. This will involve drafting manuals, policies, procedures, monitoring programmes, work plans, crib sheets, newsletters, bulletins, intranet sites, etc. These documents and the infrastructure they represent comprise the Compliance infrastructure.
6. Carrying out training and awareness activities to ensure that all staff are aware of the requirements that apply to them, know what to do in order to comply with them and are aware of the consequences they face if they do not comply.
7. Conducting review work to ensure that the requirements identified are being complied with.
8. Implementing corrective action where instances of non-compliance or other problems that need to be addressed have been identified.
9. Engaging in advisory work to provide guidance to staff on how to comply with relevant requirements in the context of issues and problems that are raised during normal business activities.
10. Keeping on top of regulatory developments and changes within their firm so that they can ensure their policies and procedures remain up to date and their businesses well informed.
11. Managing relations with regulators in order to ensure that both sides are kept up to date on regulatory developments and that there are no unpleasant surprises.
12. Engaging in regulatory reporting to meet specific rule requirements.
13. Identifying and measuring Compliance risks in order to be able to assess the impact and likelihood of a particular risk materializing. Understanding what the implications of the risk are, and how the risk can be addressed.
14. Undertaking management reporting to ensure that senior staff are aware of where the firm currently sits within the regulatory environment.

Further detailed guidance about the day-to-day tasks to which these responsibilities give rise is provided in Chapter 10 and Appendices A and B.

2.2.2 What Are the Characteristics of a Good Compliance Officer?

As well as having your department in optimal shape (this is considered in Section 2.3 below) it is also important that you examine your own characteristics, strengths and weaknesses to see whether you need to raise your personal game in terms of what you bring to the business and how well you can perform the previously mentioned tasks. After all, the business pays for the Compliance Officer so it is only fair that they should get their money's worth. What, then, does a good Compliance Officer look like? What are we to aspire to? It goes without saying that we should be tall and toned with dazzling good looks and a winning smile. But, in addition, if you or I were ever to win the prestigious accolade of 'Best Compliance Officer Who Ever Walked the Earth', then we would probably have many of the following attributes.

Attribute

- Confident – We would not be the sort of person to be intimidated by a 'lout with clout', a person with authority who also has a thuggish mentality and who will try to intimidate and cow us into bending the rules to suit his or her purposes.

- Good at preparing and delivering training – able to put across the Compliance message in an upbeat and easily digestible way that keeps the business's attention rather than making them switch off and not listen to a word we say.
- Analytical.
- Able to communicate with the business at all levels.
- A good knowledge of the business units for which we are responsible so that we are familiar with the people, the plans, the projects, the problems, etc., and are able to adapt our Compliance model to this.
- A good understanding of the whole regulatory universe within which our firms operate – it's not enough simply to know the rules, that is just the starting point; we also have to know where the rules have originated, why they are required, and understand how they affect products, services and the firm itself.
- Able to pay close attention to detail, particularly for reading new rules, monitoring work and investigations.
- Inventive and creative when it comes to working with the rules so that the story does not end with a 'No'. In reality the word 'No' should only ever begin the story – 'No, you can't do that, but let's see how we can change things slightly so that this proposal does tick all the right boxes'.
- Strong enough to say 'No' even when under a lot of pressure to say 'Yes'. Despite the above item, we do very much need to have the word 'No' in our vocabulary and not be afraid to use it. We should not be pressured into saying 'Yes' by egos in the Front Office. (If you do not feel comfortable standing your ground when staff more senior than you are agitating for a 'Yes', then perhaps Compliance is not for you.)
- A good sales and PR person in order to be able to 'sell' the concept of Compliance to the rest of the firm.
- Strong report writing skills so that regulatory matters can be brought to the attention of senior management coherently and succinctly.
- Able to concentrate for long periods.
- Quick to learn and take in new situations.
- Commercially sensitive and pragmatic enough to take a risk-based approach when making decisions that affect the business.
- Able to use IT systems sufficiently well as to be capable of designing training material, using surveillance systems, producing exception reports and the myriad of other uses of IT in the world of Compliance.
- Capable of managing a project such as implementing new Compliance initiatives and running remedial action plans.
- Confident enough to voice our opinions even if they are extremely unpopular.
- Able to make a quick decision.
- Confident enough *not* to make a quick decision in cases where detailed consideration is required.
- Able to make a considered decision by thinking laterally and drawing together all the strands of a particular issue and weighing up what is best for the regulator, the firm, the group as a whole and the customer (and your own mental well being!).
- Diplomatic and skilled in the art of persuasion and in negotiating for a desired outcome. This involves not constantly 'crying wolf' and threatening the business that the big bad regulator will get them. In reality, the odds are that they won't. We

(Continued)

need to be ready with more convincing and realistic reasons than that to comply with a rule, such as having to hand some specific examples of regulatory messes that firms similar to our own have found themselves in – fines, public censure, compensation payouts, extradition orders, negative front page news stories, etc.

- Confident enough to challenge the status quo and make waves at the top of the firm.
- Thick skinned.
- Customer services-focused – It's important to remember that while we have a 'policeman' role, we are also providers of regulatory services to the business, who ultimately pay our wages. In this respect, we have to keep our in-house customers (the business) happy.
- Ready to question our own behaviour and accept that we might have made a wrong decision.
- Fully up to speed with current regulatory trends and able to work with these in the context of our own firm. This means having the ability to practise 'just-in-time Compliance' by taking control of an issue at the right moment, not just the day before the regulator comes in as you will then not have enough time to put things right. Nor should you be so far ahead that your work is stale and needs to be updated by the time the rest of the regulated community wakes up to a new trend that you spotted ages ago.
- Have gravitas and authority so that the business is more inclined to take your views seriously and act upon them.
- Patience – it can sometimes take aeons for the Compliance message to sink in . . . and lastly . . .
- Enthusiastic about our work as Compliance Officers. (Otherwise, with the amount of grief it can give you it's just not worth it!)

2.3 COMPLIANCE: GOOD AND BAD

2.3.1 What Are the Characteristics of a Good Compliance Regime?

Once you are clear about the division of responsibilities for Compliance within your own firm and the type of tasks you need to undertake, you need to decide how you will actually operate your Compliance department and the nature of the Compliance function that is appropriate for your firm. As previously noted, we have been provided with some guidance in this area from various sources (Basel, IOSCO, MiFID, the FSA) but it is vitally important that, while taking account of what these bodies say, you should also make arrangements that suit your own particular firm. Do you really want a 'best in class' Compliance department or will 'solid and dependable' do just as well? Rolls Royce Compliance departments may achieve no more in your firm than the Ford Escort version, which costs less, requires fewer staff to keep in optimal condition, and perhaps has more perspective and sense of real priorities.

Based on the requirements, guidance and observations of the bodies listed above the rest of this section describes a set of common characteristics that tend to be present in many successful

Compliance departments and functions. See how many boxes you can tick below – the more ticks, the more likely it is that the Compliance regime at your firm is fit for purpose.

Internal arrangements

---

1. The Compliance department is independent of the business both in terms of line management and pay structure so that regulatory decisions are not skewed by remuneration considerations.
2. Appropriate staffing arrangements are in place:

   - the Compliance department has enough staff;
   - staff are well qualified with appropriate experience and interpersonal skills;
   - succession planning is in place to minimize the impact of key staff moving on;
   - staff responsibilities and reporting lines are clearly documented; and
   - a training and development plan is in place for each department member, with staff able to attend training when necessary (note the skills and competences for Compliance and anti-money laundering staff prepared by the Financial Services Skills Council – see Appendix 1.

3. The Compliance department has a thorough understanding of the business and its products, services and aspirations.
4. Internal departmental controls and procedures are clearly documented and up to date.
5. A business continuity plan is in place and has been tested (recently!)
6. The Compliance universe has been fully mapped and measures have been implemented to address all applicable requirements – see Chapter 7.
7. Regulatory risks across the whole firm have been identified and a risk mitigation and management programme is in place.
8. The risk mitigation and management programme is monitored and updated on an ongoing basis – in the realms of financial services regulation things are never static and you need to be able to move quicker than the regulator and predict their next area of focus. You have pretty much the same sources of information as the regulator in relation to national and international regulatory development, so think strategically.
9. The risk assessment methodology used is clearly defined and documented.
10. Key regulatory requirements are communicated to the business on a timely basis.
11. The Compliance department has enough office and desk space – security is adequate in terms of being able to keep sensitive documents under lock and key.
12. The Compliance department has enough equipment – computers, fax machines, scanners, photocopiers, Bloomberg terminals, reference books, software, access to on-line databases etc.
13. The Compliance department has an adequate budget for travel to overseas offices for supervision and monitoring purposes.
14. Independent external consultants are periodically invited into the firm to assess the adequacy of the Compliance department.
15. The benefits of sound Compliance arrangements are clearly communicated to the business and where possible a monetary value is placed on Compliance 'wins'.

(Continued)

16. Compliance controls and systems are embedded into existing systems so as to minimize costs.
17. The Compliance model is proactive rather than reactive with a well defined plan of action against which performance can be measured.
18. Compliance monitoring is undertaken to identify potential issues so that they can be corrected before they become problems and remedial action plans are implemented when control weakness and breaches are identified.
19. Management reporting systems are set up so as to give a clear indication of the effectiveness of the Compliance model (if you are so effective that all runs smoothly then the sad truth is that you might be forgotten; out of sight, out of mind – so make sure that you are constantly getting 'good press' and that people get to know about the near misses, disasters averted, regulatory action pre-empted etc.)
20. A risk based approach is taken so that most effort is placed on managing the areas in which your firm stands to lose the most.

Interaction with the rest of the firm

1. The term 'Compliance Risk' is clearly defined and is understood across the firm.
2. Compliance has direct access to the chief executive officer so as to be able to voice any concerns without being intercepted by people further up the reporting line.
3. The Head of Compliance has appropriate status within the firm.
4. There are regular meetings between Compliance and senior management so that both sides remain fully updated and can factor developments into their respective plans.
5. There is Compliance buy-in from staff at all levels within the firm, and especially from senior management.
6. Senior management accept their Compliance responsibilities and take these responsibilities seriously.
7. Senior management understand the key elements of the regulatory regime and how it impacts them and the activities and aspirations of the firm.
8. Senior management lend their full support to the Compliance department – you can get everything right within the team but if it is not possible to roll out a successful model because of senior management resistance then you are facing a very hard battle. (You can fight the fight or go somewhere else for an easier life where someone else has already taken on senior management and come out on top.)
9. The Compliance department has free access to all staff and records within the firm and has the right to challenge any department, employee or practice in relation to which it has a concern.
10. The Compliance department is seen as a business partner rather than a business preventer.
11. Compliance representatives are invited to all key business meetings so that Compliance has a full understanding of business plans and priorities and can tailor its activities accordingly.

12. An individual's regulatory understanding and actions form part of the annual appraisal and bonus system.
13. The business takes Compliance advice and requests on board as their interests are aligned with those of the Compliance department.
14. A Compliance risk committee is in place which is mandated with taking complex regulatory decisions. As well as Compliance staff the committee's membership comprises senior business management to demonstrate their ownership of Compliance-related issues.
15. Senior management is kept fully informed of Compliance activities and priorities by means of regular meetings and briefings.
16. The Compliance department is mindful of the need for commerciality when taking regulatory decisions that will affect the business and undertakes 'regulatory engineering' to work with the rules to make them fit a desired business outcome.
17. The business involves Compliance in new initiatives at an early stage as it is recognized that this will make any regulatory issues easier to address.
18. Compliance input is welcomed at all levels of the firm as the benefits that go with sound Compliance systems are acknowledged by all.
19. The Compliance department has good links with other control departments in terms of shared resources and exchange of knowledge. Where there is overlap between functions performed by the Compliance department and another unit, the extent of their respective responsibilities is clearly defined.
20. The Compliance department undertakes a regular cost-benefit analysis to demonstrate how they are adding value to the firm (you work for a financial institution where 'money talks' so you might as well speak the language of your colleagues when reminding them of all that you do for them).
21. The Compliance department uses customer satisfaction surveys to see how the function is perceived by the business and to identify areas where improvements are needed.
22. The Compliance department is subject to periodic review by Internal Audit or another appropriate department to assess its level of service and to highlight any areas where procedures and controls need to be strengthened.
23. Staff throughout the firm understand that the role of the Compliance department is that of 'facilitator' and that it is not there to 'do Compliance' on their behalf – all staff take responsibility for their own regulatory actions.
24. Regular reports measuring Compliance risk are provided to senior management.
25. The relationship between the Compliance department and the rest of the firm is formalized in an official document such as a memorandum of understanding or Compliance Charter (see in Chapter 3).

Interaction with Third Parties

1. Good relations with regulators.
2. Good relations with exchanges and clearing houses.
3. Strong network of other Compliance Officers so that you can 'phone a friend' if you're not quite sure what to do about a particular issue you have to deal with.

(Continued)

4. Membership of industry bodies, trade associations etc., so that you can keep up with current developments in the world of Compliance.
5. Clear understanding of what the relevant trade associations have to offer so that guidance can be obtained readily in times of need.
6. Help shape regulatory policy by responding to consultation papers and joining interest groups to lobby rules makers.

2.3.2 What Are the Characteristics of a Bad Compliance Regime?

The less successful your Compliance department and the Compliance regime you have implemented in your firm, the more likely it is that you will receive regular criticism from your colleagues in the business. This does not make for a happy working life and you should do all in your power to ensure that Compliance is not seen as little more than an incredibly expensive and burdensome insurance policy against regulatory risk. It simply cannot be an 'optional extra' that is 'applied' a few days prior to the launch of a new initiative, nor should it be seen as a necessary evil that can only serve to hinder business and reduce profit.

Therefore, if you do not want to come to work in a regulatory battle ground each day, try to remove the following elements from your Compliance regime. It will help you to avoid winning the Compliance booby prize ... and the animosity of all of your colleagues.

1. Lack of independence. The Compliance department reports to the business and therefore finds it difficult to make decisions that are necessary from a regulatory point of view but are not seen as business friendly. This also means that you have no place to go if you are not getting business buy-in.
2. A remuneration package structured so that Compliance staff salary is directly related to profitability of deals done. If adding an extra 25K to your bonus depends on whether or not you say 'Yes' to a particular transaction, then some of the less steadfast among us may be tempted to give in.
3. High staff turnaround so that the Compliance team does not have a sound collective understanding of the Compliance model that is being implemented, or of the firm and its objectives.
4. Lots of short-term temps in the Compliance department who are just 'passing through' and have no loyalty to your team's mission.
5. The Compliance team is understaffed.
6. Compliance staff do not receive adequate compensation and feel undervalued. The Compliance department staff are unenthusiastic about the firm and their work.
7. Compliance staff do not understand the specific products and services offered by your firm.
8. Compliance staff do not understand the specific regulations and legislation that apply to your firm.
9. Failure to engage with relevant regulators on an ongoing, business-as-usual basis.

10. Lack of a Compliance vision. Compliance department actions are driven by the events of the day rather than by a strategic plan of action.
11. Procedures and controls that are not reviewed regularly, running the risk of working with 'stale' arrangements that were effective some years ago but are no longer fit for purpose.
12. Failure to communicate with the business other than to issue orders and instructions about Compliance requirements.
13. Failure to engage with the business to determine ways in which Compliance can work to minimize the impact of regulatory requirements on business development. You then have 'Team Business' v. 'Team Compliance', which is not pretty.
14. Failure to give adequate guidance and training to staff about the relevant requirements and how your firm is affected.
15. Lack of Compliance systems and controls.
16. Lack of commercialism when taking decisions that will directly affect the business.
17. Compliance staff not confident enough to stand up to the business if a particular activity has to be stopped for regulatory reasons.
18. Failure to identify new regulatory requirements and determine how your firm will be affected.
19. Internal Compliance department procedures are not documented, or if they are documented, are not up to date or extensive enough.
20. Lack of clear and documented Compliance policies and manuals to be used by the business.
21. Compliance problems and remediation are not reported to senior management.
22. Corrective action plans are not implemented when Compliance problems are identified.
23. Compliance remit does not cover all the firm's activities.
24. Your team reports to a Head of Compliance who is based overseas and does not understand the requirements of the local regulatory regime, but allows your local Compliance function little independence of action.
25. Compliance approach is not risk based or flexible.
26. The Compliance department works to a strict programme that does not allow for contingencies.
27. Time is spent addressing small and easy wins because it is considered too difficult to tackle the bigger problems.

It is so important to be aware these things and eliminate them that it is advisable to undertake an annual self-assessment to check that your own department does not display any of the above characteristics.

2.3.3   Danger Signals

Undoubtedly, the removal of the above elements from your Compliance regime is easier for some of us than for others. The more that the following characteristics are displayed by your firm or by individual departments within it, the more effort you need to put into refining your Compliance model and selling the benefits of Compliance to the business.

1. No CEO or senior management buy-in with regard to Compliance requirements.
2. Senior management do not accept responsibility for Compliance, or do not take their responsibilities seriously.
3. Frequent tensions and disputes with the business in relation to regulatory strategy.
4. Your firm has not recently been subject to a regulatory review so the business has forgotten just how tough and unpleasant inspection visits can be. (It is amazing how quickly Compliance becomes everyone's best friend prior to a regulatory audit.)
5. The firm has a high number of staff from overseas jurisdictions, perhaps with more relaxed regulatory regimes. Such staff are not accustomed to working with your local regulatory model.
6. Your firm is struggling financially and there is pressure on staff to perform. This can put the emphasis on short-term gain rather than long-term viability, which can lead to Compliance corners being cut.
7. Matrix management is in place, meaning that a large proportion of your staff report to managers in overseas jurisdictions where there is a lack of understanding of local regulatory requirements and their importance.
8. Remuneration structure takes no account of an individual's regulatory mind-set.
9. Compliance is not embedded in business strategy, is consulted as a last minute afterthought (if at all) and is seen as one last hurdle to overcome before a new initiative can be launched rather than as a partner that can enhance business operations.
10. Compliance is considered the responsibility of the Compliance department alone – staff take no responsibility for their own actions and do not think for themselves about the regulatory implications of their activities.
11. Advice, guidance and requests from the Compliance department are regularly ignored by the business.
12. Historically there has been a weak Compliance department.
13. Your firm has a high proportion of prima donnas and star performers who have a reputation for greatness to maintain and who feel pressure to keep their number one slots.
14. Management does not concern itself with Compliance issues and does not get involved with Compliance strategy planning.

If you find yourself working for a firm where several of the above characteristics are present (and you don't decide to change job!) refer to Chapter 10 for guidance on how to deal with a lack of cooperation.

2.4   THE ARGUMENT FOR COMPLIANCE

2.4.1   What Are the Benefits of Compliance, Regulation and the Compliance Officer?

Earlier in the text we looked at the natural tension that must exist between the business and the Compliance department in order to strike the right balance between commercial interest and regulatory necessity. Though this tension is generally felt to be one of the less desirable elements of Compliance work, we are lucky that things are changing, and have been for some time, as the industry wakes up to the benefits of financial services regulation and the advantages of having a well-structured and competent Compliance department. However, just in case anyone ever dares to question why your firm 'has to spend so much time and money on compliance' (sound familiar?) you may wish to have in your arsenal a ready list of the benefits that regulation and Compliance bring to the financial services industry in general and to your own company in particular.

The UK has had its fair share of financial scandals and is not immune to the effects of similar scandals in other countries.

How many of the following do you recall?

The collapse of Barings Bank

The famous rogue trader, Nick Leeson engaged in inadequately supervised trading activity while also acting as Head of Operations, running up losses that led to the bank being sold to ING for £1.

Robert Maxwell and the Mirror pension scheme

Robert Maxwell diverted millions of pounds from his employees' pension funds to use for his own purposes.

The Collapse Bank of Credit and Commerce International (BCCI)

BCCI, nicknamed the Bank of Cocaine and Criminals International, collapsed in 1991 with enormous debts following fraud committed on a massive scale. The events at BCCI even spawned their own EU directive – the Post BCCI Directive to strengthen prudential supervision across Europe.

The Flaming Ferraris

The flamboyant antics of the three traders concerned meant that their attempts to manipulate the Swedish Stock Exchange OMX Index in 1998 captured the imagination of both the media and the public.

The Near-Collapse of Equitable Life

Cunning use of actuarial techniques enabled Equitable Life to continue to promise policy holders more money than was available to them, leaving thousands of investors with below expected retirement funds.

The Mis-selling of Split Capital Trusts

The way that many split cap trusts were managed and invested led to them presenting a much greater investment risk than was disclosed to a large number of investors by their investment advisers. Thousands lost out.

(Continued)

The Mis-selling of Endowments

Many home owners using an endowment policy as a means of paying off their mortgage have been left with shortfalls as the risks associated with the endowment mortgage were not adequately explained to them.

The Mis-selling of pensions

Workers who would have been better off at retirement if they had either joined, or remained with, their employer's pension scheme were advised to leave their employer's scheme, or not join it in the first place.

The Collapse of Enron

Institutional fraud and accounting irregularities on a mammoth scale, coupled with energy market manipulation, led to the bankruptcy of trading giant Enron. Investors, many of them also employees, suffered substantial losses as share values plummeted, with massive employee pension plan losses. One of the accounting scandals – not to mention Tyco, World.com and others – credited with (or blamed for) the implementation of the Sarbanes–Oxley Act in the US.

Allied Irish Bank

Rogue trader John Rusnak lost hundreds of millions of dollars as an FX trader.

Northern Rock

A questionable funding structure resulted in the first run on a UK bank in living memory (see commentary in the section on the Financial Services Compensation Scheme in Appendix 1).

Griffin Trading Company

Unauthorized trading at GLH Derivatives led to major client money shortfalls at Griffin (the firm through which it traded Eurex futures).

Long-Term Capital Management

The spectacular losses of hedge fund LTCM sent shockwaves of fear around the financial community as concerns about systemic risk (a knock-on effect on other institutions) and dubious hedging techniques were splashed across the headlines.

Deutsche Morgan Grenfell's European Growth Trust

Unauthorized trading by fund manager Peter Young led to multi-million pound investor losses.

Payment Protection Insurance (PPI)

At the time of writing the Competition Commission is investigating the PPI market following allegations that it is frequently too expensive, has sold insurance to consumers who will not be able to claim on it, and specifically excludes several of the situations that can most commonly result in repayment problems.

If you told the people who suffered as a result of these scandals (clients and/or employees) that Compliance was a waste of time and money, you might get lynched. But when things are going well and through our daily duties and vigilance we prevent a similar scandal from occurring, it can sometimes seem that no – one wants to know, because all of that ticking and bashing and reading of rulebooks is not very sexy. How many situations that could have blown up into similar scandals have been identified and addressed by the poor, humble Compliance Officer before they even got near the headlines? We will never know.

To deal more with the specifics, read through the following sections that pinpoint some of the most identifiable benefits pertaining to financial regulation and the Compliance function. And make sure you quote them freely if anyone tries to denigrate our role!

Benefits to clients

- Many of the detailed Compliance rules are aimed directly at ensuring that customers get a fair deal. If you can comply with these rules then you will be improving the customer experience with all the competitive advantages that this brings, such as loyalty, trust and 'recommendability'. If we serve our customers well, there is also less risk that we will find ourselves subject to litigation or a complaint to the FSA on the part of an unsatisfied client.
- The improved systems that are required to comply with the customer-focused rules – for example, reporting, customer agreements, notifications – mean that the service your firm can deliver is more dependable, thus increasing customer loyalty.
- Competitive advantage: our customers expect to be treated fairly and the conduct of business rules seek to put the client's best interests first, preventing the feeding frenzy that may lead to unsuspecting investors being bled dry and killing any prospect of a long-term relationship with the firm. If your firm has a reputation for integrity and fairness then it will benefit from increased client loyalty.
- All of the above should lead to increased business and, therefore, increased profit.

Corporate governance benefits

- Many regulatory requirements not concerned directly with improving the customer experience are aimed at enhancing internal systems and controls, and this has the effect of improving the efficiency of the firm. This is probably the aim of all the management gurus who have never even given the FSA, the SEC and others a second thought. Think of this aspect as a lucky by-product of the fact that your firm is regulated!
- The formal requirement to apply robust corporate governance systems, rather than having this left to chance, should help achieve better accountability at all levels when apportionment and oversight controls are implemented;
- Management information should be improved as a result of the various measures that need to be put in place to determine the success of your Compliance model.

Monetary benefits

- Good Compliance arrangements normally call for, and result in, improved efficiency (as seen above) and business process efficiencies generally lead to reduced costs.
- Obviously if you maintain high standards of regulatory Compliance your firm is less likely to lose money through compensation payouts or litigation.
- Equally, having a robust Compliance regime means that you are much less likely to have to pay out money in fines, and with the level of fines rising year on year now is a very good time to keep this in mind.
- The stronger your Compliance systems and controls, the more leniently your firm will be treated under Basel II, thus lowering your capital charges and freeing up money for deals to be done.
- As noted above, many Compliance requirements are directly aimed at ensuring that clients are well treated. Logically, this should lead to increased customer satisfaction and thus increased profit.
- Some would even go so far as to say that the Compliance department is a 'profit centre in reverse' – think how much money is 'saved' by preventing fines, supporting the firm's good reputation and by freeing up regulatory capital by contributing to the risk control framework. When you consider these things, it becomes a lot easier to justify the costs of Compliance.

Reputational Benefits – Clients, press, regulators

- *The media* – Good Compliance systems and controls will save your firm from being media fodder for a press extravaganza. The last thing you need is your firm making headline news for all the wrong reasons.
- *The regulators* – A robust Compliance infrastructure means less chance of regulatory censure, and if you do get into trouble, your penalty is likely to be lighter if you can show that, overall, Compliance systems are working well and that whatever problem you had was just a one off that has been/can be easily remedied. We also make sure that our firms maintain good relations with the regulator so that they are less likely to take a heavy-handed approach if something does go awry.
- *Clients* – See comments on previous page concerning customer satisfaction.
- And talking globally, it is in all of our interests to protect the reputation of the UK financial services industry. We do not want to see business lost to the other centres who would love to take a piece of our action: the financial services industry is very important for the UK economy (29 759 firms, 165 544 individuals, 5% of the UK's GDP, as quoted from an the FSA speech of 2006[3]) and by helping to ensure that high regulatory standards are maintained, we play our part in protecting it.

---

[3] Speech by Callum McCarthy, 13 February 2006: Risk based regulation: the FSA's experience.

Benefits to your Firm and your Colleagues

- We read the rulebooks, the consultation papers, the discussion documents, etc., and attend the regulatory seminars so that other staff don't have to. (Do you think your Chief Executive has any idea how many the FSA consultation papers you have waded through in the past year?)
- Once we've figured out what the relevant requirements are we take the time to digest them and transform them into easy to follow bite-sized chunks. This way, the business can get on with dealing, advising, financing, making money, etc., without having to spend time poring over complicated rules and requirements trying to work out what applies to them and what doesn't.
- We know the rulebooks inside out (or we should do if we're worth our pay packet). Before a new line of business is commenced, or before a deal is closed, there is a whole array of regulation to be navigated. But luckily, as Compliance Officers we know our way through it like the back of our hand! We can create a route map for the business, warning our colleagues of the directions that go nowhere, of the routes to be avoided at all costs as they lead to regulatory danger zones, and of the routes that lead smoothly and rapidly to the other side of the regulatory jungle!
- Our knowledge of the rules also means that we know when an exemption applies, or when it is likely that a waiver can be obtained. Everyone loves a shortcut!
- Our industry awareness means that we know what the regulator's current 'hot buttons' are. These are the problems that we really don't want to see in our firms as we know that the regulator is focusing on them and will take a very hard line if any irregularities are discovered.
- We spot potential problems before the regulator has a chance to suspect them. No matter how agitated people get at the thought of an internal Compliance review, most are aware how much more unpleasant it could be if the regulator checked and found something amiss.
- We guide our firms from business plan to commercial success to enable them to reach their goals without taking a nasty detour down the road to regulatory censure and all its associated horrors, such as fines, prosecutions and loss of reputation.
- But not only do we protect our firms from the dangers of rule breaches, we also shield them from overzealous regulation. We play our part in moulding our own regulatory environment by joining trade associations and discussion groups and by responding to consultation papers in order to shape regulation in a way that is business friendly and workable, not only in the context of the rulebook, but also in business practice.
- We also protect our colleagues from vindictive, irresponsible clients who do not know what they are doing, but fasten on to the slightest little problem in the hope that they can blame us for their bad investment decisions and be compensated. As Compliance Officers we can ensure that all our regulatory ducks are in a row. That way we can make sure that these misguided clients have no case if they try to raise a suit against us.
- We act as the Jiminy Crickets of the financial world, reining in the over-enthusiastic traders, for example, and helping them put some perspective back into the relationship between profit and good business ethics.

Why do we have Financial Services Regulation?

This text is dedicated to examining the Compliance function, but as the agenda for a large part of what we do is set by our regulators, it is worth spending some time looking at what our regulators are expected to achieve and what their own objectives are.

Financial services is one of many industries that is overseen by a regulatory body. In the UK we have, for example, the Environment Agency, the Food Standards Agency, the Trading Standards Agency, the Driving Standards Agency, Companies House and the Civil Aviation Authority. Even though the scope of interest of all of these bodies varies greatly, they all have the common, high level aim of supervising a particular sector or activity that has an impact on the general public.

Focusing on the financial services sector alone, I have only encountered one jurisdiction that does not have *at least* one regulator. And again, even though the scope of these bodies will vary from country to country and from sector to sector, all will have a common set of high level objectives.

---

1. Monitoring the solvency/capital adequacy of the firms they regulate.
2. Consumer protection.
3. Market confidence – ensuring that markets are fair, efficient and transparent.
4. Market stability – reducing the risk of a systemic failure.
5. Supervision of market conduct to prevent crime and sharp practices.

See Appendix 1 for the statutory objectives of the FSA.

All of the above would seem quite laudable, and it would be difficult to argue with the intentions of our regulators. However, we may want to take issue with the various inconsistencies that exist from jurisdiction to jurisdiction and even within a single regulatory regime.

Whereas the issue of differences in regulations from country to country is gradually being addressed by international bodies such as the European Union, the Basel Committee on Banking Supervision and the International Organization of Securities Commissions, there are sometimes inconsistencies within our own local regime that are not getting much air time. Let's look at a few examples from the UK:

- Why are certain products immune from the FSA conduct of business regulation? If a company wants to raise money by means of share or bond issuance, then these activities are highly regulated; but if a company raises money by means of a syndicated loan, the conduct of business rules do not apply to those arranging the facility.
- Similarly, if someone trades a share or a bond, the conduct of business rules apply; whereas if someone trades another broadly comparable instrument such as a participation in a loan, a promissory note or a bill of exchange, the conduct of business rules do *not* apply.
- Why is the consumer credit industry not regulated with the same vigour as other financial services in the retail space? Surely with consumer protection in financial services as a key regulatory objective it would be wise to do something about all of the hideously irresponsible advertising that we currently see for cheap money – credit cards, personal loans, etc.

- The FSA applies the whole gamut of its regulation to those wanting to spend even the smallest mounts of money on buying 'safe' investments such as gilts, but it does not regulate buy-to-let mortgages that are equally taken out for investment purposes and expose the consumer to far more risk than buying £ 1000 worth of government bonds or FTSE 100 shares.

What do you think?

2.4.2   What Are the Costs of Compliance?

It's all very well knowing the benefits of regulation and Compliance. But we are living in the real world and we know that no matter how beneficial and desirable Compliance and regulation may be, they can regularly be on the receiving end of hardcore criticism. To enable us to cope when our department or profession is being lambasted, it helps to know the nature of complaint. You can then go some way towards preparing for it, perhaps having some choice counter-augments up your sleeve to help to strengthen your case. Some of the most common lines of criticism and complaint that you are likely to encounter are listed below.

Departmental costs – direct costs that result from having a certain number of people sitting in the Compliance department

1. *Remuneration packages* – Salary, bonus, pension, etc.
2. *Office space* – Have you any idea how much it costs just to maintain one desk for a year? Ask your Administration department and you will be surprised. Then multiply that figure by the number of people in your team and you will have reached quite a tidy sum.
3. *Equipment* – We have already seen that, to be effective, there is certain equipment that a Compliance department needs, such as computers, fax machines, IT programmes, folders and cabinets, scanners, etc.
4. *Training* – If Compliance staff are going to work effectively they have to understand their firm's business, products, services, etc., not to mention all the relevant regulations and legislation.
5. *Travel* – If your firm has overseas offices for which you are responsible, then it would be difficult to make a case for not visiting them to 'kick the tyres'.

Opportunity costs – indirect costs that result from business lost due to Compliance-related matters

1. *Training* – When your dealers are sitting in your training presentation they are unlikely to be doing deals at the same time.
2. *Rejection of trade or counterparty* – If the Compliance department rejects a particular piece of business or new relationship for regulatory reasons then, evidently, no money will be made from it.

(Continued)

3. *Compliance administration* – Time spent by the business on Compliance matters such as seeking approval for PA trades, gathering KYC documentation, performing T&C assessments, etc., reduces the time they can spend on the phone speaking to clients and pumping up the balance sheet.
4. *Remedial exercises* – If you discover a serious regulatory problem, it is likely to require considerable time and money to resolve.

2.5 COMPLIANCE AS A PROFESSION

Everything we have said so far about the Compliance function seems innocuous enough, so why should Compliance Officers receive such a bad press? We are hardly the most popular people in the bank, but all we want to do is help! We simply want to help our firms and our colleagues to keep out of trouble with the regulators, so why are we so unpopular?

A lot of it is due to perception, and Compliance is certainly a job in need of an image makeover. People do not generally like to be told what to do (arguably even less so where they work in front-line financial services industry roles!) and no one likes a 'nag'. And all too often Compliance Officers are seen as the 'nagging wives' of the financial services industry – don't leave your dirty socks on the floor, put your used plate in the dishwasher, mow the lawn, fix the car, don't accept that gift, obtain my approval before you buy those shares, don't take your client out to dinner unless I say you can, start studying for your exams now. . .!

Another way of looking at it is that we are like medics, but instead of looking after our colleagues' physical health, we look after their regulatory health! Although everyone knows that they should be eating five pieces of fruit and veg each day to stay healthy, many people don't do it, and don't want the message constantly pushed down their throat. Similarly, most people working in financial services know that there are certain actions they need to take for their own benefit, but what they *need* to do and what they actually *want* to do are two very different things, and they don't want the hassle of being constantly reminded of it.

Pity the plight of the Compliance Officer! Why do we want to put ourselves in the position of having to go head to head with a recalcitrant trader, with little by way of thanks or recognition if we make a good call, and with the prospect of being the centre of attention only if we get things wrong? Why do we work in a profession towards which so many people seem to have an in-built antipathy and is so much in need of some 'public relations magic'? We aren't badly paid, in general, but we're hardly on the same footing as those in the profit centres; and each day we have to deal with the issues the Front Office find so tedious! And to top it all, the Compliance Officer who makes a wrong call faces the prospect of some meaty regulatory and/or legal sanction, not to mention a loss of personal reputation (make sure you are covered by your firm's directors and officer's liability insurance). As an aside, don't automatically assume that the regulator has it any easier. Remember Andrei Andreyevich Kozlov, the former Deputy Chairman of the Central Bank of Russia, who was murdered in September 2006 shortly after making a speech in which he spoke out against money launderers?

In case you are ever having a bad day and need some encouragement, here are some reminders about why working in Compliance is actually a truly interesting area:

- Although you may perform very repetitive tasks at the start your career, Compliance work does become extremely varied and offers exposure to most parts of the firm (see Chapter 9 and Appendices C and D). Working in Compliance therefore gives you a much better understanding of how your firm and the industry in general work than many people who specialize in just one area – a bond trader, for example, knows a lot about bond trading and someone working in the Settlements team knows how to settle trades, but how much exposure do they have to other areas of financial services?

- Depending on your field of Compliance, it can be a very people-centred role that offers an almost unique opportunity to forge relationships with almost everyone in the firm. Alternatively, if you are a more retiring type, there is plenty of scope to work more in the background doing policy work, writing procedures, assessing forthcoming regulatory changes, etc.

- Even though Compliance work is so broad, there is definitely scope to specialize if a particular areas interests you or matches your background, for example

  - Lawyers – financial crime (money laundering, fraud, insider dealing and market abuse);
  - Accountants – prudential reporting and controls;
  - Auditors – Compliance monitoring (which often involves serious amounts of foreign travel if you have an international remit);
  - Trainers – Compliance development programmes, training and competence;
  - Programmers – computer-based controls and surveillance systems.

- As the Compliance profession matures it is, arguably, becoming ever more interesting. Much of the box ticking mentality has gone and regulatory work has an increasing focus on strategy. Box ticking is still there, of course, and it has to be, but there is now much more scope for Compliance Officers to get involved with strategic decision making, when considering the regulatory implications of a planned new business model or venture, for example. Hopefully, with time, this type of value-added Compliance will turn on its head the old image of the Compliance Officer with their foot on the business brake rather than the accelerator.

- As the financial services industry grows in complexity, there is a corresponding broadening in the scope of the Compliance function which also makes it a more interesting area in which to work: new products and trade structures are being devised, new markets are opening up, outsourcing is becoming increasingly popular, more work is being done on a cross-border basis, and changes to extradition laws (see Box 4 on 'Extradition' on page 323) mean that we need to be more mindful of overseas requirements.

- For the more philosophical among us there are regularly issues of an ethical nature to grapple with. This is because there is more to Compliance than simply ensuring that a particular set of rules is complied with. We often need to get in touch with the spirit of a particular requirement rather than simply adhering strictly to what it says on the page. Some things are simply not right whether or not they are governed by a particular regulation. This means devising ways of working within the control framework in such a way that business can be done ethically, asking the question, 'How would I feel if I were on the receiving end of this arrangement?'

- The world of Compliance can also be quite dramatic from a crime-busting point of view! You will know what I mean if you have ever alerted the police to suspected criminal activity and been involved in an undercover operation to get the suspects onto your premises, their movements secretly filmed and their conversations secretly recorded to enable arrests to be made.

- Compliance also gives you the chance to hone your project management and problem-solving skills. It is very fulfilling to see a remediation or improvement programme in which you have taken part or led come to fruition.
- You sometimes have to be incredibly creative in terms of finding a thousand and one ways to say 'No' without actually ever uttering that word, as the sound of it is almost guaranteed to immediately raise the hackles of your colleagues on the business side. You also need to be creative when it comes to 'working a rule' to find a way of making it fit with your firm's business plans.

So there we have it! We can now feel reassured that we are not all mad and that there are actually some attractions to doing the job we have chosen! It is just one of the hazards of the profession that even if we are the best Compliance Officer in the world, there will always be some tension between the Compliance department and the business, and that's the way it should be. If there is no friction then something is not right: either the front office is totally cowed by Compliance, which is likely to hinder business development; or, more likely, the Compliance department does not know how to say 'No' and the business is pushing things too far.

Either way, things won't stay in that friction-free state for long as either the firm will go under due to lack of innovation, growth and development or there will be a Compliance scandal from which your firm will be unable to recover. If either of the above occurs, you may well have no business left to have friction with!

3
The Compliance Contract

Chapters 4–9 of this text provide guidance on the key elements of the 'world' within which your firm operates, and give you an idea of the type of knowledge that you and your team should have and the activities your department should engage in if you are to run a successful Compliance regime within your firm. Once you have assimilated and understood all of the above, it's time to spread the good news to the rest of the firm! As we know all too well, Compliance is never going to be the most popular department within the firm, so the more you can do to promote your services to your colleagues in other parts of the organisation the better. As the saying goes, 'if you sling enough mud some of it will stick', and although this is normally used in a negative context, it also works in reverse. If you say enough positive things about the Compliance function, then some of them will eventually stick in the minds of your colleagues. You had better just be certain that all the positive things you say are true!

As with most things, there are several ways of promoting Compliance and in this instance, it is best to use a combination of all of them! Some of the ways of ensuring that you are understood are noted below:

1. Make sure that you get Board and senior management buy-in about the extent of your responsibilities and the nature of your activities.
2. Prepare a Compliance Mission Statement (see below) and do not be sparing with its use – include it in the Compliance Manual and display it on the firm's intranet site. You could also use it (or an abbreviated version) as a 'tag line' on any e-mails sent by Compliance department staff and as a footer in any Compliance documents, reports, procedures or policies, etc.
3. Prepare an official Compliance Charter (see below) and have it approved formally by the Board.
4. Give a summary of Compliance responsibilities, activities and benefits in the Compliance manual and on your firm's intranet site.
5. Conduct training to ensure that staff are aware of what the Compliance department does, why it is there and how it can help them.
6. Launch an 'advertising campaign' to ensure that you are constantly visible to the rest of the firm. For example, you could

   - display posters about what the team has to offer;
   - organize customer satisfaction surveys (with the rest of the firm being the 'customers' of your department, rather than quizzing your firm's actual client base!);
   - run a Compliance competition;
   - send out Compliance e-mail bulletins;
   - produce a newsletter;

- prepare leaflets or small brochures about your activities and leave them lying around the office for people to read;
- organize social events for the rest of the firm; and
- organize social events in which you invite management to have lunch with the Compliance team and give them the opportunity to discuss how they feel Compliance is working, what is going well, what they want, what they don't want, what their concerns are, etc.

You can undoubtedly think of other things that would work in the context of your own firm. Of the above methods for broadcasting your message, two require further comment at this stage: the Compliance Mission Statement and the Compliance Charter.

3.1 THE COMPLIANCE MISSION STATEMENT

Your mission statement should provide a succinct definition of the most fundamental aims of the Compliance department. It has slightly different uses for those outside the department and those within it.

- *Purpose of the mission statement for Compliance department staff*
  For those within the department the Compliance Mission Statement can serve as a reminder of what being a member of the team really means, why people have chosen to work in Compliance and what they want to achieve. It can also be used to help to prioritize tasks and focus on what is really important.
- *Purpose of the mission statement for other staff*
  For those outside the department, the Compliance Mission Statement should be a brief reminder of why your department exists. It goes without saying that you should make it as positive as possible for the business – a mission statement that focuses solely on keeping the regulator in ecstasies while saying nothing about helping the firm is clearly not destined to make your life easy.

For department members and outsiders alike, your mission statement should provide a ready response to the question: 'Why does the Compliance department exist?' A considerable amount of literature has been produced about the concept of the mission statement and the general consensus seems to be that it should be short (preferably no longer than a few sentences), punchy, positive and very easy to understand.

Based on some of the matters that we looked at in Chapter 2, Sections 2.3 and 2.4, such as the benefits of compliance and the key features of a successful Compliance department, sample mission statements for a Compliance team might be:

- *To provide XYZ Bank with successful Compliance solutions that satisfy regulatory requirements while promoting successful business practices.*

- *To ensure that EFG Ltd attains high standards of regulatory Compliance by providing a practical, efficient and business friendly Compliance solution.*

- *To promote the highest standards of regulatory Compliance in such a way as to enhance business practices and thus add value to the whole firm.*

3.2   THE COMPLIANCE CHARTER

The Compliance Charter expands on the key concepts contained within the Mission Statement. It can be used to serve the dual purposes of promoting the services offered to the firm by the Compliance department while clearly defining the scope and limitations of the department's responsibilities and powers. To a certain extent, it can be considered as a contract for services between the department and the rest of the firm – the Compliance department has the opportunity to indicate formally what it will do for the firm as a whole while defining the basis on which it will operate. Senior management can then endorse this so that everyone knows what the position is. This should provide a basis for managing any future differences, disputes, requests for additional resources or requirements for material corrective action.

When drafting the charter it will help you to get business buy-in if you use the same sort of language that is used by the rest of the firm. Is there any jargon that is specific to your company; any motto; any company-wide mission statements? Are business communications within your firm scattered with MBA speak? Are there certain words and phrases that seem to crop up all the time? If you write your charter using the 'house language' then your colleagues are much more likely to accept it.

3.2.1   Contents of a Compliance Charter

The following sections provide some suggestions for items that may usefully be included in a Compliance Charter.

Contents

Definition of Compliance Risk

It is useful to include a definition of Compliance risk in the Charter – you may wish to use the definition provided by the Basel Committee on Banking Supervision and noted in Section 2.1 of Chapter 2.

Overall Responsibility for Compliance

In line with major national and international regulators (see previous chapter) the Charter should make it clear that responsibility for Compliance rests with senior management and that it is the role of the Compliance department to assist senior management with their responsibilities.

The Charter should also make it clear that all staff members are responsible for their own regulatory actions and for complying with relevant rules, legislation, standards, etc. Compliance should not be seen as something that is 'done' by the Compliance department but rather an ethic that is shared by the whole of the firm. To strengthen this concept you could also add that each employee's 'Compliance ethic' will be taken into consideration during the annual appraisal.

Scope and Limitations of Compliance Department Responsibilities

Define the elements that will comprise your universe in terms of

- departments, business units, legal entities, etc.;
- legislation, rules, codes of practice, etc.

(Continued)

There may be times when Compliance activities are undertaken by other departments within the firm, or are even outsourced. If this is the case, the responsibilities each department or person concerned should be clearly defined so that nothing falls through the gaps.

As you don't want to be blamed for another department's failings you should also include matters for which the Compliance department will not be responsible. This will vary from firm to firm but areas that might be excluded from your remit include data protection legislation, compliance with company law, health and safety law, complaints handling, regulatory financial reporting, training and competence. An area where there is debate in this respect is anti-money laundering, with the function sometimes being managed by the Compliance department and at other times being operated as a separate discipline.

High-Level Compliance Department Objectives

Use this section to really sell the activities of the Compliance department and promote what you have to offer to the rest of the firm. This section should not be too specific and should simply summarize your goals. It is likely to be broadly similar for most Compliance departments and should include a statement that the Compliance department will undertake to

- ensure that an infrastructure is in place that is capable of providing for Compliance with relevant requirements;
- ensure that an ethical approach is taken by the firm and that its policies and procedures will allow for staff to act with integrity, even where their actions are not governed by any specific rules or requirements;
- seek to work with the business in order to promote successful Compliance solutions, as opposed to simply dictating requirements;
- constantly seek to improve efficiencies in regulatory procedures in order to add value to the business;
- seek constant and proactive dialogue with the business to understand its needs and objectives.

Day-to-Day Activities

Chapter 10 and Appendices A and B provide plenty of guidance on the type of day-to-day activities with which a Compliance department should involve itself, and from there you should select those that are relevant to your firm and add any additional ones of your own.

There is no need to go into too much detail here as this is not the place to describe all the routine tasks that your job involves. You should simply set out at a high level the activities in which the Compliance department will engage on an ongoing basis.

You should be careful not to make this section too prescriptive as that would detract from your flexibility to follow a risk-based approach.

Compliance Department Powers

Much of the Compliance Charter is dedicated to setting out how the Compliance department can support the rest of the firm – the services that the business has the right to expect from you and your team. But as with everything, the business has to understand that with rights come responsibilities. The business has to understand that if you are to provide it with the sterling service you wish to offer, it has to provide you with the authority and the means to offer that service.

This is your opportunity to set out what you require to do you job properly. Again, this is going to vary from firm to firm, but there should be common themes representing the minimum requirements that the Compliance department needs in order to be successful. These matters are likely to, or indeed should, includes the following:

- a senior staff member with appropriate standing within the firm should be appointed to run the Compliance department;
- the Compliance department should have the ability to act independently. It should not report to the business and should be represented at board level.

The Compliance department should also have

- The ability to have direct access to independent persons with sufficient authority to be in a position to intervene if a firm's regulatory health is a stake: the CEO, the Board, Audit Committee, non-executive directors, etc. There should be nothing that prevents the Compliance Officer from escalating significant and genuine concerns right to the top of the organization in cases where you consider this appropriate.
- Permission to work with HR to have influence over the type of regulatory breach that should constitute a sanctionable offence, breach of employment contract, gross misconduct, etc., and the types of internal sanctions that should be applied to such breaches. The Compliance department will be ineffective unless there are very clear sanctions for those who break the rules.
- Permission to access any document or record of the firm, including personal documents, if it is reasonably believed that these are needed for a regulatory purpose.
- Adequate resources in terms of staff, computers, office space, training, travel budget, etc.
- The right to expect cooperation from other departments within the firm in pursuit of Compliance activities.

Compliance Responsibilities of the Rest of the Firm

Make it clear that you expect your colleagues in the rest of the firm to contribute to the success of the Compliance function. You could include their responsibility to

- involve Compliance in new business initiatives and new products;
- complete Compliance training;
- keep up to date with changes to regulatory policies and procedures;

(Continued)

- notify Compliance of complaints and rule breaches;
- coordinate any discussions or meetings with regulators through the Compliance department;
- ask for guidance when they have any Compliance queries or concerns; and
- report suspicions of money laundering to Compliance (if that is the appropriate reporting chain).

Performance Measurement

- Once everyone's responsibilities have been established it's important to set out how both sides (Compliance and business) can measure performance under the Compliance Charter and what needs to happen if either side does not meet one of its obligations. How can you prove that you are doing a good job? How can you demonstrate that the business is not cooperating?
- It is advisable for Internal Audit to review the adequacy of your firm's regulatory infrastructure and compliance with the Charter at least once a year.

Senior Management Reporting

In this section you should establish the types of management information that will be required to quantify Compliance performance. What sort of matter does senior management want and/or need to be made aware of by the department? How should this information be reported? How frequently? Further guidance in this area is available on page 188 of Appendix A.

Escalation Procedures

You need to establish escalation procedures on both sides. What will you do if you consider that the business is not informing you of important developments? What do you want the business to do if they are not happy with any element of the Compliance regime you have implemented? Hopefully you will never need to have recourse to this part of the Charter, but should there ever be problems it is useful to have a prearranged way of dealing with them. Just as you don't want to experience a total lack of cooperation from the business, the business does not want you to run off to the regulator every five minutes to help you to sort out your differences. (The regulator does not want you to do this either!)

Getting the Charter Approved

Ensure that you do not simply complete the Charter within the Compliance department and present it to management as a *fait accompli*. If you take this approach you will not get any real 'buy-in' from the business who will simply view the Charter as another Compliance department document that has nothing in particular to do with them. In order to extract real value from the Charter, you also need to persuade the business to buy into the concept.

Present it to them in such a way that they can see how it benefits them; ask for their input; let senior management review it and debate it, in your absence if necessary, to tailor it in ways that suit them better. If the Charter goes through a few versions before both sides are happy, then that is a good thing – the more involvement management have had in producing this document the more they will view it as belonging to them as well as to the Compliance department, and the more cooperation you should receive as a result.

One of the most important reasons to get business buy-in is to make it more difficult for management to complain about what the Compliance department does or does not do at a later date. If the business has signed up to the Charter and approved it at Board level, then in voicing any criticisms they must understand that it is their own Compliance model they are criticizing, not just that of the Compliance department.

Changing the Charter

The Compliance Charter will probably not remain static for long periods of time. It's probably best to review it on an annual basis so that both parties (i.e Compliance and business) can make changes to keep pace with any developments in business, regulation, markets, management, processes, etc. Any changes, or indeed any decision to keep the Charter as it is for another 12 months should be noted in a Board meeting minute.

A Final Word of Warning

Do not make the Compliance Charter too detailed or prescriptive, especially in terms of fixed procedures and Compliance department deliverables: you don't want to overburden other departments, or make a rod for your own back. Beware of overkill.

4

Mapping Your Compliance Universe

There comes a time when those who are serious about working in Compliance, and are in it for the long term, need to get to grips with how their activities, and those of their firm, fit into the wider legislative and regulatory universe within which they operate. But first, let's qualify that comment! If you are happy to live your life in a Compliance bunker, coming to work each day to simply read rules and bide your time until you can leave again in the evening, then, I admit, you don't really need to know very much about how your firm is placed in the wider regulatory environment. But if you were that sort of person then you probably would not be reading this text.

On the other hand if you want to be in a position to lead your firm successfully through the complexities of the Compliance universe then it really is vital to understand how your firm is placed. So, once you have determined the high level scope of your responsibilities in the Compliance Charter (see Chapter 3) you will then need to tackle the more detailed aspects of your environment. To do so successfully you will need to take on board a vast amount of information that should form the building blocks of the Compliance regime that you implement in your firm, and should cover the following broad areas:

- Operating entities within your group.
- Business units and support departments within each operating entity.
- External service providers.
- The regulatory environment in which you are operating

  - regulators and other standard setting bodies;
  - legislation, regulations, best practice codes, etc.

- Products, services and business activities.
- Commonly used documentation relating to trading, regulatory matters and other relevant areas.

You will notice that even though your profession is 'simply' that of Compliance Officer, several of the areas listed above are outside the narrow scope of regulatory Compliance. And there is a purpose for this that goes beyond simply satisfying your idle curiosity! You may not feel that as a Compliance Officer you need to know how a syndicated loan works or what the Human Resources department does. However, it is knowledge of fields other than your own – even if extremely cursory in some cases – that puts your activities into context and thus broadens your understanding of the universe in which you are working.

It is, for example, all very well having an in-depth knowledge of the rules on financial promotions, but if you don't know what your firm is advertising or promoting, how these products and services work, or who they are targeted at and why, then your word-perfect textbook regulatory knowledge will not get you very far.

Besides, the more you know about how your firm works, the more credibility you build up with the business; and the more credibility you have, the more buy-in you get. As you must already know, the business is liable to ask you anything at any time, and if you cannot answer the questions within what they consider a reasonable time (usually immediately) you will lose their confidence. In most cases the business does not care about the niceties of what it considers to be the fine distinction between a form that is required by the Human Resources department rather than by Compliance; or about an agreement that must be sent to a client for tax rather than regulatory purposes. Those things don't matter to many Front Office people, so don't let yourself down.

I'm not suggesting that you try to learn every last detail about every single part of your firm – from how the receptionist organizes her files to how to book complex structured transactions in the settlement systems – but the ability to speak to a trader with some authority and knowledge about what an ISDA agreement is, for example, why it is required and who within the firm can help them further, will certainly stand you in better stead than admitting that you have no idea what one is, why it's required or whether your firm actually uses them.

It's evidently not possible at this point to provide a generic bible, setting out all the information you need to obtain relevant to your firm. Luckily, however, there are two things that can be done to give the information-gathering process some structure.

1. The basic information-gathering model in Chapter 5 provides guidance on the type of data that you will need to gather when undertaking a fact-finding exercise on your firm, its group and the individual departments within it. The model is designed as a 'catch-all' but if you adapt it to suit your own situation, complete it and subsequently keep it up to date, it will form a key tool for defining what you are actually responsible for in your own specific role.

   When you are completing your fact-finding mission, you may find that you are having particular difficulty obtaining some of the information suggested. If this happens there are two possibilities:

   (a) The information is not relevant to your business – for example, you may not have any tied agents, in which case you will clearly not be able to gather any data in this area.
   (b) You have a problem – for example, your firm has many tied agents but nobody seems to be responsible for the relationships or know much (beyond the very basics) about any of the third parties concerned. This is all the more reason to press on with your fact find so that you can be the one to find out what the situation is and bring it under control.

2. This text also helps with the information-gathering exercise by providing basic summaries of the key component parts of any Compliance universe. Such information is provided on products, documentation, regulators, legislation and on other departments you are likely to have in your firm. It does not promise to be comprehensive but if in your particular situation you need to cover some additional points that are not covered here – for example, information about some overseas regulators – you can adapt the fact-finding models provided to your individual circumstances.

And a final comment before the fact finding begins in earnest. At this stage, just keep to information gathering, getting comfortable and familiar with your universe. Only when you have reached that stage is it time to start any type of analysis: how is product X affected by rule Y; are this department's procedures compliant with relevant laws; are there any regulatory requirements relevant to such and such a document, and if so, what are they?

The following chapters turn from 'Mapping your Compliance Universe' in concept, as described above, to the practical business of getting it done: breaking down into their component parts your firm's activities and the environments in which they operate.

Specifically, the following areas are covered:

- Chapter 5: Mapping your Corporate Universe.
- Chapter 6: Regulators and Other Industry Bodies.
- Chapter 7: The Legislative Environment and Rules Mapping.
- Chapter 8: Financial Products, Services and Documentation.

5
Mapping Your Corporate Universe

This chapter provides guidance on the type of basic standing data that you should have on the operating entities, business units and external services providers that fall within your remit.

5.1 OPERATING ENTITIES

First comes a very basic task: make a list of all the operating entities within your group for which you have responsibility. Then make a list of the operating entities for which you do not have responsibility. For some, this will be very straightforward, but for others, less so. For example, if you are the Compliance Officer for a single regulated firm located in the UK which has no parent company, subsidiaries or other affiliates, this area of your universe will be less complex than for others working for multi-branch, international financial groups. Which of the following do you have responsibility for?

- UK branch offices.
- Overseas branch offices.
- UK representative offices of group firms overseas.
- Overseas representative offices of a UK entity;
- More than one UK-regulated firm within your own group.
- Non-regulated firms within your own group. (Watch out – these might not be regulated by the FSA, but perhaps they are governed by other requirements such as your corporate best practice standards and policies, data protection law, rules set by a lead regulator based overseas, etc. You also need to check that some clever clogs does not suddenly decide to book a trade through one of these unregulated entities that could result in it undertaking unregulated investment business.)
- Special purpose vehicles.
- Investment funds.
- Nominee companies.
- Joint ventures partially owned by other firms.
- Dormant entities – see comments above for non-regulated firms.

For each entity that is key to your responsibilities you will want to keep a basic information log (which you will need to update on a regular basis) covering the type of information listed below.

What about entities that you are not responsible for? Just use your judgement on a case by case basis. If there is an overseas group office on the other side of the world that has been dormant for years and never had any involvement with your company anyway, then perhaps you simply need to know that it exists and who the main point of contact should be; nothing more. For other entities perhaps you should keep slightly more information – you never know when things will change and it will suddenly become vital to know more.

Information required	Comments
Full name	• Note what any abbreviations stand for. • Also make sure you use the correct corporate designation, e.g. Plc, Ltd, AG, SA, etc.
Previous name	• It's amazing how long old names stick. If an entity you are responsible for was previously known by another name, then you had better know about it. • Some people will probably continue to refer to it by its previous name and you need to know what they are talking about. And if you are reading through old files you need to know which names refer to entities for you are responsible but are now known by another name.
Registered address	You need to know which address should go on official legal agreements, contracts and other documents.
Place of business address	• You need to know where to go when you pay the office a visit. • A single entity may have several operating addresses, even within one city if activities are spread across a number of sites.
Key contact name, phone number, e-mail address fax	You have no excuse for not being able to get in touch when you need to.
Website address	This is very important to know to enable you to read up on the entity and find out more about it, and also because websites are deemed to be financial promotions and need to comply with relevant requirements.
Place of incorporation *Date of incorporation* *Company registration number* *Tax registration number*	Basic corporate info that it does no harm to have at your fingertips.
Entity type	Is the entity a limited company, a public limited company, partnership, limited partnership, fund, special purpose vehicle, representative office, branch office, etc.?
Name of local regulator/s	Remember that there may be more than one regulator, so make sure that you note down the details of all of them.
Local regulatory approval date/s *Local regulator approval/ registration number/s*	
Capitalization	This will impact • regulatory capital resources; • the amount of money that a firm can lend; • terms on which it can borrow; • type/size of transactions that can be undertaken and correspondingly regulatory capital requirements. The above will also be a factor in the frequency and intensity of reporting required by the regulator.
Financial year end	This will have an impact on regulatory financial reporting dates.
Owners and other affiliates	• More than just useful information to know – you need to be aware of who the firm's 'Controllers' are and with whom it has 'Close Links', for purposes of regulatory applications and reporting. • You should also be aware of the department or person to whom you should be sending management information reports in relation to the Compliance status of the entity.

- Additionally, if a parent or parents are regulated in an overseas jurisdiction there may be further overseas legislation and regulation to apply.

Listings

Is the entity listed on a stock exchange? If so, there will be listing rules to comply with.

Subsidiaries
Representative offices
Branch offices

- The FSA has various rules relating to entities which it considers to be closely linked to any of the firms it regulates and one of its threshold conditions for authorization is that a firm's close links must not inhibit the FSA's supervision of it.
- If the entity for which you have responsibility has any subsidiaries, rep offices, branch offices, SPVs, etc., then you had better know as much about these as you do about the entity itself.

Powers of attorney

You need to know who has legal authority to sign on behalf of the entity; who can commit the entity to transactions; who can sign returns to the regulator; who can bind the firm to service contracts, etc.

Chief executive and directors

- Senior staff will need FSA approval, or registration with overseas regulators if the entity is in another jurisdiction.
- See Appendix D for guidance on how Compliance requirements impact senior management and the board of directors.

Company secretary

- Useful source of corporate information.
- See Appendix D for guidance on how Compliance requirements impact Company Secretariat.

Committees

Real power often lies in the hands of committees, and you need to know how they work and the members with whom you are most likely to come into contact. For example, you may find yourself having to deal with committees covering the following areas: training, conflicts, new business, Compliance risk. Get hold of the terms of reference of each relevant committee and find out who the members are.

Compliance Officer
Money Laundering
Reporting Officer

These are your peers and you need to be on good terms with them and be able to get in contact with them at short notice – they will probably be useful sources of advice, guidance and support.

Other key staff

- It is useful to know who has the following roles: Chief Operating Officer, Chief Finance Officer, Head of Internal Audit, Head of Operational Risk, Head of Human Resources, Head of Legal, Head of Operations.
- It goes without saying that you should also know the name of the heads of each business unit.
- If you have the contact details of the above people to hand, all the better.

Auditors

- You will need to form a good working relationship with the entity's auditors – they are responsible for carrying out financial audits and for undertaking various other functions on behalf of regulators.
- If you have a good relationship with your auditors you may also be able to obtain a little unofficial and free advice from them on Compliance queries that you have. Your auditors will probably have dealings with many regulated firms and should be able to give you a feel for the types of controls in place in other firms similar to your own.

(Continued)

Information required	Comments
Legal advisers	• If an entity has a strong link with a particular law firm then this relationship should be particularly valuable for obtaining regulatory advice that is specifically tailored to the business undertaken.
Corporate or business service providers	• Each entity may have any number of service providers – from the cleaner to the contractors who remove confidential papers for shredding. • Evidently some of these service providers will have some relevance to Compliance. • If any services have been outsourced to third parties then there are the FSA requirements to comply with – see page 182 of Appendix A for guidance on outsourcing arrangements in general and Appendix 21 for guidance on the outsourcing agreement.
Business units	• Prepare a list of all business-related departments – both front and back office (further information about the type of details required here is provided below). • Prepare a list of all other departments, e.g. Legal, Human Resources, Financial Reporting. • See Chapter 9 and Appendices C and D for guidance on the activities of other departments within the firm and how they impact compliance arrangements.

5.2   BUSINESS UNITS

Once you have determined the operating entities that you are responsible for, and have some basic information about them, you will need to familiarise yourself with the business units and other departments within these entities. You should aim to be familiar with the following type of information for each business unit, and to update your knowledge frequently. See Chapter 9 and Appendices C and D for guidance on the activities undertaken by various business units within financial services firms.

Information required	Comments
Name *Previous name*	As with each separate legal entity, it is useful to know what all abbreviations in a name stand for, and, where relevant, any name(s) by which the department was previously known.
Division	• In larger groups/companies individual departments will be grouped together into divisions that will have their own objectives, procedures, business models, etc. • You need to know which division your department fits into.

International offices	• Some departments operate internationally, with staff in various locations, all operating as one team. • This adds an additional level of complexity for the Compliance Officer as there will be staff in overseas locations to get to know as well as additional regulatory requirements from foreign regulators to contend with.
Main internal business contacts	• It's useful to know which other service departments work with the business units for which you are responsible. • Staff in such departments can provide you with useful information and can also collaborate with you on regulatory tasks – for example, you can work with Human Resources on a training plan or you could work with the Legal department on preparing client agreements. • These tasks will all be made easier if you have good contacts throughout the firm.
Key contact name, phone number, e-mail address fax	You need to be able to keep in touch!
Authorized signatories	Knowing this allows you to detect a document that has been signed by someone who does not have the internal authority to do so.
Legal advisers *Business consultants* *Other external service providers*	• Knowledge of who the preferred legal advisers and business consultants are is, at the very least, useful background information. • However, you are likely to find yourself communicating with these people yourself on occasion in order to resolve various regulatory issues – for example, terms required in a legal contract, so it helps to know who you will be dealing with. • Knowing who the external professional contacts are is useful also because a good relationship with them allows you to ask them for the odd piece of informal advice and guidance. • You also need to be able to identify any service providers who could be deemed to be carrying out an outsourced function on behalf of your company in order to apply the FSA rules on outsourcing. • See page 182 for guidance on outsourcing arrangements and Appendix 21 for guidance on the outsourcing agreement.
Intranet usage	An intranet site is a useful means of finding out more about a business, as well as being a useful vehicle for posting Compliance notices, forms, checklists, procedures manuals, etc.
Senior management	• You will need to know, and be on good terms with, the manager of each business unit for which you have responsibility. • These senior managers are the link between you and the business being undertaken 'at the coal face'. If you can get these managers on your side your job will be much easier as they will support you in delivering your Compliance message. They will also help to ensure that their staff comply with relevant requirements and generally set a positive 'tone from the top'. • Remember also that the FSA makes senior management responsible for Compliance, so you need to be able to identify people falling into this category in order to remind and/or brief them of their responsibilities in this area. • Further guidance about senior management can be found on page 253 of Appendix D.

(Continued)

Information required	Comments
Other staff	• You will need a full staff list for the each department for which you have responsibility so that you can keep track of who needs a regulatory registration, who is/needs to be covered by the FSA training and competency rules, who is being disciplined, who is transferring between departments, who is leaving and will thus need a regulatory reference, etc. • Try to get to know as many staff in the department as possible – if you are on good terms with somebody it certainly helps when it comes time to deliver a (potentially unpopular) Compliance message to that person. • Determine whether there are any 'star performers' who may be tempted to cut compliance corners to increase or maintain commissions. • Determine whether there are any Appointed Representatives.
Management's main Compliance concerns	Obviously this is very important to know as you will have to work with management to resolve these matters.
Products, services and activities	You should be familiar with the full range of products (e.g. bonds, syndicated loans) and services (e.g. custody) offered by each department. Guidance on several financial products can be found in Appendices 7–18.
Exchange involvement	If any of the business you are responsible for is conducted on exchange, then exchange trading rules will add an extra layer to the regulations you must be familiar with.
Unique selling points	As background information it is useful to know what makes the business or company that you are working for special.
How is income generated?	• Knowing this information enables you to check whether or not fees are being charged fairly and whether correct disclosure is being made to clients. • Fee structures can also create conflicts of interest – an adviser may be tempted to recommend a trade to a client in order to generate commission rather than because that trade is in the client's best interests. • It is also useful to understand remuneration policy. Ideally, employees' remuneration will be linked in some way to their regulatory performance. It would not be suitable for someone to be paid a large bonus because he or she had generated massive profits by disregarding regulatory risk.
Trade and customer documentation used	• List the trade documentation the department uses, e.g. ISDAs. • List all customer documentation used by the department, e.g. classification letters. • List all regulatory agreements used by the department, e.g. client money trust letter. • List any other agreements in place, e.g. service level agreements, soft commission agreements, etc. • (For further information on documentation see Chapter 8 and Appendices 19 and 20.)
Financial target for the year	• This is not only useful background information, but knowing what the target income is can highlight to you situations in which people may be prepared to cut corners, take risks and ignore regulatory requirements. • For example, if certain staff or a department are very much behind target, they may be more prepared to enter into a transaction with a 'dodgy' client if they think it will help them to make their target.

Advertising and marketing	• Promotional material is a good source of background information on the department that has issued it. • But you also need to know which marketing material is being produced so that you can review it to ensure that it complies with any relevant regulatory requirements.
Target client base	• Getting to know the type of client your firm focuses on is very important as it tells you which parts of the FSA rulebook to apply. • As good background information, it is also helpful to know the jurisdiction and entity type that is targeted.
Most valued clients (current and target)	• Win favours by speeding through requests that relate to the department's top customers. • You should also think about whether the good relationship with the department's top customers has resulted in favouritism that works to the detriment of other clients.
Relevant trade associations	• These can be useful sources of background information on the products and services offered by your department. • Such associations may also have codes of conduct that your department has chosen to comply with.
IT systems	• These are useful to know as background information. • You may also be able to use business systems to prepare reports that would be useful to Compliance for monitoring purposes.
Top deals of previous 12 months *Worst deals of previous 12 months*	Useful background information.
Competition	• Useful background information, especially if you read in the press that a key competitor has had regulatory problems – it could mean changes to your business patterns as clients leave the competitor and come to you, or it could mean less business as clients leave the market in general, seeing it as too risky. • Whatever the effect on the business, it is definitely worth checking to see what went wrong at your competitor so that you can ensure the same mistakes are not also being made by your own firm.
Challenges	• Knowing the challenges that your department faces helps you to get more in tune with their plans. • It can also indicate the areas in which people may be tempted to take the most risks and thus the areas that should be kept under closest scrutiny.
Regulatory environment (rules map)	You need to identify all potential sources of legislation, regulation and best practice codes that could affect your business. Further information on rules mapping is provided in Chapter 7 and Appendix A and further information on relevant legislation is provided in Appendices 3–6.
Manuals, procedurals, policy documents	• Useful sources of background information. • You should also review these to ensure that they do not contain any procedures that do not provide for compliance with relevant requirements. • You may wish to add some regulatory references to these documents.
Risks	• You should be aware of the key risks affecting the department, along with how they are managed and any remedial action that should be taken. • Obviously, not all risks are of direct concern to Compliance, but an awareness of risks in other areas provides you with useful background information on issues affecting the department's activities.

(Continued)

Information required	Comments
	• Determine which steps, if any, need to be taken by the Compliance department.
Conflicts of interest	• You need to carry out a thorough exercise, logging all the potential conflicts of interest that could affect the department, together with how they are managed and mitigated. • You should also identify any gaps and form a plan to carry out remedial action as soon as possible. • Conflicts of interest are a key topic for regulators worldwide and you cannot afford to get this wrong. • Further information is available on page 146 in Appendix A.
Recent regulatory issues	• You absolutely need to know the regulatory history of the department. • If there have been no recent regulatory issues, then all well and good – try to keep it that way. • If, however, there have been problems you need to know everything about them, such as: how and why they arose; who was responsible; are those people still at the firm; is the regulator still monitoring the situation; is remedial action still ongoing; is there a risk that the problem will arise again?
Regulatory hot topics	• Determine whether there have been any recent regulatory sanctions relevant to the department. • Determine whether there are any current regulatory issues in the market in general affecting the type of business undertaken by the department you are reviewing – for example, read the financial press and check regulatory websites to see if any relevant policy documents have been issued recently. • Are there any issues affecting the type of products and services relevant to this department?
Changes in previous 12 months	This is useful information to put where you are today into context.
Changes planned for next 12 months	• This is vital information. You need to know how the business plans to evolve to enable you to address in good time any compliance issues that this might give rise to. • Determine the unit's plans for the next twelve months and assess the impact that this will have on Compliance, products, structure, services, etc.

5.3   EXTERNAL SERVICE PROVIDERS

Also forming part of the regulatory universe are the non-group companies that have an impact on the ability of your firm to meet its regulatory requirements. Such third parties include

- UK and overseas brokers and introducing brokers;
- business consultants, agents and advisers;
- appointed representatives;
- tied agents;

- firms both in the UK and overseas to which a particular part of the regulatory process has been outsourced or for which a service is performed on an insourced basis; and
- managers, distributors, custodians and sponsors of investment funds.

The information you will need about these non-group entities will vary depending on the nature of the relationship, but as a minimum should consist of the following:

Information required	Comments
Contact details	Address, telephone number, website.
Relationship manager	Key contact person at the third party entity.
Internal relationship manager	Which business unit and staff member within your firm 'owns' the relationship with this entity?
Key dates	• When did the relationship commence? or • What is the proposed start date if this is a new relationship? • Is there a set date when the relationship is due to terminate or to be reviewed?
KYC	• Is there a need to carry out KYC on this entity? • If so, has KYC been carried out and are documentary records up to date?
Nature of relationship	Which services and/or products are provided to your firm by this third party?
Regulated status	• Is this entity regulated either in the UK or overseas? • If regulated, what is its regulatory status? • What is its regulatory history?
Background	What is the history of the relationship to date – is this perceived to be a successful relationship and, if not, what are the issues? Is anything being done to improve the situation?
Plans	Will there be any changes to the relationship in the near future?
Outsourcing	• Could this relationship be deemed to constitute material outsourcing under the FSA regulatory regime? • If so, are relevant regulatory requirements being complied with (see page 182 of Appendix A)?
Monitoring and oversight	• Is there a need to carry out monitoring visits to review the service standards provided by the other firm? • Or does the other firm have the right to come in and carry out monitoring reviews of your own company?
Contractual agreement	• Review the contract between your firm and the third party so as to gain a better understanding of the relationship. • If the arrangement involves outsourcing, the agreement must meet specific regulatory content requirements – see Appendix 21.
Fees	• On what basis is this entity paid for its services? • Is disclosure made to clients if necessary? • Could this arrangement constitute a soft commission arrangement?
Internal requirements	• Are there any internal policies or procedures that apply to your firm's relationship with this third party?

For further guidance concerning relations with third parties see page 137 of Appendix A.

6
Regulators and Other Industry Bodies

When mapping your regulatory universe you will have identified the regulators and other organizations and agencies that form part of the environment within which your firm operates. Obviously, it is vital to have a really detailed knowledge of those organizations that have true rule-making power and the ability to get you into trouble if things go wrong. But the successful Compliance Officers do not stop there. They understand the value of getting to know all the industry bodies that are linked to the type of business in which they and their firms are involved and which include

- government departments – national and international;
- central banks;
- trade associations;
- international organizations;
- exchanges and clearing houses, on which more guidance is provided below;
- law enforcement bodies;
- informal unions of financial services firms who take a joint stance in a particular area; and
- consumer groups.

And don't forget the press, which is very powerful when voicing opinions and influencing thought and strategy in areas of interest to it. Several types of non-regulatory industry bodies are listed above and these are of relevance for many reasons:

- They may help to shape regulatory policy by lobbying the FSA or the government (perhaps you feel strongly about an issue and want to get involved).
- They may set best practice standards that are adopted by firms in your field of business (you do not want to be left behind). This is becoming increasingly important with the FSA's move towards principles-based regulation (see Box 1 ('Acting a Principle') on page 317 and Box 7 ('Industry Guidance') on page 328) as a result of which we have the prospect of many more industry-based codes of conduct to guide us rather than the prescriptive rules we normally deal with
- They may provide guidance about particular areas of regulation and regulatory developments.
- They may deliver training.
- They may provide networking opportunities. Some organizations have regular meetings that can present good opportunities for meeting other people in the industry to find out what is happening in other firms, the types of issues they are facing and how they implement particular rules. And the more people you know, the more people you can call upon for guidance if you have a problem you are not sure how to tackle.

For each regulator, standard setting body or industry association you identify as relevant, it is also advisable to make a note of how it affects your own firm, and the person within your team who is responsible for managing the relationship and following developments.

Appendix 1 provides summary details of some of the regulators and other industry bodies that are most likely to be of relevance in the UK (even though several of them are based overseas and/or have a global remit). If you have an international brief, you should seek out similar bodies in the jurisdictions that are of relevance to your particular role.

6.1 EXCHANGES

Alongside regulators, central banks and governments, exchanges are some of the most signific-ant players in the regulatory arena as they are required by their own supervisors to implement robust rules for the companies they list and the entities that trade on them. The phenomenon of the exchange can be traced back several hundred years, but in the past 20 it has probably gone though as much change as in all of its previous existence. It is important for Compliance Officers to keep track of these developments if they are to have a thorough understanding of the industry in which they operate.

Exchanges were traditionally owned and operated by the member firms that used their markets and there was a tendency for them to be viewed as some sort of national status symbol embodying a country's industrial capacity, economic prowess and overall financial existence. But patriotism and emotion are now being cast aside and many exchanges have demutualized to become simply a specialized type of company, often operating internationally, trying to make a profit and facing competition (as we will see below), just like any other. However, despite the changes, their traditional functions remain more or less unchanged, as summarized here.

Corporate Fund Raising

Stock exchanges provide a vehicle for companies to 'go public' or 'list' by issuing equity shares, thereby increasing the range of people willing and able to fund them and, if things go according to plan, increasing the amount of cash they have to develop their business. After the initial public offering (IPO), companies can then continue to raise funds through stock exchanges either by means of subsequent new issues of shares, or by issuing listed corporate bonds. This role of providing companies with a means of raising the funds they need to expand means that exchanges play a pivotal role in a nation's economy. Note that not all exchanges have a listing function.

Trading and Liquidity

Once an investment has been listed on an exchange, the exchange then offers a central environment for trading in IT. The organized market place offered by the exchange allows investors to find buyers for the asset they wish to dispose of, and sellers of what they want to acquire. When the exchange uses a market-making system to ensure liquidity in certain classes of share (see below), investors know that they will always be able to find a buyer or a seller.

Price Discovery and Benchmarking

Another important aspect of the centralized market place is that it facilitates the determination of fair prices for what is on offer – anyone who is charging something that seems to be exhorbitant will need to adjust their pricing, or be priced out of the market. Exchanges therefore instill confidence in the financial markets by giving comfort that investors have not been over charged for something they have bought, and that they have received a fair value for what they have sold. Pricing is key in the financial markets and price levels determined by exchanges may be used for many things, including

- stock valuation, e.g. PE ratio, quick ratio, etc.;
- formulating market indices, which are used as
  - benchmarks for gauging the mood of the economy in general;
  - benchmarks for gauging the mood of a particular market such as base metals or oil;
  - assessing performance of individual products or collective funds;
  - the basis for other products, such as contracts for difference;
  - the basis for derivatives contracts and structured products.

- valuing collective investment scheme units;
- portfolio valuation; and
- determining when margin calls should be made.

Organized Market Place

Exchanges offer an organized and structured market place where trading occurs in a controlled and tested environment. The assurance this gives to participants is vital for maintaining confidence in the financial markets as a whole and can be bolstered still more when an exchange teams up with a central counterparty and or clearing house, with the associated settlement security these bodies can provide.

Strategizing

Derivatives exchanges offer market participants the opportunity to engage in a number of strategies, for example to maximize their income through speculating or avert risk by locking in a known price for a future date (hedging).

Corporate Restructuring

Stock exchanges provide a facility for takeovers via tender offer (see Appendix 8).

Regulation

With exchanges providing all the key functions offered above, it is vital that they should do so in a fair, reliable and transparent manner if participants are to maintain their trust in the markets. Indeed, so crucial are exchanges to the operation of healthy financial markets that they are required to impose stringent rules on their participants, as well as being regulated themselves. Their rules cover a wide range of activities including

- listing (in the UK requirements are set by the FSA);
- setting criteria for membership;

- trade times and sizes;
- Transparency:

  - listed companies are required to disclose material information about themselves as soon as possible as a key element of the fight against market abuse);
  - post-trade price and conditions reporting;
  - pre-trade order publication requirements.

- approval of new exchange traded products;
- facilitating the resolution of disputes between participants;
- surveillance to identify market abuse and any other inappropriate activity; and
- disciplinary arrangements.

As well as the traditional activities noted above, exchanges are increasingly taking on a marketing role and heavily promoting their services in the face of increasing competition not only from other exchanges but also from a variety of alternative trading mechanisms and venues. Increasing globalization means that international companies no longer choose automatically to list in their country of incorporation. It also means that exchanges in one country may establish trading venues in another. A number of concerns have been expressed about how this increased competition among exchanges could lead to conflicts between their commercial aspirations and their regulatory responsibilities with most debate focusing on the following areas:

- *Lower standards* – Competition between exchanges could lead to a lowering of admission criteria for member firms, thus damaging market integrity. This has certainly been an argument put forward about AIM by certain competitor exchanges (or maybe it's just sour grapes as it has been so successful?).
- *Regulatory investment* – Exchanges may be inclined to spend less money on their regulatory infrastructure to free up funds for spending on activities that will have a more direct impact on their profitability.
- *Regulatory fund raising* – Could exchanges be tempted to use financial penalties on market participants as a way of generating income? This is unlikely in the long term as such a strategy would undoubtedly scare off their membership, but as a short-term quick fix to financial difficulty it could conceivably take place.
- *Regulation of rivals* – Where exchanges regulate rival firms (either as market participants or listed companies) that provide competing execution venues there may be an inclination to subject them to disadvantageously harsh regulatory scrutiny and practice.
- *Public service* – As exchanges are performing a public role that is so fundamental to a country's economy, some feel that it is too risky to leave the provision of such an important service to the uncertainties of the commercial world and the pursuit of profit rather than the public good.

In order to combat these perceived dangers exchanges must comply with rules set by the relevant national regulator. Many have also found their regulatory responsibilities being stripped away from them: in the UK, for example, the LSE is no longer the competent authority for listings.

Although exchanges generally share the characteristics previously described, there are also considerable variables in terms of how they operate and what they offer. Some of the key differentials are as follows:

- *Product offering* – Some exchanges offer a means by which companies can raise funds and list, whereas others do not provide a listing facility. Still others do not list securities at all, offering only derivative contracts. Certain exchanges also provide facilities for trading currency and commodities.
- *Trading style* – This may be done face to face across the floor of the exchange (known as 'open outcry'), via screens and phones, by means of the exchange's own electronic dealing system, or by a combination of these.
- *Trading method* – In its simplest form an exchange may merely be a meeting point of potential buyers and sellers of a certain asset, without any special mechanism to bring the interests of the two sides together. This mechanism (or lack of one) is not seen in many modern exchanges because it does not support the key requirement they now have to provide: the expectation of a certain amount of liquidity – i.e. the ready availability of buyers and sellers, and vice versa.

Modern exchanges use two principal mechanisms to achieve this, the first being the longer established and less technologically complex:

- A 'market-making system' directly supports liquidity in the market in shares or other products, especially in the shares of smaller companies which don't enjoy 'natural' liquidity. In these cases brokers will, in return for certain privileges, undertake to make a market (quote a buy and sell price) in certain products.
- Another mechanism, used predominantly for investments with more 'natural' liquidity – e.g. shares trading in the top indices, such as the FTSE 100 – is the electronic order book. Here, a bid and ask order of any size can be entered, with a range of possible restrictions, anonymously, and will be met if and to the extent that there is a buy or sell order to correspond to it.

For the Compliance Officer perhaps the biggest differentiator is status. Of the exchange functions listed above there are few (e.g. listing and market index formulation) that can only be offered by a 'traditional' exchange: there are certainly other mechanisms whereby companies can raise funds, trades can be struck and prices gauged. This is where the rivals to traditional exchanges are found.

Until a few years ago, the chief alternative to trading on exchange was to trade directly with another counterparty, called trading 'over the counter' or (OTC). But developments in the world of IT, and especially the growth of the internet, have led to the emergence of a range of hybrid facilities that are not traditional exchanges but which no longer seem to fit the OTC mould: we now have the 'unofficial', or pseudo-exchange.

Our regulators have defined what they consider to be a bona fides exchange. In the UK, for example, an exchange in the regulatory sense of the world is one that has met and complies with the relevant requirements set out in FSMA and in the FSMA 2000 (Recognition Requirements for Investment Exchanges and Clearing Houses) Regulations 2001. Anything else may look like an exchange and act like an exchange, but it is simply not going to give investors the regulatory certainty that is required to obtain the FSA seal of approval and be permitted to wear the 'exchange' label. As the jargon for referring to the different types of trading venue can be confusing, guidance is provided below.

Venue type	Comment
Recognized investment exchanges (RIEs)	RIEs are exchanges established in the UK that meet the FSA's approval criteria, and which are thereafter supervised by the FSA on an ongoing basis.
Designated investment exchanges (DIEs)	DIEs are exchanges that are not active in the UK but are deemed by the FSA to provide consumers with adequate levels of protection.
Regulated market	RIEs may offer more than one separate market and not all of these will meet the 'regulated market' criteria. The London Stock Exchange's Domestic Market, for example, is 'regulated' whereas AIM is not (being an 'exchange regulated market' instead).
Exchange regulated market	Offers a lighter-touch regulatory regime for new and smaller companies wanting to gain access to public funds. Securities are still classed as 'listed' but listing rules as applicable to 'regulated markets' do not apply. Under MiFID, strict pre- and post-trade transparency requirements do apply.
Multilateral trading facilities (MTFs)[1]	MTFs (a term coined by MiFID) provide the same type of trading facilities as exchanges but without the requirement for regulation as such (although authorization to conduct investment business *is* required). Trading is conducted electronically, directly between the two counterparties.
Systematic Internalizers[1]	Systematic Internalizers (yet another MiFID term) are investment firms which on a regular basis are able to execute client orders internally as they hold large inventories of securities.
Electronic cross networks or electronic communication networks (ECN)[1]	Another name for an MTF.
Alternative trading system (ATS)[1]	Another name for an MTF.
Bulletin boards (via the internet)[1]	Bulletin boards offer facilities whereby sellers can advertise their wares and buyers can take a look at what is on offer.

[1] OTC trading.

With these unofficial exchanges there is reduced (if any) regulatory vetting and investors are to a certain extent in uncharted territory where anything might happen. So why would anyone want to take the risk of using them for investment? The main answers are flexibility and cost:

- *Flexibility* – When investors come together directly they can invest in more or less any way they choose, as long as they can find someone else to sit on the other side of their trade. They are not constrained by exchange approved investments or contracts.
- *Cost* – As these pseudo-exchanges often have only a limited physical presence and do not have a whole infrastructure of rules and requirements to maintain, prices can be kept low.

What does all this mean for the financial services industry as a whole? Well, it probably means considerable angst and more change, because as exchanges try to defend themselves from the alternative trading venues, they are forming cross-border alliances in which some countries lose control over their national exchange. As we have seen, even though exchanges are essentially corporate entities with a specialized function, they are often seen as national status symbols and flag fliers and many people get rather excitable about the idea of their country's national exchange going into foreign ownership.

Not so long ago, plans were afoot to form a European 'mega' exchange with a merging of eight or nine leading exchanges, but perhaps not surprisingly their management could not agree terms. Since that time, however, we have seen a number of lesser alliances, for example, the London Stock Exchange with Borsa Italiana and Euronext with LIFFE.

All of this should not go unnoticed by the Compliance Officer as the regulatory implications of international exchange alliances have the potential to be far reaching. We saw a good example of this in 2006 when it became clear that NASDAQ was interested in buying the London Stock Exchange. This led to concerns about whether, as a subsidiary of a US entity, the LSE would be required to comply with the hyper-restrictive Sarbanes–Oxley Act (see Appendix 6) to which has been attributed a considerable flight of new listings from New York to London, where the listings regime is deemed to be more flexible and pragmatic.

The UK government was quick to respond and passed the Investment Exchanges and Clearing Houses Act 2006 (IEC Act) thus ensuring that irrespective of the jurisdiction of the owners of an exchange, national rules will apply. In the end the deal did not go through, NASDAQ gave up on the LSE and turned its attentions to the Swedish exchange. How long will it be before Sweden passes a piece of legislation like the IEC Act?

There are some concerns that the multitude of trading venues will lead to a fragmentation of liquidity, but on the whole the view seems to be that a consolidation of European exchanges makes sense from a business perspective: our patchwork approach and lack of streamlining arguably put us as a competitive disadvantage to our rivals in the USA due to the higher costs that ensue. But the US also essentially has one national regulatory system whereas Europe does not. Despite the convergence that we are achieving with MiFID (see Appendix 5 and Box 9 on page 331), our regulatory landscape is anything but uniform and we have some way to go before we are ready to accept a single European exchange.

So, in the meantime we are left with the diversity of trading venues and the competition for liquidity that we see today. This has several implications for the Compliance Officer

- a greater number of execution venues means that there are ever more rules and requirements to keep track of;
- best execution can be harder to establish as there are so many venues through which to execute;
- there is a greater number of regulatory relationships to be maintained, bringing the potential for additional regulatory visits, increased supervision, possible disciplinary action, etc.;
- it becomes important to know the difference between the various types of execution venue – the Market Abuse Directive only applies to regulated markets, and not all facilities fall into this category; and
- there is greater settlement/counterparty risk as fewer trades are conducted on an exchange with a central counterparty.

Further details about some individual exchanges and clearing houses can be found in Appendix 2.

6.2   CLEARING HOUSES

Clearing houses are to exchanges what the Back Office is to the Front Office in the financial services firm, their role being to facilitate the settlement of trades that have been conducted on the financial markets they support. They are often associated with a particular investment exchange although they can also be used for the settlement of trades that have been undertaken off exchange (i.e. over the counter, or OTC). In essence, clearing houses match buyers and sellers, making sure that buyers receive the assets they have paid for and that sellers receive the monies they are owed. They also facilitate the payment and receipt of initial and variation margin.

At a high level, two settlement models are used by clearing houses: one model uses a system of novation to a central counterparty, whereas the other allows buyers and sellers to face and settle with each other directly. Where novation is involved, settlement/credit risk for participants is greatly reduced as the clearing house automatically becomes the counterparty to both sides of every trade (i.e. the buyer to every seller and the seller to every buyer). The clearing house has various means of protecting itself, and its members, financially from such events, such as imposing initial and variation margin requirements and setting minimum capital adequacy requirements for membership. Novation also facilitates netting so that instead of having to make and receive numerous daily deliveries of cash to a range of counterparties, a single payment can be made or received and delivery of securities and amounts owed may be set off against amounts receivable. Finally, novation also permits anonymity as firms do not necessarily know entity with whom they have transacted, as settlement is always with the clearing house. This means that sensitive trading strategies remain confidential.

Where there is no novation, settlement/credit risk remains with the counterparty to a trade, and if they are unable to pay for the assets they have bought, a seller who has already delivered the assets will take a credit hit.

The Financial Services Authority has the right (and duty) to recognize and supervise clearing houses active in the UK. In order to achieve 'recognized' status the FSA must be satisfied that the clearing house complies with the requirements of the Financial Services and Markets Act 2000 (FSMA), section XVIII, and the Recognition Requirements for Investment Exchanges and Clearing Houses Regulations 2001. The status as a recognized clearing house under FSMA removes the need for authorization to conduct investment business that would otherwise apply. It also acts as a safeguard in that only the most trustworthy and well-managed organizations will be granted, and maintain, recognized status. Further information about the FSA's supervision of recognized clearing houses can be found in its Recognized Investment Exchanges and Recognized Clearing Houses Sourcebook.

Guidance on the two Recognized Clearing Houses in the UK can be found in Appendix 2.

7

The Legislative Environment and Rules Mapping

As a successful Compliance Officer you will already have, or will be in the process of creating, a list of all the pieces of legislation that are applicable to your firm's activities. And in order to operate to your full potential, once you know which legislation applies you need to be able to find your way around it, because there will invariably be times when you are not sure what a particular rule is designed to achieve, where it comes from and whether there is any chance of being sent to jail if you or your colleagues fail to comply with it.

Sometimes, the only way to really get to grips with what is required is to go back to primary sources, i.e. the relevant sections of the piece of legislation that gave rise to the requirement in the first place. Of course, legislation is also useful for defining key terms and concepts – for example, the FSA's Glossary often simply refers the reader to the relevant section of FSMA, or other even more impenetrable texts such as EU directives, which is not particularly helpful unless you have copies of the legislation to hand, or know where you can easily get hold of them.

Obviously, for the majority of financial services firms operating in the UK, FSMA is **the** key piece of legislation. But that doesn't mean that other legislation can be ignored. There are many other laws with which you need to be familiar that directly affect financial services activities, several of which impose some quite meaty penalties for non-compliance.

This last point is of particular importance if you are not lucky enough to have Compliance-friendly senior management. If you have at your finger-tips a good knowledge of the personal liability that the 'top brass' of your firm face under each relevant piece of legislation, and if you can give management some juicy examples of counterparts finding out about this liability in person, and happen to sprinkle in such pieces of information at choice moments in a discussion about why a particular control needs to be introduced (despite its cost or supposed inconvenience), then it is amazing how willing even the most reluctant of bosses can become to act upon what you say. Applicable regulatory legislation falls into three broad categories:

1. Legislation designed specifically to establish the legal framework for the financial services industry, eg the Financial Services and Markets Act 2000.
2. Law applicable to certain types of financial services activity only, e.g. the Bills of Exchange Act
3. Law that is of more or less general relevance, but has a significant impact on financial services, e.g. the Proceeds of Crime Act 2002.

It should also be remembered that there is a considerable amount of overseas legislation that is of relevance to UK financial services firms. For an example of why this should be, see Box 6 ('Going Global') on page 326.

Once you have identified the key pieces of legislation that are of relevance to your firm you should determine those for which the Compliance department has primary responsibility and those that are administered by another department. This can then be noted in the Compliance Charter (see page 43 of Chapter 3) so that there is no confusion over who is required to do what.

It is also a good idea to put a risk management and mitigation programme in place for each law for which you have responsibility within your firm. Matters that you might cover are summarized below.

Issue	Comment
Responsibility	If you have a large department, and/or a considerable number of laws to be aware of, you may wish to assign responsibility for particular pieces of legislation to individual team members.
Applicability	Determine the extent to which the law is applicable to you. List the business units, activities and products to which it is relevant.
Risks	Establish what you consider to be the key risks for your firm in relation to each piece of legislation.
Controls	Document the controls that have been implemented in relation to each risk identified.
Weaknesses	Identify any weakness in the control framework relating to the risks identified.
Action plan	Prepare a corrective action plan designed to address the weaknesses you have identified. Make sure that you record and track progress on a regular basis.
Review frequency	Based on the overall level of risk presented to your firm by the piece of legislation, determine how frequently you should monitor compliance with its requirements. Review frequency may differ for different sections of the law.
Risk	What overall risk rating do you attribute to this law? Your risk rating may be based on a number of factors such as • seriousness of penalties that can be imposed by the law • frequency with which penalties are imposed • extent to which the law is applicable to your firm – does it apply across the board, or only to one small part of what you do? • is compliance with the law the primary responsibility of the Compliance department? Or is primary responsibility with another department with only a peripheral impact on the Compliance department?

Appendices 3–6 comprise a summary of some of the key pieces of legislation that are of relevance to UK financial services firms. If you have an international brief, you will need to research the legislation relating to the jurisdictions that are relevant to your particular role.

The text of UK legislation can be found easily on the internet and two websites are particularly useful:

• *Office of Public Sector Information* (http://www.opsi.gov.uk/)
  This is probably the easiest to use but bear in mind that just because the text of a law can be found on the site, it does not mean that it is still in force, or that significant sections of it

have not been either repealed of amended by subsequent legislation. It also does not contain legislation dating back more than about 20 years.

- *The UK Statute Law Database* (http://www.statutelaw.gov.uk/)
  Operated by the Ministry of Justice this website is slightly more difficult to navigate than the previous one, but it does contain useful details of how a particular piece of legislation has been amended and how it will be affected by amendments that are not yet in force. It also has legislation dating back far further than the OPSI site.

7.1   RULES MAPPING

Once you have identified all the various sources of requirements that affect your firm (legislation, regulation, industry best practice, etc.) you will be well on the way to getting to grips with three of the most fundamental concerns that the Compliance Officer should have

- the requirements that your firm needs to comply with now;
- how planned changes in your firm's activities will be affected by current regulation; and
- how planned changes to the regulatory universe will impact your firm.

The only way you can really get to grips with these three fundamental points is by rolling up your sleeves and getting your hands dirty with some solid rules mapping. Now, rules mapping may well be one of the most boring activities known to humanity – no one ever said it wasn't. But as a successful Compliance Officer, there is no escaping it (unless you can pursuade a trusty colleague to do it for you!).

Rules mapping needs to be done at two levels:

1. *High level* – Understand the regulatory framework in the jurisdiction in which you work.
2. *Detailed level* – Understand how the jurisdiction's regulatory framework affects the operations of your own firm.

A brief summary of the high-level UK financial services regulatory environment is provided in Chapter 1. This should also serve as a guide to the sort of information that you should gather about the regulatory environment in place in any overseas jurisdiction where there is an entity for which you have responsibility.

7.2   DETAILED RULES MAPPING FOR YOUR OWN FIRM

First, the high-level rules map is going to be fairly similar for all firms in the same jurisdiction. Once you have established this framework however, you need to add some detail, because different firms undertake different types of activity, meaning that they will be affected in different ways by the high-level arrangements in their jurisdiction. Not all parts of each law, for example, will apply to every firm.

During this more detailed stage of the rules-mapping process you need to establish how all the various components of a particular jurisdiction's regulatory regime impact your own firm in the context of the products and services it provides. To help you do this, Appendices 1 to 6 provide guidance on some of the key pieces of legislation and the main regulators and other standard setting bodies that form part of the regulatory universe not only in the UK, but internationally. These chapters can be used for a sort of 'pick and mix' selection process to identify the legislation, regulators, etc., that are relevant. This will enable you to prepare a detailed model that is tailored to fit the individual circumstances of each firm for which you are responsible. Also, do not forget to include any internal policies and procedures that your firm has implemented as these also form part of your regulatory universe.

If your firm is relatively small with only one line of business then a single regulatory map is likely to be sufficient, but for many Compliance Officers the story is not going to end there: once you go beyond the very high level requirements that apply to all, there are going to be separate requirements that are relevant to the business activities each a firm conducts. For example, if you drill down into the detail of the FSA rulebook, you will realize that not all parts of it are relevant in all cases. If you don't have an asset management function, for example, the Collective Investment Scheme sourcebook does not need to play a particularly significant part in your life.

There are two approaches that can be taken to this more detailed rules mapping – the bottom-up or the top-down approach:

- *Bottom-up approach* – Take a department, product, activity, etc., and establish all the different regulations, legislation, etc., that apply (some guidance is provided in Appendices 3–6, 24, C and D that can be used as a starting point).
- *Top-down approach* – By far the most detailed and time-consuming part of the rules-mapping process. Take a set of regulations or a piece of legislation and determine how each requirement applies to the various departments, products, activities, etc., relevant to your firm. It is possible to go into a lot of detail when doing this and if it is an area you are not familiar with it is definitely worth getting as detailed as possible. The table on page 75 provides a possible format for a top-down rules map for a hypothetical firm with four separate departments: Equity Sales, Proprietary Trading, Investment Research and Corporate Finance. Some of the comments on applicability may change from firm to firm depending on their specific activities (e.g. if a firm has an Equity Sales department that does not do any distance marketing, then COBS 5 will not be relevant). Other comments on applicability should be uniform across all firms (e.g. no firm should have an Equity Sales team involved with claims handling for long-term insurance and therefore COBS 17 should never be relevant).

  Note that even though this table is provided under the heading 'detailed rules mapping' there is certainly scope to do mapping on a much more detailed level than that included here. Ideally, after having identified a set of requirements that are applicable to a particular department then another table should be created for that particular set of requirements. As an example, the table shows that COBS 2: Conduct of Business Obligations is applicable to the Equity Sales department. But COBS 2 has four subsections and these can also be mapped for applicability.

This process, although painfully tedious, is really worth while. It's amazing how the process of breaking down a set of requirements into their most basic units, and having the discipline to work out exactly what is required, how it applies to your firm, and exactly how your firm complies with the particular requirement, can expose weaknesses in the Compliance infra-structure that you would not necessarily have noticed before. Even if you do not expose any weaknesses, it is also a great learning tool for really getting to grips with the detail of a rule or requirement.

Further information about rules mapping can be found on page 138 of Appendix A.

Sample Rules Map: This table shows a rules map prepared for a hypothetical company with four different Front Office departments: Sales and Trading, Proprietary Trading, Research and Corporate Finance.

Ref	Rules	Departmental Applicability			
		Equity Sales	Proprietary Trading	Research	Corporate Finance
COBS 1	Application	Applicable, but for reference purposes only: explains the scope of COBS requirements.	Applicable, but for reference purposes only: explains the scope of COBS requirements.	Applicable, but for reference purposes only: explains the scope of COBS requirements.	Applicable, but for reference purposes only: explains the scope of COBS requirements.
COBS 2	Conduct of business obligations	Applicable	Applicable	Applicable	Applicable
COBS 3	Client categor-isation	Applicable	Applicable	Applicable	Applicable
COBS 4	Communicating with clients, including financial promotions	Applicable	Applicable	Applicable	Applicable
COBS 5	Distance com-munications	Applicable: extensive dis-tance marketing activities conducted.	Not applicable as applies only to 'consumers' as defined by the FSA.	Not applicable: the Research Department does not carry out any distance marketing.	Not applicable as applies only to 'consumers' as defined by the FSA.
COBS 6	Information about the firm, its services and remuneration	Applicable	Applicable	Applicable	Applicable
COBS 7	Insurance mediation	Not applicable: no insurance business undertaken.	Not applicable: no insurance business undertaken.	Not applicable: no insurance business undertaken.	Not applicable: no insurance business undertaken.

(Continued)

Ref	Rules	Departmental Applicability			
		Equity Sales	Proprietary Trading	Research	Corporate Finance
COBS 8	Client agreements	Applicable	Not applicable: no client business undertaken.	Not Applicable: no designated investment business undertaken.	Applicable
COBS 9	Suitability (including basic advice)	Applicable	Not applicable: no personal recommendations made.	Not applicable: no personal recommendations made.	Applicable only where personal recommen- dations are given.
COBS 10	Appropriate- ness (for non- advised services)	Applicable	Not applicable: no relevant activities undertaken.	Not applicable: no relevant activities undertaken.	Not applicable: no relevant activities undertaken.
COBS 11	Dealing and managing	Applicable	Applicable	Not applicable: no relevant activities undertaken.	Not applicable: no relevant activities undertaken.
COBS 12	Investment research	Not applicable: no preparation or distribution of investment research.	Not applicable: no preparation or distribution of investment research.	Applicable	Not applicable: no preparation or distribution of investment research.
COBS 13	Preparing product information	Not applicable: no relevant activities undertaken.	Not applicable: no relevant activities undertaken.	Not applicable: no relevant activities undertaken.	Not applicable: no relevant activities undertaken.
COBS 14	Providing product information to clients	Not applicable: no relevant activities undertaken.	Not applicable: no relevant activities undertaken.	Not applicable: no relevant activities undertaken.	Not applicable: no relevant activities undertaken.
COBS 15	Cancellation	Not applicable: no relevant activities undertaken.	Not applicable: no relevant activities undertaken.	Not applicable: no relevant activities undertaken.	Not applicable: no relevant activities undertaken.
COBS 16	Reporting information to clients	Indirect relevance: transactions are reportable but reports sent by Back Office.	Indirect relevance: transactions are reportable but reports sent by Back Office.	Not applicable: no relevant activities undertaken.	Not applicable: no relevant activities undertaken.

COBS 17	Claims handling for long-term care insurance	Not applicable: no insurance business undertaken.	Not applicable: no insurance business undertaken.	Not applicable: no insurance business undertaken.	Not applicable: no insurance business undertaken.
COBS 18	Specialist Regimes	Only rules on stock lending are of relevance.	Not applicable: no relevant business undertaken.	Not applicable: no relevant business undertaken.	Only rules on corporate finance business are of relevance.
COBS 19	Pensions supplementary provisions	Not applicable: no pensions work undertaken.	Not applicable: no pensions work undertaken.	Not applicable: no pensions work undertaken.	Not applicable: no pensions work undertaken.
COBS 20	With-profits	Not applicable: no insurance business undertaken.	Not applicable: no insurance business undertaken.	Not applicable: no insurance business undertaken.	Not applicable: no insurance business undertaken.
COBS 21	Permitted Links	Not applicable: no insurance business undertaken.	Not applicable: no insurance business undertaken.	Not applicable: no insurance business undertaken.	Not applicable: no insurance business undertaken.

7.3   RULES MAPPING FOR AN OVERSEAS JURISDICTION

For each jurisdiction for which you are responsible you need to understand at least as much about its regulatory regime(s) as has been described for the UK in Chapter 1. When you have completed this task you may have a much longer list of sources of requirements than you have for the UK: overseas, you often find that each different area of financial services activity is governed by a separate regulator – one regulator for banking, for example, another for insurance and another for broking.

And of course once you are aware of all applicable laws, regulators, rules etc., then you can start the more detailed mapping of requirements as detailed in this chapter.

8
Financial Products, Services and Documentation

8.1 PRODUCTS AND SERVICES

It is difficult to be successful as a Compliance Officer unless you understand the full range of products and services offered by your firm. If you do not understand this basic element of your working environment you are liable to give wrong or inappropriate advice, potentially getting yourself, your firm and your colleagues into trouble. It also lays you wide open to being hoodwinked: if you are trying to tackle a Compliance query that has come your way and a trader or fund manager is able to 'blind you with science' because you don't know your swaps from your collars, you may well find yourself being 'engineered' into giving a 'Yes' when your response should really be a 'No, not in any circumstances'.

And just as important are the matters of credibility and good-will. Your Front Office colleagues want to feel that they are dealing with someone who knows what they are talking about, and specifically, someone who knows the firm's business. You will get a lot more 'business buy-in' if you are capable of having a sensible conversation about the key products relevant to the departments for which you are responsible. Think about it – if, for example, someone asks you about the regulatory implications of a credit default swap that they are working on and you have no idea what that is, then you are going to lose credibility (and waste time) if this has to be explained to you before you can give your view.

Needless to say there is an enormous range of financial products and services on offer and it seems as if new variations of these are being invented all the time. You clearly cannot be an expert in all of them – or perhaps if you were you would not be working in Compliance! But you should at the very least

- Know which products and services your firm is permitted to trade/offer. This will depend on the scope of your firm's regulatory licences. (Details of the permissions for each regulated firm are published on the FSA's website, but many regulators issue individual licences.)
- Be aware of which of these products and services have received internal approval. (This may not always tally with your firm's regulatory permissions.)
- Confirm which products and services your firm is actually offering and involved in right now. (While you may have regulatory and management approval to provide advice in relation to commodity futures, for example, there may be no department currently doing this.)
- Be clear about the basis on which your firm is involved with each product (see the table on the following page).

Once you have established the above in relation to each entity and/or department for which you have responsibility (and that was the easy part), then is the time to really start to put in some serious work. You need to have at least a basic understanding of the products and services offered by your firm: How do they work? What are they used for? How are they affected by the regulatory universe in which you operate?

Basis of service	Description
Execution only dealing	Client gives trade instruction with no advice provided by you.
Advisory	Client pays for your advice but need not pay heed to or act on your recommendation.
Discretionary management	You make investment decisions on behalf of your client or a set of clients, within an agreed set of parameters, without having to seek permission prior to undertaking each individual trade.
Proprietary trading	There are no clients involved – you follow the trading strategy that you think will lead your firm to financial victory!

8.2   UNDERSTANDING PRODUCTS AND SERVICES IN CONTEXT

On first encounter many financial products may seem impenetrably complex. Rest assured, however, that no matter how 'funky' a transaction may appear, the basic concepts upon which the vast majority of products and services are based are very straightforward:

- one person is buying and another person is selling; and/ or
- one person is lending and another person is borrowing.

Another way of looking at it is that, on the one side, there are consumers of financial products and services, and, on the other, there are firms and individuals whose business it is to supply those products and services.

The next time someone comes to you with something really 'rinkydink', try to break it down using the concepts mentioned above and see if your understanding is enhanced.

The requirements and expectations of the financial services consumer vary greatly and so does the product offering available, but it is nevertheless possible to break these down into just a few basic categories (which are not, of course, exhaustive), as summarized below.

In Appendices 7–18 you will find a basic introduction to the financial markets and some high-level guidance on some of the most well-known financial products and services. (If you need any more detailed information there are plenty of courses to attend or textbooks to consult.) Also provided in these appendices are some suggestions about key compliance concerns for each product type, sources of regulatory requirements and relevant industry organizations.

Consumer needs	Comment/example	Sample product/service
Extra funding	• Businesses need funding to expand, or to buy some new equipment. • Individuals need funding in order to buy a house, or to go on a high street spending spree.	• Share issue • Private equity • Trade finance • Loan
Financial peace of mind	• If a company will have a metals consignment to sell in one year's time, it will be beneficial for that company to agree a price today rather than risk the price of that metal taking a nose dive by the time it is ready for sale. • If an individual fears losing his job, he feels better if he can 'buy' a certain level of income that will be available to him if he finds himself without work.	• Bank guarantees • Futures • Income protection insurance
Currency exchange	• If a UK retailer imports shoes from Italy, it needs to pay for the goods by exchanging sterling for euros. • If you go on holiday to New York, you need to buy some dollars.	• Foreign exchange services
Security	Companies and individuals both want to know that if they have a million pounds today, they will also have at least a million pounds tomorrow (unless they are willing to accept the risk of losing it by 'gambling' on doubling their money).	• Deposit accounts • Money market funds • Certificates of deposit
Wealth accumulation	Companies and individuals would both be very pleased to find a way of not only securing their million pounds for tomorrow, but also turning it into a little bit extra.	• Gilts • Term accounts
Tax planning	Companies and individuals are both keen to reduce the amount of cash they hand over to the tax man.	• Tax advice • Individual savings accounts • Tax avoidance schemes, such as trusts
Advice and expertise	Many companies and individuals have a financial plan but do not know how to achieve it. A mining company, for example, knows the best way of getting gold out of the ground but is not necessarily going to know the best way to raise money to buy a new mine. Likewise, you may know very well how to drive a Ferrari but may be stumped when it comes to finding the money to buy one.	• Financial advice • Discretionary investment management
Fun	A lot of people get an enormous amount of pleasure out of pursuing a hobby in watching the markets, whether by 'beating the market', by watching a trusty portfolio of 'safe' blue chips go up in value, or by dabbling in something a bit more exotic!	• Stock broking services • Spread betting

8.3 DOCUMENTATION

Inextricably linked with your firm's products, services and activities is the documentation that holds it all together: the pieces of paper that establish exactly what one party expects from the other and how it is to be achieved. There are basically four types of documentation with which the Compliance Officer needs to be familiar:

Agreement type	Comments
Trading agreements	• These agreements describe the relationship between the supplier and consumer of a given financial service.
	• The agreements are not regulatory documents – their contents are not specified by regulators nor is their usage a regulatory requirement (although they may have an impact on regulatory capital calculations).
	• It is not generally necessary to have a detailed knowledge of trading documentation, but at least a little background information about the agreements used by your firm is vital: if you look blank when a trader talks to you about an ISDA for example, and then you expect that person to treat you with any credibility going forward, then you have just reduced your chances of this happening. Don't give people an excuse not to take you seriously.
	• In smaller firms without a separate Legal and/or Documentation department it can frequently fall to the Compliance Officer to ensure that trade documentation arrangements run smoothly.
	• There are proforma agreements in place for many types of trade that have been prepared by industry associations focusing on particular types of business.
	• Where there are no proformas, other documentation in this category will need to be prepared on an ad hoc basis by a firm's Legal department or by external advisers.
Customer documentation (for account opening and operating)	• Account opening documents are used to establish the basis on which a firm will manage its overall relationship with its customers.
	• Other documents in this category are required on an ongoing basis to notify customers of activity on their account for example, or to reflect changes in the firm's relationship with an existing customer.
	• Several of the documents are required for regulatory purposes whereas others are simply used as a matter of best practice and convenience.
	• The Compliance department is sometimes responsible for sending out these documents and should always be involved in their drafting to make sure that any regulatory contents requirements are complied with.
	• Compliance Officers should have a good knowledge of the documentation in this category that is in use in their firm.
Tax documentation	• Tax authorities are interested in the activities of the consumers of financial services, their identity and the location of the beneficial owners of the assets involved. Their interest is such that a suite of forms and declarations have been prepared for firms to give to their customers to ensure that correct tax information is collected.
	• Tax documentation does not relate to any specific Compliance requirements but, nevertheless, it is useful to have at least a cursory knowledge of this area.
	• In smaller firms, as is the case with trading agreements, it can frequently fall to the Compliance Officer to ensure that tax documentation arrangements run smoothly.
Regulatory documentation	• The final category of documentation relates to miscellaneous requirements stipulated by the FSA and/or other regulators.
	• Compliance Officers should have a good knowledge of documentation in this category.

Appendices 19–22 provide a brief introduction to some of the most commonly used documentation.

9
Compliance Outside the Compliance Department

Who needs to know about Compliance and regulatory requirements within your firm? The Compliance department? Your Investment Managers? The Legal department? Operations? Human Resources? The receptionist? The simple answer is that *everyone* working for a regulated firm needs to know about Compliance. The level of knowledge required will clearly vary greatly depending on a person's role and position within the firm but it is hard to think of anyone who you can categorically say does not need even the slightest awareness of how Compliance requirements bear on their role. Even a driver or messenger or temporary secretary needs to know not to act on price-sensitive information, for example, or not to leave documents lying around in case client details get into the wrong hands. At the other end of the scale, the Heads of Front and Back Office functions arguably need to be as familiar as you are with Compliance requirements in their specific area. It is your job to get them there. In order to do so you need to understand what they do – first, to establish which rules have an impact on them and, second, to meet them on their own ground, and not have the wool pulled over your eyes.

The Compliance Officer should therefore know which departments there are within their firm, establish the type and extent of regulatory knowledge that is required by the people within each of these departments, and then make sure they all know what is expected of them by providing training or by writing manuals or briefing notes, or by a variety of other means as described on page 126 of Appendix A.

If you don't do this then you are simply not meeting your responsibilities – people who work in financial services need to be aware that there are various rules and regulations that apply to them, and that if they breach these requirements they may be subject to serious penalties. It is only fair that you tell your colleagues what their responsibilities and liabilities are so that they are adequately protected from inadvertent breaches. If you don't do this you are also letting your firm down by failing to make sure that everyone is clear about what is expected of them.

In general the departments within a financial services firm are separated into two broad categories, the first being the Front Office and the second the Back Office and support areas. Additionally, senior management and the board of directors could be said to be in a separate category that sits above the other two. The final sections of this chapter provide a brief overview of the Front and Back Office with more detailed guidance located in Appendix C (Front Office) and Appendix D (Back Office, support functions and senior management), which take you in greater depth through typical Front and Back Office departments and cover the following:

- general background information to establish the principal activities of each department;
- regulatory and legislative requirements so that:

– you are aware of the key areas in which problems may arise with respect to each department; and
– employees of the relevant departments can be notified of requirements applicable to them so that these can be factored into their day-to-day activities.

- situations in which there is overlap between Compliance and another department (particularly in the Back Office and other support functions) so that you know

  – who may have information that is of use to you;
  – who may be of assistance in tackling a regulatory issue;
  – who it would be useful for you to pass information to; and
  – who will be reviewing your performance.

Obviously each firm is organized differently in that the names of the departments may vary from one institution to the next, and the scope of responsibilities for each department will not be uniform in all cases. But, in general, issues of the nature of those set out in Appendices C and D will be relevant.

9.1   THE FRONT OFFICE

The 'Front Office' is the term used to refer to the parts of the firm that are customer facing and revenue generating. Appendix C provides a brief summary of four Front Office functions that are found in many firms:

- Customer Sales and Trading
- Investment Management
- Corporate Finance and Investment Banking
- Research.

Because such a wide range of activities may be undertaken by the Front Office the Compliance requirements and controls covered in Appendix C do not apply uniformly:

- Some do not apply to all activities;
- Some apply to all activities but with varying effect due to the differing nature of the products and services involved; and
- The applicability of others depends of the type of customer concerned.

Due to the variation listed above and given the complexity of many of the rules involved, Appendix C aims more to highlight the principle and generic concepts behind a rule or requirement of which both Compliance and the Front Office rather should be aware, than to cover each regulatory nuance.

9.2   THE BACK OFFICE AND OTHER SUPPORT FUNCTIONS

Back Office departments support the revenue-generating activities of Front Office staff – for example, ensuring that trades settle correctly, providing information to clients, monitoring risk and making sure that systems and controls are working satisfactorily. Fewer detailed Compliance requirements apply to these areas but even so, there are important regulations that are of relevance (and it is important not to forget this when you are drawing up your training plan).

It's not all one way, however. There is likely to be some degree of overlap between the responsibilities of the Compliance department and the Back Office and support functions within your firm. Take advantage of this to collaborate as much as possible with relevant staff in terms of relying on them for vigilance, gaining information and advice, and implementing joint initiatives.

The Back Office material in Appendix D gives a short explanation of the activities of each area, highlights the ways in which there may be synergies with Compliance and briefly describes the relevant regulatory requirements. Finally, remember that even where a function is outsourced (which many firms choose to do with activities such as settlement and client reporting) responsibility for making sure that Compliance standards are met still rests with your firm. You can outsource the function, but not the responsibility.

10
Key Compliance Department Activities

This chapter considers the types of activities with which Compliance Officers are involved on a day-to-day basis. These can be split roughly into

- routine activities; and
- advisory work, when Compliance is taken 'off piste' and you are asked to tackle something new and unfamiliar.

10.1   ROUTINE ACTIVITIES

Financial services firms are involved in widely differing types of business, and if you compare your own regulatory and corporate universe with that of a colleague in another firm, even if they are involved in a broadly similar line of business, you will be surprised at the number of differences there are. No matter how different the line of business, however, Compliance departments generally have a fairly similar brief and will thus be involved in a similar set of routine activities. (Remember that all Compliance departments should have similar objectives, as discussed in Chapter 2.)

These basic, work-a-day activities constitute the foundation of your firm's Compliance regime and while they are certainly not rocket science you have to get them right: there's too much at stake under FSMA and in terms of your own reputation within the firm if you don't. Once you understand what the rules require and the internal procedures your firm has implemented, you will find that these functions are fairly straightforward and you will soon be doing many of them on auto pilot.

Even though they are not generally considered to be the 'sexy' side of Compliance, you really should look on them as your friends; they offer you a certain amount of security as you know exactly what you are doing – a conveyor belt of Compliance issues to process: how to report a suspicious transaction; how to process personal account trades; how to deal with a gift received from a client . . . and so on. And for those new to Compliance, processing such matters is a good way to begin.

Appendices A and B set out the key activities that will be undertaken by the majority of Compliance departments (although, depending on the firm, they may be the responsibly of another department, for example, Operations, Legal, etc.). It also provides guidance on the key requirements relating to these activities and the practical steps that need to be taken to ensure Compliance with them.

And a final word – the guidance in Appendices A and B are largely based on the current FSMA regulatory regime (although it does not slavishly follow the detail of each rule). Requirements change from regulator to regulator, jurisdiction to jurisdiction and even from year to year. To a certain extent it's not so much the detail that is important – the key to getting things right is to understand the principles and concepts involved, and to be clear about the underlying intention of a rule or requirement. Indeed, the importance of detailed rules looks set to play an ever reducing role in future with the rise of principles-based regulation – see Box 1 on page 317.

10.2   OFF PISTE COMPLIANCE: ADVISORY WORK

A large part of this text is dedicated to 'mapping' your Compliance universe to enable you to find your way around it as quickly and as easily as possible (as with the previous section of this chapter for example, providing suggested 'routes' for the accomplishment of several key tasks). But there does come a time when there is no map and you need to go 'off piste'. This is the other side of Compliance – ad hoc advisory and project work in uncharted territory – and you need to be just as comfortable with this as you are with the routine. This field of Compliance can be a bit like riding on a regulatory rollercoaster, offering lots of thrills and spills along the way; daunting, but also very satisfying. It will keep you on your toes and present you with new challenges every day – challenges that will really enable (or force) you to think laterally and develop solutions that will guide your firm successfully through 'the regulatory jungle'. But this area of Compliance is also where the most danger lies for you as a Compliance Officer – get this part of your job wrong and you're in serious trouble. Get it right, and this is your opportunity to show your chief executive just how beneficial a Compliance department can be: marrying regulatory certainty with improved internal efficiency and customer service.

Of course, this text cannot even begin to provide guidance on all the queries and issues that may come your way. Nor can it teach you to think on your feet or manage expectations, which are key skills for undertaking successful advisory work. It also cannot take account of the fact that, depending on their experience and background, a routine enquiry for one Compliance Officer is going to constitute a catapult into the unknown for another. What this text can do however is provide some pointers to the type of issue that you should consider when one of your business managers approaches you with a pressing and complex query, or even something quite straightforward that you simply have not encountered before.

You can take comfort from the fact that even though the types of issue that you can be presented with vary so greatly, there is at least a relatively standard approach that you can take whenever tackling something new. You can apply much the same model whether you are dealing with something arising in the context of 'business as usual' that is slightly out of the ordinary (e.g. My client wants to give me an anaconda as a gift, can I accept it?) that you can if you are being presented with something that constitutes a totally new departure for your firm and its business (e.g. We want to set up a suite of branches in Chile, how do we go about it?)

This process has three stages:

1. Understanding as much as possible about the new situation/query with which you have been presented.
2. When you have enough understanding of what the new situation is, or what precisely the query relates to, determining what exactly the regulatory implications are.
3. Deciding how the matter is best addressed – devising your plan, and following though.

The next section of this chapter is dedicated to helping you to put these three steps into practice.

10.2.1   Understanding What It Is All About

No matter how experienced you are, you cannot possibly understand every single aspect of the financial services industry, every single regulatory requirement, or how the two interact. You will inevitably be faced with situations in which you are asked a question about something that you know little, if anything, about. It sounds obvious, but if there is a query or issue that you need to think about for more than a few minutes, this will probably be because you have been presented with something new – either a familiar issue in a novel context, or something that you have never been confronted with before (and perhaps didn't even know existed!).

Paradoxically, before we come to look in detail about what to do in order to tackle the unfamiliar we need to look at what you absolutely must *not* do: never allow yourself to be rushed into giving an answer before you feel comfortable doing so. You really must not get pressued into giving a response before you have been able to consider all the issues. If you do, you are not going to do yourself or your firm any favours. You may think that a successful Compliance Officer would be able to give a quick-fire response, but this is only true if you know exactly what you are talking about. Otherwise, you risk making a mess. Looked at from a very simple level, if you give the go-ahead to something you do not understand you could be showing the green light to a serious rule breach. And conversely, if you say 'no' to something that you do not fully understand, you could be preventing your firm from carrying out a perfectly legitimate, not to mention profitable, business activity. And remember – that will affect *your* bonus too!

The following table gives examples of some of the basic questions that you can ask to get a deeper understanding of issues on which you may be required to pass judgement.

Theme	Comment
Who	• Who within your firm is involved with the query? • Which departments are involved? • Which operating entities are involved? • Are any third parties involved, eg consultants, appointed representatives, lawyers? • What type of client is involved? • Which regulators will be involved?
What	What exactly does the query involve: • New service? • Innovative trade structure? • Which products? • Which legislation?

(Continued)

Theme	Comment
Why	Why is there a query in the first place? Why can't things carry on as they were before?
When	• When is the answer needed? • When is the change going to take place, or has it already occurred? • Have there already been any developments that you have not been told about?
Where	• Which jurisdictions will this situation affect? • Which locations within the UK will be involved? • Where will the target clients be based? • Where will any joint venture partners be based? • Where will any third party service providers be based?

Once you have the basics as described above, here are some suggestions for finding out more about a situation that you are struggling to understand.

- Tell the person asking you the question to put the query in writing. This will buy you some time, and it will also give you something concrete to go on.
- In order to get some background information ask to see any documents that have been written about the new situation or query. Documents you could ask for include business plans, mandates from previous similar transactions, credit applications, business proposals.
- Keep asking questions and don't stop until you feel you have all the information you need. You might find it useful to speak with the following people:

  - The person who has come to you for advice or guidance.
  - The boss of the person who has come to you for guidance – they are likely to be more experienced and better able to explain things to you.
  - A more junior colleague in the department generating the query – junior staff are often more willing then their seniors to take time out to talk to Compliance (they have more time, they have more to prove and it can make them feel important that someone is taking the time to talk to them!). You may also not feel so bad about asking junior staff 'stupid' questions when you would not like to reveal your ignorance to their more senior colleagues.
  - Members of your own Compliance department.
  - Compliance contacts in other firms – keep it confidential of course and only talk in generalities.
  - Contacts working for industry associations that focus on a field relating to your query.
  - Staff in other departments in your firm that may also be affected by the matter that has been brought to your attention. Depending on the situation you could think about asking for advice from staff in Legal, Documentation, Operations, Finance, Internal Audit, Human Resources and Information Security.

- When you are talking the situation through it often helps to break things down into stages or to draw diagrams showing flows of cash and assets.
- Drawing a diagram of a complex trade structure is also useful for making confusing proposals seem more straightforward.
- Check all definitions and rules and requirements in the area in relation to which you have been given a query. Go back to primary sources even if you feel that you know a rule well; check it again in the context of the new situation; read the guidance in the rule book; study the Glossary; look at relevant pieces of legislation.
- Type a key word or phrase into Google.
- Look at your textbooks or reference books to find material on the area on which you are being questioned.
- Check internal procedures manuals and policy documents for requirements in that area.
- Look up definitions in dictionaries of financial terms.

10.2.2 What Are the Regulatory Implications?

When you feel that you have a full understanding of the new situation or query that is being presented to you then you will be in a position to make a judgement about its regulatory implications. Again, it must be stressed that there can be no 'one size fits all' approach as the range of matters that will be brought to you is so great that it is obviously not possible to supply an exhaustive list of issues that you will want to consider that will cover every possible situation. All the same, the following list does provide a flavour of the type of questions you will want to ask yourself and others when reaching a determination about a new situation. The items you should be questioning can be split into two broad categories:

1. What should be done about a situation that has already occurred?
2. Can a proposed new arrangement be implemented?

Questions for Situations that have Already Occurred

Area	Query
Regulatory approval	Does your firm have the appropriate regulatory authorization to engage in the activity you are being asked about?
Applicable rules and requirements	Has there been a breach of any of the following requirements? • Legal. • Regulatory (consider regulators, exchanges and clearing houses). • Best practice. • Contractual. • Codes of conduct. • Internal procedures.

(Continued)

Area	Query
Staff authorization	Does the person to whom the query relates have the authority to do what was done in terms of: • your firm's internal arrangements? • the training and competence rules? • the Approved Persons rules?
Data security	Has there been a breach of confidentiality, data protection or information security?
Counterparty impact	• Will a client be disadvantaged as a result of what has happened? • What category of client has been affected? • Might you have to pay compensation?
Threshold conditions	Does the matter have any impact on the firm's continuing compliance with the FSA's Threshold Conditions for authorization?
Fitness and propriety	Does the matter have any impact on the Approved Persons rules or a controller's fitness and propriety?
Compliance resources	Are there adequate Compliance resources for addressing what has happened or is the issue so serious that additional staff will be required as part of a remediation project?
Breaches and complaints	• Have you been advised of a situation that will need remedial action? • Is further investigatory work required? • Could this situation be symptomatic of a wider problem? • How exactly did the situation arise? • Is it likely to occur again? • Does any immediate preventative action need to be taken? • Does the matter form part of a pattern of events that is already under review? • Has there been a complaint from an eligible complainant? If so, have the appropriate complaints handling rules been followed?
Money laundering	• Is there a possibility that money laundering has taken place? • Has the required report been made either to the Money Laundering Reporting Officer or to SOCA. • Are you concerned that 'tipping off' has taken place?
Market abuse	• Is there a possibility that market abuse has taken place? • Do you need to report a suspicion of market abuse to the FSA?
Fraud	• Does it appear that there has been a fraud? • Is your fraud officer or department aware of what has happened? • Are they already investigating the situation?
Outsourcing	• Does the problem that has arisen result from something that has occurred at a service provider? • Has there been a breach of a service contract?
Operational losses	• Has an operational loss been incurred? • If so, is the Operational Risk department aware of the situation or should you notify them?

Reporting and notifications	• Do you need to notify a regulator of what has taken place? • Does a report need to be made to senior management or head office? • Does a suspicious activity report need to be filed? • Do you need to notify another department? • Should you seek legal guidance?
Finding out more	• If you need to find out more about a situation, who can you ask? • Which documentation can you review? • Will key conversations have been subject to voice recording?

Questions Relating to Proposed New Arrangements

Area	Query
Regulatory approval	• Does your firm have the regulatory authorization to engage in the activity that you are being asked about, or will a new permission be required? • Will you need to obtain any overseas regulatory approvals?
Rules mapping	• Which pieces of legislation apply to the matter that you are being asked about? • Which regulations apply to the matter you are being asked about? • Do you need to take any overseas requirements into account? • Are staff within your firm familiar with processes involving these requirements? • Is there any clear regulatory or legislative reason why a proposed new activity you are being asked about cannot take place?
Exchanges	• Does the situation mean that a new exchange membership will be required? • If so, how long will membership approval take? • Does anyone within the firm have experience of the relevant exchange rules? • Who will prepare the application? • What are the initial and ongoing costs involved?
Clearing houses	• Will new clearing house relationships be required? • If so, how long will membership approval take? • Does anyone within the firm have experience of the relevant clearing house rules? • Who will prepare the application? • What are the initial and ongoing costs involved?
Regulatory capital	• How will a new activity you are being asked about impact regulatory capital? • Is your Finance/Regulatory Reporting department aware of the plans or do you need to inform them?
Training and competence	• Do existing Front Office and Operations staff have the correct status under the T&C rules to take on the new activity? • If new staff are required, which T&C status will be required? • What training will be required to prepare staff for the new activity?

(Continued)

Area	Query
Approved Persons	• Do current staff have the correct status under the Approved Persons regime to undertake a proposed new activity? • Which Approved Persons status will any new staff be required to have?

Internal approval	• Has relevant senior management given their approval for the proposal?
	• Do all relevant support departments know about this development? Departments you may wish to liaise with include (see Appendix D):
	
	    − IT;
	    − legal;
	    − operations;
	    − tax;
	    − finance;
	    − human resources; and
	    − marketing.

Staff authorization	• Do the people involved have the appropriate level of internal authority to do what is being proposed? • If not, are their plans sanctioned by their management (in which case you also need to talk to them). • Would it be appropriate to grant the missing authorization?
IT systems	• Are the required IT systems in place to support the new activity? • Does the IT department know about the plans, or do you need to tell them? • Will any additional Compliance systems be required or will changes be required to existing systems; for example, your trade surveillance software may not be configured to cover a particular new product that someone wants to trade.
Responsibility	• Is there a clear reporting line that will demonstrate ultimate senior management responsibility for the new activity? • Does the senior manager responsible have experience of the type of regulatory issue to which the new situation gives rise?

Counterparty impact	• What effect will the new activity have on the firm's client base? Will a new type of clients be taken on, such as
	
	    − retail clients?
	    − professional clients?
	    − eligible market counterparties?
	
	• Will services be provided on a new basis, such as
	
	    − advisory?
	    − discretionary?
	    − execution only?
	    − through an agent?
	
	• Do staff within your firm have the experience to support the new type of client or basis of service?

Staff resources	• Are there adequate staff in the following departments to carry out and support the new activity:

                              – Front Office;
                              – operations;
                              – compliance;
                              – credit;
                              – legal;
                              – marketing;
                              – IT;
                              – finance;
                              – human resources; and
                              – risk

Complaints

- Will the new situation give rise to eligible complainants as defined by the FSA?
- If so, are there appropriate systems and controls in place?
- Has your firm had complaints in a similar area in the past?
- If so, has appropriate remedial action been taken so that such complaints are unlikely to arise again?

Documentation

- Will the new situation give rise to any additional documentation requirements?
- If so, does someone in the firm have the experience to draft or negotiate this documentation, or will external input be required?

Client assets

- Do the arrangements you are being asked about give rise to any changes to client assets services, such as

    – client money?
    – custody?
    – collateral?
    – mandates over a third party bank account?

Compliance resources

- Are there adequate Compliance resources for dealing with the new situation?
- Will temporary staff be needed for a project or will permanent staff be required to have ongoing responsibility for an entirely new area of business?

Continuity planning

- Does the business continuity plan need to be updated to take account of the new situation?
- Will this be completed by the time the plan is to 'go live'?

Money laundering

- Do you need to update your firm's anti-money laundering arrangements to take account of a new product or service?
- Do you understand all of the money-laundering risks associated with the new product or service?

Topicality

- In relation to the proposal, are there currently any regulatory 'hot topics' that you should take into consideration: a large fine, a scandal in the press, a 'Dear CEO' letter etc.?
- You will want to be extra careful to get things right if the answer to the above question is 'Yes' as regulatory scrutiny is likely to be heightened.

Conflicts of interest

- What are the potential conflicts of interest in relation to the matter you are being asked about?
- Ensure that you have listed all potential conflicts and how they can be managed and mitigated.
- Or does the situation give rise to a conflict that is so substantial that you really cannot proceed?

(Continued)

Area	Query
Internal procedures	• Does what you are being asked about breach any internal procedures? • Will the Compliance manual need to be altered? • Will a new procedures manual be required? • Will new policy documents be required?
Voice recording	• Will voice recording need to be applied to a new activity that you are being asked about? • If so, does the firm have enough capacity on its voice-recording system or will changes to the IT infrastructure be required?
Outsourcing	• Does the matter you are being asked about involve a new outsourcing arrangement? • If so, could this constitute 'material outsourcing' under the FSA regulatory regime? • Or will the matter involve your firm engaging in an activity for a third party – insourcing? • Are any service level agreements required?
Record keeping	• What are the record-keeping requirements associated with the situation you are being asked about? • Will a change to current procedures be required?
Regulatory sanctions	• What are the regulatory sanctions that your firm could face if things go wrong in the new area? • Is it worth the risk?
Financial promotions	• Will financial promotions be issued for a new service or product offering? • Which jurisdictions will the promotional material be issued into and do you know what the advertising rules are? • What sort of client will the promotional material be targeted at?
General	• What is the doomsday scenario – if you give the go-ahead to a new project, what are the worst things that could go wrong and what could be the consequences? • Would the regulator care very much if these things happened, or are they immaterial? See Chapter 11 for guidance on what the regulator's 'hot buttons' are.

10.2.3 Your Plan of Attack

Looking at What Has Already Happened

Somebody comes to you with a potential problem. You investigate a bit and find out that you really are not best pleased with what has been going on. What are you going to do now? You're obviously going to have to tell someone to stop what they've been doing and do something else instead. But in all but the simplest of cases, things are not going to stop there. You are frequently going to have to implement some sort of remedial action plan to correct what has occurred – the list below gives guidance on the types of issue that you should consider when trying to put things right.

Issue	Comment
Policies and procedures	• Are new policies and procedures going to be required in order to cover this situation, or to prevent it from arising again?
Training	• Has the situation highlighted any training needs? • Remember that you or other members of Compliance might also need training.
Disciplinary action	• Is internal disciplinary action appropriate? • Have you engaged with HR to determine how best to proceed?
Competence	• Has somebody done something so serious that it could compromise their 'competent' status under the T&C regime? • Should you no longer deem this person as competent? Or can the situation simply be remedied by the provision of additional training?
Approved Persons Regime	• Has somebody done something so serious that it could affect their fitness and propriety under the Approved Persons regime? • If so, have you notified the FSA?
Notifications	Who needs to be notified of the new situation? • senior management; • the FSA; • head office; • another regulator; • the police; and • a client.
Continuity planning	• Does the business continuity plan need to be invoked? • Does the business continuity plan need to be updated to take account of what has happened?
Outsourcing	• Can you pursue a third party for damages? • Do you need to find a more reliable service provider?

New Situations/Initiatives/Proposals

Clearly, once you have worked out exactly what the situation is that you are being presented with, you need to decide what to do next. You have various options:

• Say 'No', you cannot do what you are proposing in any circumstances. End of story.
• 'Fiddle about' a bit with the proposed plan to make it workable, then say 'go ahead'.
• Say 'Yes' straight away – there may be no regulatory issues involved in what you are being asked about.
• Make the most of the fact that senior management is responsible for Compliance: write a brief note summarizing the issues and let the bosses decide if they want to take on the

risk. You can use this approach when the matters at stake are not clear cut – the project being proposed has the potential to lead to very serious rule breaches, but there is nothing inherently wrong. This way, senior management are aware of what might happen, and aware that they would be responsible for any trouble. But they can balance that with the business benefit as, after all, your firm is there to do business, not to 'do compliance'. If you take this route, it really helps to provide senior management with recent examples of things that have gone wrong in the relevant area – regulatory fines and sanctions, for example.

- If you find that you are being presented with new and complex proposals with some regularity you would probably benefit from establishing a committee or other forum to discuss new business initiatives. You can gather colleagues from the various areas of the firm who are most likely to be affected by changes and use the meetings to identify potential problems and how they can be addressed. This helps to prevent the situation in which you spend ages considering the regulatory implications of a new business plan only to find that the Legal department, for example, has discovered a reason why the new initiative cannot go ahead.

- If you are regularly presented with complex new plans, you can make matters run more smoothly by arranging for the business do some ground work before the new plans come to you. For example, you could establish a procedure under which you will not consider new proposals unless you have a certain minimum amount of information. You can use the suggestions listed earlier in this chapter to prepare a template setting out the information you wish to be provided with.

- Make a plan – some of the things that you give the go-ahead to will not require much work, of course. But if you have just said 'yes' to the establishment of a new branch, for example, then you have a considerable amount of work ahead of you. Work out exactly what needs to be done from a regulatory perspective and who needs to do it. Let the business see your plan and make it clear that they cannot go ahead until all matters have been addressed.

Help!

Still don't know what to do? Then forget *all* the detail mentioned above for a while and think about your gut reaction:

- does the proposal pass the 'smell' test?
- does it pass the 'front page of the Financial Times' test?
- do you think most people would be ashamed to admit to the matter that you are considering?
- would you be reluctant to let the regulator find out about it?
- would you rather your colleagues did not find out about it?
- if everyone in a particular department, firm or sector wanted to do what you are being asked to consider, would this have an overall positive or negative impact on the UK financial services industry?

Sometimes these simple questions can help to guide you in the right direction.

And if you have exhausted all the options suggested in this chapter and *still* don't know what to do, then you really need to admit it. Some matters simply cannot be dealt with within the Compliance department or indeed within your firm. Perhaps you really *should* know what to do. But if you don't, there's simply too much riding on it to make a mistake. Seek professional advice and go on a course. You'll know what to do next time.

10.3   COMPLIANCE CONUNDRUMS

As we have seen above, despite the fact that in the UK we work with a rulebook running to thousands of pages of specific rules and general guidance, there are times when Compliance can seem to be one big grey area. The number of real-life situations that fit a rule neatly and have a simple yes/no answer is really very small. Most Compliance questions are messy. This is one of the most confusing (and most rewarding) parts of the job.

Appendix E provides some examples of the kinds of real-world, tangled scenarios that show what the Compliance world is all about. Some of the examples are greatly simplified to get to the core 'Compliance' issue, but all are representative of the types of issue that you are likely to meet in the real world. The 'comments and solutions' try to propose strategies you should adopt when faced with a dilemma, and to steer you towards a perspective which combines

- knowledge of and respect for the rules;
- pragmatism and proportionality; and
- commercial understanding

... because most dilemmas will call for a measure of each of these.

The remainder of this chapter deals with what is probably the biggest of all conundrums for the Compliance professional: how to tackle a basic lack of cooperation from the business. Some Compliance departments have the luxury of an open and constructive relationship with a conscientious and circumspect business function, whose Compliance awareness will do much of their work for them; the others will probably find that the core weakness of their relationship with business units gives rise to one 'Compliance moment' after another, not to mention a determined resistance to any solutions Compliance might propose. Get the business on side first of all, and many of the scenarios set out in the Appendix will never arise; if you don't you may well make your job impossible.

10.4   DEALING WITH A LACK OF COOPERATION

Dealing with a lack of cooperation from the business is one of the most difficult challenges you will face as a Compliance Officer. Other things are much more within your control: you learn about a new rule by looking it up in the rulebook; you document your procedures by writing a manual; you identify instances of non-compliance by conducting review work. You *make* someone comply by ... doing *what* exactly? By engaging in mind control, hypnosis, recruiting your own Compliance armed forces?

If any of the danger signals identified in Chapter 2, Section 2.3.3, are true of your firm, then it is likely that you will be meeting resistance on a fairly regular basis. And even if the danger signals are not present, no matter how reasonable you are, or how reasonable your colleagues generally are, there will still be the odd occasion when you come across the 'lout with clout' – a person with authority who also has a thuggish mentality and will try to intimidate you into saying what he or she wants to hear by

- telling you that you do not understand;
- telling you that you are missing the point;
- saying what a poor service Compliance provides, how it is poor value for money;

- saying that they will complain to your boss about your obstructive attitude (Just try to get to your boss first, and if they are decent he or she will support you!);
- shouting; and
- being abusive.

You may find yourself in the situation of knowing all there is to know about Compliance, regulation and your firm, and you may have the most beautifully drafted and formatted Compliance manual in the world. But if you cannot get anyone to take notice of what you tell them, or to read or pay attention to your lovely manual, then with the best will in the world you are not going to do a very good job.

Here are some of the tactics you can try when faced with a lack of cooperation or with people acting in a way that does not make for a healthy regulatory environment within your firm.

1. Don't get to that stage in the first place – train and explain so that the business has no inclination to do something wrong in the first place.
2. Have a good think about whether what you are saying is correct – after all you might be wrong, and back-tracking is not the end of the world.
3. Simply tell the individuals not to do what they are doing and inform them of what you want them to do instead – nice and simple but frequently very effective.
4. Ask them to reread the relevant section of the Compliance or procedures manual that relates to what you want them to do.
5. Nag and cajole, and return later to see if the individuals are now doing what you want.
6. Remind them of the internal penalties that they may face if they do not do as you ask.
7. Remind them of the legal, regulatory and reputational penalties they may face if they do not do as you ask.
8. Tell their boss what they are up to (or not up to as the case may be) and encourage their boss to put pressure on them as well.
9. Come up with an alternative, workable solution – perhaps an even more business friendly way of doing what they wanted to do.
10. Get advice from colleagues about what they have done in similar situations.
11. Ask your Compliance contacts in other firms for their opinion – perhaps you are being too risk averse.
12. Ask yourself if what you want the people to do is really important – perhaps this is not a fight worth having and you need to conserve your energy for the bombshell that is around the corner.
13. Let the individuals explain why they do not want to do as you say and, if convinced, let them carry on as they were – perhaps you did not initially understand them and are actually asking them to do something irrelevant, or even incorrect.
14. Put the matter on hold and bring it up for general discussion during a team meeting.
15. Put the matter on hold and ensure that it is covered in the next Compliance or Internal Audit review.
16. If what the other people are doing affects another department, tell an appropriate person who can back you up – HR, Regulatory Reporting, Training, etc.
17. Tell your boss so that he or she can also bear down on the miscreants. Alternatively, it may be within your boss's remit to approve the situation that you are concerned about on an exception basis, whereas you do not have this authority.

18. Tell your boss's boss if your own manager is not giving you the support you need. Pass the buck upwards as far as possible if you truly are stuck and things are going really badly – you are not paid enough to deal with this sort of nonsense!

19. Tell Internal Audit, Head Office Compliance, or External Audit and they may be able to include the matter in their next review of the area that is concerning you.

20. Or perhaps you will agree that the business will carry the risk of going against your decision – after all, our regulators are very clear that responsibility for Compliance rests with senior management, so perhaps you should just leave them to it.

21. And if none of the above works and you really are convinced of the fact that you are right, and that the problem you are aware of is very serious, tell the FSA (last resort only in the vast majority of cases).

One final note on this matter before moving on. If you feel that something inappropriate is going on and you are not getting the support you require, then you should make brief notes of discussions that you have had with others in order to record their responses. You should also note down the rationale for decisions that you have taken. The last thing you want is to find yourself blamed for having identified a problem and then having done nothing about it!

11
Comply or Die – When Things go Wrong

Of course nothing ever happens in your firm (or my firm for that matter) that would cause the regulator to raise a disapproving eyebrow. However, knowing what is likely to make things go wrong, and what happens when they do, does serve a very useful purpose (other than the obvious voyeuristic pleasure that is to be derived from rubber-necking the bad girls and boys to see what they have been up to, and what will happen to them as a result)!

There are two main reasons for knowing about this:

- An awareness of the main roads to regulatory and legislative catastrophe – and, conversely, what is likely to feature (if at all) as a mere blip on the regulator's radar – is a useful tool in prioritizing work tasks and resources. Why spend time fretting about something insignificant that is happening on the equities desk when something much more hair-raising is afoot in Operations?
- The prospect of regulatory and/or legal censure can be a handy tactic for 'extracting' Compliance from a recalcitrant workforce – if some maverick has decided to 'opt out' of your Compliance arrangements, a cautionary tale about what happened to someone else who also could see no point in following that procedure can often do wonders to focus the mind. You see, even though 'doing Compliance stuff' may not be fun, it is a lot more fun than going to jail, the ultimate penalty that all financial services practitioners must contend with.

  Note, however, that the use of such 'scare tactics' should only be employed as a last resort. It is much better to achieve Compliance through a collective wish to do the right thing than through a desire not to be thrown into jail. In the long run, this is going to have far more lasting and deep-rooted results. So, not be the best way to go about the business of 'doing Compliance' but if other methods have not worked it can undoubtedly be a very useful tool.

This chapter deals principally with enforcement in the UK under the FSMA regime, although three points of qualification are required:

- As noted in Chapter 1, there are other regulatory regimes in place in the UK and each has its own methods of detecting and punishing malpractice.
- Appendices 3–6 provide guidance on a number of pieces of legislation applicable to the financial services industry in the UK. These give rise to additional sanctions outside the scope of the FSMA regime which must also be considered.
- Each jurisdiction in which you operate will have its own enforcement regime and you should ensure that you and your colleagues have a clear understanding of how it works, with a knowledge along the lines of that set out below for the UK.

From the FSA's perspective there needs to be a mechanism for penalizing and remedying poor practice to assist it in meeting its four statutory objectives (market confidence, public awareness, consumer protection, reducing financial crime), all of which are negatively affected by low standards and inappropriate behaviour. Consequently, its enforcement regime is designed to

- deter undesirable conduct;
- promote high standards of market and regulatory behaviour;
- provide a mechanism for compensation and restitution;
- ensure that corrective and remedial action can be prescribed; and
- penalize bad behaviour.

The disciplinary and enforcement process is based on an extensive and complex legislative and regulatory framework, with the FSA's main powers in this area being granted to it under FSMA. FSMA grants the FSA wide-ranging disciplinary authority and the right to take both civil and criminal action against firms and individuals, whether or not they are regulated under it. The FSA also has powers under a number of other pieces of legislation (see Appendix 24).

Luckily, the FSA is not given a free rein over how it exercises these powers and must comply with strict procedural requirements. It must also act in accordance with the Human Rights Act 1998 (see Appendix 3). Actions taken must be proportionate and fair and are subject to intense scrutiny, not only via the official channels but also by the media, which is very vocal when it comes to expressing its views about how the FSA has handled a case.

But most people do not care too much about the theory behind the regulator's powers and activities in this area. All they really want to know is 'Does it affect us?' and, more importantly, 'How can we avoid getting into trouble?' The focus of this chapter is consequently as follows:

1. To establish the means the regulator has of finding out about the skeletons in your Compliance closet.
2. To identify what presses the regulator's hot buttons – what are the key things that they really do not want to see in your firm?
3. To set out what the regulator can do to find out more about what's been going on once it has a hunch that something is not right.
4. The avenues that are open to you if your firm or your colleagues are subject to FSA scrutiny.
5. To summarize what might happen if it does turn out that your firm, or someone employed by it, has misbehaved.

11.1   SOMEONE's WATCHING YOU

Just like your mother when you were a rebellious teenager, the FSA has the uncanny ability of finding out about your misdemeanours no matter how clever you think you have been. Unlike your mother though, the ability to know what has been going on does not stem from some unfathomable talent for engaging in remote viewing and being in five places at once, but from a well-established set of arrangements and requirements that enable the FSA to exercise its supervision over the firms it regulates.

The FSA imposes requirements on its firms to supply it with certain information on a regular basis and it also has the right to call for additional information whenever it considers it appropriate. Serendipity, however, also has its part to play, and there are various 'random' ways in which you may be caught red handed!

The following lists describe some of the main ways in which the FSA can discover what your firm has been doing. When considering what it says, you should bear in mind that all regulatory contact should be governed by the overriding requirement to be open and cooperative with the FSA, as set out in Principle 11.

Regular reporting and notification requirements

Auditors reports

- Each regulated firm must have an appropriate auditor which must be granted adequate access to its records.
- The FSA takes the role of the auditor very seriously and indeed it is a criminal offence to give false or misleading information to an auditor under s346 of FSMA.
- The auditor's main duty is to make three key submissions to the FSA. These are

  - the audit report, including information on the firm's regulatory reporting activities during the period covered by the report;
  - the internal controls letter which either comments on the firm's internal controls (if this happens, it is bad) or confirms that the auditor has no comments (if this happens, it is good); and
  - the client assets report covering a firm's compliance with the Client Assets rules.

- Not only do the auditor's reports supply a wealth of information to the FSA that it may wish to follow up on, but the reports themselves also give rise to certain notification requirements on the part of the firm being audited.

Actuaries reports

The rules relating to actuarial reports are broadly similar to those concerning auditor reports but cover only a limited range of firms such as long-term insurers and friendly societies.

Application to vary Part IV approvals

If you submit a request to vary your permission, the scrutiny to which you will be the subject during the approval process may alert the FSA to some misdemeanours on your part of which it was previously unaware, for example you may be carrying on the activity already: unauthorized investment business.

Rule waiver or modification request

If you submit a request to the FSA to obtain a rule waiver or modification, you may find that not only does your request not get approved, but that you have inadvertently alerted the FSA to something going on in your firm that it is not happy with.

(Continued)

Contacting the FSA for guidance

As with requests to vary your Part IV approval or to obtain a rule waiver or modification, if you contact the FSA for guidance about a particular matter you may find yourself alerting them to something they do not like the smell of and that they consider requires further investigation.

Approved Persons reporting

The FSA can find out a lot of information (not all of which it might look favourably upon) from the various forms submitted to it in relation to Approved Persons. Two good examples are

- you are careless enough to submit a request for someone to be approved to conduct an activity which your firm does not have permission to undertake;
- you notify the FSA that someone has been dismissed for gross misconduct – the FSA may well be in contact in order to find out more about the context in which this gross misconduct occurred, and whether it is symptomatic of control or procedural failings.

Controller and close links reporting

The FSA must be informed of certain matters concerning a firm's controllers or other close links that it has. Such notification enables the FSA to satisfy itself that a firm is continuing to meet the FSA's threshold conditions for approval – if your company is to be controlled by, or to have close links with, a disreputable firm then the FSA is likely to take a keen interest in this.

Appointed representative reporting

This is similar to Approved Persons reporting (above) but covers appointed representatives instead.

Miscellaneous notification requirements

There is a very wide range of matters of which the FSA requires to be notified in relation to the firms it regulates. Such notification requirements include (but there are many others):

- suspicions of market abuse;
- the intention to establish a new branch;
- a material rule breach;
- entering into a material outsourcing arrangement; and
- evidence of fraud having been committed against the firm.

Reporting requirements

A number of regular and ongoing reporting requirements are imposed on firms by the FSA in order to consolidate its understanding of their activities and to identify breaches of requirements. The matters covered by regular reporting requirements include

- capital adequacy;
- appointed representatives; and
- list of overseas regulators for any regulated entity within the firm's group.

Transaction reporting

Firms are required to report various transaction types to the FSA to enable it to monitor and assess matters such as whether a firm is doing business beyond the scope of its permitted activities and to assist it in the detection of market abuse.

Powers that the FSA has to gather information over and above the normal reporting requirements detailed above

Periodic inspection visits

- The FSA has the authority to conduct monitoring visits of the firms that it regulates.
- These visits may be either planned or unplanned and the amount of detail that the FSA gives a firm about the people it wishes to interview and the records it wishes to view will vary.
- The FSA must also have similar access to a firm's suppliers under a material outsourcing contact as it does to the firm itself.

Risk assessment visits

The FSA takes a risk-based approach to regulation and as part of the process of assessing risk within a particular firm and across the financial markets in general, the FSA undertakes periodic risk assessment visits. See Box 2 ('ARROW') on page 320.

Mystery shopping

The FSA 'plant' may call up or visit your firm so that standards of advice and recommendations can be assessed along with the appropriateness of the sales techniques employed. Retail firms are most likely to experience mystery shopping.

(Continued)

Communications with other regulatory bodies

- The FSA is expected to cooperate with other regulators based both in the UK and overseas.
- If one of these regulators contacts the FSA to request further information about a firm they are investigating, this is likely to suggest to the FSA that there is something worth investigating there too.
- Communications with overseas regulators will be of particular relevance to firms that are part of an international group or who provide cross-border services.
- The FSA may also be alerted to misdemeanours by an investment exchange if a firm they regulate has breached that exchange's rules.

Serendipitous methods by which the FSA may find out about what your firm has been doing

Financial promotions

- Just like the rest of us, FSA staff are consumers of the mass media. That means that if they see or hear a financial promotion that they do not think is appropriate, you may well find yourself getting a call to explain its contents, and why you allowed it to be issued.
- But that's not all. The FSA actively encourages members of the public to report misleading financial promotions and has a dedicated telephone hotline for this purpose. Watch out!

Newspaper or press article

An article in the press or even a TV or radio programme that mentions your firm may alert the FSA to developments of which it was not aware, and it may want to find out more about it or why it did not or receive prior notice.

During investigation of another firm

If you are particularly unlucky the FSA will start out by investigating another firm, get wind of the fact that you have had some dealings with them, and then take an interest in their involvement with your own firm as well.

Complaints by clients to the FSA or to the Financial Ombudsman Service (FOS)

Disaffected clients can obviously get on the phone to either the FSA or the FOS and tell them all about their dissatisfaction with the services that your firm has provided. Whether the complaint is justified, or whether it is all just hot air, if the allegations are serious enough, and have a degree of credibility, it would be hard for the FSA to ignore them and not contact you to find out more.

Whistle blowing

- Under the Public Interest Disclosure Act 1998 (PIDA) employees are protected if they 'blow thewhistle' about certain practices they believe to be occurring at their place of employment.
- Such practices include criminal offences and failures to comply with legal obligations.
- The FSA encourages firms to implement internal whistle-blowing procedures but under PIDA the FSA is itself officially designated a person to which such disclosures may also be made.
- If a disgruntled employee, for example, makes a credible report to the FSA that your firm is committing a criminal offence or is not complying with a legislative requirement, then it is not likely to be long before you get a call.

Complaint from another firm

If you treat other firms badly as clients or business partners they may complain about your actions to the FSA.

And what if you find out that something is wrong that the FSA has not spotted? You are going to need to make a decision about whether it is material enough to disclose to the regulator. And that is one of the hardest decisions you are likely to have to take as a Compliance Officer: you can't necessarily count on being treated leniently simply because you have 'fessed up'. But if you don't, things will get a whole lot worse if the regulator *does* find out. One of the most important things to do if you find a problem and decide not to tell the regulator is to document the reasons for your decision. This will help you to justify your approach if ever called upon to do so.

11.2   THE FSA HAS 'HOT BUTTONS'

Not all regulatory breaches are created equal. There can be no question that rule breaches of any kind are to be avoided as far as possible, but obviously some breaches are not going to provoke as much interest from the FSA as others. An isolated failure to record the name of the person who took a client's order does not rank with repeated market abuse in FTSE 100 takeover activity.

Luckily, in the context of its risk-based approach to regulation, the FSA has clearly indicated the issues it will take seriously: in this respect there are no hidden goal posts and the approach taken by the FSA will always be dictated by the impact that a particular issue could have on the FSA's statutory objectives as detailed above. In this respect, at a high level, the FSA will always have regard to

- the impact that a particular matter could have on market confidence;
- whether the matter under review is detrimental to the public's understanding of the financial services industry;
- the degree to which consumer understanding of financial services may suffer as a result of a firm or individual's activities;
- whether the issue being investigated involves financial crime.

At a more detailed level, the following gives guidance on the matters that the FSA will consider when deciding how seriously it should take a breach, a suspected breach or a near miss.

- Has there been an actual rule breach? Note that this extends beyond the FSA rules to include, for example
  - The Unfair Terms Regulations
  - The JMLSG Guidance Notes
  - The City Code on Takeovers and Mergers.
- Has there been a breach of any relevant legislation?
- Was there an intention to breach a rule?
- Is there evidence of financial crime, e.g. money laundering or market abuse?
- Is there evidence of the matter having occurred repeatedly?
- Can the matter be considered so serious that the firm in question no longer meets the FSA's Threshold Conditions?
- Has there been a breach of the Code of Practice for Approved Persons?
- How likely is the matter to reccur?
- How long ago did it take place?
- Were any retail customers involved?
- Did the firm or an employee's actions lead to financial loss by a client?
- Had the firm provided training in relation to how to avoid a particular breach? Was the training adequate?
- Has appropriate remedial action been taken?
- How well does the firm or individual understand the implications of what has occurred?
- How cooperative has the firm or individual been with the FSA?
- Is the matter indicative of inadequate internal systems and controls, or is it a 'one off'?
- To what extent could the firm or individual have taken action to avoid the matter arising in the first place?
- To what extent will the interests of consumers be served by pursuing the matter?
- Is there evidence of a lack of management control in relation to what is being investigated?
- Does the matter result in a breach of the firm's regulatory approval?
- Is an Approved Person acting outside the scope of their approval?
- What is the previous record of the firm or individual – has previous disciplinary action been taken?
- To what extent was the incident or activity under review premeditated?
- Did the person undertaking the activity know that it constituted a rule breach or that it was otherwise not appropriate in some other way?
- Did the firm or individual act recklessly?
- Did the firm notify the FSA of the matter as soon as it was aware of it?
- Is the matter connected to any other 'misdeeds' on the part of the firm or individual?
- Will the action be punished by another regulator?

- Was there a breach of the FSA's principles for businesses?
- Is there any evidence to suggest negligence on the part of the firm's management?
- Has there been a breach of an individual requirement imposed on the firm by the FSA?
- Has there been a breach of a firm's internal policies and procedures?
- Has there been a breach of the Code of Market Conduct?
- Is there any evidence that false or misleading information has been provided to the FSA in an attempt to prevent the matter being discovered?
- Was the action contrary to FSA guidance, either in the rule book, or provided on an individual basis?
- Did the firm seek guidance on how to address the matter being reviewed?
- Has there been a breach of a Prohibition Order?

11.3   WHAT THE FSA CAN DO TO FIND OUT MORE

Once the FSA has the idea that it does not quite approve of what might be going on within your firm there are further ways in which it can set about gathering information. The majority of these extend beyond the powers that the FSA has to gather information during the normal course of its relationship with you.

How the FSA can find out more

Request for further information

- At the very lowest level or initial stages of concern the FSA is likely simply to call up a firm and request some more information about the matter that is of interest by holding informal discussions or by requesting access to certain records. Time limits on the provision of the additional information may be imposed.
- The matter may stop at this point, or the FSA may then use tougher tactics: if it does not feel that it is getting the cooperation from a firm that it considers appropriate by simply being polite and asking for information during the course of their normal relationship, then it has the option of getting heavy: the FSA has the right to demand access to certain information, within a specified timeframe, even if you do not wish to share it.

Compulsory and voluntary interviews

As well as being able to ask people to attend an interview on a voluntary basis, the FSA can also compel them to be interviewed. Interviews will often be recorded and where they are given under caution because a person is suspected of a criminal offence they will be subject to the relevant PACE[1] code to ensure that the right balance is struck between the power of the authorities and the interviewee's rights and freedoms.

---

[1]   Police and Criminal Evidence Act 1984.

(Continued)

Formal investigation

If the FSA really does not like the picture that is being built up of what a firm or an individual has been up to, it can mount a formal investigation. It may conduct the investigation itself, or appoint other people to investigate on its behalf.

Skilled persons report

If the FSA does not conduct an investigation itself it may require a firm or connected person to appoint an approved 'skilled person' to produce a report on the firm's activities.

Search and seizure powers

The FSA has the ability to obtain a search warrant permitting the seizure of documents and other information and the taking of steps to prevent such material being tampered with or destroyed. Search warrants will generally only be used if the FSA believes it will not be able to obtain the documents or records it requires by other means.

Liaison with Financial Ombudsman Service

Where there has been a complaint from an 'eligible complainant' the Financial Ombudsman Service may conduct its own enquiries. Such enquires may involve a firm handing over relevant documents which may subsequently be passed to the FSA.

Liaison with other regulatory authorities

The FSA has prepared guidelines with a number of other authorities for cooperating during investigations and it may call upon one of these authorities to provide it with information to which it has not previously been party. Such other authorities include

- The Serious Fraud Office
- The Crown Prosecution Service
- The Crown Office.

11.4   WHAT TO DO IF YOU ARE BEING INVESTIGATED OR ARE SUBJECT TO DISCIPLINARY ACTION

If you find yourself subject to an FSA investigation the key thing to remember is to be open and cooperative (Principle 11). No matter how great the temptation, do not build a bonfire and burn the evidence; do not flee the country and do not keep your computer's delete button pressed down for a week. Tell the FSA what they want to know, and let them see what they want to see. Don't try to be too clever and think that you can outsmart them – no matter how much it hurts the reality is that they are more powerful than you are and you don't want to antagonize them. This does not mean giving in: however the outcome of FSA cases is not a foregone conclusion, as we shall see below. But, on balance, it will not help your case to dissimulate, and the more uncooperative you are, the more likely you are to scupper your chances of winning an appeal if things were ever to get that far. The list below describes your main options.

Potential courses of action to persons under investigation or subject to disciplinary action

---

Enlist professional help

- One of the first and most important things that should be done by a person with whom the FSA has indicated its displeasure is to enlist professional help. You could turn to
  - lawyers;
  - accountants;
  - Compliance consultants; and
  - all of the above.
- These professionals will hopefully know more about the FSA's enforcement process than you do, and will have experience of dealing with investigations and helping other firms to come through them.
- You are likely to pay a lot of money for their services, but better that than go to jail!

Make a representation to the FSA

On receipt of notice that the FSA intends to take disciplinary action, the recipient can make a representation in support of their case (either in writing or orally) on his or her own behalf. Such representations should be made within a specified time frame.

Independent Complaints Commissioner

FSMA requires the FSA to establish arrangements for investigating complaints about its activities and, accordingly, the FSA has appointed an Independent Complaints Commissioner. Those who are not happy with the way the FSA is behaving towards them may apply to the Complaints Commissioner for their complaint to be investigated.

Financial Services and Markets Tribunal

- The Financial Services and Markets Tribunal has been established to ensure that certain FSA disciplinary decisions can be subject to review.
- Although it is established under FSMA, it is independent from the FSA and the sort of matters that can be referred to the Tribunal include
  - the removal of Approved Person status;
  - disciplinary actions against regulated firms;
  - a decision by the FSA to vary a firm's regulatory approval;
  - disciplinary actions relating to market abuse.

- There have recently been some well-publicized cases in which the Tribunal has ruled against the FSA. These include the L&G mis-selling case (see Box 8 on page 330)

and the case of Paul Davidson (nicknamed 'the Plumber') in relation to allegations of market abuse.
- Be very careful, however, if you decide to go down this route – former Canaccord Capital broker Tim Baldwin was recently cleared by the Tribunal of the accusations made against him by the FSA that he had engaged in market abuse. However, he was still required to pay a considerable legal fee for the case he mounted against the FSA and, in the end, these fees were considerably more than his original fine. Mr Baldwin has come out of the whole affair with a nasty hole in his pocket although the damage to his reputation has been nicely repaired.
- Further information about the Tribunal is available in Appendix 1.

Mediation

The FSA's independent mediation scheme can be used to try to help the parties involved to reach a settlement. Under this scheme a neutral mediator is appointed to assist with negotiation and it is available in most enforcement cases, although notably not in those involving the FSA bringing a criminal prosecution.

Go to the press

If you really feel as though you are being treated badly by the FSA there is obviously the (unorthodox) option of contacting the press and hoping that they will take up the campaign on your behalf. No guarantees of success here, and it may well backfire. A risky route to take but in desperate cases you may feel that you have nothing to lose.

Challenge under the Human Rights Act 1998

The Human Rights Act prohibits public authorities (such as the FSA)from acting in a way that is contrary to the European Convention on Human Rights. If you consider that actions on the part of the FSA have breached such rights you may be able to challenge the action in court.

Appeal for the support of you trade association

If you consider that you are not receiving fair treatment from the FSA you could contact a trade association, such as those detailed in Appendix 1, to see if they will support your case in the interests of their membership.

Judicial review Civil Procedure Rule 1998 – Part 54

- You could also try contesting the FSA's (or the FOS's) decisions by means of a judicial review in accordance with the Civil Procedure Rule 1998 (Part 54) if you wish to challenge the lawfulness of decisions or actions taken by these bodies.
- If the court were to judge that the FSA or the FOS had indeed acted unlawfully, then it has the power to grant a remedy such as a quashing order or a prohibiting order. It is important to remember that a judicial review is not an appeal and simply challenges the way in which decisions have been made in terms of whether the correct procedures have been followed.

11.5 CONSEQUENCES OF RULE BREACHES AND OTHER REGULATORY MISDEMEANOURS

Compliance may not be fun, but it is undoubtedly a lot more fun than getting it wrong and feeling the full force of the regulator's wrath, or even going to jail. As acknowledged before, nothing would ever go wrong in either your firm or mine! But just out of interest, the list below gives a summary of the various horrible things that might happen to all those wayward firms out there (along with their wayward staff and wayward Compliance Officers), should they decide that adhering to regulatory requirements is not for them.

For the more serious courses of action that the FSA may take, the regulator must follow the formal enforcement process. This is set out in the FSA's Decision Procedure and Penalties Module and involves (in the simplest terms) the FSA publishing notices about disciplinary action that it intends to take, has subsequently decided to take, and the date that the action will take effect (see Box 12 ('The Enforcement Process') on page 336).

Potential outcome

No action

If you are very lucky, the FSA will decide that nothing was wrong after all and that no action whatsoever is required. Alternatively, the FSA may at one point have intended to take disciplinary action but then thought better of it. In this situation, a notice of discontinuance will be issued detailing the actions previously set out in a warning notice or a decision notice that are now not going to be taken.

Informal requirement that something should be done differently, or request to keep the FSA informed

- If it turns out that the FSA is not too concerned about what your firm is up to it may just give an informal suggestion as to what could/should be done differently. Or it might ask you to keep it informed of future developments relating to the area in which it was interested.
- If this happens, it is a good idea to carry out a full review and, thereafter, monitor the 'problem area' regularly to satisfy yourself that you have covered all your bases, and to pre-empt your next routine inspection visit.

Individual guidance

- One degree more serious than the 'informal requirement' for a firm to conduct its affairs in a particular way is for the FSA to issue individual guidance, which will generally be in writing and will normally be discussed with the firm prior to being issued.
- There are various circumstances in which individual guidance may be given, for example, to specify how a rulebook requirement applies to a particular firm or where the nature of a firm's activities requires guidance in addition to that contained in the rulebook.

(Continued)

Variance of a Part IV permission at the FSA's own initiative (individual requirements)

If the FSA has specific concerns about a firm's business it may vary that firm's regulatory approval.

- This can happen for various reasons such as the FSA being concerned that a firm no longer satisfies the threshold conditions for authorization due to inadequate systems and controls, for example, or as a result of the introduction of new products not already covered by existing arrangements.
- A Part IV permission may be varied by imposing either a statutory limitation or requirement.
- An individual limitation might relate to the type of activities that a firm can engage in, the category of client it may deal with or the type of investment it may offer.
- An individual requirement might relate to capital adequacy or the submission of specific reports.
- The FSA may also vary a Part IV permission in support of an overseas regulator.
- The FSA will not formally vary a firm's Part IV permission if it feels that the same result can be achieved within the normal course of the regulatory relationship with the firm in question.

Cancellation of Part IV permission

If the FSA has very serious misgivings about a firm it has the authority to cancel its Part IV permission altogether. It may also cancel a firm's Part IV permission in support of an overseas regulator.

Injunctions

- The FSA has the power to apply to the courts under FSMA and the Unfair Contract Terms Regulations to obtain an injunction if it appears likely that a person's actions are in conflict with the FSA's objectives.
- Injunctions may be made to
  - prevent use of an unfair term in a contract;
  - freeze assets;
  - restrain a course of conduct; and
  - remedy a course of conduct.

Withdrawal of Approved Person status

- If the FSA considers that an Approved Person no longer meets the Fit and Proper criteria it has the power to withdraw that person's approval or prevent him or her from conducting a specified activity. This action may also be accompanied by a prohibition order (see below).

Prohibition of individuals

- Prohibition orders can be issued against any individual whether or not he or she is an Approved Person and may, among other things:

- prevent a person from undertaking a function in relation to any regulated activity;
- prevent a person from working for a specific regulated firm;
- prevent a person form working for a particular type of firm; and
- prevent a person from carrying out particular activities.

- Prohibition orders will be made when the FSA considers that a person does not meet its Fit and Proper criteria.
- Prohibition orders may be revoked by the FSA after a certain period has elapsed. The individual concerned may also apply to the FSA for the order to be revoked or varied.

Restitution, redress and compensation

- Under FSMA the FSA has the power to order compensation to be paid or to apply to the courts for a restitution order.
- When deciding whether or not to make a restitution order the FSA will consider several factors including

  - the number of persons affected;
  - the costs of securing redress;
  - whether another regulator may secure redress; and
  - whether a person may bring their own proceedings.

- Additionally, the Financial Ombudsman Service may require firms to pay compensation or to take other action that it considers appropriate.

Insolvency orders

The FSA may apply to the courts to obtain insolvency orders of various kinds if it considers that it would be in the public interest to do so. Such orders will be sought in situations in which the FSA considers that the entity involved cannot, or is unlikely to be able to, repay its debts. The FSA itself need not be a creditor of that person.

Public censure

The FSA may issue a public censure against a firm or an individual in a number of circumstances including:

- Breach of a Statement of Principle for Approved Persons.
- Market abuse.

Fine

- The FSA may impose financial penalties on both firms and individuals.
- It is not permissible to take out an insurance contract against the possibility of incurring an the FSA fine.
- With the exception of the late submission of reports, there is no set scale of fines – the FSA has the authority to determine the size of fine that is appropriate, depending on the seriousness of the action being sanctioned.

(Continued)

- In certain circumstances early payment of a financial penalty may result in a discount, but be warned, as the level of the FSA fines is following an upward trend - as shown in the table.

Year	Number of fines	Total value of fines
2000/01	79	£5 847 748
2001/02	76	£10 062 597
2002/03	16	£10 119 000
2003/04	21	£12 425 000
2004/05	31	£22 249 000
2005/06	17	£17 430 860
2006/07	32	£14 661 143

Source: The FSA website, 10/11/07

The FSA prosecution

- FSMA gives the FSA the power to prosecute certain criminal offences including
  - market abuse;
  - insider dealing; and
  - Breach of the Money Laundering Regulations.
- The FSA will take account of the seriousness of the offence before it decides to prosecute, and in relation to money laundering offences the FSA will also consider whether there has been a breach of the JMLSG Guidance Notes (see Appendix 1).
- Take heart from the fact that in all likelihood the FSA does not really want to take you to court if it can help it. After all, it may well not win the case, or it might be shown up during an appeal, which would play havoc with its credibility in the industry and beyond.

The FSA caution

The FSA may decide to issue a caution rather than prosecute. Any such cautions will be recorded on the Police National Computer and will form part of the person's 'regulatory record' maintained by the FSA.

Private warning

- In cases where the FSA is not happy with a firm's or an Approved Person's behaviour, but does not wish to undertake formal disciplinary proceedings, it may decide to issue a private warning.
- Such cases will tend to relate to more minor breaches, and/or breaches in relation to which immediate and appropriate remedial action has been taken.
- Private warnings are formal written documents that form part of the recipient's 'regulatory history'.

Notification to, and assistance of, an authority other than the FSA

The FSA may pass information about misdemeanours to other authorities such as the Takeover Panel or an overseas regulator, and it may also appoint investigators and conduct interviews at the request of an overseas regulator. As a worst case scenario this may result in extradition (see Box 4 ('Extradition') on page 323 in relation to the 'NatWest 3').

Action by an authority other than the FSA

In cases where the FSA decides not to take disciplinary action itself, this may be because the matter it was investigating is actually going to be to taken up by another regulatory/investigatory agency such as

- a recognized investment exchange;
- an overseas regulator or enforcement agency;
- the Serious Fraud Office;
- the Department for Business, Enterprise and Regulatory Reform;
- the Crown Prosecution Service;
- the Association of Chief Police Officers in England, Wales and Northern Ireland;
- The Crown Office.

Action taken by another authority does not automatically preclude the FSA from taking action itself.

Action for damages

Breaches of certain rules and legislative requirements are actionable at the suit of private persons (and in some cases other persons) who have suffered loss as a result of the breach. The rules to which these rights apply are set out at the end of each section of the FSA Handbook.

Unenforceability of agreements

There are various cases in which agreements will not be enforceable if they are made in breach of certain key FSMA requirements. Such cases include

- agreements relating to regulated activities that are entered into in breach of the General Prohibition; and
- agreements made as a result of unlawful communications.

Referral to non-FSA-related complaints scheme

The Financial Services Ombudsman may decide to refer a complaint that has been brought to it to another complaints determination body.

(Continued)

Damage to corporate and personal reputation

If your name, or that of your firm, features in the headlines for all the wrong reasons then it is unlikely to do much for your chances of winning either top customers or new job offers. Also remember that when you go for a job that requires Approved Persons status, disciplinary action on the part of the FSA, or other regulators, needs to be disclosed; and as the FSA has to do the approving, you can't just pretend that nothing ever happened.

Breach of employment contract

The consequences of breaching an employment contract obviously vary from firm to firm. It may result in loss of privileges (e.g. no bonus), or a qualified reference that will follow you if you try to change your employer. As a 'worst case' scenario you may find yourself being dismissed, or being 'advised' to fall on your sword. On the bright side, this course is often taken on a non-adversarial and confidential basis and may do the least harm to your future employment prospects (especially if you were in the wrong!).

Strategic closure of firm

Following significant regulatory problems the overseas owners of UK firms may simply decide that it is not worth the effort to do business in the UK and may decide to withdraw, leaving you and your colleagues without a job.

The ultimate price for non-compliance . . .

If your business feels uncomfortable with the prospect of FSA enforcement action, then you should explain to them how lucky they are that they are not subject to Chinese regulations. There have been at least two cases in the last few years of banking irregularities in the People's Republic of China leading to the imposition of the death penalty for the people involved.

Other, less extreme, examples of enforcement actions that have been taken in the UK can be found in Appendix A. As noted at the beginning of the chapter, a few well-chosen references to these and other similar cases can often be enough to stop even the most seasoned of regulatory mischief-makers in their tracks (for a while, at least). That's why it is a good idea to have a system in place for distributing news about relevant regulatory actions to your management and colleagues. For these purposes you should be able to find something relevant to you in Appendix 23. There you will find cases involving a wide cross-section of firms and individuals. You will see actions taken against the largest and the smallest of firms as well as against individuals; people just like us and our colleagues, firms just like our own; real people and firms of the type you come across in your daily life who have found themselves, through either circumstance or something more sinister, at the centre of a regulatory action of which some will find it hard to recover.

Appendix A
Routine Compliance Activities

This appendix contains details of some of the routine activities most commonly undertaken by the Compliance Officer. It is important to remember that the guidance provided on each area provides summary guidance only and you should tailor the procedures and controls within your own firm to the specific requirements of your business activities and customer base.

Activity	
Compliance culture, ethics and integrity	122
Maintenance of compliance manual	123
Maintenance of compliance policies and procedures	125
Regulatory training	126
Undertaking and supervising remedial action plans	127
Internal relations	128
Annual Compliance Plan	129
Maintenance of Compliance department charter	130
Annual compliance attestation	130
Supervising other entities within the group	131
Maintenance of compliance and regulatory risks register	131
Sample risks register – Research department	133
Advisory and project work	134
Management of relationship with regulators, clearing houses, exchanges, etc.	135
Regulatory visits	136
Regulatory service providers	137
Responding to consultation papers and industry developments	138
Rules-mapping and reviewing new legislative and regulatory developments to assess relevance	138
Periodic regulatory reporting to the FSA	139
Ad hoc reporting to the FSA	140
Payments of fees to the FSA	140
Membership of professional bodies	141
Keeping up to date	141

(Continued)

Activity	
Disciplinary procedures	142
Passporting	143
Regulatory agreements and documentation	145
Conflicts of interest	146
Market abuse	149
Insider information definition under the FSMA 2000	154
Named or commonly known market manipulation techniques	156
Chinese walls	157
Insider lists	159
Watch and restricted list maintenance	160
Personal account dealing	162
Inducements	165
Approval of financial promotions	167
Handling complaints and litigation	169
Handling rule breaches	170
Administration of training and competence regime	171
Administration of Approved Persons regime	174
Approval of new or non-standard transactions	177
Voice-recording arrangements	178
Data Protection Compliance	179
Corporate knowledge	180
Record keeping	181
New offices	182
Outsourcing	182
Whistle blowing	184
Client categorization	185
Management information	188
Fraud	190
Compliance monitoring	191

Topic	Compliance culture, ethics and integrity
Objective	Ensure that the corporate culture within your firm is one that consistently promotes ethical business practices.
Explanation	• All the training that you can give and all the policies and procedures that you can write will do no good if your firm has a poor compliance culture: staff will simply seek to find ways around the standards that you introduce unless they are committed to the principles that underpin them.

- Having a culture of ethics and integrity within the firm is becoming more and more important with the growing trend for regulators to move away from rules-based regulation and more towards principles-based regimes, as seen with the introduction of the FSA's 'Treating Customers Fairly Initiative' and the recent stream-lining of the rulebook: People could find themselves subject to disciplinary action even if no rules have been broken simply because it was considered by the regulator that they have not acted fairly.
- It should also be remembered that acting ethically is in all of our best interests – if the UK gets a reputation for being a 'dodgy' place to do business then internationally mobile firms will waste little time in finding somewhere else to transact.

Actions Required

1. Ensuring that people act with a conscience is not straightforward – there is no manual that you can write, no procedure that you can introduce that can be guaranteed to bring about the desired mindset in your colleagues. It is more a question of instilling in staff a respect for fair play and openness towards customers, fellow employees and the industry as a whole.
2. This may be done by setting a good example and continuously questioning the firm's behaviour towards others even if an action is not explicitly prohibited. This is where the Compliance department comes into its own in acting as the firm's regulatory compass or its corporate conscience.
3. Senior management should also play a vital role in fostering a culture of Compliance within the firm and they should be well aware of their responsibility to set a good example to the rest of the firm.
4. You may find it appropriate to provide ethics training based on the specific activities that your firm is involved with.
5. Under the Public Information Disclosure Act firms should implement whistle-blowing procedures. These procedures are likely to be an appropriate route for staff to use to report instances of unethical behaviour or actions that are not compatible with a sound Compliance culture.
6. Another idea is to introduce a Reputational Risk and Ethics Committee in which plans can be appraised for their moral integrity and in which questionable behaviour on the part of an employee can be considered to determine whether any disciplinary or corrective action should be taken.
7. Some firms choose to have a Code of Ethics covering not just regulatory issues but also every aspect of behaviour within the firm ('borrowing' from the stationery cupboard, surfing the net during work time, embellishing the CV to try to get a promotion, etc.).

Further information   See Appendix 24.

Topic	**Maintenance of Compliance manual**
Objective	• Documenting the essential details of the firm's regulatory systems and controls in a Compliance manual.
Explanation	• There is no formal obligation in the UK for firms to have a Compliance manual but the existence of such a document is certainly a regulatory expectation. Such a document ensures staff understand what is expected of them from a regulatory perspective and lets them know what the potential penalties are if these expectations are not met.

(Continued)

Topic	**Maintenance of Compliance manual**
	• Also, having a comprehensive Compliance manual is a useful tool for the Compliance Officer; like an insurance policy – as long as you have covered a requirement in your Compliance manual, and made the document known to staff, then they will not be able to blame any wrong-doing on the fact that you had not told them what the rules were. • Writing a comprehensive Compliance manual is a time-consuming job and some firms choose to pay a consultant or law firm to do it for them. • Make sure that you look at some sample manuals written by the people you are considering commissioning to complete this task: you need to get something that will work for your firm – a 2000-page manuscript may be very comprehensive but realistically it will not be read by anyone. Not even by you! • Contrast the Compliance manual, which is normally written at a fairly high level and is applicable to all staff with Compliance policies and procedures that should be more detailed and have a more targeted applicability.

Actions required	1. Write your manual – Compliance manuals typically include the following sections:
	
	   – brief description of what Compliance is and why it is important;
	   – brief description of the Compliance function within your firm;
	   – high level summary of your firm's Compliance universe;
	   – details of the key requirements relevant to your firm;
	   – how relevant requirements impact your staff;
	   – what employees need to do to comply;
	   – what penalties there are if things go wrong; and
	   – sources of further information and guidance.
	
	2. Implement a system to make sure that all new staff sign a Compliance declaration indicating that they
	
	   – have read the Compliance manual;
	   – understand its contents; and
	   – agree to comply with the requirements it details.
	
	3. You should update your Compliance manual regularly – annually is good, perhaps with update bulletins in between if there is a really big change that you need to make staff aware of. After an update you should ensure that staff sign a fresh Compliance declaration.
	4. Make your Compliance manual available on the intranet – that way you save trees and no one can say that they have not been provided with a copy of it.
	5. Add a clause in the firm's standard employment contract to the effect that staff must comply with the terms of the Compliance manual and that a breach of its requirements is a disciplinary offence.

Further information	See Appendix 24.

Topic	**Maintenance of compliance policies and procedures**
Objective	Ensure that your firm has all appropriate policies and procedures so that staff are aware of the regulatory and best practice standards to which they must adhere in performing their activities.

Explanation	• There are a variety of mandatory or best practice policy and procedure documents that firms should prepare. These include
	
	   – conflicts of interest (FSA);
	   – customer executions (FSA);
	   – anti-money laundering (JMLSG); and
	   – whistle-blowing (Public Interest Disclosure Act 1998).
	
	• You may also wish to prepare other policy and procedural documents tailored to the specific activities of your own firm such as
	
	   – fraud;
	   – chinese walls arrangements;
	   – voice recording; and
	   – data security.
	
	• Providing appropriate policies and procedures is part of the training function – you cannot expect staff to know what to do unless you tell them. Not all procedures and requirements are intuitive.
	• Having a solid set of policies and procedures manuals helps to protect your position and that of the firm if things go wrong – if employees act inappropriately they will not be able to blame their actions on a lack of awareness.
	• Policies and procedures manuals go beyond the Compliance manual in that the former are generally more detailed and do not necessarily apply uniformly across the firm, whereas the latter is normally at a higher level and is applicable to all employees.

Actions required	1. Determine the areas where the FSA requires a written policy applicable to your firm. 2. Consider which other areas you think would benefit from having a written policy. Write your policies and procedures taking into account any relevant regulatory or legislative requirements and your firm's own practices and activities. 3. Try not to make the documents too long and complex, otherwise people will not bother to read them (counterproductive), and if they are too prescriptive they may generate a multitude of immaterial policy breaches that will need to be revised each time there is a minor change. 4. If your firm is part of a larger group it is useful to consider whether your policies should be developed with a view to rolling them out to other group entities, or whether other group entities already have policies that would be useful for you to use, if not in full, then at least to give you ideas and a template. Note that anti-money-laundering policies and conflicts policies should cover the whole group. 5. Ensure that you understand the policy approval process in your firm – you may need to have your document approved by the board, given an internal reference number, noted by a central policy administration team, etc. 6. Ensure that your policies and procedures are available to all who need to use them – publication on the intranet is normally a good idea. 7. When a new policy or procedure is published you should give training to those who will be affected.

(Continued)

Topic	Maintenance of compliance policies and procedures
	8. It is also a good idea to have relevant staff sign an undertaking indicating that they have read the policy, understand it and agree to comply with it
	9. You should conduct periodic monitoring to ensure that your Compliance policies and procedures are being complied with. Internal Audit will probably also do this so it is a good idea for you to spot any breaches first to give you a chance to put things right.
	10. You should review your policies and procedures on a regular basis to ensure that they are kept up to date in terms of legal and regulatory developments and your firm's activities.
Further information	See Appendix 24.

Topic	Regulatory training
Objective	Ensure that staff are aware of the Compliance requirements that are applicable to them.
Explanation	• Even where there is no formal requirement to train, it is vital to do so because you cannot expect your staff to comply with relevant requirements if you do not tell them what these requirements are – it's hardly fair not to do this.
	• The provision of training also helps to protect your position and that of the firm if things go wrong – if employees act inappropriately they will not be able to blame their actions on a lack of awareness if they have been thoroughly trained in the relevant area.
Actions required	1. Identify any areas in relation to which training is mandatory for your firm – a well-known example of this is anti-money-laundering awareness.
	2. Identify other areas in which you consider training would be advisable. These ideas may come from various sources such as
	– internal weaknesses that you have noticed;
	– internal weaknesses that have been identified by another reviewer such as Internal or External Audit;
	– requests from other departments or management;
	– changes to the activities of your firm thereby generating additional Compliance requirements;
	– current regulatory action against other firms – you wish to avoid making the same mistakes; and
	– matters that are getting regular press coverage – you don't want to be next on the front pages.
	3. Once you have identified the areas in which you need to give training, prepare a training plan – a yearly plan is a good idea.
	4. Try to tailor your training as much as possible; not all departments need the same training because they are not all involved in the same activities, so you should take account of this when you are devising your plan and preparing your training material.

5. There are a number of ways that your training can be delivered including

   - formal presentations you make yourself;
   - inviting a training company to give training at your office;
   - sending staff on external courses;
   - running workshops and practical sessions;
   - round table discussions;
   - computer programs;
   - sending regulatory bulletins to relevant staff by e-mail; and
   - requiring certain documents to be read.

6. You should try to get senior management buy-in for your training so that they can take their part in ensuring that all staff participate.
7. You should list the names of all required participants and then keep a record of the staff who have completed the training – for face-to-face training it is a good idea to use sign-in sheets. And some firms also provide certificates of attendance.
8. Any staff who have not completed the training within a set time period should be reported to management.
9. It is important to give special consideration to induction training. What minimum level of regulatory knowledge do you wish staff to have when they start at your firm? You should prepare a regulatory training programme for new joiners and an induction pack as well, containing documents such as the Compliance manual and the policies and procedures that will apply to their activities.
10. Think also about what training you will provide to temporary staff and contractors. If they will be with you for only a very short space of time it may not be appropriate for them to receive the full induction training and pack but, nevertheless, a certain level of guidance is definitely appropriate.
11. Ensure that you liaise with the Human Resources department so that you are made aware of new staff – permanent, temporary and contractors – otherwise you will not be aware of the full population of staff who require training.

Further information   See Appendix 24.

Topic	**Undertaking and supervising remedial action plans**
Objective	Ensure that any control weaknesses and any legislative and regulatory breaches are appropriately and promptly addressed.

Explanation	• The Compliance function will find itself subject to some sort of review or assessment at some point.
	• Such reviews may be undertaken by a variety of people including
	
	  – regulators;
	  – exchanges;
	  – internal audit;
	  – external audit; and
	  – the Head Office Compliance team (if your firm is part of a larger group).
	
	• Following a review the Compliance Officer will generally be presented with a list of corrective actions that need to be taken in order to either address rule breaches or strengthen the control infrastructure.

(Continued)

Topic	Undertaking and supervising remedial action plans
Actions required	1. Endeavour to receive as early a warning as possible of any impending review – that way you can do a bit of a 'tidy up' before the auditors arrive.
	2. Prepare staff for the fact that a review will be undertaken: tell them who will be undertaking the review, what the review is for, and the type of questions that may be asked.
	3. Once a review is complete, try to ensure that you hold a close-out meeting with the review team so that you get an idea as soon as possible of the matters that will be raised in their report.
	4. If there are any findings that you do not agree with, ensure that you notify the review team and provide evidence that their findings are not correct or representative.
	5. Try to ensure that you get an opportunity to negotiate on the corrective action that will be recorded in the report. You do not want to be held to implementing measures that are totally impractical, even if you do agree that the issues they are designed to tackle do need to be addressed.
	6. Once you have a final list of issues and corrective actions note these down in a database, indicate which member of the Compliance team is responsible for which action and the date by which it must be completed.
	7. If necessary, make regular reports to senior management on the progress you are making.
	8. Keep a full record of the action that has been taken to address each point so that you can show this to the review team should they decide to follow up on any of their findings.
	9. You may also need to conduct some review work to ensure that any new policies, procedures or practices are being observed.
	10. Some matters raised may not be the responsibility of the Compliance department to rectify even though they have a regulatory impact. If this is the case you should implement a similar plan to that described above in supervising any other department that is involved in the corrective action activities – you do not want their failings to tarnish your good name!
Further information	See Appendix 24.

Topic	Internal relations
Objective	Maintain good relations with other departments within the firm so that a useful exchange of information can take place.
Explanation	• The compliance department can benefit from information obtained and used by many other departments throughout the firm.
	• Similarly, the above departments may benefit from knowledge obtained by the Compliance department.
	• The departments that it may be of most use to liaise with include
	– internal audit;
	– legal;
	– operational risk;
	– marketing;
	– credit; and
	– human resources.

Actions required	1. Determine which of the departments within the firm will be of most benefit in terms of the exchange of information.
	2. Form a contact with a key member of each department.
	3. Have yourself added to mailing and distribution lists so that you regularly receive information.
	4. Explain to your contact the nature of the information that you think it would be useful to receive, for example, details of

               – frauds;
               – serious control breaches; and
               – disciplinary action.

	5. Have regular meetings with your contacts so that you can keep up to date with developments in their department.
	6. Find out what information you produce or receive may be of benefit to your contacts and arrange for this information to be distributed to them.
Further information	See Appendix D.

Topic	**Annual Compliance Plan**
Objective	Ensure that the Compliance department's work has a focus and that its output is measurable.
Explanation	• Most things tend to drift if there is no plan and the activities of the Compliance department are no different – a plan helps set priorities and focuses the mind on what is important.
	• A plan also helps you and other parts of the firm to measure your performance and understand the Compliance department's contribution.
Actions required	1. Many people find that planning is best done on an annual basis although other time periods can be used.
	2. Determine the actions that your department needs to have achieved by the time 12 months is up.
	3. These matters may include

               – recruitment of more staff;
               – provision of staff training;
               – preparing new policies and procedures;
               – revision of existing polices and procedures;
               – joining a particular industry body;
               – conducting certain monitoring reviews; and
               – automating certain processes that are currently undertaken manually.

4. Your priorities may be set by

               – requests from other departments;
               – current areas of regulatory focus;
               – recent disciplinary action either within the firm or by the FSA; and
               – changes to your firm's business model.

5. Set a deadline for each activity.
6. Assign responsibility for each activity.
7. Regularly follow up on progress.
8. Leave some slack in the plan so that unexpected events can be dealt with, and do not follow the plan too rigidly. Times change, and what might have seemed vital in January may be irrelevant by June.

(Continued)

Topic	**Annual Compliance Plan**
	9. A key part of the planning process is the preparation of the budget – there is no point in preparing a plan that requires £1m if you only have £1000 in the kitty!
Further information	–

Topic	**Maintenance of Compliance department charter**
Objective	Ensure that the Compliance Charter remains appropriate and up to date and that its requirements are complied with.
Explanation	As noted in Chapter 3 it is useful to have a Compliance Charter that sets out the regulatory rights and responsibilities of the Compliance department *vis-à-vis* the rest of the firm.
Actions required	Prepare a Compliance Charter in line with the guidance provided in Chapter 3 and ensure that this charter remains up to date, relevant and known to the rest of the firm.
Further information	See Chapter 3.

Topic	**Annual Compliance attestation**
Objective	Ensure that staff maintain an awareness of Compliance polices, procedures and manuals.
Explanation	It never goes amiss to remind your colleagues of their Compliance obligations – a manual that was read a year ago may have been changed, procedures may have been altered or training may no longer be fresh in their minds.
Actions required	1. It is a good idea to require staff to sign an annual Compliance declaration or attestation. 2. You may choose to have the attestation cover whatever you wish. For example, you may choose to have staff confirm – compliance with the Compliance manual and Compliance policies and procedures; – that all PA dealing has been conducted in accordance with the firm's policy; – that all gifts and benefits have been handled in accordance with the firm's policy; and – that no information has changed in relation to details supplied to the FSA for Approved Persons registration, or providing new details where there has been a change. 3. Set a date by which all attestations must have been returned. 4. Keep a log of staff who have signed the attestation, and those who have not done so yet. 5. Staff who have not signed the attestation by the required date should be identified to senior management.
Further information	–

Topic	**Supervising other entities within the group**
Objective	Ensure that all Compliance departments within the group are managed so as to provide appropriate regulatory services to the group entities for which they are responsible.
Explanation	• If you work for a firm that is part of a large group then there is likely to be a central Compliance department situated in head office. • If your own department is highest within the structure, with responsibility for coordinating the activities of teams in other entities, then you should implement sound arrangements for exercising this oversight. You do not want to be held responsible for people, issues or activities of which you have no understanding or knowledge. • The more uniform the approach you can adopt, while remaining open to local differences in methodology and regulation, the better.
Actions required	1. Compile a list of all the other Compliance departments that you are responsible for supervising. 2. For each department, make sure you know who the staff are and what they do, especially the Compliance Head. 3. You should also know which firms each department provides Compliance services for. 4. Decide which of the Compliance services, activities, policies and procedures you wish to roll out across the whole group. For example, can you have a single Compliance manual covering all entities, can there be a single location where personal account dealing requests are processed or where training records for the group are kept? 5. Also be aware that certain policies need to be implemented on a group level (e.g. for firms based in the UK, conflicts of interest and anti-money laundering). 6. Ensure that you undertake adequate supervisory activities over remote Compliance departments. Some of the processes you may put in place include – organizing regular meetings of all the Compliance departments, whether face to face or by video or telephone conference; – establishing regular written reporting requirements; – establishing ah hoc notification requirements; – imposing minimum training and knowledge requirements across all the teams; – preparing a single set of Compliance procedures that must be followed by all Compliance teams; – undertaking monitoring activity of the remote Compliance departments; and – regularly visiting the remote departments and ensuring that their staff also come and visit your department.
Further information	See Chapter 5.

Topic	**Maintenance of Compliance and regulatory risks register**
Objective	Ensure that you are aware of the main risks faced by your firm, as well as how these are managed and mitigated.
Explanation	Increasing emphasis is placed on a risk-based approach to Compliance, and one of the building blocks of this approach is to prepare a risk register.

(Continued)

Topic	**Maintenance of Compliance and regulatory risks register**
Actions required	1. Decide on the aspects of the business that you want to risk assess. Some of the areas that you may choose include – individual regulations; – pieces of legislation; – products; – services; – departments; and – whole entities. 2. Decide upon a risk-rating methodology. Risk measurements that you may choose include – likelihood of a regulatory or legislative breach; – impact of a regulatory or legislative breach; – whether the issue/area is currently a 'hot topic' with the FSA, another regulator or the media, thereby potentially generating regulatory attention; – whether the issue/area has recently give rise to considerable disciplinary action on the part of a regulator; – whether the issue/area has been noted as an area of focus by the regulator; – the importance of an issue/ area to the firm; – internal regulatory history – whether the issue/area has been subject to a negative Compliance monitoring or Internal Audit report, or whether Operational Risk highlights this issue/area as one of concern; – whether a material number of customer complaints have been generated in relation to this issue/area; and – whether the firm has staff who are experienced in dealing with this issue/area. Each of these factors, and any others that you are using, can be assigned a risk value. 3. Identify the risks associated with each area that you are assessing and give each risk a rating in accordance with the methodology identified above. 4. When you have noted all the Compliance risks relating to a particular area you should note down how each risk is managed or mitigated. This will also help you identify areas where additional controls need to be implemented. 5. You should also set risk tolerance levels: you may decide risk values correspond to an area being high, medium or low risk. 6. The table on the opposite page provides an example of how a risk register may be formatted. 7. When you have conducted your risk assessment and noted areas where remedial action is required you should be able to see which areas need particular attention, and this can be fed into the annual Compliance plan (see page 129). 8. The risk assessment can also be used for Compliance monitoring purposes (see page 191) to identify issues/areas that should be reviewed. 9. The risk register should be updated on a regular basis in line with developments to the firm in particular, and to the industry in general.
Further information	–

Sample risks register – Research department

Table showing some of the regulatory risks faced by a hypothetical Research department as well as the mechanisms that have been implemented to mitigate those risks, and actions that will be taken in future to further strengthen the control environment. Risks are rated out of 3, with 3 representing the highest level of risk.

Risk	Existing control/s	Action/s to be taken
Research leaked to internal department before being distributed to clients. **Risk Rating: 2** *(would be high impact but strong controls are in place)*	• Use of electronic distribution system means that all recipients of research, including internal department, receive reports at the same time. • Research team has received training on the importance of ensuring simultaneous distribution of research to all recipients.	• Conduct periodic audit of electronic distribution system to ensure it is working properly. • Provide refresher training on simultaneous distribution.
Research issued in collusion with the Investment Management department in order to impact the price of a security for the benefit of the Investment Management team. **Risk Rating: 2** *(would be high impact but strong controls are in place).*	• Both Investment Management and Research team staff have received training in relation to the need for independence of research. • Compliance conducts regular manual reviews to identify any correlation between research and investment management transactions.	• Investigate the possibility of implementing an automatic system for identifying any correlations between research reports issued and investment management transactions undertaken.
Research Analyst trades prior to research distribution. **Risk Rating: 2** *(would be high impact but strong controls are in place).*	All Research Analyst trades must be approved by line management and Compliance prior to execution.	Commence periodic retrospective review of Research Analyst trades to identify any transactions that may have been completed prior to research report distribution.
Research Analyst agrees contents of research with issuer. **Risk Rating: 2** *(would be high impact but strong controls are in place).*	• Research department procedures clearly prohibit this activity. • Colluding with issuers to agree the contents of a research report is a named disciplinary offence within the firm. • All Research Analysts must sign an undertaking indicating that their research is independent.	• No additional action being considered at present.

(Continued)

Risk	Existing control/s	Action/s to be taken
Failure to include required disclaimers on research reports. **Risk Rating: 1** *(strong control in place and impact probably not as significant as with some other risks).*	All research reports are checked to ensure they include the appropriate disclaimers prior to distribution.	No additional actions being considered at present.
New Head of Research based overseas and does not have good understanding of the UK regulatory regime for research. **Risk Rating: 2** *(potentially high risk situation but strong controls are in place).*	• Existing Research team members are experienced in UK regulatory requirements for research. • Research department procedures incorporate UK regulatory requirements.	• Provide training to new Head of Research in relation to UK regulatory requirements. • Compliance to undertake enhanced supervision of Research activities until new Head of Research has more familiarity with UK requirements.
Research Team not located behind a Chinese wall. **Risk rating: 3** *(high-risk situation in relation to which mitigating controls can have only limited impact).*	• Research department is not located near the other Front Office departments although there is no physical segregation. • All staff in the firm have received training about the need for Research activities to be independent.	• Arrange for the Research department to be moved to an access-restricted office as soon as possible. • Introduce appropriate procedures to underpin the physical segregation and provide training to all relevant staff.

Topic	Advisory and project work
Objective	Ensure that you provide sound advice in relation to regulatory matters and that any project work you undertake considers all applicable regulatory, legislative and best practice requirements.
Explanation	• Not all Compliance activities are 'off the shelf' such as the provision of induction training, approving personal account trades or processing Approved Persons registrations. • The majority of issues to be tackled are much more complex and involve lateral thinking instead of just following a simple set of procedures.
Actions required	1. When you are required to provide some regulatory advice or engage in project work you should find out as much as possible about what is required. 2. You should also agree a deadline with the person who has asked for your input – you may be expected to give some advice on the spot, whereas more complex issues may take a matter of months to address adequately.

3. You can use the information in Chapter 10 on Off Piste Compliance as a guide to the types of issues that you should consider.
4. Remember to let the person to whom you are delivering your advice or project work know if you are not going to meet your deadline so that this can be extended or the scope of the advice or project can be modified.

Further information	–

Topic	**Management of relationship with regulators, clearing houses, exchanges etc.**
Objective	Maintenance of good relations with regulators and regulatory bodies of relevance to the firm.
Explanation	The Compliance Officer should ensure that the firm deals with regulators and regulatory bodies in an open and cooperative manner.
Actions required	1. Identify all regulators and regulatory bodies of relevance to the firm. This may include stock exchanges, clearing houses, international bodies and government departments. For further examples see Appendices 1 and 2. 2. Once a list has been established as per (1) above, make sure that you are aware of the key contacts at each regulator/regulatory body. Note their names, contacts details and areas of responsibility. 3. Ensure that all Compliance department staff and key individuals within the firm know who the key regulatory contacts are so that they can respond with the required urgency if they take a message from one of them. 4. Identify all regular and ad hoc reporting and notification requirements and ensure that these are made on a timely basis. 5. Respond to additional requests for information from regulators promptly, which involves ensuring that records are easily accessible and that staff know the importance of communicating with regulators openly and truthfully. 6. Make staff aware that if they receive a phone call from someone purporting to be a regulator, then this should be reported to Compliance immediately and no response should be given until it has been ascertained that the request for information is genuine; there have been cases of people making bogus claims to be regulators in order to try to obtain confidential information about firms or their clients. 7. Ensure that staff send copies of any regulatory communications they receive to the Compliance department. 8. Maintain a regulatory correspondence file so that records of all communications with regulators are close at hand. 9. In order to ensure that Compliance has full control over the relationship with regulators you may choose to ban staff from contacting regulators unless their contact is preapproved by Compliance and the results of the communications are reported to Compliance as soon as possible after the event. 10. Ensure that any connected persons such as material outsourcing providers, Appointed Representatives and other firms within the group are aware of the above requirements.
Further information	–

Topic	Regulatory visits
Objective	Ensure that regulatory visits are conducted as successfully as possible.
Explanation	• Regulatory visits are key to a firm's relationships with its regulators and considerable planning and effort should be put into ensuring that these go as smoothly and successfully as possible. • Firms will generally receive ample notice of a routine regulatory visit but this is not always the case, especially when the regulator is conducting a investigation. • Regulatory visits may be conducted by a number of organizations such as – the local regulator; – a regulator of an overseas jurisdiction in which your firm has a branch or provides services on a cross-border basis; – a regulator of another firm within the group; – an investment exchange; and – the regulator of a company to which your firm provides material outsourcing services.
Actions required	1. Upon receipt of notice of a regulatory inspection visit you should try to obtain as much detail as possible about – the reasons for the visit; – the matters to be reviewed; – the documents and records to be reviewed; – the people to be interviewed; and – the regulatory staff who will be visiting the firm and the roles of each one. 2. If the timing of a visit is not convenient, due for example to key staff absence or an inspection by another regulator, it may be possible to reschedule the visit depending on the urgency and materiality of the inspection. 3. Ensure that office space and perhaps computer terminals and phones are available for the use of the inspection team. 4. Collate all documentation ready for inspection as soon as it is requested. 5. Notify the staff that the FSA wishes to interview and provide them with guidance on what may be asked of them. 6. Remind staff of their duty to communicate openly and truthfully with regulators. 7. Check with the FSA whether they wish, or will permit, a member of the Compliance team to accompany staff during their interviews and, if so, make sure that a suitably senior and knowledgeable member of the department is available for each interview. 8. Send a general notification to the whole of the firm indicating the dates that the regulatory visit will take place, and reminding staff that they should be 'on their best behaviour'. 9. Ensure that the regulator has free access to all parts of the premises. 10. If a report requiring corrective action is issued by the regulator after their visit try to discuss the findings with the inspection team prior to the report being finalized. This gives you a chance to correct any misunderstandings, explain any mitigating circumstances and influence the corrective action required and target dates for completion. 11. Once finalized, ensure that the regulatory report is communicated to senior management and implement a plan to address and rectify all matters raised. Monitor progress until all actions have been completed and make regular progress reports to senior management.

12. The regulator may also wish to visit persons connected with the firm such as material outsourcing providers, Appointed Representatives and other firms within the group – in such cases, similar arrangements as those listed above should be implemented.

Further information   See ARROW, Box 2 on page 320.

Topic	**Regulatory service providers**
Objective	Ensure that the firm maintains relations only with reputable service providers and that where there are regulatory implications, any applicable rule requirements have been addressed prior to the relationship being formalized.

Explanation	• Various service providers are used to perform functions that are covered by the FSA rules.
	• Such service providers include those offering the following types of service:
	  – custody;
	  – holding client money deposits; and
	  – clearing and settlement.
	• The Compliance department should ensure that new relationships are established in accordance with the FSA requirements and that they remain appropriate.

Actions required	*Existing relationships*
	1. List all service providers that have a regulatory impact on the firm. This may include
	  (a) external audit;
	  (b) regulatory lawyers;
	  (c) training providers (to both the Compliance department and the firm as a whole);
	  (d) providers of IT support to any specialist computer systems used by the department;
	  (e) news services such as Complinet;
	  (f) publishers/distributors of regulatory magazines and journals;
	  (g) consultants and professional compliance advisers; and
	  (h) parties to whom a compliance-related activity has been outsourced.
	2. Review their contracts to ensure that they comply with FSA requirements.
	3. Conduct periodic reviews to ensure that
	  – each relationships remains appropriate; and
	  – fees paid are not excessive and are in line with those envisaged in the agreement.
	4. Ensure that you have a named contact at each service provider.
	New relationships
	5. Implement procedures whereby staff responsible for new relationships with a regulatory impact are aware of the relevant regulatory requirements.

(Continued)

Topic	**Regulatory service providers**
	6. You may decide that Compliance should approve all such new relationships; alternatively, you should ensure that procedures are in place so that only suitably qualified and senior persons within the firm may do so.
	7. Perform due diligence on the proposed new service provider to ensure that they are appropriate persons with whom to enter into a business relationship.
Further information	–

Topic	**Responding to consultation papers and industry developments**
Objective	Play a part in directing regulatory strategy.
Explanation	• The FSA issues many consultation papers to which they invite comment to help to ensure that the measures introduced are necessary, workable, proportionate and will not put the UK at a regulatory disadvantage.
	• Industry groups regularly get together in an attempt to influence regulatory decision making, set best practice standards and provide a united response to relevant developments within the industry.
	• Financial services are a key part of the UK economy and regulatory policy can have a major impact on the UK as a place to conduct financial services activities.
	• If the UK is to maintain its leading position in global finance then its regulatory position must remain strong (we have seen what happened in the USA as a result of the introduction of the burdensome Sarbanes–Oxley Act, and we should endeavour to ensure that the UK regulatory regime, while remaining robust, does not put the UK at a competitive disadvantage through unnecessary rigours).
Actions required	1. Keep up to date in relation to both industry and regulatory developments both in the UK and overseas.
	2. Review the FSA or other regulatory consultation papers and comment when the subject relates to an area of your experience or expertise.
	3. Join industry groups and contribute to the policy-making process (if you can't be bothered to cast your vote then you should not complain if you don't like the regulations you get).
Further information	–

Topic	**Rules-mapping and reviewing new legislative and regulatory developments to assess relevance**
Objective	Ensure that the firm complies with all relevant Compliance requirements.
Explanation	If you do not know what the rules and requirements are that affect your firm, then you obviously cannot ensure that it complies with them.
Actions required	1. Identify all sources of Compliance-related requirements that impact the operation of the firm. This may include requirements from

    - legislation;
    - regulations;
    - industry codes;
    - recognized best practice; and
    - internal policy.

2. Analyse the above sources and requirements and document how each one impacts the firm.
3. You may wish also to risk-rate each source of requirements to help to prioritize your work. Measures for risk rating that can be used include

    - number of departments or products in the firm affected by the requirement;
    - nature of disciplinary action resulting from a breach of a requirement;
    - number of recent disciplinary cases there have been involving the law, regulation, etc.; and
    - complexity of requirements and how well they are understood by the firm and by the Compliance department.

4. If your firm has multiple departments, various subsidiaries, a wide range of products, etc., it may be useful to complete a rules map for each of these.
5. Once completed, the above rules maps should be kept up to date and relevant requirements should be communicated both within the Compliance department and across the firm.
6. A sample rules map can be found on page 75.

Further information	See Chapter 7.

Topic	**Periodic regulatory reporting to the FSA**
Objective	Ensure that all regular reports to regulators are made on a timely basis and contain all required information.
Explanation	Regulated firms are required to make a number of regular reports to their supervisors. Details of the regular reports required by the FSA are set out in SUP 16, but if your firm has overseas connections, there are also likely to be overseas reporting requirements to comply with.

Actions required	1. Analyse all relevant sources of regulatory requirements and identify all rules requiring regular reports to be made to supervisors.
	2. The Compliance department is not necessarily responsible for all reports so identify the department that is responsible for each one.
	3. Based on the information above, prepare a reporting diary showing
	
	    - name of report to be made;
	    - regulator or other organisation to whom the report is to be made;
	    - contents of report to be made;
	    - reporting frequency;
	    - reporting dates; and
	    - person/department responsible for making the report.
	
	4. Where a report is made by another department make sure that you have an understanding of what the report contains and why it is required.
	5. It goes without saying that the contents of each report should be accurate and that a record should be kept of each report sent.

(Continued)

Topic	**Periodic regulatory reporting to the FSA**
	6. The FSA specifies a number of ways in which reports may be delivered. If the usual postal service is being used it is wise to obtain a receipt to evidence delivery date. 7. You may wish to conduct periodic monitoring to ensure that reporting is taking place as required, although it is likely that if the regulator has not received a report they require, they would notify the firm of this matter. 8. Failure to submit a report on time may result in the firm having to pay an administrative fee or in some form of disciplinary action.
Further information	See Appendix 24.

Topic	**Ad hoc reporting to the FSA**
Objective	Ensure that all ad hoc reports and notifications are provided to regulators on a timely basis and contain all required information.
Explanation	Regulated firms are required to make a number of ad hoc reports and notifications to their supervisors. Unfortunately there is no single list where all of these requirements are compiled and so this is something that each firm will need to prepare for itself.
Actions required	1. Analyse all relevant sources of regulatory requirements and identify all rules requiring ad hoc reports and notifications to be made to supervisors. 2. Prepare a list of notifiable reporting requirements and note the following information: – nature of report/notification to be made; – timing requirements; – supervisor/organization to whom report is to be made; – source of requirement; and – potential disciplinary consequences of failure to make a report. 3. Ensure that all staff are aware of the notification and reporting requirements so that they can let the Compliance department know if a relevant event occurs; if you are not told of relevant events then you cannot report them, and not all notifications relate to matters for which the Compliance department is responsible. 4. Obviously the details of each notification should be correct and a record should be retained of each notification sent.
Further information	See Appendix 24.

Topic	**Payment of fees to the FSA**
Objective	Ensure that FSA fees are paid in full and on a timely basis.
Explanation	• Once a firm is regulated, various fees are payable to the FSA both on an annual and ad hoc basis.

- The FSA has numerous fee-paying requirements, including those related to

  - initial authorization;
  - applications for a listing;
  - individual recognition of an overseas collective investment scheme;
  - approval and vetting of a prospectus;
  - transaction reporting;
  - funding the Financial Ombudsman Service; and
  - funding the Financial Services Compensation Scheme.

Actions required	1. Review the FSA's fee paying manual and identify all fees that must be paid by the firm.
	2. Prepare a list of applicable fees noting the amount and frequency of the fees payable and their due dates.
	3. Allocate responsibility for keeping track of the fees calendar and making sure that fees are paid.
Further information	See Appendix 24.

Topic	**Membership of professional bodies**
Objective	Make use of the services offered by professional bodies related to the work of the Compliance department and contribute to their operation.
Explanation	Professional bodies are of great use to the Compliance Officer – their members can be sources of advice and guidance, they often publish a variety of documents that are useful background reading or that set best practice standards, and they liaise with regulators and other standard setters so as to shape the regulatory infrastructure.
Actions required	1. Review the professional bodies that may be of use to you – do not think only of Compliance-related organizations as some of the bodies of wider interest have sub-committees or groups that focus on regulatory matters.
	2. Join up to the groups that you think will be most useful to you. Make use of everything that they have to offer, but share your own knowledge too, and contribute whatever you can to group initiatives.
Further information	See Appendix 1.

Topic	**Keeping up to date**
Objective	Maintain a thorough understanding of legislative, regulatory and industry developments that affect your firm.
Explanation	If you do not keep up to date you will not be in a position to provide appropriate and timely advice and input when required – the firm is paying for your services and in return it is your responsibility to provide the best service that you possibly can.
Actions required	1. Make a list of all the key and peripheral areas in relation to which you need to keep up to date. This may include
	– laws;
	– regulations;
	– trends;

Topic	Keeping up to date

- best practice;
- new types of financial crime;
- new compliance methodologies;
- EU initiatives; and
- developments in overseas markets.

2. If the team is large enough, assign one person or unit to focus on each specific area; for example, one person may focus on financial crime and another on EU initiatives.
3. Ensure that knowledge is kept up to date by making use of the various training providers and other sources of information that are available. These include

   - reviewing regulatory web sites;
   - reviewing consultation papers and discussion documents;
   - reviewing government department web sites;
   - reading the industry press such as the *Financial Times, The Financial News, Compliance Monitor, Compliance Recorder*, etc.;
   - subscribing to internet news services such as Complinet, Mondaq, etc.;
   - using the Google Alerts function on the internet to be notified automatically of particular areas of interest;
   - attending training courses;
   - attending conferences and seminars (many law and accountancy firms provide excellent free seminars);
   - attend meetings and discussion groups held by relevant professional bodies;
   - obtaining relevant industry qualifications; and
   - liaising with other Compliance departments within your group.

4. Keeping up to date should not be an isolated activity. Be proactive – you should be continually reviewing the knowledge you have gained against the products, services, activities and plans of your firm to assess what the impact is and to determine whether you need to take any Compliance action – training, revising procedures, conducting a review, etc.
5. You may wish to set a training and development plan for the department with new joiners having to undertake a certain set of development activities before they can be considered fully integrated into the team.
6. Such activities may include

   - attending courses;
   - reading relevant documents or periodicals; and
   - obtaining specified qualifications.

Further information	–

Topic	Disciplinary procedures
Objective	Ensure that there are appropriate procedures in place to discipline staff for a breach of Compliance rules or policy.
Explanation	A disciplinary policy acts as a deterrent to staff from breaching Compliance requirements and shows the regulators that your firm takes regulatory compliance seriously. Without clear disciplinary procedures it can also be harder to dismiss an employee for inappropriate conduct.

Actions required	1. Liaise with Human Resources and the Legal department to draft a disciplinary policy that clearly identifies unacceptable behaviours and indicates the potential consequences of such behaviour.

2. You should ensure that all staff know they are expected to comply with all applicable Compliance rules, policies and procedures and that failure to do so may result in disciplinary action. Some methods of doing this are to have a clause in the standard terms of employment to this effect, or to have a statement in each Compliance policy/procedure/manual that a failure to comply with the document may result in disciplinary action.

3. Disciplinary cases are extremely sensitive matters as they can cost a person his livelihood if a qualified withdrawal from the Approved Person's register makes future employment difficult.

4. It goes without saying then that you must be absolutely sure of all the facts before taking any disciplinary action, to the extent that you would be capable of backing your case up in court, as your action may result in a claim for unfair dismissal or discrimination.

5. Your record keeping in this area should be impeccable and as these records concern very delicate issues, you must be sure that they are maintained in compliance with applicable data protection legislation.

6. In this context you should also consider your policy on employee references – if another firm asks you for a reference on the employee who has been disciplined, how much detail, if any, will you give? As the provision of a negative references can sometimes land companies in court it is advisable to speak with your Legal department or an employment lawyer for advice if you are asked for a reference in such circumstances.

7. When a staff member needs to be disciplined there are a number of related matters that need to be considered, including:

- whether any other staff members are involved;
- whether there is any evidence of fraud;
- whether any customers have been disadvantaged;
- whether the FSA needs to be informed;
- whether the matter calls into question the individual's fitness and propriety under FIT; and
- whether the issue represents a breach of the FSA's Code of Conduct for Approved Persons.

Further information   –

Topic	**Passporting**
Objective	Ensure that all passporting arrangements are operated in accordance with the requirements set out under the relevant EU directive, and that adequate compliance control is exercised over such arrangements.
Explanation	• Firms with their head office in one EEA state are permitted to provide certain defined financial services into other EEA states without having to gain separate approval from the states into which the services are provided.

Topic	Passporting

- The state where the firm is based is called the home state.
- The state into which the services are provided is called the host state.
- There are various passporting regimes in operation depending on the type of financial services being undertaken – insurance, UCITS management, etc.
- Passported services may be provided in two ways:

  - by establishing a branch in another state; and
  - by providing 'cross border' services, i.e. providing services into the host state from a base in the home state.

Actions required

Passporting via a branch

1. Ensure that management knows to inform Compliance when a new branch is established.
2. Determine the business model and planned activities of the branch to assess whether it falls within one of the passporting regimes and, if so, which one.
3. As part of the planning stages before the opening of the branch you should find out as much as possible about the local regulatory environment to determine which local regulations will be applicable to the proposed activities.
4. On the basis of the services to be provided and the nature of the local regulatory environment, you should implement a local regulatory infrastructure for the new branch, for example, who will be the Compliance Officer, what will be in the Compliance manual, how will reports be made to head office, etc.?
5. Notify the FSA of the intention to open the branch in accordance with the notification requirements set out at SUP 13.5.1 SUP 13 Annex 1 or 2.
6. After notification the branch should not be opened until the FSA has notified the firm that it has provided a consent notice to the host state regulator.
7. Once the branch is open you should review its activities on a regular basis to ensure that it complies with all relevant regulatory requirements in both home and host state.
8. Management reporting to head office should also take place on an ongoing basis.
9. Notify the FSA of any changes to the branch operating arrangements in accordance with SUP 13.8.

Passporting via the provision of cross-border services

10. Ensure that management knows to inform Compliance when a new cross-border service is being provided from the home state. This is likely to be more tricky than with the opening of a new branch which is a fairly major event and is unlikely to go unnoticed by you. What systems can you implement to ensure that you are made aware if an over-enthusiastic salesperson suddenly decides to try to tap the Spanish or German market?
11. To raise awareness you should provide training on passporting to management and Front Office staff and also cover passporting in the Compliance manual.
12. You may also want to carry out periodic monitoring to review the addresses of new customers being set up, and the addresses to which confirmations and other customer correspondence is being sent as this may help you to identify services being conducted into jurisdictions for which you have not completed the correct passporting process.

13. When made aware of a new cross-border passporting arrangement find out as much as possible about the services to be provided to determine whether they fall within the scope of one of the EU's passporting regimes and, if so, notify the FSA in accordance with SUP 13.4.2 and SUP 13 Annex 3.

14. Investigate the regulatory environment in the host state in order to determine any regulatory requirements that the firm must comply with in its provision of the cross-border services and provide training to the relevant staff. You may also want to provide written guidance.

15. Ensure that the provision of the relevant cross-border services is not commenced until the FSA has confirmed to the firm that it has provided the host state regulator with a consent notice.

16. Once the cross-border services are being provided you should review the arrangements on a regular basis to ensure that all relevant regulatory requirements in both home and host state are being complied with.

17. Notify the FSA of any changes to the basis on which the cross-border services are provided in accordance with SUP 13.8.

General

18. You should keep very careful records of your firm's passporting permissions. Such records should include, for each country:

   - date application made to the FSA;
   - date notification of approval received from the FSA;
   - whether services are provided via a branch, or on a cross border basis;
   - nature of services approved; and
   - relevant host state regulatory requirements.

Further information	See Appendix 24.

Topic	Regulatory agreements and documentation
Objective	Ensure that templates for regulatory documentation contain all the required clauses.
Explanation	The FSA has stipulated a considerable number of documents that must be used by regulated firms and these documents must contain certain required details, must be sent within specified timeframes, and sometimes require a written response from a client or other third party.

Actions required	1. Review your firm's activities *vis-à-vis* the FSA rules and determine which regulatory documentation is required.
	2. Further details are provided in Appendices 19 and 21 but good examples are
	
	   - client agreement/terms of business;
	   - trade confirmations;
	   - periodic statements;
	   - outsourcing agreements;
	   - client money trust letters;

(Continued)

Topic	Regulatory agreements and documentation
	− client assets trust letters; − custody agreements; and − mini prospectuses.
	3. Review templates for each document and ensure that these contain all the required clauses; add any clauses that are missing or prepare new templates if required.
	4. You may wish to complete this exercise in conjunction with the Legal department.
	5. Ensure that the people responsible for preparing and sending out the documents know which are the required clauses and that these may not be removed or altered without reference to Compliance.
	6. Also ensure that the people responsible for sending out the documents know when they must be used and what the deadlines are for dispatch.
	7. As it is generally not the Compliance department that is responsible for preparing client statements, custody agreements, etc., you should conduct periodic reviews to ensure that the templates that you approved have not been altered and that documents are being dispatched within the required timescales, with written responses from clients obtained where necessary.
Further information	See Appendices 19 and 21.

Topic	Conflicts of interest
Objective	Ensure that all actual and potential conflicts of interest affecting the firm are identified and are thereafter subject to appropriate management and mitigation.

Explanation	• A conflict of interest occurs when the interests of a client are at odds with the interests of the firm, an employee or another client.
	• The fact that a transaction or situation gives rise to the potential for a conflict of interest does not necessarily mean that the firm cannot proceed, as long as appropriate conflicts management arrangements are implemented.
	• The interests of a party receiving a service and the party providing it are of course never completely aligned. In the client's ideal world they would receive your services free of charge and would buy your assets from you at cost. Legitimate business interests are not the target here. Conflicts arise rather when there is an imbalance of power, information or resources whose existence is known to one party but not the other, and is exploited to the detriment of the latter.
	• Typical situations that may give rise to a conflict of interest include the following:
	  − The firm has an interest in a transaction taking place that the customer does not know about, e.g. it will receive an inducement or is returning a favour.
	  − The firm is trying to make a gain or avoid a loss to the detriment of the client.
	  − One client is being favoured at the expense of another.

- Detailed examples of conflicts of interest that may be encountered in a financial services firm are provided in Appendix E.

Actions required

1. The key components of a conflicts of interest regime are

   - implementing arrangements to identify any actual or potential conflicts of interest;
   - implementing arrangements to manage and mitigate the conflicts identified;
   - documenting control policies and procedures;
   - staff training and awareness; and
   - monitoring.

   Where firms are part of a group of companies, a group-wide 'conflicts of interest' regime should be implemented.

   Conflicts identification

2. There are two types of conflict that may be identified:

   - **generic** situations that exist on an ongoing basis, e.g. the potentially competing interests of the Sales team and the Research department; and
   - those that arise on an **ad hoc** basis, e.g. two Corporate Finance clients wishing to buy the same target company.

3. For **generic situations** you should prepare a log identifying all the potential conflicts to which your firm is susceptible. The log should also note how you will manage each situation. If your firm is large it is best to do this exercise for each department separately as each unit will be subject to different types of conflict.

4. The conflicts log that is produced should be reviewed regularly in line with business, staff, product and market development and operating environment to ensure that it is kept up to date.

5. Use the above log to identify any corrective action that needs to be taken to strengthen the control environment, and ensure that this is implemented.

6. It is less straightforward to identify **ad hoc conflicts.** The various means of doing this include the following:

   - Develop a good knowledge of your firm's day-to-day business and its clients so that you become aware of potentially conflicting situations as they arise.
   - Rely on staff vigilance – Front Office staff should know which situations may give rise to conflicts and should notify you when they think such a situation may arise.
   - Attend regular Front Office business unit meetings in which current and future projects and transactions are discussed.
   - Receive regular business pipeline reports so that you can see which departments and clients are doing what.
   - Ensure that Research reports are approved by Compliance prior to issue so that they can be checked for conflicts with other business being conducted by the firm.
   - Require personal account trades to be pre-approved by Compliance to enable you to decline any transactions that might disadvantage a client.

(Continued)

Topic	Conflicts of interest

- Require inducements to be pre-approved by Compliance to enable you to decline requests relating to any gifts or benefits that might disadvantage a client.
- Implement electronic conflicts clearance system so that you are automatically alerted if a conflict arises. Typically, such systems work by requiring details of all corporate finance or investment banking transactions to be fed into a transaction database. The system then looks for matches in terms of client name, transaction name, etc., and a warning e-mail is sent to Compliance so that the situation can be investigated.
- Use a watch and restricted list to log details of transactions that may give rise to conflicts of interest so that new transactions can be checked against this before being agreed.
- Access to any transaction database or watch and restricted list should be severely restricted and no new mandate should be agreed until the conflicts check has been completed.

Conflicts management

7. Again, conflicts management techniques vary, depending on whether the situation is generic or ad hoc. Some of the most commonly used methods of controlling **generic conflicts** are to:

- Implement permanent Chinese walls to segregate sensitive departments;
- Implement appropriate reporting lines so that two potentially conflicted departments (e.g. Proprietary Trading and Investment Management) do not report to the same person; and
- Ensure that the firm's remuneration policy does not put undue pressure on employees to meet tough sales targets to the detriment of client interest.

8. Some of the most common ways of controlling **ad hoc conflicts** are as follows:

- Refuse to approve inappropriate inducements or personal account trades.
- Notify clients of specific conflicts of interest that impact their current relationship with the firm, warning them of the risks of such a situation, and seeking their explicit approval to proceed.
- Arrange a temporary Chinese wall – this may be needed where there are two teams within a single department working on conflicting mandates. Stay close to transactions and staff that are subject to temporary Chinese walls and review to ensure that the arrangement is working appropriately. Continuously review to assess whether the management of the conflict needs to change.
- Decline to take on a mandate that conflicts with work the firm is already conducting for another client.

Documented policies and procedures

9. Internal procedures for the identification, management and mitigation of conflicts of interest should be clearly set out in writing so that staff understand exactly what their responsibilities are in this area. The FSA details some specific contents requirements for the firm's conflicts of interest policy, with particular attention paid to corporate finance business.

Training and awareness

10. Train staff on the conflicts of interests that they are most likely to encounter in their specific departments and on how each should be managed.
11. Ensure that staff are fully familiar with the firm's conflicts of interest policy and procedures.

Monitoring

12. Undertake regular Compliance monitoring to

- identify conflicts of which the firm was not previously aware;
- ensure that conflicts identification controls are working properly;
- ensure that conflicts management controls are working properly; and
- assess whether the conflicts policy and procedures are being complied with.

Further information   See Appendix 24.

Topic	**Market abuse**
Objective	Ensure that the firm does not commit market abuse either for its own account, or to assist a client, and that suspicions of market abuse are identified and reported to the FSA where appropriate.
Explanation	• Market abuse distorts the transparent and efficient workings of the markets and creates unfair advantage for unscrupulous participants who seek to benefit unfairly from

- information that is price sensitive and has not been made public; and/or
- manipulating the price of listed investments for their own purposes.

- Market abuse is being taken ever more seriously by the FSA and is right at the heart of two of its four statutory objectives, namely, of maintaining confidence in the UK financial system, and of preventing the UK markets from being used for financial crime. Market abuse is all about markets being used dishonestly; if this goes unchecked in a given market, confidence in that market will be lost, leading people to take their business elsewhere.
- For the offence of market abuse to take place the abusive activities must have been undertaken in relation to a 'qualifying investment' traded on a 'prescribed market' (or in relation to which an application for trading on a prescribed market has been made).
- A 'qualifying investment' is one covered by the Regulated Activities Order (see Appendix 3).
- A 'prescribed market' is an exchange established and approved as a regulated market within the EEA.
- The FSA identifies several ways in which market abuse may be carried out. These are summarized below, though it should be noted that many specific definitions are used both by the FSA and the Criminal Justice Act 1993, and space does not permit the inclusion of all of these here. At a high level there are two types of market abuse:

- actions that involve insider dealing (and related concepts); and
- those that involve market manipulation.

(Continued)

Topic	**Market abuse**

	• Actions amounting to insider dealing are

- insider dealing itself;
- improper disclosure (of inside information); and
- misuse of (inside or relevant) information.

• Actions amounting to market manipulation are

- manipulating transactions;
- manipulating devices;
- dissemination; and
- misleading behaviour and distortion.

• Note that there does not have to have been an intention to engage in market abuse for an offence to be committed.
• Suspicions of market abuse must be reported to the FSA. However, many people consider that the FSA has not been particularly successful in prosecuting cases of suspected market abuse to date, so we may see activity cranked up in this area during the next few years.
• For each form of abuse defined the FSA provides examples (in its Code of Market Conduct) of behaviour it does NOT capture. These are not 'safe harbours' as much as attempts to give more definition to the vague boundaries within which the offences exist: they do give helpful, though still generalized, examples of what is 'on-side', but of course these examples are not exhaustive: in essence they state that normal commercial behaviour motivated by something other than a desire to commit market abuse will *normally* not amount to an offence.

Insider dealing

• This takes place when an insider deals or attempts to deal, or encourages another person to deal

- in a qualifying investment or related investment; and
- on the basis of inside information relating to the investment in question.

• The terms 'insider' and 'inside information' are very tightly defined and several factors set out by the FSA must be present for information to qualify as such. See definitions on page 154.
• *Example*: You learn from an insider that a company will announce unexpected and substantial losses, so you sell your holding of shares before the announcement in order to avoid a loss when the share price subsequently falls.
• Possible signs of insider dealing include an urgency to trade (especially in a way which is out of the ordinary for the client in question), trade instructions given irrespective of seemingly unfavourable pricing and repeated trading between two clients in the same asset.
• It is interesting (and somewhat disheartening) to note that one of the UK's most recent prosecutions for insider dealing was actually against a Compliance Officer who had access to inside information by virtue of his role and who was imprisoned for conspiracy to commit insider dealing.

Improper disclosure

• This takes place when an insider discloses inside information to another person, otherwise than as legitimately required as a result of his employment, profession or duties.

- *Example*: As an insider, you know that your company will announce unexpected and substantial losses and you tell another person of this fact before the official announcement has been made so that person can sell, thus avoiding a loss.

Misuse of information

- Similar to insider dealing but with wider scope in that it applies not only to 'inside information', but also to 'relevant information'.
- Relevant information is information that does not meet the specific definition of inside information but is not generally available and is likely to have an impact on trading decisions made concerning a qualifying investment. For instance, inside information needs to be precise, but relevant information does not.
- *Example*: You learn through your employment with a company that its relations with several key clients are suffering because of poor client service, and you sell your shares in the company in the expectation that your employer's share price will decline if those clients move elsewhere.

Manipulating transactions

- Trading so as to give false or misleading impression as to the supply, demand for or price of a qualifying investment or in such a way as to impact the price of a qualifying investment (price positioning).
- *Example*: You collude with another trader to repeatedly buy and sell shares in a particular issue so as to make it seem that there is considerable demand, thus causing the price to rise, at which point you sell your proprietary holding at a price that you would not otherwise have been able to achieve.

Manipulating devices

- Engaging in a trading strategy that involves the dissemination of misleading information in the qualifying investments concerned.
- *Example*: You buy a large proprietary position in the shares of Company A. You then spread false information about the positive future prospects of Company A, wait for the rise in the price of Company A's shares resulting from your positive market commentary, and then sell your shares at a price higher than you would otherwise have been able to.

Dissemination

- Spreading information that is likely to give a false or misleading impression as to a qualifying investment.

- *Example*: You use an internet bulletin board to record a false rumour that a listed company (that you hold in your portfolio) is about to be subject to a takeover bid in order to benefit from the resultant price rise.

Misleading behaviour and distortion

- Activities that would be likely to give a false impression as to the price, demand, supply or value of a qualifying investment but are not undertaken directly in relation to that qualifying investment. Two possible examples are behaviour undertaken in relation to

  - a commodity such as sugar, as sugar futures traded on Euronext.Liffe are qualifying investments; and
  - an OTC equity derivative contract based on an LSE listed equity, as such an equity would be a qualifying investment.

- *Example*: You arrange for consignments of sugar to be transported in such a way as to give a false impression of the demand for sugar, thereby affecting the price of sugar contracts traded on Euronext.Liffe.

(Continued)

Topic	Market abuse

Actions required	1. The essential elements of your anti-market abuse regime should involve

    – identifying the types of market abuse to which your firm is most susceptible;
    – implementing preventative controls;
    – implementing detective controls;
    – implementing an internal and external reporting system for suspicions of market abuse;
    – record keeping;
    – staff training and awareness; and
    – monitoring.

Identification

2. Identify the types of market abuse to which your firm is most susceptible. If the firm is large and engages in multiple activities, it is best to do this exercise for each department as each unit will be vulnerable to different types of market abuse.
3. Plenty of examples can be found in the FSA's Code of Market Conduct.

Preventative controls

4. The preventative controls you may wish to use include

    – regular training, tailored (largely, but not exclusively) to the specific types of market abuse that each department is most likely to encounter;
    – provision of written guidance on controlling market abuse;
    – use of Chinese walls designed to prevent the inappropriate flow of information from one part of the firm to another;
    – watch and restricted lists used to control and monitor trading; and
    – personal account dealing controls used to control inappropriate staff dealing.

Detective controls

5. There is increasing regulatory expectation that firms will operate electronic surveillance systems to identify suspicions of market abuse. These systems can be programmed to identify situations which may indicate market abuse, e.g. a large proprietary position taken in an issuer a day before a takeover announcement for a transaction with which the firm's Corporate Finance department is involved and about which it may have inside information.
6. Of course, electronic and automated surveillance systems should not be used exclusively and trading activity should also be subject to periodic manual review. However, if thousands of trades are being executed in one day, irregularities are more likely to go unnoticed.

Reporting

7. Implement a system whereby any suspicions of market abuse (whether identified through staff vigilance or electronically) are brought to the attention of the Compliance department.
8. Suspicions of market abuse that cannot be resolved or satisfactorily explained must be reported to the FSA.

9. It may also be necessary to make a report to the Serious Organized Crime Agency (SOCA) as given the criminality of market abuse any proceeds from it can be considered the proceeds of crime, which brings it within the scope of anti-money laundering legislation and controls.

Record keeping

10. The type of records you should maintain in relation to suspicions of market abuse include
    - date suspicion identified;
    - dates between which suspicious behaviour took place;
    - nature of suspicion;
    - staff members involved;
    - person reporting suspicion;
    - department involved;
    - details of client/s involved;
    - details of product or service involved;
    - whether the suspicion was reported to the FSA;
    - whether a report was made to SOCA;
    - remedial action taken;
    - whether the suspicion was reported to senior management;
    - whether any disciplinary action took place;
    - whether a customer complained (and if so, details);
    - whether legal guidance was obtained as to how to proceed (and if so, details);
    - whether customer compensation was paid, and if so how much; and
    - date investigation of suspicion is considered complete.

Staff training and awareness

11. Ensure that staff are aware of the actions that constitute market abuse and the serious penalties associated with it.
12. It is useful to tailor the examples of market abuse used for training purposes to situations that are relevant to your firm's own activities.
13. As well as giving face-to-face training sessions, written guidance material is also important, and many firms also implement a market abuse policy.

Monitoring

14. In addition, regular monitoring should be undertaken by the Compliance monitoring team to identify, for example

    - suspected cases of market abuse that have gone unnoticed and that need to be investigated;
    - failures in electronic surveillance;
    - changes that need to be made to electronic surveillance to reflect changes to business;
    - instances of market abuse suspicions that have been identified but not adequately followed up;
    - cases of market abuse that should have been reported to the FSA but were not; and
    - staff members who have not undertaken the required market abuse training.

Further information   See Appendix 24.

Inside information definition under the Financial Services and Markets Act 2000

There is a separate definition of insider dealing under the Criminal Justice Act 1993 s.52 but it is narrower and is encompassed by the elements below.

Inside information (general)	Information relating to ***qualifying investments***, or ***related investments***, which are not commodity derivatives, which (a) is of a ***precise*** nature; (b) is not generally available; (c) relates, directly or indirectly, to one or more issuers of the ***qualifying investments*** or to one or more of the ***qualifying investments***; and (d) would, if generally available, be likely to have a ***significant effect*** on the price of the ***qualifying investments*** or on the price of ***related investments***.
Inside information (commodity derivatives)	Information relating to **qualifying investments**, or **related investments**, which are commodity derivatives, which (a) is of a ***precise*** nature; (b) is not generally available; (c) relates, directly or indirectly, to one or more such derivatives; and (d) users of markets in which the derivatives are traded would expect to receive in accordance with ***accepted market practices*** on those markets.
Inside information (order information)	With respect to the function of executing orders in any ***qualifying investments*** or ***related investments***, information given by a client and related to their pending orders which (a) is of a ***precise*** nature; (b) is not generally available; (c) relates, directly or indirectly, to one or more issuers of the ***qualifying investments*** or to one or more of the ***qualifying investments***; and (d) would, if generally available, be likely to have a ***significant effect*** on the price of the ***qualifying investments*** or on the price of ***related investments***.
Qualifying investments	• Any investment that has been 'prescribed' as such by HM Treasury in the Financial Services and Markets Act 2000 (Prescribed Markets and Qualifying Investments) Order 2001 (SI 2001/996).

- This covers all investments of a kind specified for the purposes of section 22/ Schedule 2 of FSMA such as shares and corporate and government bonds.

Related investments

An investment of which the price or value is based on the price or value of a *qualifying investment*. This includes instruments such as futures, options and swaps.

Precise

- For information to be precise it must relate to

  - current circumstances; or
  - circumstances that are reasonably believed to be about to occur; or
  - an event that has taken place; or
  - an event that may reasonably be expected to take place.

- The information about the event or circumstance should be adequately specific for someone to be able to use it to form a view as to how it will impact relevant *qualifying investments* or *related investments*.

Significant effect

For information to have a significant effect on price it must be the type of information which a reasonable investor could be expected to use when making an investment decision.

Accepted market practices

- Information relating either directly or indirectly to a commodity derivative and which is

  - made available to users of such markets as a matter of routine; or
  - subject to a disclosure requirement as a result of

    - a statutory provision;
    - market rules;
    - a contract on the commodity market or commodity derivatives market; or
    - accepted customs on the commodity market or commodity derivatives market.

An insider is someone who holds inside information in one of the following situations:
- belonging to the administrative, management or supervisory bodies of an issuer of *qualifying investments*;
- having a shareholding in an issuer of *qualifying investments*;
- having access to the information through the exercise of his employment, profession or duties;
- as a result of their criminal activities; and
- having obtained the information by other means which he knows, or could reasonably be expected to know, is *inside information*.

Named or commonly known market manipulation techniques

Market manipulation has given rise to a somewhat esoteric vocabulary of its own with some of the principal named and/or commonly recognized techniques described in the following table.

Name	Explanation
False and/or misleading transactions	
Wash trades	Transactions in investments by connected or colluding parties undertaken on the basis that actual beneficial ownership and market risk exposure will remain with the seller, but giving the impression to other parties that these have passed to the buyer. (CESR's definition specifies that repurchase and stock lending transactions do not fall into this category.)
Painting the tape	Engaging in one or more published transactions to give the impression of increased trading activity in an investment.
Improper matched orders	Buy and sell orders entered into at or near the same time by prior arrangement between colluding parties. (This does not refer to legitimate exchange activity such as crosses.)
Orders placed with no intention of execution	Entry of published (e.g. order book) buy or sell orders away from the market to give the impression of supply or demand for an investment, the orders being deleted before execution. (A variation is the market-moving order, entered (in smaller size) at better than the last bid/ask, and incurring only a limited trading loss if the order cannot be deleted in time.)
Price positioning	
Marking the close	Trading at or near the close of a market in order to influence the closing/reference price of a security or its derivative.
Colluding in the after market of an Initial Public Offer	Parties who have received allocations of an IPO entering the secondary market act in concert to generate interest in the stock and force its price up, disposing of their holdings when they have done so.
Abusive squeeze	Exploiting a commanding position in the supply of a security or commodity underlying physically delivered derivative contracts in order to profit in periods of concentrated demand, e.g. on derivative expiry dates.
Creating a floor in the price pattern	Trading, usually by issuers of securities, so as to sustain their share price artificially and protect the issuer against rating agency scrutiny, or a run on its shares.
Excessive bid/ask spreads	Manipulation of the bid/ask spreads by market makers or specialist brokers to maintain the apparent value of an investment at an artificial level, away from the fair value implied by actual supply and demand.

Trading on one market to improperly position the price of a financial instrument on a related market	Trading in one investment to influence the reference price of another trading elsewhere (chiefly in respect of derivatives and their underlying(s)).

Fictitious devices/deception

Concealing ownership	Transactions transferring legal ownership of an investment from one party to another which effectively holds it on behalf of the first, usually to avoid disclosure of assets/interests requirements.
Pump and dump	Taking a position in a security and then inflating its value by disseminating positive information about, or buying further into, the stock, selling out when the price has risen.
Trash and cash	The opposite of the above: shorting a security and disseminating negative information, or shorting further, to deflate its price, then closing the whole position when it is in profit.
Opening a position and closing it immediately after its public disclosure.	A prominent long-term investor such as a portfolio manager makes public a transaction in an investment but disposes of it shortly afterwards.

Topic	**Chinese walls**
Objective	To ensure that the inappropriate flow of information within the firm is minimized.
Explanation	• The use of Chinese walls is well known through the financial services industry as a mechanism for preventing inappropriate information flow from one part of a firm to another (both physically and electronically).
	• Their use is particularly relevant in the context of controlling market abuse and conflicts of interest, and departments located behind a Chinese wall are generally those handling non-public price-sensitive information, or those handling information that could give rise to a significant conflict of interest in relation to the activities of other areas of the firm.
	• Classic situations in which Chinese walls may be used include
	– to prevent information about forthcoming research being made known to proprietary traders; and
	– to prevent information about a corporate finance mandate being made known to fund managers.
	• Departments that regularly handle information that may give rise to a conflict of interest or to market abuse should be located behind a Chinese wall so that access to the information they control can be restricted.
	• The departments located behind a Chinese wall, in a restricted access area, are often referred to as 'private side' departments.
	• The departments not behind a Chinese wall are often referred to as 'public side' departments.

(Continued)

Topic	Chinese walls

| | • Due to their seniority, some staff, such as directors, may need access to information both on the private and the public side of the wall. Such staff are commonly referred to as being 'above the wall'.
• It may sometimes be necessary to temporarily involve a public side staff member in a private side transaction. Such staff are commonly referred to as 'wall crossers'.
• Although Chinese walls controls (see below) are relatively intensive in terms of the administration they require to be effective, it should be stressed to the firm that they actually afford several business benefits including

  – enabling businesses to be conducted in the same firm that may otherwise not be considered compatible; for example, acting for two separate bidders in a takeover situation;
  – providing a defense from allegations of market abuse; and
  – providing a defense from action for damages taken against the firm under FSMA s.150. |
| *Actions required* | 1. Review the activities of all of the departments of your firm and note whether or not you consider that they should be located behind a Chinese wall. Write a justification so as to provide an audit trail for your decisions. Teams frequently located behind a Chinese wall due to the sensitivity of the information they hold include

  – research;
  – new issues;
  – mergers and cquisitions;
  – investment banking;
  – corporate lending; and
  – private equity.

2. Arrange for physical barriers to be erected to prevent ready access to private side departments. This may include some fairly expensive building work so make sure that you have senior management buy-in for this as it may well be costly.
3. To be truly effective, Chinese walls should result in total physical segregation, and access to a private side department should be restricted. Most firms nowadays have electronic door controls operated by an electronic pass or by finger print recognition.
4. Computer systems access to private side information should also be fully restricted and the computer files of staff behind a Chinese wall should only be accessible by appropriately authorized staff in the relevant department.
5. Notify all staff at the outset of their employment as to whether they are located on the private side or the public side, or whether they will be above the wall. Written guidance should be provided to each category of employee so that they are aware of what their respective rights and responsibilities are for their status.
6. Operate strict controls over staff gaining access to a Chinese wall department whether this be on a permanent basis, as a temporary wall crosser, as for a staff member who will be above the wall. Such access rights should only be granted following approval from the relevant line manager and the Compliance department, and a justification for why access is required should also be noted. |

7. You may wish to record access and approval to Chinese walls areas on a record form and/or database showing

   – name of person for whom access is required;
   – nature of access required, e.g.:

     o independent access to department;
     o access to department only when accompanied by a private side staff member (i.e. non-independent); or
     o access to computer files only.

   – reasons access required;
   – date access required to commence;
   – date access will no longer be required (where access is to be temporary);
   – person/people approving access;
   – date access approved.

8. Document your Chinese walls arrangements and controls so that guidance is available to all staff.
9. Chinese walls are not necessarily permanent arrangements and it may be necessary to establish temporary arrangements to cover a particular transaction, for example the situation referred to above in which a firm acts for two separate bidders for a single takeover target. In such a case it would not be appropriate to build new permanent walls to separate the two deal teams, but you are otherwise likely to be able to segregate the two teams and implement controls similar to those described above to permanent walls.
10. Your Chinese walls should be subject to regular monitoring, both by the Compliance department and by relevant departmental heads. Matters that you may wish to monitor include

    – unauthorized access to a Chinese walls area – either physical or via computer;
    – failure of electronic access controls on doors to Chinese wall areas;
    – log not being maintained of wall crossers;
    – failure to give guidance to new staff as to what the implications are of being on the public or private side, or being above the wall; and
    – new departments or actives that require Chinese walls arrangements to be extended or changed.

Further information   See Appendix 24.

Topic	Insider lists
Objective	Ensure that an adequately detailed, populated and up-to-date list is maintained of all staff with access to inside information.
Explanation	• In order to control and deter market abuse, listed companies are required to prepare insider lists detailing the people acting on their behalf (whether employees, or on a contractual basis) who have access to inside information relating to them.
• In order to facilitate issuer compliance with insider list requirements, firms should implement insider list arrangements where their staff hold inside information on their listed clients. This is most likely to be of relevance for members of the firm's corporate finance or investment banking teams.

(Continued)

Topic	Insider lists
Actions required	1. Determine the departments and people within the firm that are most likely to have access to inside information. 2. Implement arrangements whereby the information required by the FSA to be maintained on insider lists can be captured. Such records include − names of insiders; − entity in relation to which each person is an insider; − reasons for their needing to be insiders; − date on which each person became an insider; and − date when each person ceased to be an insider. 3. Each time a staff member's name is added to an insider list the person should acknowledge in writing that − his name is on the list for that particular entity; − he agrees with the date in relation to which he can first be attributed with being in possession of inside information; and − he is aware of the penalties for breaching relevant requirements (ideally these should be summarized on the acknowledgement form with guidance as to where further details can be obtained). Staff should also acknowledge in writing when they are removed from the insider list to confirm that they no longer have access to inside information on that particular issuer. 4. Decide who will be the custodian of the insider lists – this may either be the Compliance department, or relevant departmental heads. 5. Prepare written procedures on the use of insider lists within your firm. 6. Provide staff training in relation to when and why insider lists are required and the penalties they may face if they breach relevant requirements. 7. Conduct periodic monitoring to ensure that insider lists are being made and maintained appropriately. 8. Remember – confidential and price sensitive information should be shared on a need to know basis only.
Further information	See Appendix 24.

Topic	Watch and restricted list maintenance
Objective	Ensure that trading does not take place with or in prohibited or restricted entities.
Explanation	• Although the watch and restricted lists are not defined terms in the FSA Handbook they are widely known and used throughout the financial services industry. • Watch and restricted lists are used for a variety of reasons including − controlling inappropriate information flow; − preventing or managing conflicts of interest; − preventing or identifying suspicions of market abuse;

- preventing breaches of exclusivity arrangements; and
- preventing the commencement of a business relationship with parties that the firm does not wish to become involved with for whatever reason (reputational issues, for example).

- Although similar in nature, the watch and restricted lists have different uses. These may vary somewhat from firm to firm but in general, their use can be summarized as follows:

Watch list

- Used to record the names of entities in relation to which the firm has non-public and price-sensitive information; AND
- The circumstances that have given rise to this information have not been publicly announced, e.g. an *intended* takeover bid.
- This list is not distributed across the firm.
- Trading in entities on the watch list by staff in the department that has generated, the watch list entry is forbidden either on a personal, customer or proprietary basis.
- Other members of the firm may trade in watch list entities (as long as there are appropriate Chinese wall arrangements in place), but such trading should be subject to review to ensure that the trading is not improper (e.g. based on inside information).

Restricted list

- Used to record the names of entities in relation to which the firm has non public and price sensitive information; AND
- The circumstances that have given rise to this information have already been publicly announced, e.g. a *known* takeover bid (as such entities will often start out recorded on the watch list and then be transferred to the restricted list).
- Also may be used to list entities in which trading should be restricted for various other reasons, such as

  - impending research publication; or
  - reputation issues, which may mean it is not desirable for the firm to be seen to be involved with a particular entity; or
  - the entity having a bad credit history with the firm; or
  - the entity being engaged in a dispute or litigation against the firm.

- This list may be distributed across the firm.
- No member of the firm may trade in an entity on the restricted list.
- The watch and restricted lists are generally maintained by the Compliance department. In larger firms, administration of the lists and other sensitive information is the responsibility of 'the control room' whose staff undertake many of the control activities described below.

Actions required

1. Implement arrangements for the preparation of the watch and restricted lists:

   - Define the circumstances in the context of your firm that will give rise to an entry on either list.
   - Prepare a paper or electronic form that staff can use to make the notification (see below).
   - Document these arrangements.
   - Provide regular training in relation to them.

(Continued)

Topic	**Watch and restricted list maintenance**

2. The watch and restricted lists notification form should include details such as

   – name of company to be added to a list;
   – whether the company should be added to the watch or the restricted list;
   – person requesting that the company be added to the list;
   – department;
   – reason entity needs to be added to the list;
   – whether the entity is listed and, if so, on which stock exchange; and
   – staff members who are party to the sensitive information about the entity being added to the list.

3. You should also include on the form scope for the entity to be moved from the watch to the restricted list (and reasons and person giving the instruction), and scope for the entity to be removed from a list (plus reasons for this and person giving the instruction).

4. Define the circumstances in which the watch and restricted lists should be used. For example, lists should be checked prior to

   – approving a personal account trade (the person may have had access to inside information);
   – accepting a corporate finance mandate on an exclusive basis (the firm may already have entered into a exclusivity arrangement with another customer in relation to the same project);
   – forming a new customer relationship (the firm may have had a bad credit relationship with the entity in the past and may not wish to undertake further business with them); and
   – issuing research (the research may be contrary to advice that is being given in a corporate finance relationship, eg Research team says sell as they consider the company a poor prospect whereas Corporate Finance are trying to find buyers as they consider the prospects good).

5. You may grant certain exceptions to the prohibition on doing business with entities recorded on either list – for example, executing a trade that is conducted to facilitate an unsolicited customer order.

6. Undertake staff training to ensure that the correct use of the watch and restricted lists is known to the relevant employees.

7. Conduct periodic monitoring to ensure that information recorded on the watch and restricted lists remains current and to identify trading in entities recorded on one of the lists.

Further information	See Appendix 24.

Topic	**Personal account dealing**
Objective	To ensure that employees do not engage in inappropriate personal account dealing.
Explanation	• Examples of inappropriate personal (PA) account dealing include

   – trading in a manner that disadvantages a client;
   – engaging in market abuse, especially insider dealing;

  - employees spending too much time contemplating the progress of their personal investment portfolios rather than carrying out their job; and
  - employees running up large personal losses to the extent that it could impact their suitability to work for the firm – being financially sound is one of the FSA's criteria for assessing fitness and propriety.

- It is also prohibited to procure someone else to trade on your behalf so as to hide the above situations from an employer.
- The PA dealing requirements do not apply in a number of situations including

  - trades that have not been undertaken at the employee's own discretion; and
  - purchase of a life insurance policy.

- You may choose to exclude more junior staff who are not involved with designated investment business from your PA dealing regime, but many firms decide not to take advantage of this exemption for best practice purposes (remember that market abuse, insider dealing and reputational issues have a far wider reach than the FSA rules), and for administrative convenience.
- The PA dealing rules applying to Research analysts are particularly strict.
- Appointed Representatives and outsourcing service providers should also be covered by your PA dealing regime.

Actions required

1. The essential elements of your PA dealing regime should include

   - requiring staff to obtain pre-approval for their personal trades;
   - ensuring that you are promptly notified of all PA trades executed;
   - monitoring;
   - preparing a PA dealing policy setting out the essential details of the firm's controls; and
   - provision of staff training so that they are aware of what is expected of them in this area.

Pre-approval

2. Pre-approval is not strictly a requirement under the FSA rules. However, it certainly makes sense in terms of identifying and preventing inappropriate trades before they take place unless you

   - require all PA trades to be undertaken through your own firm;
   - distinguish all staff accounts from other accounts in the trading system;
   - have systems in place to ensure that inappropriate PA orders are not accepted for trading; and
   - can extract reports showing PA trades so that these can be scrutinized after the event.

3. Ensure that you have a prompt approval system in place – you don't want your colleagues to blame your slow response for losing money as the markets have moved against them.

4. Decide how approval will take place – you may use a paper form needing a signature, or you could use an electronic request and approval system.

(Continued)

Topic	Personal account dealing

5. Decide who will have authority for approving trades. Will it be just Compliance, just line management, a director, or a combination of the above?
6. Decide what criteria will be used for approving and rejecting trades, and how 'danger' situations will be identified. Examples of the types of transaction prohibited by some firms include trades in

- shares issued by a client of the firm;
- shares issued by your own firm;
- participations in a collective investment scheme managed by the firm;
- investments in an industry covered by the firm; and
- investments in a company with which the firm has a legal dispute.

Other firms choose to make a blanket prohibition on spread betting as substantial losses can be made relatively quickly due to rapid movements in positions. Not only might this have an impact on the financial standing of the employee concerned but it might also cause them to spend more time watching their own trades than those of their clients.
7. A good way to identify impropriety is to check PA dealing requests for matches on the watch and restricted lists.
8. Ensure that people with responsibility for PA approvals understand what the approval criteria are, what the process is for approving a trade, when they should seek your guidance and which records they need to retain.
9. You may decide that approvals should only be valid for a number of days after which another approval will need to be obtained.
10. You may also decide to impose a holding period (e.g. investments bought may not be sold within 30 days) in order to prevent excessive trading.

Notification of PA trades

11. As detailed above, the IT systems in some firms allow for PA trades to be automatically notified to the Compliance department.
12. Most firms, however, will have to rely on staff members to supply them with a copy of the contract note, or having a duplicate contract note sent directly from the broker.

Monitoring

13. Once notified of a trade you should review it to ensure that any approval conditions were met, e.g. was it undertaken within the stipulated number of days, has the minimum holding period been breached?
14. Monitoring is particularly important for trades that have not been pre-approved and you will need to carry out some vetting on all or some of them for appropriateness (see guidance above).
15. Pay particular attention to monitoring successful trading! If someone is consistently successful with their deals – i.e. trading consistently to avoid loss or make a profit – how does this guy get lucky all the time? Is he the best stock picker in town, or is he trading off the back off inside information?
16. You may also decide to monitor for particularly unsuccessful trading. Remember that financial soundness is part of the FSA's fit and proper test and if an employee is suffering from considerable financial strain he may be tempted to take risks in the workplace that he would not otherwise contemplate.

Policy and training

17. Decide who your policy will apply to. Will it be all staff, even if not involved with designated investment business? What about implementing a group-wide policy encompassing affiliates all over the world?

18. The essential details of the firm's PA trading procedures should be documented in a policy, along with guidance about what the potential penalties are for a breach.

19. Training should also be undertaken so that staff understand the policy and everything that is expected of them in this area.

20. In order to ensure maximum awareness some firms make compliance with the PA dealing policy a condition of recruitment, and include this clause in their employment contracts.

21. Another idea is to have all staff sign a declaration confirming that they understand the firm's PA dealing rules and agree to comply with them. Related to this is the annual process some firms implement of requiring staff to sign a declaration confirming that all of their trades during the previous year were undertaken in accordance with the PA dealing policy.

Further information	See Appendix 24.

Topic	Inducements
Objective	Ensure that adequate arrangements are in place to prevent the offer or receipt of inappropriate inducements such as gifts and benefits of any kind.
Explanation	• The inappropriate offer and receipt of gifts and benefits in financial services can create a serious conflict of interest in which firms may be induced to act in such a way as to disregard the best interests of a client or clients: – What if, in return for a substantial gift from a client, a salesperson agrees always to allocate trades in a way that gives an unfair advantage to that client over others? – What if a fund manager offers a substantial gift to a broker to encourage that broker to execute trades in a way that gives that fund manager an unfair advantage over other clients? • The FSA defines inducements very widely as – fees; – commissions; and – non-monetary benefits. • This definition is generally considered to include things like – attendance at seminars and conferences; – research; – subscription to journals or electronic information providers; and – presents such as wine, watches, pens, etc. • The FSA allows fees, commissions and non monetary benefits only in three specific situations: – they are paid or provided to or by the client or their representative; or

(Continued)

Topic	Inducements
	– they are paid by or for a third party but does not impair the firm's duty to act in the client's best interests AND an appropriate disclosure is made to the client AND the inducement is designed to enhance customer service; or – they are proper fees paid to facilitate business such as those relating to custody and settlement, regulatory levies, etc. • At a high level, inducements may be of two varieties: – Those offered/received on an ongoing basis, e.g. a subscription to a journal. – Those offered/received on an ad hoc basis, e.g. a gift given by a client as a sign of appreciation for the successful completion of a complex transaction. • Some firms are happy for employees to accept gifts but require payment of an equivalent amount of the value of the gift to either the firm or a charity. In these circumstances, a full audit trail should be retained.
Actions required	1. Make a log of the ongoing arrangements your firm has in relation to inducements. Information to be captured includes – nature of inducement; – how the arrangement works; – other parties involved, i.e. who offers or receives the inducement; – monetary value of inducement; – date arrangement started; – name of employee within your firm who is responsible; – explanation as to how clients have been notified of the arrangement; – explanation as to how this inducement is either necessary, or enhances customer service; and – explanation as to how the inducement cannot be deemed to conflict with the firm's duty to act in its clients' best interests. 2. In order to complete the above log you should speak to a variety of staff across the firm, including senior management, Front Office, the marketing department, who may be in change of corporate entertainment arrangements, and Accounts who are responsible for processing and approving payments. 3. In the context of your firm, decide which forms of inducement are acceptable and which are not. You may decide to place a blanket ban on some types of inducement (for example, cash payments) whereas others you may deem to be acceptable as long as their value is below a minimal predetermined value. You may also consider it necessary to terminate some of the arrangements listed in (1) above. 4. Implement arrangements whereby Compliance is notified of all new inducements to be offered or received above the threshold value referred to in (3) above so that a decision can be taken as to their appropriateness. Make a record of these along the lines of those indicated in (1) above – you may find it useful to make an approval check list to make sure you have covered everything. 5. In some cases you may wish to withhold approval for receipt of a particular gift because you consider it either excessive or inappropriate but you fear that it may be considered a snub to the party offering the gift. In such circumstances, you may decide that the gift can be accepted but should be raffled internally, or given to charity.

6. Ensure that staff are aware of the firm's inducements procedures and arrangements by giving regular training in this area and by documenting the arrangement in a written policy.
7. Conduct regular monitoring to ensure that the firm's inducements policy is being complied with.

Further information   See Appendix 24.

Topic	**Approval of financial promotions**
Objective	Ensure that all financial promotions are fair, clear and not misleading and that they are in compliance with any relevant legislative or regulatory requirement.
Explanation	• Financial promotions compliance is taken very serious by the government and the FSA, to the extent that it is a breach of FSMA (not just a rules breach) for an unregulated firm to issue or approve an advertisement for financial services. • Given the above, it goes without saying that you should ensure that your firm has watertight procedures for the preparation, approval and issue of financial promotions – the FSA is particularly active in following up cases of inappropriate advertising and even has a hot line that the public can call to report what they consider to be instances of malpractice. • As well as the FSA's financial promotions rules there are several other bodies that control advertising activity in the UK and it is important to comply with any requirements that they might impose in addition to those of the FSA. Such bodies include – the Advertising Standards Authority; – the Office of Communications; – the Office of Fair Trading; and – local Trading Standards offices. • The extent of the FSA rules applicable to the issue and approval of financial promotions depends on the target audience of the material: – *Eligible counterparties* – COBS rules do not apply, although the Principles for Businesses are relevant. In particular, note Principle 7: Communications with clients, which reads: 'A firm must pay due regard to the information needs of its clients, and communicate information to them in a way which is clear, fair and not misleading.' – *Professional clients* – The higher level COBS rules apply, but not those specifically directed to retail financial promotions. – *Retail clients* – All of the COBS rules apply.
Actions required	1. Prepare a list of all the different types of financial promotion issued and/or approved by your firm. Ensure that you capture all of the different types including – websites; – advertorials;

Topic	**Approval of financial promotions approvals**

- direct mail shots;
- radio and television slots.

2. Once you have the above list, it is helpful also to note for each type of financial promotion:

   - department and manager responsible for the advertising material;
   - frequency with which issued;
   - target audience – client categorization;
   - target audience – jurisdiction;
   - product/s covered;
   - whether or not the material falls within the strict the FSA definition of a financial promotion: 'an invitation or inducement to engage in investment activity'.

3. On the basis of the details gathered above, determine the relevant legislative and regulatory requirements that apply to the financial promotions issued and approved by your firm. This can vary extensively depending on the type of advertisements and the nature of the audience. Details of some of the various sources of requirements in this area are noted below.

4. Prepare an approval checklist covering the various requirements applicable. Depending on the extent of variations in the financial promotions issued or approved by your firm, you may need only one checklist, or alternatively, you may need one checklist for each type of financial promotion.

5. You should determine which arrangements you will implement for the approval of financial promotions material. In some firms, only members of the Compliance department are authorized to do this, whereas in other firms, other suitably experienced staff members may do it.

6. The checklist/s should include the following type of information:

   - date material submitted for approval;
   - name of person approving the material;
   - your internal approval reference code;
   - time period during which material will be in circulation.
   - target audience – client type;
   - target audience – jurisdiction;
   - whether the material contains any confidential information about a firm or a client;
   - whether the information in the communication could be deemed to breach market abuse requirements;
   - confirmation of compliance with specific the FSA rules such as:
   - whether the material is clearly identifiable as a financial promotion;
   - whether the name of the firm is included;
   - whether a clear reference period for past performance details is shown; and
   - date material approved for issue.

7. Any person permitted to approve financial promotions should receive regular training to ensure that they are aware of all relevant requirements.

8. You should conduct periodic reviews to ensure that no inappropriate financial promotions have been approved, that appropriate records are being kept, that only people authorized to do so have approved financial promotions, and that the checklists you use are up to date *vis-à-vis* changes to regulation, legislation and the type of advertisement issued/approved.

Further information	See Appendix 24.

Topic	**Handling complaints and litigation**
Objective	To ensure that customer complaints are dealt with efficiently, expediently and appropriately, and where relevant, in accordance with the FSA requirements.
Explanation	• The FSA requirements on complaints handling apply only to 'eligible complainants'. It goes without saying, however, that all complaints should be treated seriously and handled accordingly. • The FSA definition of an eligible complainant includes private individuals, small businesses, some charities and some trustees with a (potential) customer relationship with a firm.

Actions required	1. Prepare a written policy and/or procedure for handling complaints. This should allow for compliance with the FSA requirements where relevant, and should cover matters such as
	
	   − definition of an eligible complainant (staff need to know which complaints the FSA rules must be applied to);
	   − process to be followed when a complaint is received;
	   − time limits within which complaints are to be dealt with;
	   − records to be maintained.
	
	2. If a complaint is particularly significant or complex guidance should be obtained from the Legal department as to how to proceed as the customer may also decide to initiate legal proceedings against the firm.
	3. You should also consider whether the complaint results from so serious a breach that the FSA should be notified. The FSA may then, of course, decide to take disciplinary action against you.
	4. Complaints that cannot be satisfactorily resolved between the firm and the customer may be referred (by the customer) to an independent complaints handling scheme such as the Financial Ombudsman Service, Finance and Leasing Association conciliation and arbitration schemes, the Pensions Advisory Service or the Pensions Ombudsman.
	5. You should conduct periodic monitoring of the complaints handling process within your firm to ensure that
	
	   − complaints are being handled in accordance with the complaints policy; and
	   − any trends can be identified for further investigation if required.

Further information	See Appendix 24.

Topic	**Handling rule breaches**
Objective	Ensure that rule breaches are identified and thereafter handled appropriately.
Explanation	Rule breaches, whether material or relatively insignificant, need to be brought to the attention of the Compliance department so that the issues raised can be addressed.
Actions required	1. Create a system for recording rule breaches. You may use a paper record or a database and the type of information to record includes the following:

- date/s of rules breach;
- nature of breach
- person responsible;
- person reporting breach;
- department involved;
- rule reference;
- remedial action taken;
- details of client/s involved;
- details of product or service involved;
- target date for breach to be resolved;
- date breach considered resolved;
- whether breach was escalated to senior management;
- whether any disciplinary action took place;
- whether a customer complained (and if so, details);
- whether legal guidance was obtained as to how to proceed (and if so, details);
- whether reported to the FSA under SUP 15; and
- whether customer compensation was paid, and if so how much.

2. Make sure that your breaches register or database is fully completed; what better invitation is there for negative comment in a regulatory or Internal Report than a rule breach record in relation to which no evidence of remedial action can be seen?
3. Make sure that employees are aware that they should be reporting breaches to the Compliance department – you may want this simply to be done by e-mail or face to face, or you may prefer to prepare a form that staff can complete and send to you.
4. You may also populate your records as a result of compliance monitoring work completed or the review work of other department such as Internal Audit or Operation Risk.
5. When you are made aware of a breach you should investigate to find out how it came about, although clearly the depth of your investigation will depend on how serious the breach is.
6. However, even breaches that seem minor are worth more than a cursory glance because they may be symptomatic of something else. What if this is the tenth time this month that the same employee has made a mistake; the same computer system has failed; the same product has been affected?
7. Rule breach statistics (number, materiality, percentage past resolution date, etc.) are frequently used as a performance measurement marker to be reported to senior management.

8. You should periodically review your breaches register or database to see what lessons can be learnt – this information could be used as the basis of training.
9. Remember that under SUP 15, details of material breaches have to be reported to the FSA.

Further information   –

Topic	**Administration of training and competence regime**
Objective	Ensure that staff achieve and maintain the required competency for the roles they are performing.
Explanation	• The FSA's training and competence (T&C) requirements apply on two levels:

- The competent employees rule – applies to all staff.
- The T&C rules apply to staff who are performing one of the key roles identified by the FSA, *but only in respect of retail clients*. Such roles include investment management and overseeing settlement arrangements in relation to discretionary management activity. The full list is set out in the FSA's rules – TC Appendix 1.

• The competent employees rule requires firms to ensure that their employees have the required skill, knowledge and expertise to discharge their specific responsibilities successfully. Honesty should also be considered to be a function of competence.
• The training and competence rules are much more prescriptive and cover matters such as

- training;
- exam requirements;
- maintaining competence;
- competency assessments; and
- supervision.

Actions required   *The competent employees rule (all staff)*

1. To a large extent it should be possible to comply with the competent employee rule simply by applying standard Human Resources best practice such as

- conducting formal recruitment interviews;
- obtaining references and evidence of qualifications prior to employment;
- having a probationary period during the first few months of employment;
- providing staff with job descriptions;
- ensuring that staff have an annual appraisal;
- ensuring that each staff member has a line manager who is responsible for supervising his work;
- providing relevant training

2. Even though there is no longer an examination obligation for staff active only in the wholesale markets many firms are choosing to impose an examination requirement as a matter of best practice.

(Continued)

Topic	Administration of training and competence regime

Training and Competence rules (staff providing retail services)

3. From the list specified by the FSA, identify all the roles covered by the training and competence rules that are undertaken by staff within your firm.
4. Identify all departments within your firm that have staff who engage in one of the activities specified by the FSA as being covered by the T&C rules.
5. Ensure that all staff who should be covered by the T & C rules

    – have been identified;
    – have been notified of their T&C status; and
    – understand the practical application of the T&C rules insofar as they impact their role.

    It is useful to have a proforma memo that can be sent to each staff member moving into a role covered by T&C.
6. Ensure that heads of departments know which staff in their teams are covered by the T&C rules as they will probably be required to act as T&C supervisors (see below).
7. *Recruitment* – For new joiners, notes from recruitment interviews should be retained as part of an initial assessment of competency. Staff should not be recruited unless satisfactory references about their previous activities and training have been received and until evidence of relevant examinations passed has been obtained.
8. *Training* – Staff should receive induction training on joining the firm, and should thereafter undertake regular training that is tailored to their individual roles and which takes account of changes in the markets, products, regulation and legislation that are relevant to the individual employee concerned.
9. *Assessing competence* – In order to attain competence, a formal assessment of competence must be conducted and the results recorded. The competency assessment should cover

    – technical knowledge and its application;
    – required skills and their application; and
    – the markets, products, legislation and regulation that are relevant to the person being assessed.
    The individuals being assessed must also evidence that they have the required examination passes for their roles.

10. *Examination passes* – The Financial Services Skills Council is the UK body that established appropriate examinations in relation to the training and competence rules:

    – Some T&C roles require exam passes prior to the employee commencing the activity.
    – In some circumstances it may be possible for an employee to obtain an exemption from the required exam passes.

11. Maintaining competence – Arrangements must be implemented to ensure that employees maintain their competence to take account of changes to the environment in which they are working – perhaps there is a new regulatory requirement affecting their role, or perhaps market practice has changed since the last time their competency was assessed, etc.

12. Supervision – Arrangements must be implemented whereby staff are subject to appropriate supervision and monitoring both before and after they have been assessed as competent.

General

13. Departmental heads (rather than the Compliance department!) are responsible for the operation of their departments and, consequently, responsibility for ensuring that their staff members comply with the training and competence rules rests soundly with them, especially where they act as T&C supervisors. Their responsibilities in this respect should be made very clear to them as if one of their direct reports misbehaves the FSA is likely ask how that person was being supervised and the criteria used to assess that person as competent.

14. Actions you make take to facilitate T&C Compliance are listed below.

   - Provide written guidance to department heads in relation to the training and competence rules and their responsibilities thereunder in relation to recruitment, supervision, competency assessments, etc.
   - Provide written guidance to staff performing a role covered by the training and competence rules in relation to

     o their status under the rules (are they already assessed as competent or a trainee, and in relation to which specific activities and products);
     o responsibility for maintaining their competent status or to work towards competency; and
     o examination passes required, etc.

   - Provide periodic training on the T&C rules to both departmental heads and their staff.
   - You may also choose to prepare certain proforma documents to facilitate compliance and record keeping, including

     o competency assessment form;
     o competency certificates; and
     o examination exemption forms.

   - Conduct periodic reviews to ensure that the T&C rules are being complied with.
   - You may also wish to liaise with Human Resources to be notified of new joiners to the firm to keep an eye on which you consider may need to be covered by the T&C rules – just in case a department head lets someone slip through the net!
   - Provide guidance to T&C supervisors in relation to their responsibilities. This should include

     o having a clear understanding of the source of and rationale for the T&C rules;
     o understanding their degree of responsibilities for the actions of staff they are supervising;

(Continued)

Topic	Administration of training and competence regime
	o knowing which T&C status each of their team has, and if this is not the same, which T&C status each requires; o knowing which roles within their departments are coved by the T&C rules; o knowing which exams are required for which roles, and associated timing requirements; o setting training and development programmes for their staff; o undertaking competency assessments. – In some circumstances T&C supervisors are required to take an appropriate exam themselves, even if they are not conducting a role covered by the T&C rules.
Further information	See Appendices D and 24.

Topic	Administration of Approved Persons regime
Objective	Ensure that the firm identifies, registers and deregisters Approved Persons appropriately, that Approved Persons are and remain fit and proper to perform a Controlled Function, and that they comply with the Approved Persons Code of Conduct.
Explanation	• The FSA requires that persons performing certain Controlled Functions must be vetted by and registered with the FSA as Approved Persons (unless an exemption applies). • Controlled Functions are those activities that are vital for the continuing sound operation of the firm and at present comprise the 16 functions specified by the FSA in SUP 10.4. These are divided into the following categories as detailed below. • Responsibility for compliance with the Approved Persons rules is usually with the Compliance department, although in some firms this responsibility is delegated in full or in part to the Human Resources department. • The Approved Persons regime is very closely linked to the Training and Competence regime and it is useful to run these two procedures in tandem.
*Governing functions**	Covers the functions of • director; • non-executive director; • chief executive; • partner; • director of unincorporated association; and • directing the affairs of a small friendly society.
*Required functions**	Covers the functions of • apportionment and oversight of responsibilities and controls; • EEA investment business oversight (for heads of business units conducting regulated investment business);

- compliance oversight;
- money laundering control; and
- various senior actuarial roles within insurance companies.

*The systems and controls function**	Covers persons with significant responsibility for - the firm's financial affairs (e.g. Head of Finance Department), - setting and managing risk appetite and exposure (e.g. Head of Risk); and - reporting on the adequacy of, and compliance with, the firm's internal systems and controls (e.g. Head of Internal Audit).
*The significant management function**	Covers persons with significant responsibility for a role not otherwise specified as a Controlled Function, e.g. the Head of the Back Office, or the Head of a Front Office department that does not undertake designated investment business.
The customer function	Covers staff with responsibility for maintaining, managing and developing client relationships e.g.: - provision of corporate finance advice; - advising on derivatives; - dealing with or for clients in securities; and - provision of investment management services.

* These functions are known as significant influence functions.

Actions required	1. Make sure that you have a register listing the details of all Approved Persons including
	
	   – name;
	   – Controlled Function/s performed;
	   – date approved for each Controlled Function.
	
	2. Ensure that procedures are implemented, most likely in conjunction with Human Resources, whereby you are informed in advance of
	
	   – new joiners;
	   – staff transferring between departments and roles;
	   – overseas staff temporarily performing a customer function in the UK; and
	   – leavers.
	
	In this way a timely determination can be made as to whether a person will need to be registered or deregistered as an Approved Person, or a change made to an existing registration.
	3. Ensure that no individuals perform a Controlled Function until they have been approved by the FSA to do so (unless an exception applies). The greatest likelihood of this requirement being breached is in the Front Office when someone moves into a Customer Function role without Compliance being notified.
	4. Exceptions from the requirement to be a Approved Person to carry out a Controlled Function are
	
	   – Performance of a significant influence function for less than 12 weeks to cover temporary or unforeseen absence of an appropriately approved staff member.
	   – People based overseas who spend no longer than 30 days in the UK in a 12-month period during which they perform a Customer Function. For the exception to be valid, such individuals must remain subject to appropriate supervision during their time in the UK.

(Continued)

Topic	Administration of Approved Persons regime

5. In relation to the exceptions listed above accurate records should be maintained of relevant dates and timescales to ensure that the exception remains valid.

6. There are various the FSA forms used in relation to the Approved Persons regime. These are

   - Form A: Application to perform a Controlled Function.
   - Form B: Notice to withdraw an application to perform a Controlled Function.
   - Form C: Notice of ceasing to perform a Controlled Function.
   - Form D: Notice of change in the personal details of an Approved Person.
   - Form E: Internal transfer of an Approved Person.

7. Such forms should be signed and vetted by Compliance (or whoever else is responsible internally) to make sure that they have been fully completed, otherwise there may be a delay in processing.

8. Before anyone becomes an Approved Person you should provide that person guidance as to what this means. You may wish to provide

   - a copy of the FSA's fact sheet on 'Becoming an Approved Person';
   - Full details of the activities that the appropriate Controlled Function comprises;
   - a copy of the Statements of Principle and Code of Practice for Approved Persons with which they will be expected to comply on an ongoing basis for the duration of their Approved Person status; and
   - summary details of their liability under the FSA's disciplinary regime (Approved Persons may be subject to disciplinary action by the FSA in a way that does not apply to non-approved staff members).

9. The firm must notify the FSA, using Form C, not later than 7 business days after a person ceases to perform a Controlled Function.

10. Think very carefully about what is written on Form C in relation to why employees ceased to perform a Controlled Function. If they were dismissed, or asked to resign due to inappropriate behaviour then the FSA wants to know about this. You should liaise with your legal department about what should be written to ensure that the firm is not left open to potential legal action on the part of employees if what is recorded prevents or hinders them securing future employment as an Approved Person.

11. When a person undertaking a Customer Function leaves the firm you should prepare and keep on file a regulatory reference for them that can be supplied to any firm that asks for such a reference in future. The details that should be recorded on the reference are set out in SUP 10.13.12(2) and include

    - details of outstanding or upheld complaints about the employee; and
    - the person's status under the Training and Competence rules.

12. Various changes to the details of an Approved Person must be notified to the FSA. Such details include

    - changes to title, name, national insurance number (to be notified within 7 business days to the firm becoming aware of the change); and
    - any matter that would impact an Approved Person's fitness and propriety (as set out in FIT).

13. To make sure that you become aware of all changes notifiable to the FSA you may wish to include notification details in the annual Compliance attestation (see page 130).
14. You should provide periodic training to remind Approved Persons of

    – the scope of their Controlled Function;
    – their obligations under the Statements of Principle and Code of Practice for Approved Persons; and
    – notification requirements to the FSA in relation to the Approved Persons rules.

15. You may also conduct periodic monitoring to ensure that staff who have not been approved to conduct a Customer Function do not engage in such activities. This could be done for example by listening to voice recordings or by reviewing order and execution records.
16. Periodic monitoring should also be carried out to ensure that any exceptions that have been applied (see above) remain valid.

Further information	See Appendices D and 24.

Topic	**Approval of new or non-standard transactions**
Objective	Ensure that no matter what activities your firm engages in all compliance issues are identified and are subject to adequate controls.
Explanation	• Your firm's activities will at some point deviate from the norm and you need to be able to assess whether the variation is acceptable, and get to grips with the associated regulatory issues. • Some features that might make a product/service/activity, etc., non-standard include – involving a new category of customer (e.g. existing wholesale product now sold to retail customers); – very large transaction; – serious risk of reputational damage, stemming perhaps from non regulatory areas such as potential damage to the environment; – service being delivered into a new and unfamiliar jurisdiction.
Actions required	1. Ensure that staff know that they should consult with the Compliance department when they want to undertake a new or non-standard activity or transaction. 2. In larger firms there is likely to be a new business committee in which such matters are discussed and approved; make sure that you or another member of the Compliance team sits on it. 3. When assessing the regulatory impact of a new or unusual product/service/activity, etc., there are evidently a number of matters to be considered. You can use the issues listed in Chapter 10 on Off Piste compliance as a starting point. 4. You will likely not feel comfortable approving all new products/services unconditionally, and some you might not feel comfortable approving at all.

(Continued)

Topic	**Approval of new or non-standard transactions**
	5. Where you give a conditional approval you may choose to impose some internal rules. For example, if it is a new product that you are being asked to assess, you may support it only on the condition that it is not sold to retail customers and that sales staff attend training before it is launched. Any such conditions that you impose should be subject to periodic monitoring to make sure they are complied with.
	6. And remember, if you cannot get comfortable with what is being proposed you may simply have to say 'no' and send the architect back to the drawing board, offering him your assistance of course, in terms of how a more appropriate plan my be devised.
	7. After a new product, service or arrangement has been launched or commenced conduct a review after about 6 months to check that everything is going according to plan.
Further information	See Chapter 10.

Topic	**Voice-recording arrangements**
Requirement	Ensure that all appropriate phone lines have voice recording applied to them, that access to voice-recorded material is subject to appropriate security controls, and that records are kept secure and for the appropriate timeframe.
Staff with voice recording requirements	• The following staff should be subject to voice recording, those who – give, receive or execute customer trades; – trade on a proprietary basis; – handle either customer or proprietary settlement instructions. • Voice recording has various uses (other than being a regulatory requirement in some markets): – It facilitates the settlement of disputes with or complaints from third parties (a telephone record can easily establish whether someone said buy instead of sell, or who passed an order for a thousand instead of a million). – It can help to meet record-keeping requirements. – It can be used by Compliance to monitor customer phone calls to ensure that suitable advice is being provided. – It can prove whether a customer trade was advisory or was execution only. (This can be useful if there is a suspicion of insider dealing, for example, and the firm can prove that it dealt to fill an unsolicited customer order rather than on a proprietary basis as a result of some 'secret' information about a forthcoming takeover gleaned from the Corporate Finance department. It is also important for suitability and appropriateness purposes.) – It can be used to provide evidence in cases of fraud, market abuse, money laundering, etc., although remember that if someone is planning to commit a crime, it is unlikely to be done on a recorded line. • Despite its many legitimate uses, voice recording can be an abuse of privacy and therefore a strong control environment is required.

Actions to be taken	1. Assess which staff fall into one of the categories listed above and therefore require voice recording, and ensure that this is applied to their phones.
	2. Review list of voice-recorded staff on a regular basis for new joiners and staff who have changed department – this is likely to generate a change to voice-recording requirements.
	3. Ensure that clients are informed that voice recording may be applied to their phone conversations; this can be done in the customer agreement.
	4. Ensure that there is a notice on phones with recorded lines alerting users to the fact that taping is in place.
	5. Periodically review the sound quality and accessibility of records to ensure that the system is working well.
	6. Make sure there are procedures in place for voice recordings to be subject to appropriate security – it is not acceptable for any person to be able to wander in and listen to someone else's telephone conversations.
	7. Voice recordings and equipment should be kept in a locked room and only authorized staff members should have access.
	8. Any request to listen to a voice recording should be approved by Compliance to ensure that the request is fair and valid and does not breach another person's privacy.
	9. Make arrangements whereby staff who are travelling but who need to undertake an activity subject to voice recording can still record their conversations: it is possible, if a little complex, to record mobile phone lines, but if this is not feasible, have staff call in to a recorded line at the firm to repeat the conversation that they have just had so that at least some form of record exists.
Further information	See Appendix 24.

Topic	**Data Protection Compliance**
Objective	Ensure that your firm handles personal data appropriately, and in compliance with relevant legislation.
Explanation	• In larger firms data protection may be the responsibility of a separate department such as Information Control or Data Security, but in smaller companies, Compliance is frequently responsible for controls and processes in this area.
	• Even if the Compliance department is not responsible for data protection it should work closely with the unit that is, as a breach of data protection requirements is also very likely to constitute a breach of the FSA principles.
	• Legislative data protection requirements apply to the personal details of individuals such as the firm's employees, customers and consultants.
	• The concept of confidentiality applies much more widely and is relevant to individuals and corporates alike.

(Continued)

Topic	**Data Protection Compliance**

Actions required	1. Identify all areas in your firm in which information is handled which falls within the remit the various pieces of data protection legislation. Such areas are likely to include
	
	  – Human Resources;
	  – Legal;
	  – Credit;
	  – Operations; and
	  – Customer services.
	
	  Remember to try to capture any 'unofficial filing systems' as well as the official ones, and note that you may also be responsible for the treatment of any personal data that is transferred to a third party as part of an outsourcing arrangement.
	2. Identify all the data protection requirements that are of relevance to your firm. In relation to the Data Protection Act 1998, for example, the overriding principles that must be complied with, as specified by the Information Commissioner, are that personal information is
	
	  – fairly and lawfully processed;
	  – processed for limited purposes;
	  – adequate, relevant and not excessive;
	  – accurate and up to date;
	  – not kept for longer than is necessary;
	  – processed in line with the data subject's rights;
	  – secure;
	  – not transferred to other countries without adequate protection.
	
	  There are also several more detailed and administratively burdensome requirements relating to matters such as data subject access requests and a firm's requirement to register with the Information Commissioner.
	3. Once relevant requirements have been identified these should be notified to the relevant departments by means of training and the provision of formal policies and procedures.
	4. Conduct periodic monitoring to confirm whether relevant requirements are being complied with.

Further information	See Appendix 24.

Topic	**Corporate knowledge**
Objective	Maintain a thorough understanding of all business units and activities undertaken by the firm.
Explanation	If you do not maintain a high level of corporate knowledge you will not be in a position to provide appropriate and timely advice and input when required – the firm is paying for your services and in return it is your responsibility to provide the best service that you possibly can.
Actions required	Do whatever it takes to get to know the firm, both Front Office, Back Office and support areas. You may consider some of the following:

- Have regular compliance update meetings with business heads.
- Attend regular departmental meetings (e.g. business development, planning).
- Attend board meetings and other committees where significant matters are discussed (or receive minutes if you cannot attend). Particularly important are new product committees and strategy committees.
- Attend training on products or services you are not familiar with.
- Get to know other departmental staff socially – communication will be easier.
- Liaise with other support areas such as Operational Risk, Internal Audit and Legal to understand the nature of the issues they are dealing with and how these may impact you.
- Liaise with HR to find out about internal disciplinary action in case this could have an impact on Compliance, and learn about new joiners and leavers so that staff can be registered and deregistered as appropriate, and covered by the Training and Competence rules where required.
- Use the temple in Chapter 5 to record the information you know about the firm/s that you are responsible for and keep this up to date.

Further information   –

Topic	**Record keeping**
Objective	Ensure that your firm retains all records required under the regulatory system.
Explanation	<ul><li>Regulated firms are required to keep a number of records.</li><li>Unfortunately there is no single list where all of these requirements are compiled and rules are scattered throughout the rule-books and relevant legislation and guidance.</li></ul>
Actions required	1. Review all applicable rules, legislation and guidance and note record-keeping requirements relevant to your firm – this is time-consuming but there is no other way, unless you pay a consultant to do it. 2. Also note the rule reference and the period for which the records need to be retained. 3. Ensure that the list of required records is well known across the firm and that it is kept up to date. If you have a large firm with many different departments, it may be wise to prepare separate schedules of record-keeping requirements for each department. 4. It is a good idea to publish record-keeping requirements on the intranet site along with other Compliance documents such as the Compliance manual. 5. Do not go overboard and keep records just for the sake of it: be especially careful with records containing personal information covered by data protection legislation – you could be committing a breach if you keep this information for longer than is necessary, or if the information you have is not correct. 6. Ensure that any confidential records are kept secure, with restricted access.
Further information	See Appendix 24.

Topic	New offices
Objective	Ensure that when a new office is established a regulatory framework is put in place to enable applicable Compliance requirements to be adhered to.
Explanation	When a new office is established, especially if it will be in a different jurisdiction, or covering a new product or service, there is plenty of scope for Compliance issues to arise if you are not given sufficient opportunity to review the plans and design an appropriate regulatory control infrastructure.

Actions required	1. Implement arrangements whereby you are notified of plans to establish new offices in good time.
	2. Find out as much as possible about the plans for the new office. As a guide you may use the notes in the section on Corporate Knowledge (see Chapter 5).
	3. Once you have determined the business plans for the branch you should prepare a rules map for it by documenting the regulatory requirements that will be applicable to it. This may be a time-consuming exercise if the office is to be in a new and unfamiliar jurisdiction, but if this is the case it is advisable to seek guidance from a local lawyer or regulatory consultant.
	4. The nature of the Compliance regime implemented for the new office will depend on the extent of its activities, the regulations that will apply and the number of staff it will have. You may be able to rely on controls already in place at head office, and simply extend them to cover the new office. Or it may be necessary to implement a totally new regime including
	
	   – a Compliance manual;
	   – Compliance policies;
	   – Compliance reporting systems both to external parties and to senior management and head office;
	   – regulatory training programme.
	
	5. If the new office will involve new activities or products and/or if it is overseas, it is likely that it will require additional regulatory approvals and you should coordinate this process by ensuring that all necessary application forms are fully completed and that any fees are paid.
	6. Even if there is no requirement for any additional regulatory approvals, consider whether a notification needs to be made of the FSA under SUP 15.5.
	7. When the office is about to open you should review any new compliance arrangements for adequacy and then provide training to relevant staff as to any regulatory expectations of them.
	8. Once the office is open you should review its compliance with relevant regulatory requirements on an ongoing basis.

Further information	See Chapter 5 and Appendix 24 (section on passporting).

Topic	Outsourcing
Objective	Ensure that outsourced services do not result in a loss of control by the firm and are conducted in such a way as to enable all applicable FSA requirements to be complied with, as though the activities were still being conducted by the firm itself.
Explanation	• There is a growing trend for services to be outsourced to either specialist firms where it is considered that they can be performed more efficiently,

- or to overseas jurisdictions where it is considered that they can be conducted more cheaply.
- Financial services activities that are commonly outsourced include
  - Back Office processing (settlement, corporate actions, etc.);
  - fund management; and
  - account valuation.

- Outsourcing can undoubtedly results in greater efficiencies and cost savings for the firm but this must not be achieved to the detriment of customer service or regulatory compliance.
- Even though a firm can outsource certain services it cannot 'outsource' responsibility and will be held responsible for breaches committed by its service providers. This means that if there is a rule breach as a result of actions taken by the outsourcing service provider, the firm cannot point the finger in their direction or blame them; the FSA will point the finger firmly back at the firm and blame it for not having appropriate systems in place for supervising the outsourcing arrangement.

Actions required

1. Prepare a log of all outsourcing relationships that your firm has entered into. Note key information such as

   - name and address of service provider;
   - name of main contact at service provider;
   - details of outsourced services;
   - names and dates of outsourcing contracts signed;
   - departments within your firm that are affected by the outsourced services;
   - whether or not the outsourced services constitute 'critical' services as per the FSA rules (see 'Note' below);
   - date on which the FSA was notified of the outsourcing arrangements (critical outsourcing only);
   - date you last reviewed the adequacy of the services provided.

2. Implement arrangements within the firm whereby no new outsourcing arrangements are implemented without Compliance approval. This is important as the FSA prohibits any form of outsourcing arrangement that would have a negative impact on

   - the firm's internal control; and/or
   - the FSA's ability to supervise and monitor the firm's compliance with relevant regulatory requirements.

3. Given the above, Compliance should review each new proposed outsourcing arrangement to assess its appropriateness. The review should cover the matters specified by the FSA, which include whether the proposed service provider

   - has the legal capacity to perform the relevant functions;
   - is capable of adequate supervision of the services rendered;
   - has the required experience to provide the relevant services;
   - (*if regulated*) has been subject to any relevant regulatory sanction or disciplinary action; and
   - (*if overseas*) whether there is any legislation in place that would prevent or hinder the FSA gaining access to relevant records or other material held by the service provider.

(Continued)

Topic	Outsourcing
	4. Ensure that each outsourcing arrangement is subject to a written contract between the firm and the service provider.
	5. Ensure that the FSA is notified of each new critical outsourcing arrangement.
	6. A risk register should be prepared identifying how all relevant risks will be managed and monitored. Appropriate mechanisms for the reporting of risks relating to each outsourced function should also be implemented. Reporting arrangements should cover reporting from the service provider to the firm, and within the firm, reporting to senior management on issues concerning outsourcing.
	7. After the commencement of an outsourcing arrangement the services must be subject to regular review to ensure that the arrangement remains appropriate. Documented arrangements should be implemented to facilitate this review.
	8. In some circumstances you may find it appropriate to provide both initial and ongoing training to staff at the service provider to ensure that they understand all relevant regulatory and legislative requirements. This is particularly the case for service providers located overseas.
	9. Outsourcing arrangements should not be terminated until due regard has been paid to how the relevant services will be performed in future and care must be taken to ensure that the cessation of an outsourcing arrangement will not have a negative impact on the firm or its customers. Consequently, such arrangements should not be terminated without the prior review and approval of Compliance.
	10. If you do not consider it appropriate for Compliance to be required to approve or review all new outsourcing relationships (or their termination) as indicated above, these functions may be delegated to another suitably knowledgeable and qualified person within the firm.
Note	• For the purposes of outsourcing, the FSA considers critical services to be those that are 'critical for the performance of regulated activities, listed activities or ancillary services'.
	• As a rule of thumb, a service can be judged critical if a control weakness or failure in relation to it would have a negative impact on the firm's ability to meet its regulatory obligations or to provide services to its customers or to continue with its regular activities.
Further information	See Appendix 24.

Topic	Whistle blowing
Objective	Ensure that the firm has procedures in place to facilitate, promote and support whistle blowing.
Explanation	• Compliance Officers cannot be in all places at all times and there are bound to be times when things go on in your absence that need to be brought to your attention. Sound whistle-blowing arrangements can facilitate this.

- Whistle-blowing arrangements are procedures whereby staff are able to make 'protected disclosures', i.e. to report instances of inappropriate activity without fear of reprisal. In the UK statutory provisions in this area are set out under the Public Interest Disclosure Act 1998 (PIDA).

Actions required

1. Set up a system whereby staff feel comfortable to report their concerns to an appropriate party without fearing recrimination. It is wise to liaise with the Legal and the Human Resources departments when doing this.
2. To ensure independence some firms choose to outsource their whistle-blowing arrangements, simply providing employees with the phone number of the third party service provider. That way, no – one with a material interest within the firm may choose to disregard the concern that has been reported.
3. Other firms choose to establish a system that is managed internally, with suitably senior and independent persons being put in charge of receiving and assessing reports.
4. Whether staff concerns are reported internally or to a third party, your arrangements should be such that any issues raised with a regulatory impact are swiftly brought to your attention.
5. Notify staff of the whistle-blowing arrangements and make sure that all are aware of the type of matters that may and may not be reported. Make it clear that vindictive reports, or reports made to settle internal disputes will not benefit from protection under PIDA. Also remind staff that even if they do seek legal redress as they feel that they have been dismissed after having made a protected disclosure, there is no guarantee that they will win, and that if costs are awarded against them the financial implications could be significant (as was the case recently with Simon Hussey, who lost a whistle-blowing claim against Nomura in late 2007).
6. You may find it useful to document your arrangements in a policy or procedures document.
7. Conduct periodic monitoring to ensure that the procedures are working effectively.

Further information   See Appendix 24.

Topic	Client categorization
Objective	Ensure that customers receive the correct categorization so that they are offered the appropriate level of protections under FSA rules, or so that the FSA rules are not applied if the person is not conducting relevant business.
Explanation	• The FSA operates a risk-based approach to consumer protection regulation with higher levels of protection being offered to the least experienced consumers. • Customer categorization is therefore a vitally important Compliance process as it determines the level of protection that a firm will apply to its different clients: if a mistake is made and a retail customer is categorized as a professional for example, then the client may be exposed to a greater level of risk than is appropriate for them as many consumer protection rules will be disapplied.

(Continued)

Topic	Client categorization
	• There are three main categories of client under COBS, with various sub-categories. These are summarized below.
Retail clients	• Inexperienced and unsophisticated investors who need the full range of protections available to them under the FSA rules. • May be individuals or small businesses.

Professional clients	• More experienced than retail clients but still need a certain level of protection – a number of the FSA rules are disapplied.
	• There are two categories:
	  – per se professional clients; and
	  – elective professional clients.

Per se professional clients	• Per se professional clients are automatically classed as professionals and include the following:
	  – regulated financial services institutions;
	  – large undertakings meeting the criteria stipulated by the FSA.
	  – governments (both regional and national);
	  – central banks; and
	  – supranational institutions such as the International Monetary Fund.
	• In specific circumstances set out by the FSA it may be possible to treat certain per se professional clients as eligible counterparties (see below).

Elective professional clients	• Clients who do not meet the criteria to be per se professional clients and who would ordinarily be classified as retail clients if it were not for the fact that they
	  – meet certain criteria set by the FSA in terms of experience and capability; AND
	  – have demonstrated a willingness to be treated as an elective professional client despite the protections that they will lose as a consequence;
	  – It may at first sight seem illogical for some people to elect to lose certain protections but they may benefit in various ways from the arrangement including the ability to gain access to asset classes and transactions that would otherwise not be available to them – many firms do not accept retail customers because of the administrative burden and risk of applying the full range of the FSA customer protection rules.

Eligible counterparty	• Highly experienced counterparties to whom only a 'light touch' regulatory protection regime need be applied.
	• There are two categories:
	  – per se eligible counterparties; and
	  – elective eligible counterparties.

Per se eligible counterparties	• Per se eligible counterparties are a subset of per se professional clients who conduct 'eligible counterparty business'.
	• Eligible counterparty business is
	  – executing orders on behalf of clients;
	  – dealing on own account;

	– receiving and transmitting orders; and
	– ancillary services related to the above.
Elective eligible counterparties	Professional clients (either per se or elective) who have requested to be treated as elective eligible counterparties.
Movement between categories	• As well as the main possibilities for movement between a client's default categorization referred to above, there are also a number of other possibilities: – per se eligible counterparty treated as professional client; – per se eligible counterparty treated as retail client; and – per se professional client treated as retail client.
Non-classified clients	• Remember that some services and products provided by financial institutions are not covered by FSA rules and therefore clients receiving these services do not need to be categorized. • Such products and services include forfaiting and trade finance.
Other possible categorization	• It is not always entirely straightforward to establish who is a client for the FSA purposes. • The following people are deemed to be clients: – potential clients; – persons who have received or who are likely to receive a financial promotion communicated or approved by the firm; and – clients of Appointed Representatives and tied agents for whom the firm has accepted responsibility. • The following people are not deemed to be clients; – corporate finance contacts; and – venture capital contacts. unless such persons have received or are likely to receive a financial promotion communicated or approved by the firm. • Be careful if you are dealing with a person acting as agent for an underlying client. In some cases it is the agent and in others the underlying client who will be deemed to be the client of your firm. The rules governing this area are set out in COBS 2.4.3.
Corporate finance contact	• A person with or for whom the firm conducts corporate finance business. • Such persons are not treated as clients as long as the firm has made it clear to them that they will not be treated as such.
Venture capital contact	• A person with or for whom the firm conducts venture capital business. • Such persons are not treated as clients as long as the firm has made it clear to them that they will not be treated as such.
Consumer	Not a categorization in itself, but a catch-all to ensure that persons receiving financial services in whatever manner – e.g. from an unauthorized person, or through a person who is the direct customer of an authorized person – are identified as being protected parties under FSMA.
Actions required	1. Ensure that staff involved in the categorization process are fully aware of the different types of client, the importance of applying the correct categorization and the consequences of getting the categorization wrong. 2. In order to achieve (1) above it is wise to provide face-to-face training and written guidance material.

(Continued)

Topic	Client categorization

	3. The FSA also requires firms to implement written policies and procedures for the client categorization process.
	4. Ensure that all clients are notified of their categorization and that any other requirements documentation and notifications required by the FSA has been sent and received back from the client. For the required contents of such notifications see Appendix 19.
	5. Ensure that categorization records are maintained in accordance with FSA requirements. Such records include
	
	  – each client's categorization;
	  – evidence that the client has been notified of his categorization;
	  – copies of client categorisation agreements.
	
	6. Conduct regular reviews to ensure that
	
	  – once categorized, clients continue to be treated in accordance with the categorization they have been given, and that the categorization remains correct; and
	  – records are maintained in accordance with the FSA requirements.
	
	7. It is useful to undertake client categorization in tandem with the KYC process as both should be completed prior to the commencement of a business relationship with a new client or counterparty.

Further information	See Appendix 24.

Topic	Management information
Objective	Ensure that senior management receive adequate information for them to be able to satisfactorily discharge their responsibilities as managers, identify trends and plan accordingly.
Explanation	• The compilation and reporting of management information is a key tool for controlling regulatory risk. • Remember that in the eyes of the FSA, senior management is responsible for Compliance. • There should be a two-way flow of information: from the firm to the Compliance department; and from the Compliance department to senior management.

Actions required	1. Decide on the information that will be reported to management. This should be specifically quantifiable and also, where possible, have a risk measurement element.
	2. Examples of information it may be useful to report include
	
	  – number of new accounts submitted for approval;
	  – number of new accounts approved;
	  – number of new accounts that were active before approval (breach);
	  – number of PA dealing requested processed;
	  – number of PA dealing requests for which no subsequent trade confirmation has been received;

- number of complaints received;
- number of complaints closed;
- number of rule breaches recorded;
- number of Approved Persons applications processed;
- number of Compliance monitoring points raised;
- number of Compliance monitoring points past their due date for completion;
- number of financial promotions approved;
- number of financial promotions issued without official approval;
- number of staff in Compliance department versus budgeted headcount;
- number of requests processed to gain access behind Chinese walls;
- number of staff trained;
- number of staff who have failed to attend a required training session;
- number of instances in which unauthorized access behind a Chinese wall was identified.

Undoubtedly you will be able to think of many more examples that are just as, if not more, appropriate to the specific activities of your firm.

3. Once you have decided on the information to be captured (your key performance indicators or KPIs) you need to determine how you will do the capturing as some KPIs lend themselves to automated capture and reporting, whereas others need to be generated manually.

4. You also need to decide which information will be reported to senior management: perhaps everything will be reported, even where there is no risk element in order to give an impression of how active the Compliance function is; or perhaps only risk indicators will be reported such as number of breaches, number of complaints, number of new accounts that were active before approval, etc.

5. Decide also how frequently the information will be reported and to whom – for example, will a brief report cross the desk of the Chief Executive at the end of every day, or will a more detailed report be made to the board of directors once a quarter (or a combination of both)?

6. Some firms choose to go one stage further with the management information function and implement something called a 'compliance dashboard', which is a real-time way of providing visual representations of how various process and procedures are operating. The dashboard approach can also be used for the real-time identification and notification of rule breaches and other risk criteria and the automatic analysis of tends.

7. This high-tech approach may only be cost effective for the busiest departments in the largest firms but it is an interesting and relatively new approach which is worth thinking about.

8. If an automated solution is used for collating and/or reporting management information, then ensure that the system has adequate IT support and is covered by your Business Continuity Plan – you don't want to spend all that money on an all-singing all-dancing software package that no – one knows how to use and that cannot be integrated into the operations of the IT department.

Further information   –

Topic	Fraud
Objective	Ensure that there are appropriate procedures in place for detecting and handling fraud.
Explanation	• Fraud is a serious problem for many companies and those operating in the financial markets are no different. The temptations are obvious – financial institutions hold valuable information about their customers' finances, which can be seen as cash cows in relation to which 'a little bit gone from here and there makes no difference'. • Larger firms normally have a dedicated Fraud team but in smaller firms the responsibility for controls in this area often lies with Compliance. • Even if there is a separate Fraud team the Compliance department is likely to be involved on a regular basis as many frauds also constitute regulatory breaches or expose weaknesses in systems and controls that have a Compliance impact.

Actions required	1. You should conduct a full review of your firm's activities to determine which types of fraud it will be most susceptible to.
	2. There are two main types of fraud to which financial institutions are vulnerable – those committed against the firm and those committed against the firm's customers. Of these two main categories there are innumerable variations, with new ones seemingly being identified every day. Examples include
	
	   – misappropriation of customer assets by staff who are meant to be safeguarding them;
	   – theft of customer identity details for personal use or sale;
	   – credit card copying;
	   – cash machine devices used to retain cards or capture card details; and
	   – creation of fake websites to obtain customer account details.
	
	3. Once you have determined the types of fraud to which the firm is most vulnerable you should assess the controls in place to make sure that any weaknesses can be addressed. Reviews should be undertaken on a regular basis as fraud techniques are constantly evolving.
	4. You should also put procedures in place so that staff know how to identify fraud and know what to do if they have a suspicion.
	5. Regular staff training is useful, preferably tailored to the sort of activities undertaken by the employees in question so that they see examples of frauds that they can relate to their own experience.
	6. A reporting regime, similar to that for reporting suspicions of money laundering, terrorist financing and market abuse, should also be implemented to ensure that you are made aware of suspicions and that they will be investigated and dealt with. You may alternatively consider the whistle-blowing reporting system suitable for this purpose.
	7. When a suspected, attempted or actual fraud has been identified it clearly must be investigated thoroughly to determine what action needs to be taken. Procedures and controls may need to be tightened, or the police, SOCA (fraud is a crime so the proceeds of it are the proceeds of crime and therefore covered by anti money laundering legislation) or the FSA may need to be informed.
	8. There may also be staff disciplinary issues and customer compensation issues to address.
	9. Keep a full record of fraud cases reported. Records to retain should be similar to those noted on page 170 for rule breaches, with the addition of whether or not the matter was reported to SOCA or the Police.

Further information	See Appendix 24.

Topic	**Compliance monitoring**
Objective	Conduct Compliance monitoring activities so that rule breaches and Compliance control weaknesses can be identified and, thereafter, subjected to appropriate remedial action.
Explanation	<ul><li>The Compliance monitoring function is similar to the role played by Internal Audit and Operational Risk in that reviews are conducted to provide comfort to senior management that the firm is in compliance with its legislative, regulatory and best practice requirements (although Internal Audit and Operational Risk have a much wider remit covering all the firm's controls).</li><li>At a high level there are two main approaches that can be taken towards Compliance monitoring work, and a combination of these is often used:</li></ul><p> – A more holistic approach looking at a variety of issues affecting a department, law, function, etc., to be reviewed. This is often conducted as a formal audit; – A more narrow approach looking at one specific aspect of Compliance such as breaches of best execution requirements. This is often conducted via electronic exception reporting.</p>

Actions required	1. A robust Compliance monitoring regime is likely to include the following features, although this will vary depending on which of the above approaches is taken:
	
	    – List all the areas that will be subject to Compliance monitoring.
	    – Risk assessment all of the above areas to determine monitoring priorities.
	    – Prepare a monitoring plan based on your risk assessment.
	    – Prepare a plan for individual reviews or tests.
	    – Prepare individual monitoring programmes.
	    – Formally notify those who are about to be reviewed.
	    – Complete monitoring work and keep records of work completed.
	    – Discuss findings with those who were reviewed.
	    – Agree the corrective action that needs to be taken.
	    – Publish a report on the results of the review work to relevant persons such as senior management and the departments subject to the review.
	    – Follow up corrective action completion with slippage escalated to senior management.
	    – Maintain a log of corrective actions required and completed.
	
	Specific actions to take
	
	2. Prepare a list of all that needs to be monitored. To make sure that everything is covered you could divide this up in various ways, including
	
	    – departments, both Front and Back Office;
	    – regulations;
	    – legislation;
	    – internal policy requirements;
	    – different offices/entities;
	    – outsourced functions; and
	    – business activities.
	
	3. Prepare a risk rating system that will enable you to determine which areas need to be monitored most frequently – evidently the areas that present the highest risk require the most frequent

(Continued)

Topic	Compliance monitoring

monitoring. You may decide, for example, that anti-money-laundering Compliance presents a greater risk to your firm than data protection Compliance, in which case, you would want to review the former with greater frequency than the latter.

4. There is no definitive list of matters that you should consider, and suggested criteria that you may use to conduct the risk rating exercise are included on page 131 (the Compliance Risk Register).

5. An automated approach to the risk-rating process can be taken by using an Excel spreadsheet or similar and giving numerical values to particular risk factors. You don't have to do it in this way, however, as long as you make a record of your rating rationale.

6. Taking the above case, for example, your decision that anti-money-laundering Compliance presents more of a risk than data protection Compliance may be based upon your view that

   – the legal penalties for breaching anti-money-laundering law are more serious than those for breaching data protection law;
   – the reputational damage caused by a breach of anti-money-laundering law is generally considered to be greater than that caused by a breach of data protection law;
   – the FSA is more active in pursuing anti-money-laundering breaches than the Information Commissioner is in monitoring data protection compliance; and
   – there are more detailed requirements relating to anti-money-laundering than there are relating to data protection compliance.

   In the context of your own firm you may also be aware that

   (a) the FSA is soon to conduct a review of your anti-money-laundering controls;
   (b) you have not provided anti-money-laundering training for over a year; and
   (c) Operational Risk has recently reported some worrying breaches to you concerning the firm's anti-money-laundering procedures.

7. Once you have risk rated all of the areas within the scope of the monitoring function, you should find some way of categorizing these into risk groups – for example, low, medium and high risk – and your high-risk areas will need to be reviewed more urgently and more frequently than your low-risk areas.

8. Based on this risk rating you should then prepare a plan of what you will monitor during the month/quarter/6 months/year to come. You should also build flexibility into your plan so that if a major issue comes up you are free to divert resources to that rather than sticking rigidly to your plan.

9. Guidance on the practical application of the two main approaches to monitoring is provided below.

Audit-based monitoring	1. Thorough planning work should be conducted prior to an audit-based review in which reviewers familiarize themselves with the area to be covered and understand the issues they may come up against.

2. A written plan should be prepared setting out matters such as

   – number of days dedicated to the review;
   – staff responsible;
   – start and end date; and
   – monitoring programmes to be used.

3. Monitoring programmes establish the tests that are to be carried out in order to assess compliance with a particular requirement. For example, a review of a sales desk may be based on a programme that incorporates testing for compliance with a variety of conduct of business requirements such as best execution, fair allocation of orders, suitability and front running.

4. Unless the review is highly confidential a copy of the plan should be sent to the head of the area/s being monitored to inform them of the audit, as a matter of courtesy, and to encourage their cooperation.

5. The audit should consist of a combination of tests and staff interviews.

6. For a sales desk review, tests may include selecting a sample of trades to ensure that suitability records have been maintained and that confirmation notes have been sent out within the required timescale.

7. For the same review of a sale desk, interviews should cover matters such as what staff consider to be the main risks affecting the department, whether they have any Compliance concerns, verifying procedures and assessing staff understanding of Compliance requirements.

   Interviews help reviewers to 'get a feel' for what is going on in the area being reviewed – in this way it may be possible to pick up on less tangible concerns that require further investigation that would not be identifiable using testing alone, e.g. concerns that a new team member has a rather gung ho attitude to Compliance or a fear that too many staff are about to leave the team and that those who remain will be under considerable pressure to meet sales targets.

8. By the time the reviewers have completed their work they should have come up with a list of findings – concerns, weaknesses, rule or legislative breaches, suggestions, etc. – that should be discussed with the senior staff responsible so that any misunderstandings can be cleared up and any remedial action can be agreed.

9. It is important to be as specific as possible in agreeing remedial action, by deciding

   - what exactly needs to be done;
   - by whom; and
   - by which date.

10. Once findings and remedial action have been agreed a monitoring report should be prepared setting out the essential details of what has been found and what has been agreed. You may also want to sum up your findings by giving the overall review a verbal or numerical rating – for example, high risk, medium risk, low risk, or a number from 1 to 5.

11. In order to increase the impact of the matters that you raise you may also choose to report on details of regulatory penalties that have recently been imposed due to weaknesses in the area where corrective action is required.

12. Prior to finalization you may also wish to issue your report in draft, to give a final opportunity for comment and correction.

13. Once the report has been issued, do not forget to thank the areas being reviewed for their cooperation and assistance during the review period. This should be done as a matter of courtesy, and also to encourage cooperation during the remedial action phase.

14. It is important to keep a log of remedial action agreed so that you can monitor the progress that is being made in strengthening controls and rectifying breaches.

(Continued)

Topic	Compliance monitoring
	15. The results of the review and progress towards completion of remedial action should be reported to senior management.
Systems-based monitoring	1. This sort of monitoring is much more targeted than the audit-based approach and is most suitable in areas where there are high volumes of tests to complete and/or where the processes being tested are automated.
	2. This method lends itself to automated exceptions reporting: criteria are programmed into a system and reports are generated either on a real-time basis, or on a specified frequency such as at daily, weekly or monthly, when an action is detected that matches the defined criteria.
	3. Such criteria may include

- customer trade before KYC approval;
- transaction with a company on the watch list;
- transactions over a particular size;
- trade confirmation not send out within required time frame.

4. Evidently, the matters listed above can be reviewed manually, but that is more time-consuming and leaves more scope for human error.
5. Your response to findings should depend on the materiality of the matter identified. For example, if a late confirmation was identified for 1 trade out of a total of 1000 for a particular day, then this is probably not particularly serious and you may not choose to follow it up; whereas if you identify that a proprietary position has been taken in a company that is just about to announce takeover plans and is being advised by your corporate finance team, then urgent investigation is definitely in order.
6. The action that is taken in relation to each finding on each exception report and notification should be recorded to provide a full audit trail.
7. If an area seems to be generating a large number of exceptions you may decide that it would be appropriate to plan an audit-based monitoring review to try to get a fuller picture of what is going on in that area, and whether there are any other weaknesses that have not been identified by the exception reporting.
8. The findings of the review work should form part of your regular reports to senior management.

Further information	–

Appendix B
Routine Anti-Money Laundering Activities

This appendix contains details of some of the routine anti-money-laundering activities most commonly undertaken by the Compliance Officer and/or the Money Laundering Reporting Officer. It is important to remember that the guidance provided on each area provides summary guidance only and you should tailor the procedures and controls within your own firm to the specific requirements of your business activities and customer base.

Activity	
KYC approvals for new relationships	195
Financial sanctions	198
Suspicions of money laundering	199
KYC reviews	200
KYC introductions from third parties	201
Third parties completing KYC on your firm	202
Provision of KYC introductions to third parties	203
Patriot Act certificate	203
Politically exposed persons	204
MLRO reporting	206
Counter terrorist financing	207

Topic	**KYC approvals for new relationships**
Objective	Ensure that no customer relationships are commenced without KYC first having been completed.
Explanation	• KYC stands for 'know your customer' and it is the term used to refer to the completion of regulatory due diligence on persons with whom a business relationship will be formed.
	• The KYC process is a key element of the fight against money laundering and terrorist financing activities in the financial markets.
	• There are various components to KYC including
	– proving the customer's identity – are they who they claim to be;
	– gaining comfort about the customer's activities and source of wealth – have the customer's funds been generated illegally;

(Continued)

Topic	**KYC approvals for new relationships**

  - demonstrating that the customer is an appropriate person for the firm to be associated with – some people may simply be judged too dangerous, from a reputational perspective for example, to deal with; and
  - building up a picture of the client's normal business activities so that any anomalies can be identified. This is useful for various purposes such as spotting suspicions of fraud and money laundering once the relationship is underway.

- In most circumstances KYC on new customers should be completed prior to forming a business relationship with a customer although limited exemptions to this are set out in the Money Laundering Regulations 2007, paragraph 9.
- Irrespective of regulatory or legislative requirements however, it makes sense from a business and reputational point of view to have a good idea of who the firm's clients are: you are unlikely to want to enter into a business relationship with a firm headed by three directors who have been declared bankrupt on several occasions, who have previously been accused of fraud, or who have previously been involved in some other sort of scandal.

Actions required

1. Identify all the departments within your firm where new customer relationships are formed.
2. Identify the types of client that your firm is most likely to deal with.
3. Prepare proforma checklists that can be used to guide staff on what KYC documentation is required. Some of the information required will be common to all types of customer (e.g. name and address) and some will be specific depending on customer type (e.g. KYC on a private company will involve different documentation requirements to those relating to an authorized unit trust).
4. KYC requirements will also vary depending on the type of product involved. For example, if you are making a loan you may also need to do KYC on the guarantors, and if you are completing KYC on a collective investment vehicle, you may wish to satisfy yourself as to the standard of KYC that is completed on the investors in the fund.
5. Additionally, KYC requirements will differ depending on the risk category of the client with additional KYC requirements applying to high-risk clients and activities. You should provide guidance on what can be deemed high-, medium- and low-risk categories of client so that KYC requirements can be tailored accordingly. Your risk assessment criteria may depend on several factors such as

   - type of products to be traded;
   - jurisdiction in which customer is based;
   - customer activities – either employment or business type;
   - type of customer – unregulated charity versus large listed company for example; and
   - whether the client is a politically exposed person, or is associated with any such persons.

6. If there is a wide variety of client and product types across your firm it is advisable to prepare pro forma checklists tailored to the specific product and client types that you are most likely to deal with.
7. If you are unable to complete satisfactory KYC on a new customer you should not commence the relationship with them, and you should consider whether the situation is suspicious and whether a report to SOCA should be made.

8. Implement arrangements whereby Front Office staff know their role in the KYC process. There are various options such as

   – Compliance approves all new clients;
   – Front Office approves all new clients, with periodic spot checks by Compliance;
   – separate KYC department approves all new clients; and
   – low-risk clients are approved by separate KYC department or Front Office and high-risk clients are approved by Compliance.

9. Arrangements should be put in place to accommodate situations in which not all of the required KYC information in accordance with your new customer approval checklists can be obtained but in which you still feel that adequate KYC information is available. Sometimes there is other evidence available to support the appropriateness of the proposed new client.

10. You may also choose to implement arrangements whereby certain low-risk relationships may be commenced prior to all KYC information having been obtained, if the situation is deemed to be low risk, and if assurances have been obtained that the missing documentation will be available within a specified timeframe. In such cases you should monitor that the missing documentation is indeed obtained and does not get forgotten once the client is taken on.

11. Part of the approval process should also comprise checking that the potential client is not listed on any internal or external control lists, such as that maintained by the Bank of England, which would indicate that they are subject to a sanctions regime.

12. A database of approved customers should be maintained that can only be updated or amended by persons authorized to do so. You may wish to include on the data base information such as

    – name of client;
    – name of relationship manager;
    – date approved;
    – any special circumstances surrounding the client's approval such as KYC information pending at date of approval;
    – type of client, e.g. individual, private company, fund, etc.; and
    – risk category of client.

13. Once a client has been approved for KYC the firm's relationship with that person should remain subject to ongoing review so that changes or concerns can be identified and investigated if necessary.

14. Once your KYC procedures are finalized, they should be documented in writing and made available to all staff members.

15. Regular staff training should also be provided in relation to KYC – the risks involved in getting this area of Compliance wrong are so great that every effort has to be taken to ensure that staff known what is expected of them.

16. You should also undertake regular monitoring to ensure that the KYC process is functioning as required. Your monitoring may include

    – identification of accounts opened without KYC approval;
    – new clients approved by persons not authorized to do so;
    – KYC documentation not obtained in accordance with your internal KYC requirements;
    – KYC checklist out of date and no longer reflecting the firm's current business or the latest legislative requirements;
    – client assigned incorrect risk category; and
    – list of approved clients not being maintained adequately.

Further information   See Appendix 24.

Topic	**Financial sanctions**
Objective	Ensure that no business is conducted in breach of current financial sanction lists.
Explanation	• Various national and international bodies such as HM Treasury, the EU Commission and the United Nations publish lists of persons and entities with which business should not be conducted.
	• Entries on sanctions lists result from various types of wrong-doing of which the persons and entities are accused of such as terrorist financing and inappropriate military activity.
	• In the UK a consolidated list of all directly applicable sanctions is published by HM Treasury which, along with the Foreign and Commonwealth Office and the Department for Business, Enterprise and Regulatory Reform, provides substantial guidance in this area.
	• Even though not covered by UK law, it is also wise to be familiar with the US sanctions regime under the OFAC, and by relevant legislation. The US sanctions regime is particularly relevant if your firm conducts business in dollars as the USA actively seeks to apply its sanctions regime extraterritorially and this is facilitated by dollar business undertaken by overseas firms: once the dollars enter the USA for clearing or processing purposes local financial services firms may find themselves obliged by law to seize them if they have suspicion that the dollar funds are connected with activity in breach of US sanctions.
Actions required	1. Ensure that you have arrangements in place to keep up to date with the sanctions regime operating in the UK – full details are listed on the Financial Sanctions pages of the Treasury's website and you may arrange for electronic alerts to be sent automatically when there is a change.
	2. If you conduct dollar business, you should also ensure that you keep up to date with the US sanctions regime. Ensure that any business that could be deemed to be in conflict with OFAC is not conducted in dollars.
	3. Implement arrangements whereby you can identify any customers or potential customers who are entered on an appropriate sanctions list:
	• *New customers* – Ensure that all new clients are checked against the sanctions list before they are approved for KYC.
	• *Existing customers* – Each time you become aware of an addition to a sanctions list you should check the list of approved clients to ensure that any matches are identified.
	4. Within reason, you should also check the sanctions list for people connected with your client, e.g. husbands and wives, where known, or shareholders or directors etc.
	5. If you find a match, you are required to freeze the assets of the persons implicated and report the match to HM Treasury as soon as possible. You should also think about whether it would be appropriate to make a report of a suspicion of money laundering or terrorist financing to SOCA even if you do not have any suspicions about the person who has generated the match. Unless you are very sure of your position in these areas it would be wise to obtain legal guidance.
	6. Carry out periodic training to ensure that staff understand the requirements of your firm's sanctions regime, the importance of complying with it and the implications of a failure to do so.
	7. Conduct regular monitoring to ensure that the sanctions regime within your firm is working adequately, including tests to check that
	– the sanctions lists used are up to date;
	– new and existing customers are checked for matches;
	– appropriate action is taken each time a match is identified.
Further information	See Appendix 24 and Appendix 4 (Trade and Financial Sanctions Legislation).

Topic	Suspicions of money laundering
Objective	Ensure that there are appropriate procedures in place for identifying and processing suspicions of money laundering and terrorist financing.
Explanation	Financial services firms are under a legal obligation to report suspicions of money laundering and terrorist financing to SOCA.
Actions required	1. You should conduct a full review of your firm's activities to determine what the key risks are for money laundering and terrorist financing in each department.

1. You should conduct a full review of your firm's activities to determine what the key risks are for money laundering and terrorist financing in each department.
2. Once you have determined where and how the firm is most vulnerable you should assess the controls in place to make sure that any weaknesses can be addressed. Reviews should be undertaken on a regular basis as fraud techniques are constantly evolving.
3. You should also put procedures in place so that staff know how to identify suspected money laundering and terrorist financing, and so that they know what to do if they do have a suspicion. Regular training is vital, as well as written guidance that is updated on a regular basis.
4. To the maximum extent possible, training should be tailored to the sort of activities undertaken by the individual employees being trained so that they see examples they can relate to their own experience.
5. Implement a reporting regime whereby you are notified of any suspicious activity that your colleagues have identified. Make reporting easy by preparing a proforma to capture all relevant information and making it available across the firm either in hard copy or electronically.
6. Information to include on the reporting form includes

   - person reporting suspicion;
   - date suspicion reported;
   - date to which suspicion relates;
   - nature of suspicion;
   - department involved;
   - clients involved; and to be completed later by Compliance:
   - whether legal guidance was obtained as to how to proceed (and if so, details thereof);
   - whether a report was made to SOCA, and if so, the outcome;
   - if a report was not made to SOCA, justification for this; and
   - date suspicion considered closed.

7. As well as relying on staff vigilance to identify suspicions of money laundering, many firms use electronic surveillance systems for this purpose as well and for larger firms the implementation of such a system is now a regulatory expectation.
8. Once a report has been made to you, you should investigate the circumstances, and if you decide that the suspicion is founded, you should make a report to SOCA. SOCA issues detailed guidance about procedures to be followed in relation to reports of suspicions of money laundering made to it and this guidance should be followed to the letter in order to avoid legal action.
9. Part of the reason that SOCA's guidance must be followed so carefully in respect of reports of suspicions of money laundering is that you must be very careful not to tip off a money launderer or terrorist financier by letting them know that you are on to them – thereby giving them time to flee the country, disguise themselves with plastic surgery, etc.! Remember that if you do 'tip off', even inadvertently, you could be found guilty of a criminal offence.
10. Suspicious activity reporting is a crucial area of Compliance due to the high penalties involved if things go wrong and it is therefore vital to have clear written procedures in place to advise staff on how to proceed if they have a suspicion.

(Continued)

Topic	Suspicions of money laundering
	11. Conduct regular monitoring of the controls implemented over suspicious activity to cover matters such as – staff training attendance; – whether the written guidance you have provided is up to date; – whether suspicions have been properly investigated; – whether adequate records of suspicions are being kept; – where applicable, whether the electronic surveillance system for detecting suspicions is working effectively. 12. Data concerning the volume and outcome of suspicious activity reports should be provided to senior management.
Further information	See Appendix 24.

Topic	KYC reviews
Objective	Ensure that KYC information held about customers remains up to date and that the firm's customer base remains appropriate.
Explanation	• KYC information should be kept up to date in order to facilitate the identification of suspicions of money laundering and terrorist financing. The customer's profile is one of the prime tools that can be used to identify suspicious activity – for example, if trading patterns suddenly change dramatically with no explanation, this may indicate that the client is money laundering or engaging in terrorist financing (or it may simply mean that KYC information has not been kept up to date and that a client is simply blowing a recent inheritance)! • The profile of individual customers evolves over time and it is important to ensure that changes are captured in the firm's records. A failure to keep client knowledge up to date means that a firm cannot truly be said to know its customers in the regulatory sense as it will not be able to properly identify deviations from a customer's normal activity levels. • The types of KYC information that may change include – company ownership; – company directors; – approved signatories; – name; – activity profile in terms of product type, trade frequency and size etc. It is important to capture as many changes as possible. • If your firm uses an electronic system to detect suspicious activity then trade frequency, type and volume data, etc., must be kept up to date or the system will generate too many false positives, which will increase the work for those operating it instead of being able to focus on real suspicions. Therefore, if your clients tells you that he will now be doing 20 trades a year instead of two because the business is growing, this new normal trading pattern should be added to his surveillance system profile or, after the client has executed more than the two trades the system expects, an exception report will be generated every time.
Actions required	1. Keep a record of the approval date of each customer to use as a reference date for a programme of periodic reviews.

2. Keep a record of whether a customer is noted as high, medium or low risk – you will want to review higher risk clients more regularly than lower risk ones.

3. On the basis of the above information, prepare a customer review timetable and distribute this to the relationship managers who should ensure that reviews are completed by the due date.

4. Progress should be reviewed on an ongoing basis and delay should be tracked on an ongoing basis with significant or unjustified slippage escalated to senior management.

5. As well as the formal review described above, relationships managers should be instructed to update the customer's profile each time they become aware of a change to the profile.

6. Ensure that changes to the profile are entered into any electronic surveillance systems used to identify suspicious activity.

7. If you are unable to complete a KYC review because the customer is unwilling to supply the information you have requested, then you should consider whether the circumstances are suspicious and whether a report to SOCA should be made.

Further information   See Appendix 24.

Topic	**KYC introductions from third parties**
Objective	Ensure that there are adequate controls surrounding the acceptance of KYC introductions made by third parties.
Explanation	• The UK's KYC framework allows for certain circumstances in which financial institution may rely on a third party to complete KYC for a new customer on their behalf. • KYC introductions are often requested from companies in the same group, when more than one firm is dealing with the same customer for a single transaction (for example, a joint corporate finance mandate) or when one firm receives regular new business introductions from another. • Whereas accepting KYC completed by a third party may seem like an easy way out from having to complete all the administration involved with obtaining KYC information, it is not without its risks. If the firm that has provided you with the introduction does not itself have adequate KYC, then you may also be held liable for any deficiencies in the files you have accepted.
Actions required	1. Determine the circumstances (if any) in which you will be willing to accept KYC introductions from third parties. Situations in which you may find it inappropriate to accept an introduction are – client is high risk; – client business is high risk; – proposed introducer has recently been penalised for failures in its KYC controls; 2. You will probably wish to ensure that ad hoc introductions are only accepted once you have approved each case separately although you may wish to give blanket approval to introductions from firms with which you have a long-term introducer relationship.

(Continued)

Topic	KYC introductions from third parties
	3. Where you plan to accept KYC introductions from a third party on a regular basis you should consider putting in place a legal contract setting out the relative rights and responsibilities of each party – although you may have difficulty persuading your introducer to do this as they may feel it makes them too exposed legally.
	4. You should record the fact that a customer was approved for due diligence via an introduction rather than by means of the usual route on your list of approved customers. And you may decide that this fact makes the customer higher risk than they would otherwise be, meaning that KYC reviews should be conducted more regularly.
	5. Your policy on accepting KYC introductions should be set out in writing and made known to the firm as a whole.
Further information	See Appendix 24.

Topic	Third parties completing KYC on your firm
Objective	Implement procedures to facilitate third party completion of KYC on your firm.
Explanation	• Just as your firm completes KYC on others, so other institutions will want to complete KYC on your own firm.
	• You are under no obligation to prepare a KYC pack to provide to third parties, but it is likely to save you time if you have one to hand so that you do not have to reproduce the material every time you receive a request.
Actions required	1. Prepare a KYC pack ready to provide to third parties. Some institutions ask for more than others and you should be careful not to give away too much information – it is best to gather public domain information rather than give details of more confidential matters.
	2. Your KYC pack should include information such as
	– full name;
	– trading name;
	– registered address;
	– business address
	– telephone and fax number;
	– web address;
	– the FSA reference number to evidence regulatory status;
	– stock exchange details if our firm is listed;
	– name of external auditor and last audited accounts;
	– directors;
	– list of approved signatories; and
	– Patriot Act certification.
	3. It might be helpful to publish the KYC pack on your website so that third parties can download this information themselves, thereby cutting down on your administration time. If you do this, make sure that that information remains up to date and be extra sure that no sensitive or confidential information is published. You should be OK with the details listed above.
Further information	See Appendix 24.

Topic	**Provision of KYC introductions to third parties**
Objective	Ensure that there are adequate controls surrounding the provision of KYC introductions to third parties.
Explanation	• The UK's KYC framework allows for certain circumstances in which KYC may be completed by one financial institution who then 'introduces' the customer to another firm without that second firm having to complete its own KYC. • KYC introductions are often requested by firms within the same group of companies, when more than one firm is dealing with the same customer for a single transaction (a syndicated loan for example) or when one firm acts as an introducing broker for others. • Firms are under no obligation to make KYC introductions and you should make a careful consideration of whether you are prepared to do this. Remember that if you 'do someone a favour' and provide them with KYC then the other firm may hold you liable for any deficiencies in the documentation you provided.

Actions required	1. Make your stance on KYC introductions known to the firm as a whole: if you will not give introduction then make this clear, whereas if you will, make it clear that all introductions must be processed by Compliance – you do not want a relationship manager to do this independently in circumstances that might not be appropriate.
	2. For each introduction proposed you should ensure that you are not aware of any reasons why the introduction should not be made. Such circumstances may include
	  – Client is new to your firm and you have not had a chance yet to build up a complete picture of them.
	  – Client is currently subject to a suspicion of money laundering.
	  – KYC file is not up to date.
	3. Where an introduction is provided robust records should be maintained including
	  – name of client that was introduced;
	  – person/s to whom introduction was made;
	  – relationship manager;
	  – reason introduction was requested;
	  – date of introduction; and
	  – information and documents provided.
	4. Your policy on accepting KYC introductions should be set out in writing and made known to the firm as a whole.

Further information	See Appendix 24.

Topic	**Patriot Act certificate**
Objective	Keep the firm's Patriot Act certificate up to date.
Explanation	• Under the US Patriot Act (sections 313 and 319) US banks and broker dealers are prohibited from operating correspondent accounts for foreign shell banks, and banks that do business with such banks. (A shell bank is one that has no physical presence in any jurisdiction.) • As a result of this requirement non-US banks seeking a correspondent relationship with a US bank or broker dealer must demonstrate that neither they nor any of their clients are shell banks.

(Continued)

Topic	**Patriot Act certificate**
	• The confirmation is obtained by requiring the foreign bank to complete a Patriot Act certificate which has a standard form (ref.: OMB 1505–0184) and on which the foreign bank must attest to its own non-shell bank status and to the fact that it does not operate accounts for such banks. • A single certificate may be used to vouch for multiple entities within a group. • Note that is requirements applies to banks only.
Actions required	1. Before opening a correspondent account in the USA, complete form OMB 1505–0184 and provide a copy to the entity with which your bank will open an account. 2. Most banks choose to publish their Patriot Act certificate on their internet site so that it is readily available to their correspondents. 3. Make sure that the information on the certificate remains up to date – if there is a change, notify your correspondents in the USA.
Further information	See Appendix 24 and Appendix 6 (the Patriot Act).

Topic	**Politically exposed persons**
Objective	Ensure that appropriate enhanced due diligence is conducted on politically exposed persons (PEPs).
Explanation	• Under the Money Laundering Regulations s.14, firms are required to conduct enhanced due diligence on PEPs due to the increased risk of corruption. • A PEP is someone who in the previous 12 months has held a prominent public position at an EU institution or at any other international body, outside the UK. Examples include – heads of state; – members of parliament; and – high ranking officers in the armed forces. • The definition also extends to immediate family members and close associates of such people. • The enhanced due diligence required should be undertaken at the outset of the relationship and thereafter, on an ongoing basis.
Actions required	1. Implement arrangements whereby PEPs may be identified at the outset of a relationship with the firm. This should involve the provision of staff training on what constitutes a PEP, and also the incorporation of checks into the identity verification process. 2. It is not always easy to determine who is a PEP – you could try the following methods: – checking with a reliable contact in the appropriate jurisdiction; – consulting a firm that specializes in conducting due diligence in the jurisdiction in question; – searching internet databases such as Worldcheck or Factiva PFA.

3. When a new client is identified as being a PEP you should make as certain as possible that they are not and have not been involved in any corruption. To do this, you can use the same mechanisms as above for identifying PEPs, and you could also conduct your own internet search to identify relevant information for yourself. You should also be as clear as possible that the PEP's source of wealth and source of funds for conducting business with your firm is legitimate.

4. Accepting a new relationship with a PEP should only take place once specific senor management approval has been obtained.

5. In order to assist senior management with the approval decision it is useful to prepare a report summarizing the information that you have on the individual concerned. Such information should include

   - why this person wants to open an account with your firm (as opposed to another firm offering similar services);
   - who will be his proposed relationship manager, and how that person knows the PEP;
   - the type of business the PEP proposes to conduct through your firm;
   - evidence of identity;
   - results of due diligence investigations into his background, and in particular, whether anything suggests that he has have been involved with corruption.

6. You should maintain a database of all PEPs that have been approved as clients of your firm to record information such as

   - name;
   - contact details;
   - basis of PEP status;
   - date of approval as a client;
   - name of relationship manager;
   - name of senior managers who approved the relationship;
   - sources of due diligence information; and
   - any specific matters that you consider need to be kept under review.

7. The PEP database is important as it facilitates the ongoing monitoring that firms are required to conduct on PEPs, which should be more rigorous than the monitoring conducted on lower risk clients.

8. Your ongoing monitoring may take various forms, including

   - scrutiny of each new transaction;
   - transaction trend analysis;
   - verifying that the actual business undertaken by the PEP conforms to that envisaged at the outset of the relationship, or that any deviations from the norm can be legitimately accounted for;
   - checking the identifies of third parties making payments to and receiving payments from each PEP;
   - commissioning regular due diligence reviews by professional security companies;
   - checking PEP search engines as mentioned above; and
   - reviewing the media for any negative press coverage.

9. The results of your ongoing monitoring should periodically be compiled in a report and presented to senor management so that they can approve the ongoing PEP relationship.

10. Your ongoing monitoring programme may vary depending on the risks presented by individual PEPs.

(Continued)

Topic	**Politically exposed persons**
	11. Be aware that existing non-PEP customers may themselves become PEPs.
	12. Provide periodic staff training in relation to the nature of PEPs, the risks posed by doing business with them and your firm's internal procedures for dealing with them.
	13. Consider a committee approach to the approval of new PEP relationships so that a number of members of your senior management may assess the proposed new relationship and share ideas and concerns prior to approval being granted.
Further information	See Appendix 24.

Topic	**MLRO reporting**
Objective	Ensure that senior management is kept up to date in terms of the adequacy of the firm's systems and controls designed to combat money laundering and terrorist financing.
Explanation	Due to the serious legal penalties that may be applied to individuals and firms found guilty of one of the several money laundering and terrorist financing offences, it is vital that senior management understand the risks that the firm is running in this area.
Actions required	1. Make regular reports to senior management concerning the firm's anti-money-laundering and counter terrorist finance controls, and the specific threats that the firm faces in these areas.
	2. You may wish to include the following type of information in your reports:
	– changes to legislation and regulation;
	– recent regulatory and legislative action taken against financial institutions;
	– number of reports of suspicions that you received during the period under review, and number subsequently reported to SOCA;
	– number of investigations undertaken by SOCA in relation to suspicions reported by you;
	– training provided, and list of any staff who have failed to attend training;
	– the key risks that your firm faces in terms of money laundering and terrorist financing, and any action that needs to be taken to mitigate these risks;
	– changes to any systems and controls in place (either recently introduced, or planned for the near future);
	– progress in relation to the KYC review timetable; and
	– results of any reviews undertaken in the area during the review period by, for example, Compliance, Internal Audit, the FSA.
	The JMLSG has published useful guidance on the contents of the MLRO report.
	3. If any project plan is detailed in the report, or requested as a result of it, you should keep an audit trail detailing what action is required, by whom, and the dates by which the actions must be completed. Regular progress reports should be made to senior management.
Further information	See Appendix 24.

Topic	Counter terrorist financing
Objective	Ensure that the firm is not used as a vehicle for financing terrorism.
Explanation	• Terrorist financing, like money laundering in general, takes place when criminals use the financial markets for their own illegal purposes. It was already recognized as a problem before the terrorist attacks of 11 September 2001 but since that time it has been increasingly in the spotlight. • The controls required to combat terrorist financing are similar to those required to prevent money laundering and can generally be covered using the same mechanism, although the legislation underpinning the two regimes is different.
Actions required	1. As a minimum, your counter terrorist finance arrangements should include – regular staff training in relation to the requirements of the Terrorism Acts 2000 and 2006, and other relevant legislation; – robust vetting of new customers and accounts to ensure that no terrorist activity or connection is suspected; – ongoing review of account and customer activity with a view to identifying suspicions of terrorist activity; – implementation of a process whereby suspicions of terrorist financing can be reported to an appropriate person internally, who will then make a report of the suspicion of terrorism to SOCA if this is deemed necessary; – thorough checking for compliance with the anti-terrorist sanctions regimes implemented by the UN, the EU, the UK and, if dollar business will be undertaken, OFAC in the USA.
Further information	See Appendix 24.

Appendix C
Compliance in the Front Office

This appendix briefly describes the activities of four typical Front Office departments before going on to look at some of the main regulatory requirements that are of relevance to them. Note that where a requirement is shown as being relevant to a particular department, this may not be true in relation to everything that they do, depending on the exact nature of the product and/or service involved. Also note that the use of the terms 'Client', 'Customer' and 'Eligible Counterparty' in this section follows their FSA definitions.

Topic	
Customer sales and trading	210
Investment management (asset management, portfolio management)	211
Corporate finance and investment banking	211
Research	212
Business and regulatory approvals	212
Relationship with Compliance department	213
Client's best interest rule	214
Provision of information about the firm	215
Client agreements	216
Best execution	218
Prompt execution	220
Client limit orders	221
Suitability	222
Appropriateness (for non-advised services)	223
Churning and switching	224
Aggregation and allocation	225
Order and execution records	226
Training and competence ('T&C')	227
Approved Persons rules	228
Inducements	229
Voice recording	230
Communicating with clients (fair, clear and not misleading communications)	230
Financial promotions	231
Client categorization	232
KYC	233
Anti-money-laundering (AML) and counter terrorist financing ('CTF') controls	235

(Continued)

Topic	
Reporting suspicions of money laundering and terrorist financing	236
Fraud prevention	236
Exclusivity	237
Investment committee	238
Investment and borrowing powers	239
Issuing research	240
Research disclaimers	241
Issuing third party research	242
Confidentiality	243
Personal account dealing	244
Conflicts of interest	246
Insider lists	247
Chinese walls	247
Watch and restricted list	248
Market abuse	248
Written policies and procedures	249
Whistle blowing	250

Customer sales and trading

- *Customer sales involves*:

  - advising customers on trading ideas;
  - receiving customer orders on an execution only basis; and
  - taking customer orders and passing them to traders for execution.

- The employees charged with maintaining customer relationships are known as Relationship Managers, Account Executives or Sales People.

- *Customer trading involves*: trading in order to facilitate customer orders (as opposed to Proprietary Trading whereby traders invest the firm's own money and do not have contact with customers).

  - No orders can be executed until the customer has given his explicit consent on a case by case basis.

- The products most commonly covered by the Customer Sales and Trading function are

  - bonds and equities traded on the secondary markets (see Appendices 8 and 9 respectively);
  - purchase of bonds and equities on the primary market;
  - products related to/based on bonds and equities such as convertibles and preference shares;

- FX (see Appendix 13);
- futures and options (see Appendix 11); and
- collective investment products like units in unit trusts and shares in investment trusts/companies (see Appendix 12).

Investment management (asset management, portfolio management)

- This function involves the discretionary management of funds belonging to third parties.
- Investment managers take investment decisions on behalf of their customers and then either execute the trade themselves or pass the execution instructions to a broker.
- Trades are executed without having to obtain customer approval on a case by case basis although the terms of the arrangement, such as risk appetite and investment objectives, are subject to prior agreement.
- The third party funds may be

  - pooled as part of a collective investment vehicle; or
  - managed as individual portfolios belonging to separate customers.

- The employees providing investment management services are known as Investment Managers, Fund Managers or Portfolio Managers.
- Virtually any product may be managed on a discretionary basis, from the mainstream bonds and shares to the more 'alternative' type of investment such as property and private equity.
- Further information about collective investment may be found in Appendix 12.

Corporate finance and investment banking

These functions encompass a large number of activities including

- advising on mergers (see Appendix 8);
- advising on takeovers/acquisitions (see Appendix 8);
- advising on divestments (sale of a corporate, usually by way of share transfer);
- advising on asset sales (sale of major assets, usually on a cash basis rather than by share transfer);
- advising on sources and types of finance;
- arranging third party finance (intermediation between borrower and lender);
- providing finance;
- providing strategic advice;
- providing corporate valuations;
- providing fairness opinions on valuations conducted by third parties;
- arranging new issues of shares and bonds (see Appendices 8 and 9);
- advising on financial restructuring;
- arranging financial restructuring; and
- distribution/recycling of risk to third parties, e.g. selling participations in a loan.

Research

- Key activities include:

  - gaining a thorough knowledge of the companies covered by the firm's research programme;
  - preparing and issuing research for internal use and for distribution to customers.

- Employees providing research services are generally referred to as Research Analysts.
- Different to the other Front Office functions in that there should not be a direct link between research produced and Research Analyst remuneration because of the scope for conflicts of interest and market abuse (see pages 246 and 248 below).

Summary of the key rules and controls that Front Office staff should be aware off

It is important to remember that the guidance below is a summary only and is not intended to be a substitute for assessing the circumstances of your own firm and putting systems and procedures in place tailored to your own activities.

Rule/control	Business and regulatory approvals
FSA client categorization impact	Client categorization does not affect requirements in this area.
Customer Sales and Trading	Yes.
Investment Management	Yes.
Corporate Finance and Investment Banking	Yes.
Research	Yes.
Requirement	Staff should be aware of the factors that govern their permitted business activities. Such limiting factors include - the firm's regulatory authorizations; - the firm's investment exchange memberships; - the employee's status under the Training and Competence (T&C) rules; - the employee's status under the Approved Persons rules; - the scope of the employee's job description or dealer mandate; - internal credit limits and regulatory capital constraints; and - the range of products for which the Back Office is equipped to provide settlement services.
Comments	- Breaches in this area are likely to be taken extremely seriously by the FSA, as an indication that a firm's systems and controls are inadequate.

- There may also be settlement issues if a trade is booked in a product that the Back Office is not geared up to process.
- In addition the firm's capital adequacy may be affected, or inaccurately represented, if unauthorized positions are taken on.

Controls

- Make sure that the scope of the firm's regulatory permissions is well 'publicized' by recording the details in the Compliance manual and desk procedures, etc.
- Provide staff with a job description and/or dealer mandate that sets out the scope of their individual permissions in terms of

  - their training and competence status;
  - their Approved Persons status;
  - products they are permitted to trade in; and
  - their various trading limits.

- Maintain a list of all the products that have been approved for trading by the firm. Ensure that this list is known to staff and that before a new product is added to it, Compliance approval and any other necessary approvals have been granted.

Further guidance   –

Rule/control	Relationship with Compliance department
FSA client categorization impact	None – client categorization is irrelevant.
Customer Sales and Trading	Yes.
Investment Management	Yes.
Corporate Finance and Investment Banking	Yes.
Research	Yes.
Requirement	<ul><li>Front Office departments should have an open relationship with Compliance and should involve the Compliance department with their plans at an early stage.</li><li>Front Office staff should also be aware of the matters that need to be notified to Compliance for follow-up action.</li></ul>
Comments	The stronger the relationship between the Front Office and Compliance, the more effective a firm's Compliance culture is likely to be.
Controls	<ul><li>Schedule regular meetings with the Front Office to discuss plans, problems, developments, etc.</li></ul>

(Continued)

Rule/control	Relationship with Compliance department

	• Ensure that Front Office staff are aware of the matters which need to be reported to Compliance including
	
	  – complaints;
	  – litigation;
	  – suspicions of money laundering;
	  – suspicions of market abuse;
	  – fraud;
	  – actual or potential rule breaches; and
	  – any other material concern about the firm's regulatory control infrastructure.
	
	• Ensure that the Compliance department is visible to the Front Office: remember the old adage 'out of sight, out of mind'. Larger firms may have line of business Compliance Officers that sit with the Front Office.
	• Also ensure that Front Office staff are familiar with the whistle-blowing procedures so that they have confidence in the procedures that will be followed if they report matters that they do not consider to be right.

Further guidance	–

Rule/control	Client's best interest rule
FSA client categorization impact	Applicable to retail and professional clients only (according to COBS 1 Annex 1) although somewhat confusingly the requirement also applies to eligible counterparties under COBS 2.1.1(2)(b).
Customer Sales and Trading	Yes.
Investment Management	Yes.
Corporate Finance and Investment Banking	Yes.
Research	Yes.
Requirement	Staff must always act in the best interests of their clients.
Comments	This rule is deceptively simple, comprising a mere couple of lines rather than the pages of text dedicated to the complexities of other requirements such as best execution or suitability for example. Yet in its 'catch all' capacity, it really is the very backbone of the principles-based regulatory regime (see page 317) with the capacity to make a breach out of just about anything: even if a specific rule has not been broken, even if there is no rule to break, *any* action taken that might be deemed to be detrimental to a client may constitute a breach of this rule. That is daunting.

It's not all bad, however, as this little rule can also serve as a sort of regulatory compass. Are you not sure which is the right way to tackle a regulatory dilemma? Then think 'client's best interest rule': and if you would not be confident explaining to the FSA how an action or outcome you are considering would be in the client's best interests, think very carefully before you go ahead with it.

Controls

- It is hard to think of any controls specifically designed to ensure compliance with this rule. Obviously it is important to comply with the rules and guidance on customer protection provided by the FSA and other bodies, but there is nothing saying that this will be enough as the rule has the potential to be so far reaching.
- Probably the most important thing to do in this context is to ensure that the firm's 'compliance culture' is such that even when there is not a specific rule, principle or piece of guidance to flag appropriate behaviour, employees are aware of the need for their actions to be guided by what is in the best interests of their clients.

Further guidance   See Appendix 24.

Rule/control	Provision of information about the firm
FSA client categorization impact	Several rules apply only to retail and professional clients but some higher level requirements also apply to dealings with all clients.
Customer Sales and Trading	Yes.
Investment Management	Yes.
Corporate Finance and Investment Banking	Yes.
Research	Yes.
Requirement	Firms must provide their customers with certain information about themselves, their services and the basis on which these services will be provided.

Comment	• The FSA has detailed client notification rules although requirements in this area also stem from several other sources.
	• Information to be provided includes
	   – execution venues;
	   – costs and charges;
	   – investment strategies;
	   – information about who customer information will be made available to;
	   – relevant investor compensation schemes;
	   – whether telephone calls will be subject to voice recording;
	   – distance marketing disclosures;
	   – details concerning arrangements for the provision of custody and client money services;
	   – details concerning discretionary management arrangements; and
	   – disclosures and disclaimers in research reports.

(Continued)

Rule/control	Provision of information about the firm

	• Three separate types of notification can be identified:
	
	  – Notifications that need to be made on a one-off basis only and can be provided in or with a customer agreement provided at the beginning of the relationship, for example, the firm's best execution policy.
	  – Notifications required on a regular basis, for example confirmation notes.
	  – Notifications required on an ad hoc basis, for example, revision of fee schedule.

Controls	• Front Office staff should have a good general awareness of the notification requirements applying to their customers.
	• They should also have a good understanding of
	
	  – the notifications that they are responsible for making themselves (and how and when to do this); and
	  – the situations in which they must instruct another department within the firm to provide a client with certain information (for example, prior to commencing the provision of custody services, the Front Office staff should instruct a custody agreement to the sent to the client).
	
	• It is advisable for Compliance to review all the notification requirements applicable to a particular department or function so these can be documented for reference and a schedule provided to staff for guidance.
	• Compliance should periodically assess whether Front Office staff are complying with the firm's notification requirements.
	• Compliance should also carry out periodic review of each department or function's schedule of notification requirements to ensure that it is kept up to date.

Further guidance	See Appendix 24.

Rule/control	Client agreements
FSA client categorization impact	• Customer agreement requirements imposed by the FSA vary depending on client categorization. • FSA client categorization is not relevant to the use of non-FSA customer agreements.
Customer Sales and Trading	Yes.
Investment Management	Yes.
Corporate Finance and Investment Banking	Yes.
Research	Yes.

Requirement	• Firms should use the Front Office agreements required by the FSA that are relevant to the nature of services they provide and the activities they engage in.
	• Such documentation should
	
	  – include all FSA stipulated clauses;
	  – be dispatched within the required timeframes; and
	  – allow for written acknowledgement of receipt, and agreement of terms, by the customer where necessary.
	
	• Firms should also use the appropriate industry agreements to cover their business activities, for example, give up agreements for relevant derivatives business and GMSLAs for securities lending.

Comments	• There are many types of agreement used to support Front Office business such as
	
	  – those required by the FSA to establish the nature of services that will be provided to a customer and the basis on which these services will be provided.
	  – those prepared by industry associations to provide standard terms for trading certain types of products.
	
	• Some documentation is completed largely by the Front Office itself (corporate finance mandates, for example) but generally, responsibility for the contents and negotiation of customer agreements rests with other departments such as Compliance, Legal, Tax and Credit.

Controls	• Compliance should provide training and guidance so that Front Office staff are aware of the various customer agreement requirements that are relevant to the activities that they carry out. Compliance responsibility here will often just include agreements required for regulatory purposes although in smaller firms Compliance may also take on responsibility for other types of trading agreement. • Even if Front Office staff are not responsible for sending or negotiating the agreements themselves it is important for them to know that before providing a new service to a customer, or undertaking any new type of activity, they should check to see that the relevant agreement is in place before proceeding. • Front Office management is responsible for ensuring that customer agreement requirements are met and Compliance should conduct periodic monitoring to check that services have not been provided before required agreements have been implemented, that the agreements implemented contain all required clauses and that the terms agreed have not been breached. • It is useful for the Front Office to maintain a list of all the trading agreements they have in place, and record when these are up for review. • It is also useful for Compliance Officers to log, and understand the usage of, each type of agreement employed by the departments for which they are responsible.
Further guidance	• See Chapter 8 and Appendices 19 to 22.

Rule/control	Best execution
FSA client categorization impact	Applicable to retail and professional clients only.
Customer Sales and Trading	Yes.
Investment Management	Yes.
Corporate Finance and Investment Banking	No – Corporate Finance and Banking staff do not generally execute trades.
Research	No – Research Analysts should not undertake sales and trading activity.
Requirement	Firms owe a duty of best execution to their clients when executing orders on their behalf. This means that firms must take all reasonable steps to execute client orders on the most favourable terms for the clients, in order to obtain the best possible result for them.

Comments	• The most favourable terms available and the best possible result depend on a number of execution factors applicable to the asset in question. Such execution factors are
	
	   – client categorization;
	   – type of order placed (particularly large or small orders are unlikely to be executed at normal market price);
	   – type of asset (it can be hard to demonstrate best execution for illiquid assets – sometimes there is only one entity willing to quote a price); and
	   – type of execution venue where the order can be executed, according to the firm's Execution policy (see below).
	
	• The above execution factors should be considered as a whole when making a decision to execute.
	• Best execution requirements are relevant whether the firm executes the order itself, or passes orders to third parties for execution. Consequently, any third parties who will be used to execute trades should be assessed for their ability to provide best execution. The arrangement should also be subject to ongoing monitoring.
	• For retail clients execution price must take account of total consideration for the transaction (cost of transaction plus costs related to execution).
	• The firm does not have to consider execution venues not included in its Execution policy, or compare its terms with the terms that another firm might be able to achieve for the client.
	• Specific execution instructions given by the client must be followed in all cases.
	• As best execution requirements apply only when a firm executes a client's order, it is important to understand exactly which instructions are covered by requirements in this area. This is not always easy to determine but some general guidance is provided below. It applies when it is reasonable to assume that the client is relying on the firm to carry out instructions on their behalf.
	• The following would generally be covered by the best execution requirement – a client's instruction to
	
	   – execute a trade at best possible market price available now;
	   – buy or sell a large block of shares over a couple of days;

– execute a trade in an illiquid stock for which there is no current market;
– execute a trade at a certain price, or better (limit order).

- The following would generally not be covered by the best execution requirement – a client's instruction to

– execute a trade at a particular price;
– execute a trade at a particular time on a specified market eg closing price on the London Stock Exchange; and
– trade in an investment not regulated under FSMA such as spot FX.

Controls

- Best execution requirements are particularly complex and involve a number of different procedures and controls.

Execution Policy

- In order to facilitate obtaining the best possible result for clients in terms of order execution firms must implement an Execution Policy establishing how the firm will rank the importance of the various execution factors when assessing how to achieve the most favourable terms for the client.
- There are several specific rules relating to the Execution Policy including requirements that the policy must

– include approved execution venues for each class of asset where it is considered that the firm will consistently be able to obtain best execution for its clients;
– cover arrangements to allow for the best possible result to be obtained for the client when orders are passed to a third party for execution;
– be applied to each client order prior to execution; and
– be given/made available to retail clients in good time before execution services are provided.

Notice and warnings

- A warning must be provided to retail clients indicating that if the client gives specific instructions in relation to the execution of a particular order then this may impact the firm's ability to follow its Execution Policy.
- A warning must also be provided to all clients if the firm's Execution Policy allows for orders to be executed outside a regulated market or MTF.

Notification and Consent

- Retail clients should be given a copy of the firm's Execution Policy prior to the firm providing any services to that client.
- Client consent must be obtained in relation to the possibility of orders being executed outside a regulated market or MTF.

Review of execution arrangements and policy

- The effectiveness of the firm's order execution arrangements and policy must be monitored on an ongoing basis with a formal review taking place at least once a year.
- In particular, the policy must be reviewed whenever there is a material change to the firm's ability to obtain the best possible result for the client.
- If deficiencies are identified, corrective action should be taken as soon as possible.
- Compliance should conduct frequent monitoring of this area.

General considerations

- As well as the matters detailed above, you may wish to consider the following type of situation in the Execution Policy:

(Continued)

Rule/control	Best execution

	– How to assess the best possible result for a client if an execution venue used by your firm is in a jurisdiction where best execution requirements do not apply.
	   – How to demonstrate best execution for an illiquid asset that only one broker will make you a price for.
	   – How to evidence best execution for particularly large or small order sizes for which there is no regular market.
	   – How to proceed if a client consistently gives execution instructions that hinder the firm's ability to obtain the best possible result, despite the client having been warned of the implications of this. (In this situation the client is putting your firm at serious risk of regulatory censure – is their business really worth it?)
	   – How can the appropriateness of an execution venue/third party be assessed and recorded.
	
	Record keeping and awareness
	
	  • Records must be retained so as to be able to demonstrate the steps taken by the firm to execute orders in accordance with the Execution Policy (see above).
	  • Compliance should provide training and guidance so that staff understand the complex requirements in this area.

Further guidance	See Appendix 24.

Rule/control	Prompt execution
FSA client categorization impact	Applicable to retail and professional clients only.
Customer Sales and Trading	Yes.
Investment Management	Yes.
Corporate Finance and Investment Banking	No – Corporate Finance and Banking staff do not generally execute trades.
Research	No – Research Analysts should not undertake trading activity.
Requirement	Once a customer has placed an order it must be executed promptly, fairly and expeditiously. Specifically, comparable orders in the same asset should be executed sequentially in terms of the time of their receipt by the firm.

Comments	Matters to consider when determining what constitutes prompt, fair and expeditious execution include
	
	  • Whether it is ever appropriate to delay a customer order – what if it is considered that prices will shortly rise or fall?
	  • What is appropriate if the firm is already busy with a very substantial order for a particular customer so that turning attention to a subsequent order for that same customer might hinder the results of the first one?

	• Whether it is permissible to delay execution of a large customer order that will have an impact on price so that other customers placing subsequent orders are not disadvantaged by the price rise.
Controls	• Compliance should provide regular training and guidance so that staff understand the requirements relating to timely execution. • Retail customers must be informed as soon as possible of any difficulty by the firm in executing their orders promptly, fairly and expeditiously. • Timely execution is the responsibility of Front Office management but should be subject to periodic review by Compliance.
Further guidance	See Appendix 24.

Rule/control	Client limit orders
FSA client categorization impact	Applies to retail and professional customers and to eligible counterparties explicitly transmitting limit orders to a firm for execution.
Customer Sales and Trading	Yes.
Investment Management	Yes.
Corporate Finance and Investment Banking	No – Corporate Finance and Banking staff do not generally execute trades.
Research	No – Research Analysts should not undertake trading activity.
Requirement	Client limit orders should be • executed as quickly as possible (unless otherwise instructed by the client) at the price specified by the client, or better; and if this is not possible: • made public as quickly as possible (transmitting the order to a regulated market or MTF for example), although this requirement is disapplied for orders that are larger than normal market size.
Comments	Requirements relating to client limit orders are there to facilitate prompt execution. However, the disapplication of the requirement to publish client limit orders of a larger than normal market size exists in order to lessen the scope for market abuse and insider dealing (as large orders may have an impact on pricing).

Controls	• Compliance should provide regular training and guidance so that staff understand the requirements relating to client limit orders. Matters that staff should be familiar with include
	
	  – the rationale behind the prompt execution rules;
	  – the regulated markets and MTFs that the firm may use to publish orders;
	  – the regulatory definition of a 'large order' under MAR; and
	  – the steps to be taken to make an order public.
	
	• Compliance with the prompt execution rules should be tested on a regular basis.

Further guidance	See Appendix 24.

Rule/control	Suitability
FSA client categorization impact	Applicable to retail and professional clients only (bearing in mind that in this context the category 'professional client' will include clients who would be eligible counterparties in the context of eligible counterparty business)
Customer Sales and Trading	Yes.
Investment Management	Yes.
Corporate Finance and Investment Banking	Yes.
Research	No.
Requirement	• Personal recommendations and advice must be suitable for each customer concerned. • Investment decisions made for customers in the context of a discretionary management relationship must be suitable for each customer concerned.
Comments	Closely linked to, but distinct from, the rules on appropriateness (see below).
Controls	• Customers should complete a suitability fact find in which they note their investment objectives, risk appetite and any other specifics about how they wish to invest (e.g. ethical investments only, Islamic-compliant assets only). • Advice should only be given/investment decisions taken in accordance with the specifications on the fact find, and personal recommendations should not be given if the customer fails to provide adequate information to allow for the suitability assessment to take place. • In certain situations a suitability report is required setting out, among other things, the reasons why it was deemed that a particular transaction was suitable for a client. Even where such a report is not strictly required for regulatory reasons it is wise for a record to be maintained showing why each piece of advice or investment decision was considered suitable for the customer concerned. • Suitability fact finds should be kept up to date and reviewed regularly for currency. • Suitability is the responsibility of the Relationship Manager/Investment Manager but should be subject to regular monitoring by Compliance. • Compliance should ensure that staff receive appropriate training and guidance in relation to suitability requirements.
Further guidance	See Appendix 24.

Rule/control	Appropriateness (for non-advised services)
FSA client categorization impact	Applicable to retail and professional clients only (bearing in mind that in this context the category 'professional client' will include clients who would be eligible counterparties in the context of eligible counterparty business).
Customer Sales and Trading	Yes.
Investment Management	No.
Corporate Finance and Investment Banking	No.
Research	No.
Requirement	Firms must assess the appropriateness of execution only customer orders relating to certain instruments.
Comments	Appropriateness requirements are similar to those relating to suitability but apply in relation to unsolicited or not personally solicited (direct offer promotions) customer services (i.e. execution only orders) for 'complex' instruments (derivatives, illiquid instruments, contingent liability investments, or other instruments on which there is not sufficient published information on which to base an informed investment decision).
Controls	• Note that if the customer contacts the firm on his own initiative, but after having received a *personalized communication* from or on behalf of the firm encouraging him to engage in a particular course of action, then the suitability rules apply, not the appropriateness rules. (A general marketing campaign is not deemed to be a personalized communication for the purposes of appropriateness.) • An appropriateness fact find should be completed at the beginning of the relationship to allow the firm to assess the customer's knowledge and experience as regards the type of investment activity envisaged. • The customers should be warned of the implications if they refuse to provide the information required to allow the firm to complete an appropriateness fact find, or do not provide adequate information in this regard. • Firms must assess the appropriateness of relevant execution only orders given to them by their customers and must warn the client if they do not consider the trade to be appropriate for them. • In the event that a firm considers a transaction inappropriate for a particular client it may try to increase the level of the customer's understanding before proceeding, by supplying product information, risk warnings and guidance, for example. • Very careful consideration should be given to completing an execution only transaction that does not meet the appropriateness criteria as it is likely to be hard to justify such action in the light of the 'client's best interest rule' and several of the FSA's Principles for Businesses such as 6 – Customers' interests and 1 – Integrity.

(Continued)

Rule/control	Appropriateness (for non-advised services)
	• The information in the appropriateness fact find should be kept up to date and records should be kept to demonstrate why a particular transaction was considered appropriate for the relevant customer. • Appropriateness is the responsibility of Front Office management but should be subject to regular monitoring by Compliance. • Compliance should ensure that staff receive appropriate training and guidance in relation to appropriateness requirements.
Further guidance	See Appendix 24.

Rule/control	Churning and switching
FSA client categorization impact	Applicable to retail and professional clients only (bearing in mind that in this context the category 'professional client' will include clients who would be eligible counterparties in the context of eligible counterparty business.
Customer Sales and Trading	Yes.
Investment Management	Yes.
Corporate Finance and Investment Banking	No.
Research	No.
Requirement	• Investment Managers must not undertake excessively frequent trades on behalf of their customers on a discretionary basis. • Account Executives must not advise customers to trade with excessive frequency.
Comments	• Churning takes place when an Account Executive advises a customer to trade with excessive frequency, or an Investment Manager undertakes an excessive number of customer trades, usually in order to generate fee income, when their remuneration is on a 'per trade' or trade value basis. • Switching is similar to churning but takes place when a Fund Manager switches customers between the sub-funds of an umbrella fund with excessive frequency. • Even trades that individually may be deemed suitable may not be suitable when assessed in sequence if they are part of an excessive trading pattern. • Churning may also take place in order to generate a false indication of the supply of or demand for a specific asset in order to manipulate the market price. In this instance, churning constitutes a form of market abuse. • Churning and switching represent conflicts of interest in which the interests of the firm and/or its staff are in conflict with the interests of the customer.
Controls	• Compliance should provide regular training and guidance so that staff understand the prohibition on churning and switching and how this impacts their day-to-day activities.

- Controls in this area are the responsibility of Front Office management but Compliance should also conduct regular reviews of account turnover so as to identify potential instances of excessive account activity.
- Both churning and switching result in trades that are not suitable for the customers concerned and therefore a strict adherence to the controls on suitability should be adequate to detect and prevent problems in this area.

Further guidance   See Appendix 24.

Rule/control	Aggregation and allocation
FSA client categorization impact	Applicable to retail and professional clients only (bearing in mind that in this context the category 'professional client' will include clients who would be eligible counterparties in the context of eligible counterparty business)
Customer Sales and Trading	Yes.
Investment Management	Yes.
Corporate Finance and Investment Banking	No.
Research	No.
Requirement	Trade aggregation and allocation must not unfairly disadvantage customers.
Comments	<ul><li>Aggregation takes place when either</li><ul><li>the orders of more than one customer, in the same asset, are combined to form a single order; or</li><li>customer orders are combined with the firm's proprietary orders in the same asset to form a single order.</li></ul><li>Allocation takes place when the assets that form part of an aggregated order are distributed among the customers concerned, and to the firm if applicable.</li><li>Aggregation may frequently be beneficial for customers as it can reduce brokerage commissions due to the larger trade sizes, but it may also lead to customer disadvantage: if the combined trade size is larger/smaller than the quantity of assets available to be purchased/sold, then it will not be possible to fill the order in full.</li></ul>
Controls	<ul><li>Aggregation should only take place if it is unlikely to work to the overall disadvantage of the customers involved.</li><li>Customers whose orders may be subject to aggregation must receive a warning that this may work to their disadvantage.</li><li>Where customer orders are subject to aggregation then subsequent allocation to individual customer accounts must take place fairly without any customer being given preference.</li></ul>

(Continued)

Rule/control	Aggregation and allocation
	• Where customer orders are aggregated with the firm's own orders, this is subject to stricter controls than if the aggregation only involves customers: priority should always be given to the customer unless it can be demonstrated that a less favourable result would have been achieved for that customer were it not for the involvement of the firm. • Aggregation and allocation requirements apply whether the firm executes the customer transactions itself, or passes transactions to a third party for execution. • Firms must prepare an order allocation policy setting out how fairness of allocation will be achieved. • Compliance should provide regular training and guidance so that staff understand the rules relating to aggregation and allocation. • The fair aggregation and allocation of customer orders is the responsibility of Front Office management but should be subject to regular review by the Compliance department.
Further guidance	See Appendix 24.

Rule/control	Order and execution records
FSA client categorization impact	Applies to all clients.
Customer Sales and Trading	Yes.
Investment Management	Yes.
Corporate Finance and Investment Banking	No – Corporate Finance and Banking staff do not generally execute trades.
Research	No – Research Analysts should not undertake trading activity.
Requirement	In order to demonstrate the fair treatment of clients (timely execution, best execution, etc.) detailed order and execution records must be maintained.

Comments	• The FSA has specified the order and execution information that should be recorded including
	
	  – name or designation of client;
	  – whether the order or execution involved a sale or a purchase;
	  – any specific client instructions concerning order execution;
	  – date and time of order receipt and execution;
	  – asset.
	
	• There are separate requirements to comply with when orders are passed to third parties for execution. These include
	
	  – name of client in relation to which the order was transmitted;
	  – name of person to whom the order was transmitted;
	  – the terms of the order that was transmitted; and
	  – date and time that the order was transmitted.

Controls	• Provide training and guidance to ensure that staff are aware of their order and execution record-keeping obligations. • The maintenance of adequate order and execution records is the responsibility of Front Office management but should be subject to regular review by Compliance.
Further guidance	See Appendix 24.

Rule/control	Training and competence
FSA client categorization impact	The detailed T&C rules apply only to staff dealing with retail clients although the higher level 'Competent Employee Rule' applies to all staff no matter what category of client they are dealing with.
Customer Sales and Trading	Yes.
Investment Management	Yes.
Corporate Finance and Investment Banking	Yes.
Research	Yes.
Requirement	All staff must achieve and maintain appropriate levels of competence for their roles.

Comments	• Training and competence requirements apply on two levels:
	
	  – All Front Office staff must comply with the Competent Employee rule.
	  – Staff undertaking certain key Front Office roles (specified by the FSA) with or for retail clients must also comply with the FSA's detailed T&C rules.
	
	• The Front Office roles covered by the T&C rules include
	
	  – advising retail clients on derivatives;
	  – advising and dealing in securities; and
	  – providing fund management services in relation to investments.
	
	• The FSA's detailed T&C rules cover matters such as
	
	  – exam passes;
	  – assessments of competence; and
	  – staff supervision.
	
	• Front Office managers are likely to be required to act as T&C supervisors for the more junior staff in their departments. Their supervisory activities should include
	
	  – observing staff when interacting with clients;
	  – reviewing client recommendations and reports prior to issue;
	  – setting a training programme; and
	  – undertaking T&C assessments to determine whether competency has been achieved or maintained.

(Continued)

Rule/control	Training and competence
	• The role of T&C supervisor carries with it a considerable amount of responsibility. If an employee for whom they are responsible starts breaching rules, then questions will undoubtedly be asked about who was supervising them, how they were being monitored, and why they were assessed as competent (if this is the case). This is not a responsibility to be taken lightly. • In order to facilitate compliance with the Competent Employee rule many firms also choose to apply the T&C rules to non-retail staff as a matter of best practice.

Controls	• Compliance should provide training and guidance to ensure that Front Office staff understand
	
	   – the status they (and their staff) have under the T&C rules;
	   – the implications of their T&C status; and
	   – how to comply with the firm's internal procedures relating to the T&C rules.
	
	• Front Office managers who act as T&C supervisors should be made fully aware of what is required of them in this capacity and should also understand the implications of getting it wrong. It is useful to provide all T&C supervisors with a hand out or leaflet summarizing their responsibilities.
	• Front Office compliance with the firm's T&C controls should be subject to regular review.

Further guidance	• See Appendix 24. • See page 171 of Appendix A.

Rule/control	Approved Persons rules
FSA client categorization impact	For Significant Influence Functions client categorization is not relevant, but the Customer Functions only apply to staff dealing with customers.
Customer Sales and Trading	Yes.
Investment Management	Yes.
Corporate Finance and Investment Banking	Yes.
Research	No.
Requirement	Staff undertaking certain functions specified by the FSA must be registered as Approved Persons.
Comments	For the Front Office, the most relevant roles under the Approved Persons rules are the: • Customer Functions (such as advising on securities and/or derivatives, giving corporate finance advice or managing investments on a discretionary basis); and • Significant Influence Functions which might include heads of important Front Office departments or divisions.

Controls	• Compliance should provide training and guidance to ensure that Front Office staff understand
	
	   − the status they (and their staff) have under the Approved Persons rules, and what the implications of this are;
	   − the specific FSA requirements with which they must comply due to their status as an Approved Person, such as the Approved Persons Code of Conduct; and
	   − how to comply with the firm's internal procedures relating to the Approved Persons rules.
	
	• Front Office compliance with the firm's Approved Persons controls should be subject to regular review.

Further guidance	• See Appendix 24. • See page 174 of Appendix A.

Rule/control	Inducements
FSA client categorization impact	None – client categorization is irrelevant.
Customer Sales and Trading	Yes.
Investment Management	Yes.
Corporate Finance and Investment Banking	Yes.
Research	Yes.
Requirement	Staff must not offer or accept any inducements that could conflict with duties owed to a customer and should comply with the procedures and controls implemented by the firm in this area.
Comments	• Rules on inducements are there to prevent the competing interests of firms and their customers and contacts from interfering with the ethical provision of financial services. • Front Office staff are on the front line in terms of managing these competing interests as they talk to customers on the one hand while also being in daily contact with service providers such as brokers and fund managers. All have their own agenda and an arrangement that suits one person may have a negative impact on others. • An example of an inappropriate inducement would be accepting a gift from a customer on the basis that, in future, that customer will receive preferential treatment. • Front Office management may be responsible for approving gifts and benefits offered or received by their staff.
Controls	• Front Office staff should understand why controls on inducements are necessary and what is likely to be deemed unacceptable. This is particularly important for any Front Office managers who are responsible for authorizing gifts and benefits.

(Continued)

Rule/control	Inducements
	• Compliance should provide regular training and guidance so that staff understand and comply with the firm's controls governing the offering and receipt of inducements. • Front Office compliance with the firm's inducements regime should be subject to regular review.
Further guidance	• See Appendix 24. • See page 165 of Appendix A.

Rule/control	Voice recording
FSA client categorization impact	None – client categorization is irrelevant.
Customer Sales and Trading	Yes.
Investment Management	Yes.
Corporate Finance and Investment Banking	Depends on the firm but voice recording is frequently only applied to staff taking or passing orders and/or executing trades, which would not normally include Research, Corporate Finance or Investment Banking.
Research	No.
Requirement	Staff involved with taking, passing and executing customer orders or providing advice over the phone should be subject to voice recording so that any disputes or queries over instructions or advice given can be readily resolved.
Controls	• Compliance should provide regular training and guidance so that staff understand and comply with the firm's voice-recording arrangements. • Front Office management should ensure that all staff in their teams who should be subject to voice recording have their lines recorded. • Front Office compliance with the firm's voice-recording requirements should be subject to regular review. • Clients should receive notification that their telephone conversations may be recorded – this can normally be achieved by disclosure in a customer agreement or terms of business.
Further guidance	• See Appendix 24. • See page 178 of Appendix A.

Rule/control	Communicating with clients (fair, clear and not misleading communications)
FSA client categorization impact	The FSA rules in this area apply to retail and professional customers only although the FSA Principle 7 (Communications with clients) also applies to eligible counterparties.

Customer Sales and Trading	Yes.
Investment Management	Yes.
Corporate Finance and Investment Banking	Yes.
Research	Yes.
Requirement	All communications with clients must be fair, clear and not misleading.
Comments	This requirement exists to protect clients and also to prevent market abuse (the making and distribution of misleading information can be used for market manipulation purposes).

Controls	• Document the ways in which the various Front Office departments may communicate with clients, for example
	
	   – over the phone;
	   – advertisements;
	   – face to face;
	   – letter;
	   – fax;
	   – e-mail;
	   – text message;
	   – electronic messaging such as Bloomberg.
	
	• Provide staff with guidance about what constitutes a fair, clear and not misleading communication in the context of their own activities. Also provide examples of what would not be acceptable.
	• Ensure that staff are aware of how misleading communications may breach market abuse requirements.
	• Front Office management is responsible for ensuring that their team's communications are fair, clear and not misleading although Compliance should also review this area on a regular basis.

Further guidance	• See Appendix 24.

Rule/control	Financial promotions
FSA client categorization impact	Requirements relating to retail clients are significantly more onerous than those applying to professional clients. Only the rules on compensation information apply to eligible counterparties.
Customer Sales and Trading	Yes.
Investment Management	Yes.
Corporate Finance and Investment Banking	Yes.
Research	Yes (independent research is not classed as a financial promotion, but non independent research should be treated as a marketing tool).

(Continued)

Rule/control	Financial promotions
Requirement	• Financial promotions must meet various requirements including the need to – be fair, clear and not misleading; – be identifiable as promotional material; – contain appropriate risk warnings; – identify the FSA as regulator; – make it clear where a matter is not regulated by the FSA; and – contain appropriate information about compensation schemes. • There are additional detailed contents requirements relating to financial promotions targeted at retail clients and relating to consumer credit arrangements.
Comments	Front Office controls surrounding the issue and approval of financial promotions, especially those aimed at retail investors, need to be particularly robust as a breach in this area is likely to be highly visible – if a sales team is launching a mass marketing campaign designed to be seen by as many people as possible then it stands to reason that it will be difficult to be discrete if things go wrong.
Controls	• Compliance should provide regular training and guidance to Front Office staff so that they – are aware of what constitutes a financial promotion; and – understand and comply with the firm's internal controls regarding the preparation, approval and issue of financial promotions. • Compliance should work with the Front Office and Legal department to ensure that where possible, standard disclaimers, disclosures and risk warnings can be used instead of having to come up with new wording each time a new financial promotion is issued. • Front Office management is responsible for the financial promotions issued by their staff although if Compliance does not approve each new financial promotion prior to issue, this area should be subject to regular Compliance review.
Further guidance	• See Appendix 24. • See page 167 of Appendix A.

Rule/control	Client categorization
FSA client categorization impact	All persons with whom a firm conducts business should go through the categorization process.
Customer Sales and Trading	Yes.
Investment Management	Yes.
Corporate Finance and Investment Banking	Yes.

Research	The Research team is less likely than others to be responsible for client categorization as it will not generally play a lead role in the new customer approvals process which is the stage at which client categorization generally takes place.
Requirement	Ensure that all parties to whom the firm provides services are categorized correctly.
Comments	Clients must be categorized in accordance with COBS rules in order to

  - determine the rules that will be applied to them;
  - determine the protections that they will receive during their relationship with the firm; and
  - assist with establishing expected trading/activity profiles (for the purposes of identifying suspicions of money laundering).

Controls	• Compliance should provide regular training and guidance so that staff

  - know the different categories of client;
  - understand the importance of correct categorization; and
  - know how to categorize their clients correctly.

  - Front Office staff must be aware of the categorization of all of their clients so that they apply the correct regulations, rules and protections to them.
  - Client categorization usually takes place at the same time as the initial KYC check. As with KYC approvals, some firms have systems whereby Compliance staff approve each new categorization whereas with others, Front Office management approve categorizations, with Compliance simply conducting periodic reviews to assess adequacy.

Further guidance	• See Appendix 24.
	• See page 185 of Appendix A.

Rule/control	KYC
FSA client categorization impact	None – client categorization is irrelevant.
Customer Sales and Trading	Yes.
Investment Management	Yes.
Corporate Finance and Investment Banking	Yes.
Research	It is less likely, although not impossible, that Research team members will be involved in the KYC process.
Requirement	KYC must be completed on all customers. KYC information must be gathered at the outset of a relationship and thereafter kept up to date on an ongoing basis.
Comments	• As Front Office staff are the 'owners' of the firm's customer relationships it is vital that staff understand the importance of completing KYC on a timely basis, and that they also understand that a breach in this area may also result in a breach of legislation for which serious penalties may be applied.

(Continued)

Rule/control	KYC
	• It is also important that Front Office staff know who exactly they should be completing KYC on: this is relatively straightforward when the firm has a direct relationship with the ultimate customer but becomes more complex when the firm is dealing through an intermediary who represents the underlying customer/s.
	• In such cases it may be possible to complete KYC on the intermediary and then rely on KYC completed by that person for the underlying relationship. But if there is any doubt as to the adequacy of KYC arrangements undertaken by the intermediary then the firm should conduct its own KYC.
	• There is a similar complication when a firm is providing investment management services to a collective investment vehicle and checks should be undertaken to ensure that the underlying investors in the fund have been subject to the appropriate KYC vetting if this is not to be done by the firm itself.

Controls	• Provide training and guidance to ensure that staff in each department
	
	  – understand the firm's KYC procedures for new relationships;
	  – understand the firm's KYC procedures for review of existing relationships; and
	  – understand their responsibilities via a vis KYC; and
	  – are aware of the legislative penalties that exist for failure to comply with such procedures.
	
	• Where the firm's deal processing systems allows, implement a system whereby a trade cannot be booked or processed unless KYC has been approved. This can also be used to generate an automatic exception report that lists staff who have tried to book trades for customers that have not been through the KYC process – such staff may then be appropriately disciplined!
	• Initial KYC approval usually takes place at the same time as the customer categorization process. As with customer categorization, some firms have systems whereby Compliance staff approve each new KYC file whereas with others, Front Office management approve KYC information, with Compliance simply conducting periodic reviews to assess adequacy.

Further guidance	• See Appendix 24. • See Appendix B.

Rule/control	Anti-money-laundering and counter terrorist financing controls
FSA client categorization impact	None – client categorization is irrelevant.
Customer Sales and Trading	Yes.
Investment Management	Yes.
Corporate Finance and Investment Banking	Yes.
Research	Yes, but requirements of less direct relevance to Research team staff as they have less direct contact with customers.
Requirement	Front Office staff must take all appropriate measures to help to reduce the risk of the firm being used for money laundering or terrorist financing activities.
Comments	Front Office staff are more likely than many others within a firm to be in a position to identify and help to prevent attempted money laundering or terrorist financing because of their direct relationship with customers, and their knowledge of customer activities.

Controls	• Some of the key matters of relevance are that Front Office staff must
	
	  – undertake regular AML and CTF training;
	  – ensure that all new customers are approved for KYC;
	  – be aware of the various sanctions regimes in place so that business is not conducted in contravention of one of these sanctions;
	  – know their customers well so that unusual activity can be identified for review in case it represents a risk of money laundering or terrorist financing;
	  – keep their customers' KYC files up to date;
	  – report suspicions of money laundering to the MLRO; and
	  – understand the requirement not to tip-off customers if they become suspicious of the customers' activities.
	
	• Compliance should provide regular training and guidance to Front Office staff so that they understand the firm's procedures and controls in this area. It is important for training to be tailored to the activities of the staff concerned for it to be truly meaningful.
	• The effectiveness of the firm's controls to counter money laundering and terrorist financing should be subject to regular Compliance review.

Further guidance	• See Appendix 24. • See Appendix B.

Rule/control	Reporting suspicions of money laundering and terrorist financing
FSA client categorization impact	None – client categorization is irrelevant.
Customer Sales and Trading	Yes.
Investment Management	Yes.
Corporate Finance and Investment Banking	Yes.
Research	Yes.
Requirement	Ensure that suspicions of money laundering and terrorist financing are identified and dealt with appropriately.
Comments	<ul><li>Due to their daily contact with clients, Front Office staff are among the best placed within the firm to identify suspicious activity. They should be in a position to judge what is a normal pattern of activity for their customers, and what is so out of the ordinary that it requires further investigation.</li><li>Front Office staff also play a key role in accepting new business and are therefore well placed to identify suspicious approaches from potential customers.</li><li>Provide training and guidance to ensure that staff in each department:<ul><li>– know how to recognize suspected money laundering and terrorist financing activity;</li><li>– know how to deal with any such suspicions in accordance with the firm's internal procedures; and</li><li>– are aware that they must not tip-off a person who is a subject of suspicion.</li></ul></li><li>Staff training on identifying suspicions of money laundering should be as tailored as possible – everyone is familiar with the archetypal image of the money launderer with a fake moustache and a bin bag full of used notes, but this does not help equity derivatives traders or corporate financiers for example, to identify what is suspicious in the context of their own activities.</li><li>Ensure that staff are aware of the protections offered to them under the firm's whistle-blowing procedures if they report a suspicion of money laundering or terrorist financing.</li></ul>
Further guidance	<ul><li>See Appendix 24.</li><li>See page 199 of Appendix B.</li></ul>

Rule/control	Fraud prevention
FSA client categorization impact	None – client categorization is irrelevant.
Customer Sales and Trading	Yes.
Investment Management	Yes.
Corporate Finance and Investment Banking	Yes.

Research	Yes.
Requirement	Ensure that suspicions of fraud are identified and dealt with appropriately.
Comments	As with any situation in which cash and funds are changing hands, the Front Office is particularly susceptible to fraud. Some of the classic situations that may affect the Front Office are

- misappropriation of client assets or funds;
- trade booking irregularities – if a trade does well, book to personal account, if it does badly, book to customer account, etc.
- claiming personal entertainment as business expenses;
- trader mis-valuing their book at the end of the day;
- customer engaged in fraudulent trading activity trying to involve the firm in their activities;
- third party setting up a website, or otherwise contacting people in the name of the firm, and inviting them to send in cash or supply account details; and
- third party calling the firm and claiming to be a customer, a regulator, etc., and requesting the provision of customer information.

Controls	• Provide training and guidance to ensure that staff in each department:

  - know how to recognize suspected fraud; and
  - know how to deal with any such suspicions in accordance with the firm's internal procedures.

- To the maximum extent possible, guidance on identifying fraud should be tailored to individual departments.
- Ensure that staff are aware of the protections offered to them under the firm's whistle-blowing procedures if they report a suspicion of fraud.

Further guidance	• See Appendix 24.
	• See page 190 of Appendix A.

Rule/control	Exclusivity
FSA client categorization impact	None – client categorization is irrelevant.
Customer Sales and Trading	No.
Investment Management	No.
Corporate Finance and Investment Banking	Yes.
Research	No.
Requirement	Ensure that where a firm agrees to provide services on an exclusive basis the appropriate arrangements are in place for this undertaking to be complied with.

(Continued)

Rule/control	**Exclusivity**
Comments	Corporate Finance and Banking customers may frequently ask for the services of the firm to be provided on an exclusive basis so as to avoid conflicts of interest; for example, a customer may not wish the firm to be advising his competitor on how to acquire the same target that he is hoping to purchase himself.
Controls	• Implement procedures whereby a record can be made of exclusivity agreements. This way the log can be checked prior to accepting a new mandate to ensure that no future transactions are accepted in conflict with existing exclusivity arrangements. • One method that can be used to manage this situation is to log all exclusivity arrangements on the watch or restricted list (as appropriate) and then consider the exclusivity issue as part of the conflicts clearance process. • Compliance should provide training and guidance so that Front Office staff understand the firm's procedures relating to exclusivity agreements. • Front Office management is responsible for ensuring that exclusivity undertakings are respected, although Compliance should periodically review the effectiveness of the controls implemented.
Further guidance	–

Rule/control	**Investment committee**
FSA client categorization impact	Client categorization is irrelevant in terms of the need for, or operation of, the investment committee although it is likely to affect the decisions taken by the committee in terms of investment strategy.
Customer Sales and Trading	Yes – if customers are given advice.
Investment Management	Yes.
Corporate Finance and Investment Banking	No.
Research	No.
Requirement	Investment decisions and advice should be in the best interests of the customers concerned and any personal or corporate interest in a transaction should be ignored.
Comments	Investment committees are often used as a key part of a firm's investment management and advice process. As well as bringing together a team of experts instead of relying on the judgement and skill of a single person, the committee approach contributes greatly to independence as it facilitates collective decision making

Controls	• Investment committees should be subject to appropriate governance:
	  – A terms of reference for each committee should be prepared and adhered to.
	  – Investment decisions and their rationale should be minuted.

- Investment strategy decisions and their rationale should be minuted.
- Care should be taken that individual members of the committee do not have any material interest in the decisions being taken.
- Procedures should be prepared so that members who find themselves conflicted on a one-off basis may be temporarily excused from participating.

- Training should be provided to investment committee members in relation to the type of conflict of interest they are most likely to encounter, and how such situations can be managed.
- Compliance should periodically review the effectiveness of the controls governing the operation and independence of the investment committee.

Further guidance	–

Rule/control	Investment and borrowing powers
FSA client categorization impact	Requirements relating to investment and borrowing powers are applicable only in relation to the management of funds. Funds available to retail clients have much stricter investment and borrowing powers than those available to professional clients or eligible counterparties.
Customer Sales and Trading	No.
Investment Management	Yes.
Corporate Finance and Investment Banking	No.
Research	No.
Requirement	A fund or other form of collective investment should at all times be invested in accordance with its investment and borrowing powers.
Comments	• The assets that a collective investment vehicle may and may not invest in, along with its ability to borrow, are set out in its incorporation documentation and will be available for review in its prospectus (or similar documents). • The investment and borrowing powers of UCITS funds are set by the UCITS Product Directive.
Controls	• Portfolio managers and Investment committee members should know and adhere to the investment and borrowing powers of each collective investment vehicle for which they have responsibility. • Investment Management departments often employ people specifically to monitor compliance with investment and borrowing powers although this does not mean that the area should not also be subject to periodic monitoring by Compliance.
Further guidance	See Appendix 5.

Rule/control	Issuing research
FSA client categorization impact	Applies to all clients except that the requirements relating to the labelling of non-independent research are disapplied for eligible counterparty business. However, as a matter of best practice, and in order to comply with market abuse legislation, the controls described below should be applied no matter what category of customer will receive the research.
Customer Sales and Trading	Yes, where issuing research.
Investment Management	Yes, where issuing research.
Corporate Finance and Investment Banking	No.
Research	Yes.
Requirement	The FSA rules on research are complex and cover requirements in several different areas: • Research procedures should be such that research is issued to all recipients, both internal and external, at the same time, thereby ensuing that no one has an unfair chance to act on the information before all recipients have had an opportunity to react to it. • Research should also be fair, clear and not misleading. • In order to avoid conflicts of interests Investment Analysts should be independent of the companies on whom they publish research, the firm (especially Corporate Finance and Sales and Trading departments) and the firm's customers (unless the research document is clearly labelled as not being independent). • Personal account and proprietary dealing in investments covered by a research report that is about to be issued should only be permitted in very restricted circumstances. • Neither the from nor its staff should accept inducements from those with a interest in the contents of the research (for example, a company wanting favourable coverage or a fund manager with a large holding of a particular investment). • Agreeing favourable research reports with the companies affected should not be permitted • Draft research must not be made available for review to issuers, even to verify factual accuracy, if the research contains a recommendation or target prices (unless the review is simply to ensure compliance with the firm's legal obligations) • In order to safeguard their independence, Research team staff should limit their participation in other areas of the firm's activity and their participation in certain activities such as the provisions of corporate finance services and pitching for new business should be prohibited altogether.

Comments	• At a high level, the FSA requirements relating to the issue of research are aimed at
	
	   – reducing the scope for conflicts of interest;
	   – reducing the scope for market abuse; and
	   – ensuring that the firm's communications are fair, clear and not misleading.

Controls

- Research is still a topical subject in the regulatory arena due to scandals involving equity research at the beginning of the decade and misdemeanours in this area are unlikely to be taken lightly.
- Robust controls need to be established surrounding the issue of research. These should include the following:
  - Ensure that the Research team understands the requirement for their material to be fair, clear and not misleading – provision of examples of what your firm does not consider to be acceptable content or wording is helpful.
  - Ensure that adequate records are kept to demonstrate the rationale behind any recommendations made in the research.
  - Identify the potential conflicts of interest that may affect the firm's Research team, ensuring that mitigating action is taken, and training staff in this regard.
  - Train staff on the ways in which research may be used for market abuse so they are clear about unacceptable behaviour.
  - Implement arrangements for the simultaneous distribution of research to customers and the firm itself. Some firms choose to use electronic distribution portals (like a specialized email system) that allow for research to be distributed to a number of people at the same time.
  - Place companies likely to feature in future research reports on the watch list so that monitoring for conflicts of interest and against personal account dealing and proprietary trading can take place.
  - Locate the Research team behind a Chinese wall.
  - Ensure that Research team reporting lines are appropriate – the team should be independent and should not report into another Front Office area.
  - Prepare written procedures covering the issuance of research and/or include research controls in the firm's conflicts of interest policy.
- Research team management is responsible for the quality of research issued and if Compliance does not review and approve each new piece of research material on a case by case basis, it should be subject to regular Compliance review.
- Ensure that Research Analyst remuneration is not directly linked to the quantity of research produced or the number of trades generated by it.

Further guidance

- See Appendix 24.

Rule/control	Research disclaimers
FSA client categorization impact	Applies to all clients except that the requirements relating to the labelling of non-independent research are disapplied for eligible counterparty business.

(Continued)

Rule/control	Research disclaimers
Customer Sales and Trading	No.
Investment Management	No.
Corporate Finance and Investment Banking	No.
Research	Yes.
Requirement	Investment research must include all relevant required disclaimers as stipulated by the FSA.

Comments	• There are extensive FSA disclaimer requirements applying to investment research and Compliance should work with Legal and the Research team so that where possible, standardized disclaimers are developed: it is much more efficient if, instead of having to come up with new wording each time a research document is issued, then only the basic variables such as analyst name and date of issue need to be changed.
	• Disclaimer contents requirements cover many areas such as
	
	  – the name and job title of the person who wrote the research;
	  – the firm's regulated status; and
	  – conflicts of interest.

Controls	• Compliance should provide regular training and guidance so that the Research team understands the requirements for appropriate disclaimers to be used on each piece of research issued. • Prepare proforma disclaimers that can be used time and time again and ensure that the permitted usage of each one is clear. • Research team management is responsible for ensuring that appropriate disclaimers are used and if Compliance does not approve each piece of research prior to issue, the use of correct disclaimers should be subject to periodic review.
Further guidance	• See Appendix 24.

Rule/control	Issuing third party research
FSA client categorization impact	Applies to all clients except that the requirements relating to the labelling of non-independent research are disapplied for eligible counterparty business. However, as a matter of best practice, and in order to comply with market abuse legislation, the controls described below should be applied no matter what category of customer will receive the research.
Customer Sales and Trading	Yes, where issuing research.
Investment Management	Yes, where issuing research.
Corporate Finance and Investment Banking	No.

Research	Yes.
Requirement	• Ensure that where third party research is distributed, this is done in accordance with any restrictions imposed by the entity that initially prepared the research. You may need to contact the originators of the research to obtain their permission and to determine on what basis you are permitted to use the material they have produced. • The firm disseminating the research must be clearly identified on the material distributed. • Certain rules may be disapplied to the distribution of third party research as long as the relevant conditions stipulated by the FSA are met.
Comments	Note that irrespective of whether FSA rules have been complied with or not, third parties are not always happy for other firms to distribute their research and it is important not to breach any copyright restrictions that limit the on-sending of such material.
Controls	• Gain approval from third parties to issue their research. If this will be a long-term and ongoing arrangement then it is probably wise to prepare a contract with the research producer establishing the basis on which your firm will distribute their material. • Ensure that third party research is clearly identifiable as such. • Prepare detailed procedures for the dissemination of third party research to ensure that all the FSA and other applicable regulatory requirements can be complied with. • Research team management is responsible for ensuring that no inappropriate use is made of third party research, although compliance with requirements in this area should be subject to regular Compliance review.
Further guidance	• See Appendix 24.

Rule/control	Confidentiality
FSA client categorization impact	For the most part client categorization is irrelevant although the requirements of the Data Protection Act 1998 only apply to individuals.
Customer Sales and Trading	Yes.
Investment Management	Yes.
Corporate Finance and Investment Banking	Yes.
Research	Yes.
Requirement	Ensure that customer information is kept confidential.
Comments	• At a high level confidentiality requirements apply on three levels: – Personal data should be kept secure so as to ensure compliance with the Data Protection Act 1998.

(Continued)

Rule/control	Confidentiality

	– Corporate information should be kept secure so as to minimize the risk of it being used for market abuse and insider dealing.
	    – Both personal and corporate information should be kept secure so as to minimize the risk of conflicts of interest.
	
	• Irrespective of any legislative or regulatory requirements however, all customers (whether individuals or corporates) will have a basic expectation that their information will be kept confidential, and this is likely to form part of any written contract that the firm enters into with its customers.
	• The type of confidential information Front Office staff are likely to have relating to individuals includes
	
	    – data included in suitability and appropriateness fact finds;
	    – client money balances;
	    – client assets holdings; and
	    – information on the firm's own employees, such as salary, date of birth and address.
	
	• The type of confidential information Front Office staff are likely to hold on corporates includes
	
	    – business plans;
	    – financial information; and
	    – current projects.

Controls	• Provide training and guidance so that staff understand the need to respect customer and employee confidentiality. • Ensure that staff have adequate lockable physical storage space. • Ensure that the firm's IT systems are set up in such a way that confidential information used by one department cannot be viewed or accessed by another. • Implement Chinese walls where required. • Include a confidentiality clause in employment contracts. • Front Office management should ensure that confidentiality controls within their departments are adequate, although this area should also be subject to periodic Compliance review.
Further guidance	See Appendix 24.

Rule/control	Personal account dealing ('PA dealing')
FSA client categorization impact	Client categorisation does not affect requirements in this area.
Customer Sales and Trading	Yes.

Investment Management	Yes.
Corporate Finance and Investment Banking	Yes.
Research	Yes
Requirement	Staff should be aware of, and comply with, the firm's PA dealing controls.
Comments	• The PA dealing rules apply when staff trade investments for their own account, or on behalf of a person connected to them such as a close family member, and are designed to combat a variety of sins including conflicts of interest and insider dealing. • Some examples of inappropriate PA dealing activity are provided in Appendix E and other matters to consider include the following:

Sales and Trading

• Relationship Managers should consider how their personal trading strategy correlates to the advice they are giving their clients. Would it be appropriate, for example, for a Relationship Manager to be selling a particular asset on a personal level, while recommending it to their customers, or vice versa?

Corporate Finance and Banking

• The personal account dealing activities of Corporate Finance and Banking staff should be subject to very careful scrutiny as the potential for insider dealing is substantial when dealing with listed companies, or companies in relation to which an application for listing has been made.
• Any dealing by staff in a company with which they currently have a mandate, or have recently had a mandate, should be treated with extreme caution due to the risk that the staff members may have inside information.

Investment Management

• Some clients will only invest in a fund if the Fund Manager has a sizeable holding in it as they consider that this shows commitment, belief in self and an alignment of interests. Other people see this as a potential for conflict of interest and frown upon the practice.

Research

• There are considerable restrictions on Investment Analysts conducting personal account trades in the securities of the companies that their research covers.
• Such trading should only be undertaken in extremely controlled circumstances, and never without the written prior approval of the Compliance (or Legal) department.
• Personal account dealing both by Research team staff, and by other staff members in securities covered by the Research team should be subject to very close Compliance scrutiny.

(Continued)

Rule/control	Personal account dealing ('PA dealing')
Controls	• Compliance should provide regular training and guidance to ensure that staff understand and adhere to the firm's PA dealing controls. • Department heads may be required to approve the PA trades of the staff reporting to them and should understand the process for this, as well as the potentially serious implications for them of approving an inappropriate PA trade. • Compliance should undertake regular reviews of PA dealing by the Front Office.
Further guidance	• See Appendix 24. • See page 162 of Appendix A.

Rule/control	Conflicts of interest
FSA client categorization impact	None – client categorization is irrelevant.
Customer Sales and Trading	Yes.
Investment Management	Yes.
Corporate Finance and Investment Banking	Yes.
Research	Yes.
Requirement	Conflicts of interest must be identified and thereafter subject to appropriate management and mitigation.
Comments	• A conflict of interest occurs when the interests of a client are at odds with the interests of the firm, an employee or another client. • There is increased scope for conflicts to arise in multi-function firms given the often competing interests of the different Front Office departments and their clients.
Controls	• Compliance should provide regular training and guidance so that Front Office staff are aware of the types of conflict of interest that may affect their work, and are able to identify them promptly and to manage them appropriately. • Front Office staff should also be trained on the processes the firm has implemented in order to manage conflicts of interest. • Samples of conflicts of interest that may arise within and between the various Front Office departments are provided in Appendix E. • Front Office management is responsible for ensuring that conflicts of interest are handled appropriately although Compliance should take an active role in this process.
Further guidance	• See Appendix 24. • See page 146 of Appendix A.

Rule/control	Insider lists
FSA client categorization impact	Listed companies (to which this requirement relates) are usually professional clients or eligible market counterparties although the nature of the controls required should not vary depending on client categorization.
Customer Sales and Trading	Less likely to be relevant.
Investment Management	Less likely to be relevant.
Corporate Finance and Investment Banking	Yes.
Research	Less likely to be relevant.
Requirement	Issuers are required to ensure that persons working for them, such as firms providing corporate finance and/or banking services, prepare insider lists.
Comments	• Requirements on insider lists are designed to combat market abuse. • Corporate Finance and Banking staff are more likely than others to become party to inside information although other staff may also be involved.
Controls	• In order to facilitate issuer compliance with insider list requirements firms should ensure that they have controls in place to record staff who are party to inside information. • Compliance should provide regular training and guidance so that staff understand and comply with the controls implemented by the firm in relation to insider lists. • Insider list controls are the responsibility of Front Office management although the area should be subject to regular Compliance review.
Further guidance	• See Appendix 24. • See page 159 of Appendix A.

Rule/control	Chinese walls
FSA client categorization impact	None – client categorization is irrelevant.
Customer Sales and Trading	Yes – awareness required although this department is not generally behind a Chinese wall.
Investment Management	Yes.
Corporate Finance and Investment Banking	Yes.
Research	Yes.
Requirement	For Chinese walls to be effective they should be demonstrably robust and known to relevant staff. It is not enough to simply erect a wall but have no controls surrounding its use.
Comments	• Chinese walls (physical and procedural barriers that prevent the inappropriate flow of information from one part of the firm to another) are key Front Office controls that enable firms engaging in competing or otherwise incompatible activities to continue on this multi-function basis.

(Continued)

Rule/control	Chinese walls
Controls	• Samples of the type of situations that the use of Chinese walls may help to prevent and/or manage are provided in Appendix E. • Compliance should provide regular training and guidance so that staff understand and comply with the controls implemented by the firm in order to support its use of Chinese walls. • Front Office compliance with the firm's Chinese walls controls should be subject to regular review although responsibility remains with management.
Further guidance	• See Appendix 24. • See page 157 of Appendix A.

Rule/control	Watch and restricted list
FSA client categorization impact	None – client categorization is irrelevant.
Customer Sales and Trading	Yes.
Investment Management	Yes.
Corporate Finance and Investment Banking	Yes.
Research	Yes.
Requirement	Staff should use the watch and restricted list in accordance with the firm's internal procedures.
Comments	• Watch and restricted lists are key Front Office controls used to monitor and restrict inappropriate or high-risk activity. • Examples of situations that may be identified or managed by use of the watch and restricted lists are provided in Appendix E.
Controls	• Compliance should provide regular training and guidance so that staff understand and comply with the controls implemented by the firm in order to support its use of the watch and restricted list. • Front Office compliance with the firm's watch and restricted list controls should be subject to regular review although responsibility remains with management.
Further guidance	• See Appendix 24. • See page 160 of Appendix A.

Rule/control	Market abuse
FSA client categorization impact	None – client categorization is irrelevant.
Customer Sales and Trading	Yes.
Investment Management	Yes.

Corporate Finance and Investment Banking	Yes.
Research	Yes.
Requirement	Front Office staff must not engage in market abuse themselves, nor encourage or assist another person to do so.
Comments	• Because of their knowledge of, and involvement with, customers, the markets, transactions and business deals, etc., Front Office staff are at greater risk than others of getting involved with market abuse. • The temptation to take unfair advantage of their knowledge or position may be particularly strong when staff are faced with aggressive targets in order to achieve their full bonus. • Examples of situations in which market abuse may be suspected can be found in Appendix E.

Controls	• Provide training and guidance to ensure that staff are aware of what constitutes market abuse in the context of their own activities. To give it maximum relevance the advice should be as tailored as possible to the business undertaken by each department.
	• Ensure that staff are familiar with the controls the firm has implemented to combat market abuse.
	• Implement arrangements whereby
	  – staff can report suspicions of market abuse to Compliance; and
	  – suspicions of market abuse are also identified by means of surveillance activities.
	• Ensure that staff are aware of the protections offered to them under the firm's whistle-blowing procedures if they report a suspicion of market abuse.
	• Front Office management is responsible for ensuring that staff comply with requirements in this area but it should also be subject to regular review by Compliance.

Further guidance	• See Appendix 24. • See page 149 of Appendix A.

Rule/control	Written policies and procedures
FSA client categorization impact	None – client categorization is irrelevant.
Customer Sales and Trading	Yes.
Investment Management	Yes.
Corporate Finance and Investment Banking	Yes.
Research	Yes.
Requirement	Firms must take reasonable care to establish and maintain the systems and controls that are appropriate to their business.

(Continued)

Rule/control	Written policies and procedures
Comments	• Although not mandatory for all areas, it is useful for systems and controls to be documented in writing. This helps staff to understand what is required of them and carry out their jobs properly as well as showing regulators that management is serious about establishing internal arrangements for compliance with relevant requirements and best practice. • Reading a department's procedures manual is a useful way for Compliance staff to gain a better understanding of its activities.

Controls	• There are requirements for formal written procedures/policies to be prepared in a number of areas that impact the Front Office, including
	
	  – best execution;
	  – aggregation and allocation; and
	  – conflicts of interest.
	
	• As a matter of best practice it may also be useful to document procedures in a number of other areas, especially those in which
	
	  – a process or activity is particularly complex;
	  – there is a high turnover of staff;
	  – a high degree of manual intervention is required; or
	  – the firm faces a particularly significant level of risk.
	
	• Policies and procedures should be kept up to date in order to reflect changes to business, the markets, products, technology, etc.
	• Procedures documents should be detailed enough to be of use, but not so detailed that it is impossible to comply with them or that they need to be amended each time there is a slight change to the control environment. An appropriate balance needs to be struck.
	• Compliance should periodically review Front Office procedures manuals to ensure that they allow for relevant regulatory and legislative requirements to be complied with.
	• Front Office management is responsible for ensuring the adequacy of its written policies and procedures and that staff follow the controls they contain.

Further guidance	–

Rule/control	Whistle blowing
FSA client categorization impact	None – client categorization is irrelevant.
Customer Sales and Trading	Yes.
Investment Management	Yes.

Corporate Finance and Investment Banking	Yes.
Research	Yes.
Requirement	Ensure that arrangements are in place for compliance with the Public Interest Disclosure Act 1998.
Comment	• PIDA allows staff to raise concerns about malpractice without the risk of suffering recriminations or reprisals as a result of having 'blown the whistle' on a colleague or customer.
	• Because so many regulatory and legislative requirements apply to Front Office activity, and because Compliance staff cannot be everywhere it is vital for Compliance Officers to be able to rely on Front Office staff vigilance.
	• For this to be a realistic possibility, Front Office staff must have total confidence in the whistle-blowing process in place at the firm.
Controls	• Provide training and guidance to ensure that staff in each department understand how and when to use the firm's whistle-blowing procedures.
Further guidance	• See Appendix 24.
	• See page 184 of Appendix A.

Appendix D

Compliance for Senior Management, the Back Office and Other Support Departments

This appendix provides a brief description of some of the Back Office and support departments that are likely to be found in the typical financial institution. It also describes some of the main regulatory requirements that are of relevance to them and summarizes the controls they are responsible for that have an impact on Compliance. Similar guidance is given in relation to senior management and the board of directors.

Department	
Senior management and the board of directors	253
Human Resources	256
Marketing	259
Finance	261
Company Secretariat	262
Internal Audit	264
IT	265
Legal	268
Operational Risk	269
Back office (Operations)	271
Tax	274

Department	Senior management and the board of directors
Typical activities	Senior management are responsible for the corporate governance of the firms in their charge. 'Corporate governance' is an expansive concept but it can be summed up as: the direction and management of corporate affairs in order to maximize shareholder (or other relevant stakeholder) value. In most firms is likely to involve the following types of activity:

- Setting strategies for the firm and reviewing their implementation.
- Reviewing performance of the firm and its employees.
- Receiving, reviewing and acting upon management information reports, and assessing whether the content and frequency of these is adequate.
- Setting remuneration policy and approving annual or periodic compensation reviews.
- Monitoring risk, and taking corrective action where appropriate.
- Reporting to shareholders and/ or other stakeholders.
- Setting the management structure and reporting lines and assessing their ongoing adequacy and appropriateness.

(Continued)

Department	Senior management and the board of directors
	• Delegating authority to individual staff members or sub-committees and ensuring that responsibilities and the scope of delegated authority are understood. • Succession planning for senior staff (who should in turn do this for their own teams). • Considering and addressing key person risk. • Considering and resolving problems that have been escalated; and last but not least, • In the eyes of our regulators, senior management are responsible for Compliance.

Areas of regulatory relevance

Senior management responsibility for Compliance	• As has been stated elsewhere in this book, in the eyes of the FSA and many other regulatory bodies, senior management is responsible for a firm's Compliance arrangements. • Day-to-day activities may have been delegated to the Compliance Officer but ultimately, the buck stops with senior management, as witnessed by the growing trend for the FSA to send out 'Dear CEO letters' when it wishes to highlight a particular regulatory concern. It does not send out 'Dear Compliance Officer letters'! • In addition to responsibility for Compliance the FSA also sets out other (extensive) responsibilities in its Senior Management Arrangements, Systems and Controls Sourcebook. • Senior management should receive full training as to the extent and nature of their regulatory responsibilities, and the consequences they may face if they do not meet these responsibilities appropriately.
Apportionment and oversight	• From a reading of the FSA's Senior Management Arrangements, Systems and Controls Sourcebook it is clear that senior management's responsibilities are extensive and that there is going to be a need to delegate. • Delegation is fine, but under the apportionment rules (SYSC 2), division of responsibilities must be clearly documented to show how each function that has been delegated ultimately feeds back into senior management. • The use of up-to-date staff organizational charts is useful for this purpose.
Approved Persons	• All directors and some senior managers will need to be registered with the FSA as Approved Persons.
Chinese walls	• In order to be able to adequately control and direct the firm, senior management are normally deemed to sit above a firm's Chinese walls to have access to all the information they require to do their work effectively. • This may be problematic when a senior manager from a public side department has access to information about private side transactions (for example a manager of a brokerage team having access to the deal pipeline of the new issues team). • In bigger firms with a sufficiently large senior management team it should be possible for only the chief executive and a couple of his closest colleagues to have free access to all information, but in many firms, there are not enough staff to arrange things in this way.

- All members of senior management who sit above a firm's Chinese walls should receive very detailed training about the nature of the conflicts of interest that they may encounter as a result of sitting 'above the wall', and how such conflicts should be managed.

Insider dealing

- Due to the extent of their responsibilities it is likely that senior management in listed firms will have access to inside information in relation to that firm.
- Personal dealing in company shares by directors should be kept under very close scrutiny to ensure their priviledged information is not abused.
- Compliance should ensure that directors and other management staff are aware of, and comply with, the restrictions on personal dealing imposed by the Model Code.

Data protection

- Due to the nature of their day-to-day activities and responsibilities, senior management will have access to a considerable amount of personal information relating to the firm's employees and clients.
- Senior management should therefore be aware of the requirements of the Data Protection Act 1998 and the procedures that the firm has implemented in order to ensure compliance with it.

Confidentiality

- Due to the nature of their day-to-day activities and responsibilities senior management will have access to a considerable amount of confidential information about the firm, its group, its clients and its employees.
- Senior management should be aware of the importance of treating this information appropriately and there should be adequate security arrangements in place to maintain confidentiality. This may include the availability of lockable storage space and the use of passwords to access information held electronically.

Company announcements

Senior management of listed firms should be careful only to disclose inform-ation about their companies in accordance with the FSA's Disclosure rules.

Market abuse

- It is very much in senior management's interests to ensure that their firm is seen in a positive light – the more successful their firm, the more successful its managers appear, and senior management may also own sizeable portfolios of shares and share options in their firms which they clearly want to see rise in value.
- In the light of the above, senior management should be aware that if they take any action with a view to giving the market a false impression of the company's prospects this is likely to constitute market abuse, which is a criminal offence.

Companies Act responsibilities

- Directors should be fully aware of their responsibilities and liabilities under Part X of the Companies Act 2006.
- If an employee also serves as a director of an overseas company, care should be taken to ensure that he is aware of his legal responsibilities as a director in the relevant jurisdiction.

Outside interests

- Under the Companies Acts 2006 directors are required to act in such a way as to promote the success of the company; they must also avoid conflicts of interest.
- Where directors have outside interests beyond the scope of the firm, or act as directors for another non-group company, this may create a conflict of interest in terms of where their allegiances lie: do they feel more loyal towards your firm and its customers? Or are they more interested in promoting the interests of the external firms of which they are directors, potentially to the detriment of your own firm or customers?

256 Essential Strategies for Financial Services Compliance

(Continued)

Department	Senior management and the board of directors
	• This is a sensitive area and a register should be maintained showing directors' outside interests and external directorships. This should be periodically reviewed for conflicts by Compliance. • Consider imposing the requirement that no external directorships should be accepted without prior Compliance approval.
Board/management meetings	• Sensitive information that may give rise to a conflict of interest will frequently be discussed at board or management meetings. • Procedures should be incorporated into the terms of reference for each committee or formal management meeting so that such situations can be dealt with appropriately and senior management should be given training in this regard. • Where meeting attendees find themselves conflicted they should generally disclose the conflict and either absent themselves from the meeting or abstain from taking part in any vote or decision making when their independence may be compromised.
Risk management	• Senior management should be constantly reviewing the risks faced by the firm, ensuring that appropriate levels of risk tolerance are set, that risk levels do not exceed these tolerances and that appropriate risk mitigation programmes are in place. • As a minimum, the FSA requires senior management to control risk in the following areas: – insurance; – financial resources (market risk, credit risk, liquidity risk etc.); – operational risk; – risk resulting from the firm being part of a larger group; – conflicts of interest; – outsourcing; – compliance; – internal audit; – financial crime; and – employees and agents.
Data protection Confidentiality	Due to their position within the firm members of senior management will often have access to confidential information about clients, staff, the firm and its group. Such information must be stored securely and should only be used for legitimate purposes.
Further guidance	See Appendix 24.

Department	Personnel/Human Resources (HR)
Typical activities	• Recruitment. • Disciplinary proceedings (including employment tribunals). • Dismissal. • Promotion. • Internal transfers and secondments. • References – inwards and outwards. • Remuneration. • Employee training, development and competency programmes. • Retention of employee personnel files. • Approved Person applications and review of ongoing employee fitness and propriety.

Areas of regulatory relevance

References	• References should be obtained for all new employees. • Offers of employment should be made subject to the receipt of adequate references. • References should be obtained prior to the commencement of employment. • Reference notes should be made for each employee who leaves the firm in case of future requests for an Approved Person reference.
Probation	All permanent staff should be subject to a 3- to 6-month period of probation during which time they should demonstrate their competence and suitability for employment by the firm (subject to legal restrictions in various jurisdictions).
Employment offers	Offers of employment should be made subject to • the receipt of adequate references; and • documentary evidence of required academic and/ or professional qualifications.
Contracts of employment	• All staff should have a contract of employment. • Continuance of employment should be made conditional on compliance with applicable regulatory and legislative requirements. • Contracts of employment should include provision for a failure to comply with regulatory requirements constituting gross misconduct.
Disciplinary cases	• HR procedures should allow for disciplinary action to be taken for breaches of regulatory and legislative requirements. • Disciplinary procedures should comply with the terms of relevant legislation such as the Human Rights Act 1998 and the Employment Act 2002.
Appraisals	• All staff should have appraisals at least annually. • Appraisals should be formal, and documented in writing. • Performance appraisals may be combined with the training and competence (T&C) assessment (see below).
Training – general	• All staff should receive regular training that is appropriate to their needs. • Certain staff will be subject to the detailed training requirements of the FSA's T&C rules. • Some HR departments have a dedicated Training Officer who coordinates training within the firm and keeps a record of training delivered and received.
Training – for Compliance department	• Various documents suggest the skills and personal qualities that Compliance staff should have. • The HR department should be able to help with forming a training and development strategy in terms of ensuring that Compliance department staff have the appropriate competencies to be able to perform their roles satisfactorily.
Approved Persons Training and competence (T&C)	• These areas are rarely the sole responsibility of the HR department although that arrangement is not unknown. • Even if HR does not take any responsibility for T&C or Approved Persons, HR management should be aware of the FSA's key requirements in these areas as they can have an impact on many areas that are within their domain, such as required qualifications, training, appraisals, etc.

(Continued)

Department	Personnel/Human Resources (HR)

Data protection	• As the custodians of the firm's personnel files, the HR department has access to a considerable amount of sensitive information about the firm's staff.
	• HR staff should therefore be aware of the requirements of the Data Protection Act 1998 and the procedures that the firm has implemented in order to ensure compliance with it.
	• In particular, HR staff should
	  – ensure that personnel files are kept secure and confidential;
	  – be familiar with requirements relating to subject access requests from staff members wishing to gain access to information that the firm holds on them; and
	  – understand that requests for employee information from an external party purporting to be a regulator or other official body should be referred to the Compliance (or Data Security) department unless they are certain that the caller is genuine.

Job descriptions	• All staff should have job descriptions in order to demonstrate apportionment of responsibility. • Job descriptions should be updated or reviewed at least annually
Remuneration strategy	• Remuneration strategies should take account of an individual's Compliance behaviour and his attitude to Compliance risk. • The firm's remuneration policy should be documented in writing.
Staff organisation charts	• All staff should have clear reporting lines. • Each area of the firm's activity should have a nominated person responsible for it. • Reporting lines and responsibilities should be documented in organizational charts which are updated on a regular basis. • HR staff should understand that dotted reported lines constitute a risk – activities undertaken by an employee with both a thick and a dotted reporting line might 'fall between the cracks' and not be subject to adequate supervision.
Induction	All new employees should receive an HR induction training session.
External directorships/ consultancies/ employment	• HR should be aware of staff who have external directorships, consultancy contracts or employment. • Where staff owe allegiances to other firms through external directorships, consultancy responsibilities and/or employment arrangements this creates scope for conflicts of interest – where would the relevant staff member's loyalty lie if the interests of a company of which he is a director compete with the interests of a client? • External employment and directorships arrangements should be subject to the written approval of senior management. • Such relationships should be subject to periodic review to ensure that they remain acceptable. • Where staff have contracts or directorships with overseas companies within the group their liabilities and responsibilities under the local legal system should be made clear to them.

HR manual	• Firms should have an HR manual that sets out the main conditions and procedures relating to key personnel matters. • At a minimum, the HR manual should cover the matters set out in this section.
Further guidance	See Appendix 24.

Department	Marketing
Typical activities	• Financial promotion. • Issuing press releases. • Internal communications. • Letterhead and signage. • Devising and managing advertising campaigns. • Promoting new product launches. • Organizing corporate entertainment. • Liaising with external advertising, marketing and PR agencies.

Areas of regulatory relevance

Nature of financial promotions	The Marketing department should be aware of the distinction between a customer communication and a financial promotion so that they know when the detailed the FSA rules on financial promotion should be applied.
Fair, clear and not misleading communications	The Marketing department should be aware that all communications they issue or approve should be clear, fair and not misleading.
Contents requirements for financial promotions	• The Marketing department should be aware that there are many detailed rules on the contents of financial promotions directed at retail customers. • Marketing staff should ensure that retail financial promotions are approved by an appropriate person (often a Compliance Officer) rather than by themselves, unless they have received the appropriate training and authorization to do so.
Cold calling	During the planning and live stages of an advertising campaign or marketing initiative the Marketing team should be mindful of the restrictions on cold calling and should not include this as part of a campaign unless they can confirm that that all regulatory requirements in this area have been considered.
Electronic and distance communications	• Marketing should be aware that there are detailed rules and requirements relating to appropriate customer communications effected at a distance or electronically. • Guidance should be obtained from Compliance prior to initiating activity in this area.
Unregulated collective investment schemes	Marketing should be aware of the restrictions on advertising and promoting unregulated collective investment schemes.

(Continued)

Department	Marketing
Consumer credit advertising	Marketing should be aware that there are detailed requirements on advertising and promoting consumer credit products and services.
Disclosure of regulatory status	• Marketing should ensure that any communications they send to retail customers include the appropriate statement as to the firm's the FSA regulated status. • The required disclosures are contained in GEN 4 Annex 1 of the FSA Handbook.

Market Abuse	• The Marketing team should be aware that promotional material can be used to commit market abuse.
	• The type of restriction that the Marketing team should be particularly aware of include the requirement not to
	
	  – disclose inside information; and/ or
	  – disseminating misleading information.

Policy on speaking to press	• The Marketing department will often be responsible for coordinating and supervising a firm's policy on speaking to the press. • This is especially important if your firm is facing negative media coverage, or if a certain aspect of your firm's activities is particularly topical (serious rules and/or legislative breaches, major customer complaints, client involved in money laundering scandal, etc.). • Contact with the press should be directed through the Marketing department so that a consistent message is conveyed and nothing inappropriate is disclosed. • It is useful to have a formal policy in this area.
Confidential information	Marketing should ensure that none of the information they distribute contains confidential details about either the firm, its group or a customer.
Research	If the Marketing department is involved with the dissemination of investment research the team should have a familiarity with the FSA's rules in this area.
Prospectuses	If the Marketing department is involved with the preparation and issue of prospectuses the team should have a familiarity with the FSA's Prospectus rules.
Inducements	• If the Marketing department manages corporate entertainment it should be familiar with the FSA's rules on inducements – corporate entertainment should not conflict with any duties owed to a client. • If in any doubt, Marketing should consult Compliance about what is appropriate.
Treating customers fairly	• Marketing and product promotion have been specifically identified by the FSA as falling within the scope of their Treating Customers Fairly initiative (see Treating Customers Fairly, Box 15 on page 340). • Marketing should have a thorough understanding of this initiative and should ensure that all their activities are compatible with it.
Further guidance	See Appendix 24.

Department	Finance
Typical activities	• The Finance department is responsible for many different functions within a firm, and may itself be split into several different units including those listed below. • There is some degree of crossover between the activities of the Compliance department and the various activities of the Finance team. Summary details are provided below.

Areas of regulatory relevance

Credit	• The Credit department is responsible for establishing and operating credit policies in keeping with the firm's business activities and credit risk appetite. Based on these policies it will assess the creditworthiness of prospective and existing counterparties of the firm, and determine what volume of business can be conducted with them, what credit limits will be imposed (effectively limiting the amount the firm may 'lend' to the counterparty), what collateral it will require, and so on. • In order to set appropriate credit limits the Credit department needs to have a sound knowledge of the firm's counterparties and consequently Credit may be able to help the Compliance department to improve their knowledge of a particular client for KYC purposes. • Individual credit applications generally contain detailed descriptions of specific trades and may thus be of use to Compliance in trying to gain a better understanding of a counterparty, or when conducting a monitoring review. • The Credit department is likely to have access to price-sensitive information (for example, on a credit application relating to financing arrangements for the takeover of a listed company) and appropriate confidentiality, Chinese walls and conflicts of interest controls should be implemented. • Credit applications for individuals are likely to be covered by the Data Protection Act 1998 and appropriate procedures and training should be implemented in this area.
Accounts Payable	• Accounts Payable is responsible for approving and processing payments made by or to the firm. • Compliance may find it useful to liaise with Accounts Payable in order to detect various irregularities such as fraud, or expense claims showing evidence of inappropriate payments or inducements. • Accounts Payable staff should be trained in relation to what may be considered suspicious or unacceptable, and should know to inform Compliance in such cases.

Financial Control	• The Financial Control department exercises a key function in any financial institution. It is engaged in many activities including
	
	   – preparation of statutory and management accounts in accordance with the relevant accounting standards;
	   – reporting to management, the FSA and company authorities such as Companies House; and
	   – preparing, monitoring and reporting the firm's regulatory Capital Resources and Capital Resources Requirements. This (very detailed) exercise involves evaluating the firm's effective permanent capital and measuring against it the value, weighted according to regulatory rules, of all of the risk positions the firm holds (investments, loans, OTC

(Continued)

Department	Finance

contracts, stock loan and so on). The sum value of risk-weighted positions must not exceed total Capital Resources.
- Compliance should be notified immediately if it appear that the firm is, or will shortly be, in breach of its Capital Resources Requirements.
- The Financial Control department can be expected to liaise with various external parties such as
  - the FSA (for prudential rule interpretation purposes);
  - statutory auditors; and
  - tax authorities.
- See Box 11, Prudential Regulation of Capital Adequacy on page 334.

Further guidance   See Appendix 24.

Department	Company Secretariat

Typical activities
- Compliance with Companies Act requirements.
- Organizing, attending and minuting board meetings.
- Maintaining the group structure chart.
- Liaising with Companies House and any investment exchanges of which the firm is a member.
- Coordinating and making official company announcements.

Areas of regulatory relevance

Organization charts
- Company Secretariat should be the guardian of the firm's structure chart, keeping track of those with whom the firm has close links such as individual shareholders and parent, subsidiary and sister companies.
- This is important information for the Compliance department to be aware of in relation to the FSA's rules on Controllers and Close Links (see below). It is also useful for general information purposes.

Close Links
- Regulated firms must ensure continuing compliance with the FSA's Threshold Conditions for authorization.
- Threshold Condition 2.3 relates to a firm's Close Links with others: firms must ensure that they do not have any Close Links with a person that may preclude the FSA from supervising the firm.
- Threshold Condition 5 (Suitability) requires a firm to ensure that persons with whom it is connected are, and remain, fit and proper.
- Company Secretariat should be aware of these requirements and should review the firm's Close Links on an ongoing basis.
- Company Secretariat should also be aware that if it looks as though the firm is likely to breach any Threshold Condition then the Compliance department should be informed immediately.

Controllers
- There are various requirements to notify the FSA in relation to controllers of a regulated firm.
- Company Secretariat will be responsible for administration concerning changes of control and may either be responsible for making these notifications or be required to inform Compliance, so that the Compliance Officer can do so.

Directors and non-executive directors
- Company Secretariat will generally be responsible for keeping a register of directors.

- Compliance and Company Secretariat should liaise closely in this regard so that
  - directors can be appropriately registered and deregistered under the Approved Persons rules; and
  - senior management responsibilities can be appropriately apportioned among directors.

Board and committee meetings and minutes

- Compliance should be aware of all material developments within the firm and a good way of keeping track is to review the minutes of board and other committee meetings that are often maintained by Company Secretariat.
- Company Secretariat should have a record of committee members and invitees. This should be reviewed periodically by Compliance for appropriateness – confidential information may be discussed at committee meetings and it may sometimes not be appropriate for certain information to be discussed in the presence of particular attendees as it could lead to a conflict of interest.

Outside interests

Company Secretariat should be aware of any outside interests of directors and should liaise with Compliance on this matter to ensure that there is no conflict with duties owed to the firm or to clients.

Data protection

- Company Secretariat is likely to hold personal information on a firm's directors, individual shareholders and potentially other senior management as well.
- The department should therefore be aware of the requirements of the Data Protection Act 1998 and the procedures that the firm has implemented in order to ensure compliance with it.

Confidentiality

- Company Secretariat is likely to hold confidential information about the firm and its group.
- Staff should be made aware of the importance of treating this information appropriately and there should be adequate security arrangements in place to maintain confidentiality. This may include the availability of lockable storage space and the use of passwords to access information held electronically.

Liaison with investment exchanges

For listed companies, Company Secretariat is often responsible for liaising with the relevant stock exchange, or discharges these responsibilities alongside the Compliance department.

Corporate governance

- Company Secretariat is often responsible for coordinating and/or managing a firm's approach to corporate governance.
- All firms should comply with the rules on senior management arrangements, systems and controls and listed firms should also comply with the Combined Code on Corporate Governance.

Disclosures to the public

- Company Secretariat is often involved with making disclosures to the public in relation to the company's internal affairs, profit, future prospects, etc.
- When a company is listed it is of vital importance that the department is aware of the laws and rules concerning insider dealing, market abuse and transparency – all disclosures should be compliant with requirements in these areas.
- Compliance (and the Legal department) should be consulted before disclosures are made if there is any doubt as to whether a disclosure is compliant or not.

Further guidance

See Appendix 24.

Department	Internal audit
Typical activities	The function of Internal Audit is to provide independent assurance to the board and senior management as to the risks a firm faces and how the firm is managing these risks. In order to achieve this, the principal Internal Audit functions can be summarized as follows: • Performing a risk review of the firm in order to prepare an annual audit plan. • Conducting reviews of the firm's activities in accordance with the above plan. • Conducting ad hoc reviews of company activities in response to changes in the internal risk environment. • Recommending corrective action so as to remedy control breaches and weaknesses. • Liaising with external audit.

Areas of regulatory relevance

Liaise with Compliance department	• The Internal Audit department can be a very useful source of information to the Compliance department in planning Compliance monitoring reviews, and it is always a good idea to consult with Internal Audit to see whether they have any relevant information to share. • Compliance should receive all Internal Audit reports as an aid to identifying areas of regulatory risk within the firm. • As a matter of course, Internal Audit should notify Compliance of any significant findings (without waiting for a report to be issued) so that any regulatory implications can be considered as soon as possible. • When planning Compliance monitoring work it is important to liaise with Internal Audit to ensure that there are no overlaps or gaps. • A Compliance department review may uncover control weaknesses that are outside the scope of the Compliance department but which need to be investigated further. In such situations the Internal Audit department should be informed so that they can carry out further review work if necessary.
Internal Audit review of Compliance	• Internal Audit can be expected to review the activities of the Compliance department on a fairly regular basis to ensure that it is fit for purpose – it pays to keep on their good side! • As well as reviewing the activities of the Compliance department, Internal Audit may also conduct reviews of the wider Compliance function and how Compliance procedures, controls and culture are embedded across the firm as a whole.
Approved Persons	• The Head of Operations may be registered with the FSA as an Approved Person conducting a Systems and Controls Function.
Confidentiality	• During the course of its review work Internal Audit is likely to have access to, and/or hold, confidential information about the firm, its group, its clients and/or its employees. • Staff should be made aware of the importance of treating this information appropriately and there should be adequate security arrangements in place to maintain confidentiality. This may include the availability of lockable storage space and the use of passwords to access information held electronically.

Chinese walls	• In conducting its review work Internal Audit staff will periodically be granted access to information held behind the firm's Chinese walls. • Such department members should be made fully aware of the nature of the information they have access to, and the corresponding procedures and controls with which they must comply.
Data protection	• During the course of its review activities the Internal Audit department is likely to have access to, use and/or compile personal data on all employees and clients. • Internal Audit should therefore be aware of the requirements of the Data Protection Act 1998 and the procedures that the firm has implemented to ensure compliance with it.
Further guidance	See Appendix 24.

Department	**IT**
Typical activities	• Maintaining existing IT systems. • Developing new IT systems. • Maintaining the telephone system. • Desk top support.

Areas of regulatory relevance

Record keeping	• The FSA imposes many record-keeping requirements on the firms it regulates and nowadays many records are kept electronically, meaning that the IT department has a vital role to play in a firm's record-keeping arrangements. • The IT department should be aware of the firm's key record-keeping requirements and should implement procedures so that all required data can be captured. • Compliance should be notified if it appears that there is likely to be a breach.
Transaction/trade reporting	• Trade and transaction reports are made to the FSA and to the relevant stock exchange electronically. • The IT department should be aware of the firm's trade and transaction reporting requirements and should notify Compliance of any problems in the IT systems covering this area.
Maintaining trading platforms	The majority of trading is done electronically (either using an exchange or via a multilateral trading facility) and the IT department should be adequately resourced to ensure that trading can continue uninterrupted.
Internet site	• The IT department will generally be responsible for maintaining the firm's internet site. • Internet sites are classed as financial promotions and should be subject to the same procedures and controls as financial promotions in any other format. • The IT and Compliance departments should implement joint procedures to prevent inappropriate and unapproved material being posted on the firm's intranet site.

(Continued)

Department	IT
	• Where information is supplied to clients via a website, IT (along with Compliance) should ensure that the information is accurate, kept up to date and is readily accessible. (This is part of an FSA requirement known as the 'website conditions'.)
Electronic products	The IT department will be instrumental in offering products electronically, such as online trading facilities, e-money and internet banking.
Data protection	• Some members of the IT department (network administrators, privileged access users or super users) will either permanently or periodically have access to personal information about staff and clients when maintaining the firm's computer systems or providing desk top support. • Such department members should therefore be aware of the requirements of the Data Protection Act 1998 and the procedures that the firm has implemented in order to ensure compliance with it.
Confidentiality	• During the course of their day-to-day activities some members of the IT department will either permanently or periodically have access to confidential information about the firm, its group, its clients and/or its employees. • Such department members should be made aware of the importance of treating this information appropriately and of never disclosing or using confidential information.
Staff surveillance	The IT department can play an instrumental role in monitoring staff behaviour with examples of controls that can be implemented including the use of electronic swipe cards to record who has entered restricted access areas of the office and the automated scanning of e-mails for sensitive words and phrases.
Chinese walls	• Some members of the IT department will permanently or periodically have either physical or electronic access to information held behind the firm's Chinese walls so as to be able to maintain IT systems and resolve IT problems. • Such department members should be made aware of the sensitive nature of the information they have access to, and the corresponding procedures and controls with which they must comply.
Data security arrangements	• IT should ensure that the firm has appropriate controls for maintaining data security. • Such controls include – password protection (including requirements for changing a password regularly, not writing it down or disclosing it, etc.); – restricted electronic access to certain areas of the firm; – firewalls; and – use of data classification policies to register material as either private or public; for example, a transaction processing system may comprise a data file, which is 'private' and a program file which is 'public'.

- Care should be taken to ensure that all electronic devices and communication systems are covered by the firm's data security arrangements. Nowadays, as well as the standard desk top computers and telephone landlines we have Blackberries, USB keys, laptops, instant messaging, etc. All of these may be used to store and/or transmit large amounts of company information and several are small enough to be easily lost.

Business continuity

The IT department is instrumental in ensuring that there is an adequate business continuity plan in place that is tested on a regular basis.

Compliance monitoring

- The IT department should be able to help the Compliance department with monitoring activities.
- Areas where electronic systems are likely to be of benefit include

  – systems for identifying suspicions of money laundering;
  – systems for identifying suspicions of market abuse;
  – non-market price transactions;
  – best execution;
  – exceptions reporting for conduct of business controls such as best execution; and
  – accessing files that have been electronically archived.

Reporting to the Serious Organized Crime Agency (SOCA)

The IT department should assist the Compliance department in maintaining its electronic link with SOCA for the reporting of suspicions of money laundering.

Compliance systems

- A number of Compliance activities can be undertaken electronically and the IT department should assist with the maintenance and development of such systems.
- Examples include

  – reporting and approval of personal account dealing;
  – reporting and approval of gifts;
  – complaints reporting and handling;
  – reporting suspicions of money laundering to the MLRO;
  – generation of key performance indicators.

Research distribution

Investment research is often distributed via an electronic platform and the IT department should assist in the maintenance of this system to ensure that all relevant customers gain access to the research at the same time.

Telephone recording

- Order, execution and settlement instructions are frequently given over the phone and telephone voice recording is commonplace (and in some cases mandatory) in order to avoid disputes and as a form of record keeping.
- The IT department is often responsible for voice-recording equipment and should have procedures in place in areas such as

  – maintenance of voice-recording equipment;
  – restricted access to voice-recording equipment; and
  – restricted access to voice-recording records.

Management information and reporting

- Management should have access to relevant information about the operation of the firm and the risks it runs.
- Such information is frequently collated and reported to management electronically, meaning that support from the IT department is vital in this area.

(Continued)

Department	IT
Customer communications	• If a firm communicates with its customers electronically it must ensure that customer information is stored and transmitted securely. • The IT department should undertake regular surveillance to ensure that the firm's security arrangements in this area are adequate.
Settlement	The IT department should ensure that the firm's electronic links to the clearing houses and settlement systems it uses are continuously operational.
Intranet site	• The IT department generally maintains and controls a firm's intranet site. • Compliance should liaise regularly with IT to ensure that Compliance policies, procedures, forms, manuals, etc., that are posted on the intranet site are accessible and up to date.
Further guidance	See Appendix 24.

Department	Legal
Typical activities	• Interpreting and advising on legislation of relevance to the firm. • Structuring transactions. • Negotiating and drafting legal contracts and trade agreements. • Handling complaints. • Handling litigation.

Areas of regulatory relevance

Liaise with Compliance department	• The Compliance department should liaise closely with the Legal department because there is overlap between their duties and routine activities in several areas.
	• Areas of relevance include
	
	   – assistance with understanding legislation which has an impact on the firm's regulatory environment; and
	   – notification to the Compliance department of serious matters of which the Legal department becomes aware that may have regulatory implications.

Data protection	• During the course of their day-to-day activities some members of the Legal department will have access to personal information about staff and clients (for example, when investigating a complaint or handling a staff disciplinary matter). • Such department members should therefore be aware of the requirements of the Data Protection Act 1998 and the procedures that the firm has implemented in order to ensure compliance with it.
Confidentiality	• Some members of the Legal department will have access to confidential information about the firm, its group its clients and/or its employees. • Such staff members should be aware of the importance of treating this information appropriately and there should be adequate security arrangements in place to maintain confidentiality. This may include the availability of lockable storage space and the use of passwords to access information held electronically.

Chinese walls	• Some members of the Legal department will periodically be granted access to information held behind the firm's Chinese walls – typical situations when this may arise include assisting with structuring a complex transaction or implementing confidentiality agreements. • Such department members should be made fully aware of the nature of the information to which they have access, and the corresponding procedures and controls with which they must comply.
Customer agreements	The Legal department should be able to assist the Compliance department in drafting customer agreements in accordance with the FSA rules, such as those in the Conduct of Business Sourcebook.
Exclusion of liability	The Legal department can help to review customer communications and promotions to ensure that there is no exclusion of liability as per COBS 2.1.2.
Complaints	The Legal department may be called upon to help with complaints handling if there is a particularly complex and serious matter to be dealt with.
Litigation	Litigation may have a regulatory impact and the Compliance department should be notified where appropriate.
Fraud	The Compliance and Legal departments will often work together in investigating cases of fraud.
Disciplinary action against the firm	The Legal department should be called upon to advise if the firm receives notification of regulatory action being taken against it by the FSA.
Disciplinary action against an employee	The Legal department can provide advice in relation to internal disciplinary procedures to ensure that where staff have broken the FSA or legislative requirements, appropriate internal action is taken which complies with employment law requirements.
Further guidance	See Appendix 24.

Department	Operational Risk
Typical activities	• The Basel Committee on Banking Supervision has defined operational risk as 'the risk of loss resulting from inadequate or failed internal processes, people and systems or from external events'. Examples of factors that might be covered by this definition include – fraud; – theft; – human error; – terrorist attacks; – IT failure; – epidemic; and – natural disasters. • Responsible for detecting, quantifying, controlling and reporting on all forms of operational risk faced by a firm.

(Continued)

Department	Operational Risk
	• Preparing and operating risk identification and measurement tools. • Reporting on risk to senior management. • Under Basel II, the Operational Risk department's findings will need to be quantified numerically and translated into risk numbers that can be fed into capital adequacy equations – the lower the level of a firm's operational risk, the lower the corresponding capital ration.

Areas of regulatory relevance

Interaction with the Compliance department	• Like Internal Audit, the Operational Risk department can be a very useful source of information for Compliance and in planning monitoring reviews and other activities: it is always a good idea to consult with Operational Risk to see whether they have any relevant information. • Procedures should be in place for Compliance and Operational Risk to share information so that Compliance is made aware immediately of any risk with a material regulatory impact that has been notified to, or identified by, Operational Risk. • Areas in which Compliance and Operational Risk are likely to be focused on the same types of control weaknesses include fraud, money laundering, market abuse and complaints.
Performance measurement and reporting	Operational Risk will probably require Compliance to prepare key performance indicators for regulatory control measurement so that as with every other department, it is possible to analyse risk statistics.
Confidentiality	• Certain members of the Operational Risk department are likely to have access to, and/or hold, confidential information about the firm, its group, its clients and/or its employees. • Such staff members should be aware of the importance of treating this information appropriately and there should be adequate security arrangements in place to maintain confidentiality. This may include the availability of lockable storage space and the use of passwords to access information held electronically.
Data protection	• During the course of its activities the Operational Risk department is likely to have access to, use and/or compile personal data on both employees and clients. • Operational Risk should therefore be aware of the requirements of the Data Protection Act 1998 and the procedures that the firm has implemented in order to ensure compliance with it.
Capital adequacy	• Operational risk capital is an important new component of Capital Resources Requirements post-Basel II and CRD. • It can be measured in varying degrees of detail, with the most sophisticated and granular (the Advanced Measurement Approaches) being the most risk-sensitive, and ostensibly being rewarded with correspondingly lower risk capital requirements. The more basic approaches (Basic Indicator and Standardized) are based on specified percentages of gross income, across the entity as a whole, or by business line.
Further guidance	See Appendix 24.

Department	Back Office (Operations)
Typical activities	• Trade settlement. • Processing outward and inward payments. • Processing corporate actions. • Safeguarding client assets and client money. • Holding collateral. • Reporting to customers. • Liaising with clearing houses. • Liaising with custodians. • Administering client accounts. • Trade reporting.

Areas of regulatory relevance

Money laundering and Market abuse	• Operations staff engaged in trade processing and settlement will have a very clear picture of the transactions that particular customers carry out. • As a result, Operations staff are in an excellent position to be able to identify suspicions of money laundering and market abuse. • Operations staff should be given regular training and guidance in terms of identifying suspicions of inappropriate activity and the subsequent reporting of such concerns.
Third party payments and receipts	• The Operations department manages the processing of customer and trade-related payments, both inward and outward. • These can constitute a greater than normal risk of money laundering as often the identity of the third party that funds are either being received from or paid to is not known; this person is not a customer of the firm but a contact of one of the firm's customers. • Procedures should be put in place to enable Operations to identify higher risk transactions of this kind so that additional vetting can be undertaken where necessary. • Periodic Compliance monitoring of this area should be carried out to assess the adequacy of controls.
Wire transaction information	• Legislation has recently been introduced to require wire transfer instructions to include the identity of the payer and for this information to remain on the instructions no matter how many institutions are involved in the processing chain. • These requirements have been introduced as part of the fight against money laundering and terrorist financing and should consequently be taken very seriously due to the global context in which we are operating. • Operations should receive training in relation to these requirements and procedures should be implemented to ensure that they are adhered to. • Periodic Compliance monitoring of this area should be carried out to assess the adequacy of controls.
Approved customers	• Depending on how the firm's systems are set up it is often possible for Operations staff to identify trades with persons who have not yet been approved as clients through the firm's official channels.

Department	Back Office (Operations)
	• Such approvals may cover matters such as lack of KYC, credit limit not yet set, customer agreement not in place, etc. • Instances of such unapproved activity should be reported to the Compliance department so that they can be dealt with appropriately.
Approved Persons	• The Head of Operations may be registered with the FSA as an Approved Person conducting a Significant Management Function.
Training and competence	• Certain Back Office activities undertaken on behalf of retail clients are subject to the FSA's rules on training and competence. Such rules apply to staff who on a day-to-day basis oversee a number of key functions including – safeguarding and administering client investments; – holding client money; and – administration relating to collective investment schemes. • Compliance should ensure that it is aware of which roles within its firm are covered by these rules – it should also ensure that the relevant people in Operations know which roles these are.
Confidentiality	• When processing trades and looking after client accounts, Operations staff will have access to confidential client information. • The Back Office will also have access to confidential information about the firm such as current and historic trading positions. • Employees should be aware of the importance of treating this information appropriately and there should be adequate security arrangements in place to maintain confidentiality. This may include the availability of lockable storage space and the use of passwords to access electronic processing systems and information held electronically.
Data protection	• The Operations department processes and has access to a significant amount of client information such as address, account number, account balances and trading history. • Operations staff should therefore be aware of the requirements of the Data Protection Act 1998 and the procedures that the firm has implemented in order to ensure compliance with it.
Chinese walls	• Operations staff will not generally have a need to work on the private side of the firm's Chinese walls. • Despite this, however, there may occasionally be times when a Front Office department working on a 'private side' deal needs to involve Operations to ensure that the transaction can be adequately processed if it is not standard for the firm. • Any Operations team members with access to private side information should be made fully aware of the nature of the information they have access to, and the corresponding procedures and controls that they must comply with.
Transaction reporting	• With certain exceptions, transactions should be reported both to the FSA and the exchange on which they were executed. • Transaction reporting is generally the responsibility of the Back Office and Compliance should ensure that staff are aware of the transactions that need to be reported and the time limits for doing this. • Transaction reporting should be subject to periodic review by Compliance to ensure that relevant requirements are being adhered to.

Client money
Safe custody
Collateral
	• The FSA's custody, collateral and client money rules are complex and they will generally be the day-to-day responsibility of the Operations department.
	• Key requirements include
	
	   – conducting risk assessments of custodians;
	   – provision of custody agreements;
	   – sending client assets statements.
	
	• Compliance should ensure that Back Office staff are familiar with their responsibilities in this area and should keep them up to date with any changes.
	• Compliance monitoring activities should be undertaken on a regular basis and the area will be subject to a once yearly review by external audit, the results of which will be reported to the FSA.
	• Operations should also be aware that collateral held by the firm in relation to non-regulated activities such as syndicated loans will not be covered by these rules.

Customer
communications
	• Back Office staff regularly communicate with clients for many reasons including to
	
	   – confirm or change settlement instructions;
	   – clear up settlement queries; and
	   – make certain reports as required by the FSA (see below).
	
	• Compliance should ensure that relevant Back Office staff are aware of the requirement to make customer communications fair, clear and not misleading.
	• Back Office should also have security procedures in place to prevent confidential information being provided over the phone to callers purporting to be a customer.

Voice recording	• Back Office staff who agree or discuss settlement instructions over the phone should be subject to voice recording.
Settlement	The Back Office should have systems in place to ensure that where it undertakes trade settlement on behalf of a client, the firm is able to deliver the relevant assets to the correct account as promptly as possible.
Trade confirmation and *Periodic reporting*	• The provision of trade confirmation notes and periodic statements will generally be the responsibility of the Back Office. • Compliance should ensure that relevant staff are aware of the content and timing requirements the FSA imposes on these communications and should keep Operations up to date of any changes. • Compliance monitoring activities should be undertaken on a regular basis to ensure that relevant requirements are being adhered to.
Hold mail	• Customers may sometimes request that communications addressed to them from the firm not be dispatched but be retained by the firm on their behalf. • Such 'hold mail' services are generally administered by the Back Office and arrangements should be in place to ensure that relevant documents are stored securely. • Operations should also be aware that hold-mail accounts constitute a higher than normal risk of money laundering as it is harder to be confident of a customer's address if they are not receiving post. • Any suspicions should be reported to the MLRO, and Compliance should subject this area to periodic review.

(Continued)

Department	Back Office (Operations)
Complaints	• Due to the regular contact that Back Office staff have with customers they may be more likely than some others within the firm to receive customer complaints and staff should therefore be familiar with the firm's complaints procedures.
Whistle blowing	• As a control department one of the functions of the Back Office is to spot instances of malpractice. • Compliance should ensure that Operations team members have confidence that they will not suffer any recriminations if they report irregularities, and they should be familiar with the firm's whistle blowing procedures.
Further guidance	See Appendix 24.

Department	Tax
Typical activities	• Ensuring that the firm pays the correct amount of tax. • Filing tax returns. • Providing advice internally in relation to – the tax treatment of certain products and services; – double taxation arrangements; – tax structuring; and – tax issues generally.

Areas of regulatory relevance

Tax disclosures	• A number of the FSA's conduct of business rules relate to tax disclosures. • These requirements include – COBS 4.5.7 and 4.7.4 – information about tax treatment in financial promotions; – COBS 5.2 and associated annexes – tax disclosures relating to E-Commerce business; and – COBS 6.1.9 – disclosure of any client tax payable by the firm.
Customer tax reporting	• Under the European Savings Tax Directive some financial services firms (those that are paying agents) are required to report information on savings income paid to individuals to HM Revenue and Customs (HMRC). • HMRC also has the power under section 20 of the Taxes Management Act 1970 to require financial institutions to provide it with details of account holders. • Customers who are found not to be paying the correct amount of tax for their offshore accounts may be accused of money laundering – your firm does not want to be implicated in this so you should have arrangements in place to detect indications of tax evasion involving customers with offshore accounts. • Also ensure that any customer information provided to HMRC is handled in accordance with the Data Protection Act 1998.
Prudential management	A number of the FSA's prudential rules relate to tax matters.

Permanent establishment	• If a firm conducts a considerable amount of business in an overseas jurisdiction it may be deemed to have a permanent establishment there even if it does not have an office there. • If this happens, the firm may be liable to pay tax in that jurisdiction (and for the record, it may also be deemed to be conducting unauthorized investment/banking business in that country).
Tax evasion/fraud/money laundering	• Tax evasion is a type of fraud and consequently any proceeds will be deemed criminal property. • Handling criminal property is likely to be deemed money laundering and any suspicion or knowledge should be reported to the MLRO and potentially also to SOCA. • Staff should be trained on how to identify potential tax fraud, especially if their activities are in more tax-sensitive areas such as working with the Front Office in relation to offshore banking and trade finance.
Transaction structuring	• Some transactions can be structured in various ways with a similar financial outcome but with a different tax (for example, withholding tax) treatment. • Some structures will be more favourable than others and it is important that such structures stay on the right side of the line that divides tax avoidance from tax evasion.
Trading taxes	• Trading taxes include stamp duty/stamp duty reserve tax on shares and VAT payable on some commodity trades. • Firm's and their clients will have to pay this tax each time they purchase shares. • Trading taxes should be disclosed to customers.
Tax forms for customers	• In some cases it is necessary for clients to complete an official tax form in order to obtain the most favourable tax treatment. • A brief summary of some of the most commonly used tax forms is provided in Appendix 22. • The tax department should be able to provide advice in relation to the use of these forms.
Suitability and advice	• Front Office staff may advise clients in relation to their personal financial planning. • Such advice may relate to counselling clients on how to maximize their tax position by, for example, ensuring that inheritance tax and capital gains tax exemptions are used. • Advice may also cover tax free wrappers such as ISAs, Child Trust Funds and pensions.
Further guidance	See Appendix 24.

Appendix E
Compliance Conundrums – What Would You Do?

This appendix consists of examples of the types of situation that occur regularly in the 'real world' which might leave you uncertain of how to proceed. Remember that the commentary provided is simply a guide on some of the key issues to consider, some of the most relevant legislative and regulatory provisions (based primarily on the UK environment) and some possible actions that you could take. It is not legal advice and should not be taken as definitive guidance on actions you should take if you ever find yourself in one of the situations described. You should adapt your responses to the specifics of your own firm's activities and customer base, and seek professional legal advice if required.

Conundrums index	
Key issues	**Dilemma/s**
Market abuse/market conduct	1, 4, 5, 6, 7, 8, 9, 10, 11, 13, 16, 17, 18, 26, 27, 32, 45, 46, 50, 51, 55, 58, 59, 60, 65, 68, 74
Client's best interest rule	1, 2, 3, 4, 6, 11, 20, 31, 39, 40, 41, 42, 49, 52, 53, 57, 69, 70, 72
Chinese walls	1, 7, 10, 13, 45, 47, 48, 50, 51, 55, 58, 60, 65
Suitability and appropriateness	2, 3, 4, 39, 40, 42, 57, 69
KYC	3, 15
Churning	4
Inducements	4, 20, 44, 53, 56, 70
Personal Account Dealing	5, 7, 8, 9, 16, 17, 18, 26, 46, 59, 67, 68, 73, 74
Insider Lists	5, 7, 9, 10, 13, 16, 26, 32, 59, 60, 74
Watch and restricted lists	7, 9, 10, 14, 26, 32, 50, 59, 60
Conflicts of Interest	10, 13, 14, 18, 19, 20, 21, 30, 44, 45, 47, 48, 53, 55, 56, 57, 58, 70, 73
Best Execution	11, 52, 53, 72
Anti-Money-Laundering Controls	11, 15, 22, 23, 24, 28, 29, 43
Voice Recording	12
Data Protection	12, 61
Confidentiality	12, 13, 14, 47, 48, 61

(Continued)

Key issues	Dilemma/s
Exclusivity	14, 47
External Directorships	19
Remuneration Policy	21, 57
Corruption	24
Approved Persons	25, 35, 37, 62
Fitness and Propriety	25, 31, 35, 37, 66, 67
Independence of research	30, 55, 56
Training and Competence	31, 35, 38, 62, 65
Senior management systems, arrangements and controls	31, 64
Permitted activities	33, 40, 62
Relations with regulators	34, 36, 37, 71
Competent Employees Rule	35, 38, 43
Risk Warnings	39
Aggregation and allocation of orders	41, 49
Investment and borrowing powers	42
Treating Customers Fairly	46, 71
Client order handling	52
Record Keeping	61, 64
Terms of business/client agreements	63
Information about the firm, its services and remuneration	63
Supervision	64, 65
Disciplinary Action	66
Research Controls	73

Dilemma 1	A Fund Manager has recently placed a pending order, which looks likely to be filled later that day, to buy a significant number of shares in ABC Company for the funds that he manages. Before the order has been filled, he learns from a Research Analyst colleague that before the end of the week they will be issuing negative research on ABC Company, and that this will likely push the share price down. The Fund Manager asks you whether he can cancel the pending order.
Key issues	• Market abuse/market conduct. • Client's best interest rule. • Chinese walls.
Comments and possible solutions	• You may feel intuitively that in order to act in the client's best interests the order should be cancelled immediately as you have been told that the share price is likely to fall soon. *However*, the likely drop in value may well be inside information, and therefore anyone acting upon it could be accused of market abuse.

- Before making your decision, consider whether the information disclosed by the Research Analyst really is price sensitive.
- Also consider whether, and where, the shares are listed as this will determine which legislative and regulatory provisions apply.
- Remember that this situation should not have arisen in the first place: the Research Analyst should know not to disclose such information about his work and some of the resultant actions you might wish to take include
  - disciplining the Research Analyst;
  - disclosing a suspicion of market abuse to the FSA;
  - providing training to the Research team and the Fund Management team on market abuse controls;
  - investigating whether there have been any previous instances of inappropriate information flows from the Research team to other areas of your firm; and
  - conducting a full review of the effectiveness of your Chinese walls.
- Given that this undesirable situation has already arisen, one of the most practical ways to tackle it is to 'freeze' the Fund Manager so that he may no longer make investment decisions until the relevant research has been released – pass his accounts for temporary management to another member of his team.

Dilemma 2	During a periodic monitoring review you see that a suitability fact find has been completed for Mr Brown (with whom your firm acts as investment adviser) which indicated that he had a very low-risk appetite, but his account manager has bought a number of AIM listed shares for him. You question the account manager who tells you that they advised Mr Brown against buying the shares, but that he insisted on going ahead anyway.
Key issues	<ul><li>Client's best interest rule.</li><li>Suitability and appropriateness.</li></ul>
Comments and possible solutions	<ul><li>AIM shares are generally considered to be higher risk than shares with a 'main market' listing as they tend to be less liquid, their issuers have less of a track record and listing rules are less stringent. The purchase of AIM shares would therefore seem incompatible with the client's very low risk appetite.</li><li>Check to see whether there is an audit trail evidencing that Mr Brown insisted on the AIM share transactions even though he was advised against them. If so, the situation is technically acceptable although you have to question whether it really complies with the spirit of the client's best interest rule.</li><li>Think about whether Mr Brown's suitability fact find is up to date; perhaps his risk appetite has changed and the fact find should have been updated to show this.</li><li>If Mr Brown still insists that he has a low risk appetite, consider whether your firm really wants him as a client: unless your records are immaculate his contradictory messages could leave you vulnerably to complaints, civil action under FSMA s150 and enforcement action by the FSA.</li></ul>

Dilemma 3	A member of your Wealth Management team asks you for advice as a prospective new client is refusing to complete a suitability fact find even though it has been explained to them that it is for their own benefit, so that the firm can give them the best possible advice. The client finds the questions intrusive and says that his education, employment etc are none of the firm's business.
Key issues	• Client's best interest rule. • Suitability. • KYC.
Comments and possible solutions	• You could try speaking to the client yourself to explain why the fact find is needed – perhaps the Account Executive has not done a good job of this. • Also explain that any other EEA firm will be subject to the same requirements in this area so the client is unlikely to find a firm willing to deal with him without a fact find. • If the client still will not complete the fact find, you will not be able to provide him with an advisory service, although depending on the type of investment involved, the firm may be able to provide execution-only services. • Question whether you really want to accept this person as a client – could his insistence on privacy also be incompatible with your KYC obligations? Does the client have something to hide? • Finally, take another look at your fact find document – perhaps it really is too intrusive.

Dilemma 4	A junior member of the Compliance team has been reviewing the portfolio management function and has noticed the following trades for a single client: • 10/6/07 – 9:23 – buy 100 shares in Company ABC; • 10/6/07 – 10:50 – buy 250 shares in Company ABC; • 10/6/07 – 1:30 – buy 175 shares in Company XYZ; • 11/6/07 – 10:01 – sell 100 shares in Company ABC; • 11/6/07 – 11:05 – buy 130 shares in Company XYZ; and • 11/6/07 – 3:45 – buy 75 shares in Company ABC. Your colleague thinks the trading pattern looks somewhat unusual and asks for your advice.
Key issues	• Client's best interest rule. • Suitability. • Churning. • Inducements. • Market abuse/market conduct.
Comments and possible solutions	• Check the client's investment objectives – perhaps he has given instructions for his account to be very actively managed in order to take advantage of intra-day price movements. • Check the performance of the shares over the period in which the trading took place to see whether the trades were in response to price movements. • Check that the client is aware of the transactions that have taken place and has not complained about them.

- Review the Fund Manager's records showing the rationale for this trading activity.
- Although the trading pattern could be perfectly acceptable it could also point to a number of improprieties, including:
  - *Churning* – Trading too frequently in order to generate commission which is earned on a per trade basis.
  - *Inappropriate inducements* – Is the Fund Manager putting excessive business through a particular broker in order to return a favour? (Check your inducements records.)
  - *Painting the tape* – Is the Fund Manager undertaking these trades in order to generate a false view of the market (market abuse)?

Dilemma 5	A member of your Treasury department asks you whether they are permitted to buy shares in your employer, which is listed on the London and New York stock exchanges.
Key issues	• Market abuse/market conduct. • Personal account dealing. • Insider lists.

Comments and possible solutions	• Whether the person can trade or not will depend on a number of factors including whether
	
	  – he has inside information about your firm or its group;
	  – the request is for a trade during a 'close period' immediately preceding a corporate announcement; and
	  – your firm permits trading in your company's shares.
	
	• Assuming that your insider list controls are working well, you can use them to check whether this person is listed as an insider.
	• Company Secretariat or Legal should be able to advise you on whether an announcement is about to be made.

Dilemma 6	One of your firm's investment managers covers Chinese shares and is considered to be an expert in that market. He regularly writes for the industry press on matters to do with the Chinese market and also frequently provides commentary on TV. You keep a record of his media involvement and decide to compare this with trading activity for his clients. You notice certain patterns emerging in that he will sometimes promote a share in the press and then, shortly after, sell that share from his clients' portfolios; on other occasions he will express negative opinions about a share, but then buy it for his clients.
Key issues	• Market abuse/market conduct. • Client's best interest rule.
Comments and possible solutions	• *Market abuse* – The Fund Manager's actions may indicate market manipulation in that he could be attempting to either raise or lower a share price in order to influence the performance of his client portfolios. Do you think he is engaging in trash and cash/pump and dump? • *Client's best interest* – If the Fund Manager is not supportive of a particular stock, then why is he buying it for his clients; and if he thinks a stock is doing well, then why is he selling it?

(Continued)

- Ask the Fund Manager to provide a full rationale for any apparently anomalous trading decisions. He may be able to explain.
- Obtain independent guidance as to whether the views expressed by the Fund Manager can be considered correct.
- If you conclude that the Fund Manager's actions were inappropriate you should consider
  - compensating the relevant clients if they lost out;
  - reporting a suspicion of market abuse to the FSA; and
  - taking disciplinary action against the Fund Manager.
- Note that as the activity relates to activities and shares on the Chinese markets (with no indication of the involvement of a 'regulated market' in the EEA) then the provisions of the Market Abuse Directive would not apply, although the FSA's market conduct principle would be relevant.

Dilemma 7	Your firm is currently providing advice to ABC Ltd, a private company, on how to secure some venture capital funding. Although it is a private company, its shares are relatively widely held and you notice that just prior to a funding deal having been secured, one of your colleagues buys shares in ABC Ltd from one of its founding members.
Key issues	• Market abuse/market conduct. • Chinese walls. • Watch and restricted lists. • Insider lists. • Personal account dealing.
Comments and possible solutions	• It seems like your internal PA dealing arrangements do not require prior approval in all cases as you did not know about the transaction until after the event; you may want to review this in the light of what has happened. • Does your PA dealing policy permit trading in issuers who are also clients? If it is silent on this point you may consider amending it to cover this situation, or providing some separate guidance. • Consider whether your colleague could have known of the ABC Ltd transaction, i.e. are your Chinese walls adequately robust? Is he recorded on the insider list? • As ABC Ltd is not listed, your colleague's action would not amount to insider dealing even if he did have sensitive information at the time of his trade (unless, potentially, another company within the ABC group is listed). However, the FSA's market conduct principle may still be relevant. Your colleague's actions also raise questions about his integrity. • If you find out that there has been a leak of information from behind the Chinese wall you will need to investigate to find out who was responsible and how this came about. Remedial and possibly disciplinary action should also be taken. • Many firms do not use watch/restricted or insider lists when dealing with companies that are not listed as market abuse (in the strict legal sense) cannot take place due to the fact that no regulated market is involved. What do you want your firm's policy to be on this? Remember that if you do not record unlisted companies on these lists, you should still have some other sort of mechanism in place for identifying conflicts of interest.

Dilemma 8	One of your senior employees is also a director of another firm, XYZ Company, owned largely by one of his friends. He asks you whether he is permitted to make a personal investment in XYZ Company.
Key issues	• Market abuse/market conduct. • Personal account dealing.
Comments and possible solutions	• Consider whether XYZ Company or its group has any listed shares in issue. If so, the provisions of the various market abuse and disclose laws will be relevant. • Determine whether the person in question could have any inside information in relation to the transaction he wants to undertake by dint of his position as a director. If so, he should clearly not be permitted to go ahead. • If you feel uncomfortable about approving the transaction even though you cannot identify any impropriety, you could warn the manager about insider dealing risk and then require him to certify in writing before trading that he does not have inside information, and that he understands that if he does come into possession of such information at any time in future, this may impact his ability to sell the shares he wishes to buy. • If neither XYZ Company nor its group is listed on a regulated market then the provisions of the Market Abuse Directive will not apply but you should still consider whether the FSA's market conduct principle, and the firm's own ethical guidelines, should be brought to bear.

Dilemma 9	Your Corporate Finance team had a mandate to provide investment advice to ABC Company (listed on the Paris Stock Exchange) that was terminated 6 months ago. A Corporate Finance team member who has joined the firm since the mandate with ABC Company was terminated now wants to buy shares in ABC Company.
Key issues	• Market abuse/market conduct. • Personal account dealing. • Insider lists. • Watch/restricted lists.
Comments and possible solutions	• Check the watch/restricted lists to see whether your firm still has any inside information on ABC Company. • Assess whether the person wishing to deal has any inside information – you should be able to check this by reviewing your insider lists, and through discussions with his line manager. You could also check whether he was involved with ABC Company during his previous employment. • It is unlikely, although not inconceivable, that the Corporate Finance team will still have any inside information 6 months after their mandate was terminated, especially if any financial statements have been issued since this time. • If you consider that the employee has inside information then he clearly cannot undertake the trade. Your internal procedures are also likely to prohibit his trade if the Corporate Finance team he works for still has inside information from their earlier mandate. • If you are sure that the employee does not have any inside information you should be able to approve the trade, but think about how this would be viewed by the market. It might give a bad impression even if there has been no impropriety. • To be conservative, you may wish to reject the trade, but if you do give approval, you could warn the employee about insider dealing risk and then require him to certify in writing before trading that he does not have inside information, and that he understands that if he does come into possession of such information at any time in future, this may impact his ability to sell the shares he wishes to buy.

Dilemma 10	Three months ago your firm provided a loan to XYZ Company, maturing in 4 years. An in-house Fund Manager now wishes to buy shares in XYZ Company for one of the funds he manages.
Key issues	• Market abuse/market conduct. • Insider lists. • Watch and restricted lists. • Chinese walls. • Conflict of interests.
Comments and possible solutions	• If XYZ Company is listed you will need to ensure that the firm does not hold any inside information that could be influencing the Fund Manager's intended trade – check your insider/watch/restricted lists – you should know automatically if this person has access to inside information, and/or whether inside information is still held by the firm. • However, 3 months after the loan was drawn down, it is relatively unlikely that this would be the case, even if the lending team had inside information in the first place. • If you suspect that the Fund Manager has inside information then clearly he should not be permitted to deal, and you should conduct a review as to how this information came into his possession if you do not think that it was in the normal course of business. Also question why he has not identified the sensitivities of the information he has. • If your Chinese walls are working well, it is unlikely that the Fund Manager has inside information but, all the same, you might consider that the situation does not feel right and not wish him to deal anyway. One way to approach this is to warn the Fund Manager of insider dealing risk and have him certify in writing that he has no such information. • Think carefully of potential conflicts of interest that could arise in future – due to their different ranking on insolvency the interests of your firm as a creditor of XZY Company are unlikely to be aligned with the interests of its shareholders (including the fund managed by your firm). If XYZ Company were to get into financial difficulty shareholders would tend to favour a long-term work-out in the interests of maintaining the company as a going concern whereas creditors would tend to prefer repayment, even through the initiation of bankruptcy proceedings.

Dilemma 11	A client gives an order for your firm to buy ABC Company shares when the price reaches 20 (they are currently trading at 25). The price gradually falls, 24, 23, 22 but then suddenly plunges to 15. You notice that the trade was filled for the customer at 20.
Key issues	• Best execution. • Client's best interest rule. • Market abuse/ market conduct. • Anti-Money-Laundering Controls.
Comments and possible solutions	• If you follow the client's instructions strictly then the trade at 20 discharges your execution obligations, but you should also consider whether it would have been in the client's best interests to trade at 15. • Ask the trader to talk you through the sequence of events, bearing in mind matters such as – prevailing market price at the time the trade was executed and whether the trader could have achieved a better price for the client before that point;

– whether there was there a reason to trade at 20 rather than 15, for example, was the trade part of a larger structure that required a particular execution price?
– was the best price, 15, available for the size of order placed by the client?

• Your concerns in this situation may include

– confirming that the trader did not execute at 15, fill client at 20 and keep the difference (a form of 'rat trading').
– market abuse and money laundering – if the client condoned a buy at 20 when they could have been bought at 15, you might be suspicious that the client was happy to lose out on the trade. Do you suspect that it was carried out for purposes other than for legitimate commercial or investment interests?

Dilemma 12

A client asks to speak to you because on reading the terms of business they have just received from your firm, they have noticed that their phone calls will be subject to voice recording and they object to this. They tell you that unless the voice recording is disapplied from their phone calls, they will not agree to do business with your firm.

Key issues

• Voice recording.
• Data protection.
• Confidentiality.

Comments and possible solutions

• Find out which department the client is dealing with as it is generally more important to have voice recording in place for departments that give and receive trade and settlement instructions (e.g. Sales and Trading and Operations).
• Determine whether there are any exchange rules that require voice recording to be in place.
• Is it company policy to record every single line used for client calls?
• Talk to the client; ask them what their concerns are and tell them about the data protection controls that you have in place to protect recorded conversations; perhaps this will allay their fears. Also explain that voice recording is there to protect the client's interests and remind them that most other firms will also have this control in place.
• It is likely to be impractical to agree to disapply voice recording for one client only. Are you sure you have the systems to comply with this? undertaking if you do decide to accommodate the client
• Ask yourself why the client objects to having their phone conversations taped. Do you consider this suspicious? Why do they not want a record of their activities? Are they going to be asking your firm to bend or break rules?

Dilemma 13

Your firm recently signed a confidentiality agreement with ABC Company, a large retail chain, in relation to the provision of corporate finance advice. The Institutional Lending team knows that a confidentiality agreement has been signed with ABC Company and as they are trying to increase their client base in the retail sector, they ask you whether they are allowed to see the information held by the Corporate Finance team who are refusing to share it.

Key issues

• Confidentiality.
• Conflicts of interest.
• Market abuse/ market conduct.
• Insider lists.
• Chinese walls.

(Continued)

Comments and possible solutions	• The Institutional Lending team may argue that as a confidentiality agreement has been signed with the firm, it should be possible to share relevant information freely within the firm, but this is very unlikely to be the case. • Check the terms of the confidentiality agreement that has been signed. It probably will permit access to confidential information only in relation to the specific transaction it covers, and not generally within the firm, thereby ruling out access with the Institutional Lending team. • Also consider market abuse and market misconduct issues: if the Corporate Finance team has inside information, then it may be an offence to pass that to colleagues in another part of the firm if this is done otherwise than in the proper course of their employment. • One of the most practical ways to tackle this situation is for the Institutional Lending team to ask the Corporate Finance team for an introduction to ABC Company on the basis that they may also be able to provide a useful banking service. That way ABC Company can decide whether there is a sound reason for making sensitive information available about themselves. • If information is shared with the Institutional Lending team this should be on the basis of a written agreement with the firm, and the relevant members of the team should be added to the insider list.
Dilemma 14	Your firm runs a private equity fund and also has an M&A team. Company XYZ is being sold and your M&A team have an advisory mandate to help a customer with their bid for it. You later notice that the firm's own private equity fund is also making a bid for Company XYZ, in competition with the M&A client.
Key issues	• Confidentiality. • Conflicts of interest. • Watch and restricted list. • Exclusivity.
Comments and possible solutions	• Check the terms of the agreement with the client – there may be a clause preventing the firm from working on a competing deal. • If there is no exclusivity you can go ahead if you think you have the appropriate infrastructure to manage the potential for cross-contamination of information between the deal teams. • Before you proceed, think about how the situation would be perceived by the M&A customer and by the market in general – you could be laying yourself open to accusations of malpractice and the potential for reputational damage is high. • At least think about notifying the M&A customer of the competing deal team situation, and the arrangements that you have implemented to protect their interests. • Be very careful to control inappropriate information flows and ensure that details of the proposal of one deal team do not leak to the other, for example if the Private Equity team gets to know the details of the client's bid, they would be able to improve upon it before making their own bid. • Make sure that physical and electronic Chinese walls are completely robust and increase your monitoring in this area. • Provide a written warning note to members of both deal teams reminding them of the sensitivities of the situation they are in and that they must observe strict confidentiality.

Dilemma 15	Your firm has recently started providing services to overseas customers where the due diligence regime is not the same as in the UK. When you ask prospective clients for KYC documentation, especially utility bills to prove their address, they often become offended and threaten to take their business to other firms which they maintain do not require them to provide such personal documentation.
Key issue	Anti-money-laundering controls.

Comments and possible solutions

- A client's address is an important aspect of their identity but obtaining a utility bill is not the only way to prove where they live.
- There is no absolute legal requirement to obtain a utility bill to verify address and this is just one of the methods suggested in the JMLSG Guidance Notes (see Appendix 1).
- What the Money Laundering Regulations 07 actually require is for firms to verify 'the customer's identity on the basis of documents, data or information obtained from a reliable and independent source'.
- In some jurisdictions post is not sent to home addresses – everything goes to a PO box because of poor postal services.
- Also, the security situation is such in certain countries that people are very wary of providing such personal information.
- In other cases, people simply find it insulting and irrelevant to have to prove themselves.
- Do your best to explain to your clients why you need to confirm their address but if you cannot get a utility bill there may be other options open to you:

  - Have the Account Executives visit the client at their home address.
  - Get a letter from their employer confirming their address.
  - Get a letter from a trusted professional, e.g. the client's lawyer or accountant to confirm their address.
  - Use the telephone directory.
  - Use the electoral role.
  - Some jurisdictions have other official address verification mechanisms such as tax records databases.

- Send the client a copy of the FSA leaflet on proving identity from the Money Made Clear range of guides which will explain to them why your firm is collecting KYC documentation. This helps to show the client that the request is official and a proper requirement, not just a whim of a nosey account executive.
- If your internal procedures are rigid think about making them more flexible so that ways of verifying an address other than a utility bill are acceptable.

Dilemma 16	A Research Analyst asks you whether he can buy shares in a company on which he issued a report 6 months ago, but has not covered since then in any detail.
Key issues	- Insider lists. - Market abuse/market conduct. - Personal account dealing.

Comments and possible solutions

- The Research Analyst should not deal if he has inside information – check your insider lists.
- Your internal policy may be that Research Analysts must not deal in any shares that he covers or has ever covered. In this case, there is no debate and the trade cannot go ahead.

(Continued)

- If you do contemplate allowing the trade, ask the Research Analyst (and his boss) if he is likely to cover the issuer again soon – if so, his actions may be viewed as suspicious by onlookers.
- Give the Research Analyst a written warning about insider dealing risk and the problems that he may face if he wishes to sell the shares at such a time when he is in possession of such information. Have him confirm in writing that he has read and understood the warning and that he does not have any inside information relating to the shares in question.
- The safest thing to do is not to approve the trade.

Dilemma 17	When carrying out a routine review of personal account trades you notice that a Research Analyst has recently issued a sell recommendation on XYZ Company, but within 2 days, bought a large number of XYZ Company shares.
Key issues	• Market abuse/market conduct. • Personal account dealing.
Comments and possible solutions	• The Research Analyst appears to have behaved in a way that is inconsistent with his recommendation – if he thinks the company is a 'sell', then why is he buying it for himself? You may suspect that he has engaged in a market abuse technique called trash and cash – spreading negative information about a company to lower its value and then buying the shares to profit as the value rises again. • Ask the Research Analyst to justify their behaviour as there may be a reasonable explanation: perhaps the analyst's research made the stock fall in value and now he thinks that the price has been corrected and so merits a buy – has he subsequently issued a buy recommendation? • If you suspect market abuse, you should report this to the FSA. • Given what has happened it seems as though there is no pre-approval for PA trades in your firm, or else the pre-approval process for PA trades does not take account of research that has recently been issued. Think about revising your procedures to address these matters. • Carry out a review of PA trades versus research recommendations and see if you can identify any other unusual situations that require further investigation.

Dilemma 18	A Fund Manager asks you whether they can buy shares in the funds that they manage.
Key issues	• Market abuse/market conduct. • Personal account dealing. • Conflicts of interest.
Comments and possible solutions	• Some clients will only invest in a fund if the Fund Manager himself has a sizeable holding in it as they consider that this shows commitment, belief in self and an alignment of interests: as his money is invested too, it is in his interests for the fund to do as well as possible. • Other people see this as a potential for conflict of interest and frown upon the practice as a Fund Manager's privileged information in respect of their fund enables them to take advantage of timing issues: buying into the fund just before good news is announced and selling just before bad news is announced. Therefore, if personal investment is permitted, it must be very closely monitored for signs of impropriety. • This is an internal policy decision that each firm needs to make for itself.

Dilemma 19   A member of your Back Office asks whether he may become a director of another company.

Key issues
- Conflicts of interest.
- External directorships.

Comments and possible solutions
- Before making a decision you should find out more information, such as

  - how much time will the person be required to dedicate to his directorship? If this is excessive, it may interfere with his working day at your firm;
  - is the other firm in an industry that competes with your own? If so, this could lead to a conflict of interests. For example, if your firm provides outsourced Back Office services and the company the person wants to join as a director also does this, then you are likely to feel that the situation presents too much of a conflict as it would be hard to see where the person's allegiances lay;
  - will the person get paid for his services and if so, could this remuneration impact his services to your own firm? and
  - does the person stand to gain any indirect benefits from the proposed directorship?

- If you decide to approve the directorship from a regulatory perspective then you should

  - liaise with HR and Company Secretariat as they may have separate procedures to follow for external directorships;
  - notify the FSA (if the employee is an Approved Person);
  - provide guidance to the person about the conflicts of interest he may encounter as a result of his directorship and how such conflicts should be managed; and
  - periodically review the continuing appropriateness of the directorship.

Dilemma 20   Your company deals with ultra high net worth individuals and one client, as a token of appreciation for services rendered, offers to repay the mortgage of one of your Investment Advisers. This involves a relatively small amount of money for the client, given their net worth, but a substantial amount of money all the same. The Investment Adviser is threatening to leave if he is not permitted to receive the gift as it would have such a material impact on the wellbeing of his family.

Key issues
- Inducements.
- Conflicts of interest.
- Client's best interest rule.

Comments and possible solutions
- What does your firm's Inducements Policy say? It is unlikely to permit a gift of this nature and size.
- Consider whether the acceptance of the gift would disadvantage any customers. Even if it appears that it would not, think about the future – if the Investment Adviser were to accept the gift it may well mean that going forward he feels beholden to the client and will feel obliged to give them preferential treatment over other customers.
- Speak to the client and explain why you do not think a gift of this size is appropriate but remember that in some cultures it is considered very insulting to reject a gift.
- Think about whether it is fair for one single employee to receive this acknowledgement. After all, he did not work alone and would have relied on the whole infrastructure provided by your firm and his colleagues.

- If the person maintains his threat to leave you should escalate this to senior management as you do not want to take the blame for driving staff away, especially if such staff are well respected.
- I can't think of any Compliance Officers who would support this mortgage repayment.

Dilemma 21	One of your firm's traders has come to you with a concern about the firm's remuneration strategy, which he says takes no account of risk. He complains that staff taking on very risky positions that are initially profitable are given extremely high bonuses, even though over the full life of the positions the firm is exposed to extreme risk. His manager thinks that he just has a chip on his shoulder as his bonus was not as high as that of some other people last time round.
Key issues	• Conflicts of interest. • Remuneration policy.
Comments and possible solutions	• The relationship between risk and remuneration is a very real concern across the financial services industry – traders take massive risks with positions that will take a few years to unwind, short-term profits come in, the trader gets a considerable bonus and leaves the firm; then the economy takes a turn for the worse and the once profitable position suddenly starts to make material losses. • Some firms are addressing this issue with remuneration strategies that take account of risk, using deferred bonuses and bonuses in the form of options so that the long-term success of the firm is linked to that of the employee. • However, unless you know that your firm's remuneration strategy is sub-optimal you need to look into this. Engage with your HR department and investigate whether things need changing – perhaps the complaint really is sour grapes on behalf of the trader. • If a policy change is required it is likely to be a hard slog as people, including senior management, are very sensitive about how they are paid.
Dilemma 22	You have recently updated your firm's customer identification procedures due to changes in the law and industry guidance. Your private client broking team is having particular difficulty in meeting the new standards that you have imposed and are threatening to walk out *en masse* to go to work for another firm where the standards are not as strict. They say that you are impeding their ability to do business and they are losing clients as a consequence.
Key issue	• Anti-money-laundering controls. • KYC.
Comments and possible solutions	• Review your new procedures – perhaps they really are too strict. • Ask the team what their specific concerns are, perhaps they have not understood what is actually being asked of them – have you provided adequate training? • Explain to the team the origin of the requirements – let them know that what you are asking them to do is actually based on law. • Benchmark your procedures against those of your peers. • Explain to the team that wherever they go, they will be faced with the same requirements to complete KYC. • Explain to the team how a robust KYC strategy protects them from legal and regulatory sanction, and damage to reputation. Give examples of some firms that have recently been fined for anti-money-laundering weaknesses. • Review the KYC information held on clients that have recently been taken on by the team to ensure that corners have not been cut. • If you cannot resolve the situation you need to escalate the matter to senior management.

Dilemma 23	A broker informs you of a suspicion that her client may be involved in money laundering. The client has just asked for a transfer of £5 million to be made to an account in the BVI, in the name of a person not known to the firm, but who the client says is her brother in law.
Key issues	Anti-money-laundering controls.
Comments and possible solutions	• Have the broker ask the client to explain the transaction (obviously this must not be done in a way that amounts to 'tipping off'). • Review the client's KYC file – does it indicate the likelihood of payments to people in BVI? Does this seem logical given the client's profile? • To whom will the payment be made? A well-known bank with headquarters in a FATF member, or one that you have never heard of with a dodgy name? This will clearly have an impact on how you feel about the payments. • Can you get any ID for the brother in law in order to verify his identity? If so, check to see whether his name is on any sanctions list. • If you cannot get comfortable with the payment you should make a report to SOCA and find a way of stalling the client until you receive SOCA's response so that you do not tip them off. Many firms would simply explain that they have very strict third party payment controls and they their internal procedures do not permit them to make such payments unless full disclosure is obtained.

Dilemma 24	Your firm has recently opened a branch in a new jurisdiction but is struggling to win any business. You understand that the market practice is to give prospective business partners small 'incentives' to ease the initial stages of the business relationship. You have prohibited your firm from doing this but your colleagues in the business argue that it is normal market practice and that all the other western banks operating in the jurisdiction do the same. If you do not allow the practice they fear that the new branch will fail, at a cost of millions of pounds to your firm. You do not want to take the blame for this.
Key issues	• Anti-money-laundering controls. • Corruption.
Comments and possible solutions	• Seek legal guidance in the country as to what is permitted under local laws and discuss the situation with your Legal department. • If possible, talk with your peers in the relevant jurisdiction to find out whether they are really behaving in the way that has been asserted, and if so, how they have made themselves comfortable with this. • There is a distinction between a blatant bribe and a 'grease payment', which is an amount paid to an official to expedite a service that is intended to be provided anyway. Bribery to influence a decision to choose your firm over another, for example, is definitely not appropriate, whereas grease payments are unfortunately sometimes the only way to get things done. The distinction between the two is sometimes very blurred. • Remember the provisions of the Foreign Corrupt Practices Act (see Appendix 6) – you do not want to get caught out by this US law. • And if your firm is accused of making or receiving inappropriate payments, gifts or incentives, you could also be pursued on charges of money laundering. • This is not a decision that the Compliance Officer should be taking alone and senior management as well as internal and external legal counsel should be involved in the discussion.

Dilemma 25	A former colleague of yours, now a good friend, has recently been offered a new job. He quotes you as a referee and his prospective employer sends you a copy of his CV relating to his time at your firm and asks you to confirm that it is correct. You notice that your friend's achievements during the time he worked with you are greatly exaggerated, but on the whole you have no reason to doubt that he will not be a very successful employee of the company he is hoping to join. You are not sure what to do.
Key issues	• Approved persons regime. • Fitness and propriety.
Comments and possible solutions	• Are you being asked to give a reference in a personal capacity, or on behalf of your company? • If it is on behalf of your company, follow your company's reference policy – most firms will only permit their references to indicate the time period and capacity in which the person worked for them rather than give any other detail, for fear of legal action. • Ask your friend about what is on the CV – perhaps you are mistaken. • If you are being asked to give a reference in a personal capacity then think very carefully about what you say if you think your friend is not being truthful. You do not want to be held liable by his prospective employer for having given a false reference. • If you are being requested to give a reference under the Approved Persons rules, you must think about how your friend's actions impact his fitness and propriety as questions in this area should be taken into consideration when references are being given.

Dilemma 26	One of the members of your Trade Finance department wishes to buy shares in one of his client companies but is not sure whether this is permitted under the firm's PA dealing policy.
Key issues	• Personal account dealing. • Market abuse/ market conduct. • Watch and restricted list. • Insider lists.

Comments and possible solutions	• Does your firm have a policy prohibiting staff from dealing in shares of their customers? In that case, the answer has to be no.
	• If not, decide on the merits of the situation.
	• Does your firm or the person have inside information on the client – check your watch/restricted insider lists and you should be able to find this out easily. Staff in the Trade Finance department are not particularly likely to hold inside information.
	• Would the trade disadvantage the client in any way?
	• Is the employee currently working on a transaction with the customer? If so, even if the employee does not have inside information when the trade is concluded, this is not going to look good.
	• If you decide to allow the trade:
	  – give the employee a written reminder about not trading on the basis of inside information, and about not being able to trade in future until such a time as they do have such information;
	  – require the employee to confirm in writing that he has no relevant inside information.

Dilemma 27	You have been asked to review a piece of research that your firm is about to issue on Company ABC. It is very positive and includes a buy/hold recommendation. Later that day, before the research is issued, a friend calls to chat, and casually tells you that she is about to place an order to sell her entire holding of Company ABC as she is disappointed with its performance. You are not sure whether you can tell your friend not to sell, based on the contents of the research report your firm will shortly issue.
Key issue	Market abuse/market conduct.
Comments and possible solutions	• You must keep quiet because if you talk to your friend about what you know, you are likely to have committed market abuse if the share is listed on a regulated market. • Even if the share is not so listed, disclosing what you know to your friend is likely to have breached the FSA's market conduct principle.

Dilemma 28	One of your colleagues tells you of a conversation that was overheard in a pub the previous night. It seemed to involve a group engaged in the illegal transport of cigarettes to avoid paying any import duty. You are not sure whether this conversation needs to be reported to SOCA as a suspicion of money laundering.
Key issue	Anti-money-laundering controls.
Comments and possible solutions	• Are you sure that what the group was discussing is really illegal? • Legally you only have to report suspicions that have come to you in the course of your business, so you would not be under a legal obligation to report what you heard. • If you are convinced of the people's illegal activities you might decide to report this to SOCA anyway, especially if you have any details that may assist them in tracking down this group. • Remember that SOCA is busy with real criminal cases and does not need to be overburdened with irrelevant reports.

Dilemma 29	You have recently recruited a new stockbroker whose client base comprises high net worth individuals, many of which you find out are based overseas and are politically exposed persons (PEPs). You are not sure how to complete satisfactory due diligence on them.
Key issue	Anti-money-laundering controls.
Comments and possible solutions	• PEPs are generally considered to present a greater than normal risk of money laundering due to the levels of corruption that are known to take place in certain government circles. • There is no reason why your firm should not do business with PEPs if it considers that their activities are above board – it should come down to your firm's own risk appetite. • Your firm should have specific procedures for doing business with PEPs – further guidance is available on page 204.

Dilemma 30	During a routine review to approve a research report prior to issue you identify a sell recommendation for a firm that you know to be a client of your Corporate Finance department. You investigate further and find that the firm is currently assisting the subject of the research to obtain funding. You are not sure whether you should allow the research report to be published.
Key issues	• Conflicts of interest. • Independence of research.
Comments and possible solutions	• The client is unlikely to be happy that one part of the firm is 'critical' of them by recommending them as a 'sell' while another part of the firm is trying to promote them to help them to raise finance. • However, the Research function is meant to be independent of the Corporate Finance team – it is not in the best interests of the Research clients for them not to be told that a firm is a poor deal if that is really the case. You may feel that this is particularly important if the Research clients are paying for the service, although this consideration should not make any difference. • Conversely, it is not in the best interests of the Corporate Finance client to have negative research issued about them by a firm that is meant to be assisting them to raise finance. • Review the customer contract for Corporate Finance, is there anything in here that will prohibit the research being sent? If so, there should not be as this has an impact on the independence of your Research function. Make sure this clause is not used again. • Have a private conversation with the Head of Corporate Finance and warn him about the situation – it would not be right for him to prevent the research from being issued, but you can at least given him warning so that he can be prepared to manage the relationship with the client when they find out. • Also find out whether the CEO of the Corporate Finance client already knows about the pending research. It is not impossible that they do as Research Analysts often talk with the companies that they cover and have them review their work (although the extent to which this is permissible is limited if a recommendation or target price is included in the research). • The most likely outcome is that the Corporate Finance mandate will be lost. Even if it is possible to keep the client on board, this could prove somewhat academic as you are unlikely to be able to assist them with their fund raising exercise if your firm is issuing negative research about them at the same time. • Guard against the Research team being put under pressure to withdraw the research report: this could happen because the successful completion of the Corporate Finance mandate may bring in a few million dollars for the firm and losing this due to a single research report that may not generate any direct revenue at all is not a happy prospect.

Dilemma 31	One of the senior members of your firm's Proprietary Equities Trading team is continually pushing the limits in terms of compliance with regulatory requirements. The number of breaches for which he is responsible leads you to believe that he should be disciplined, but his manager does not agree – saying that no serious damage has been done, and that if this person is disciplined he may leave, which would be disastrous for profits as the rest of the team is not doing very well.

Key issues

- Fitness and propriety.
- Training and competence.
- Client's best interest rules.
- Senior management systems, arrangements and controls.

Comments and possible solutions

- The person sounds like a prima donna who is dangerous for your firm. If you look into the history of many a financial scandal you will see that a large proportion involved a type of person who considered himself, and was considered by others, to be beyond reproach.
- Have other people in the firm been disciplined for doing the same or equivalent things as this person? If so, why should he receive preferential treatment just because of his seniority. This is not setting a good example.
- It should not be down to this person's manager alone whether he is disciplined. If he has breached company policy there should be an independent mechanism to go through and the person's manager should not be able to override this unilaterally.
- Discuss your concerns with the staff member involved and remind him how his behaviour is putting not only his own reputation but that of the firm at risk. Also remind him that, as a senior manager, the FSA views him as being responsible for Compliance, and ask if there is anything that you can do to assist him in discharging his responsibilities.
- Talk to HR and Legal about your concerns.
- Review the person's work practices and that of his team – there may be breaches or other situations in relation to which you need to take immediate remedial action.

Dilemma 32	A client of the Corporate Finance team is contemplating making a bid for XYZ Company at a price that your Corporate Finance team know to be greatly inflated due to the fact that they have recently completed a mandate for XYZ Company and hold confidential information on it. Given this situation you are not sure whether the firm can accept the new takeover mandate.

Key issues

- Market abuse/market conduct.
- Insider lists.
- Watch and restricted list.

Comments and possible solutions

- Is the information held by Corporate Finance on XYZ Company inside information? If the mandate ended some time ago, all relevant information is likely to be known to the market already. Check your watch/restricted list records.
- Even if the information held has not yet been disclosed the client (and its advisers – your Corporate Finance team) should legitimately gain access to it anyway during the due diligence process and your firm will thus be able to assist in making a more realistic bid price.
- Investigate whether you still owe any contractual duties to the target that would be incompatible with taking on the new mandate.

Dilemma 33

A new broker has started with your firm who has a client base located primarily in Australia and New Zealand. He says that the clients want to trade with the firm right now, but you are not sure whether you can do so as your firm has never transacted with clients in Australia or New Zealand before. In the meantime, the new broker is not doing any business and he is scared that he will lose his clients to a competitor.

Key issues

Permitted activities.

Comments and possible solutions

- Check with local lawyers to find out what the regulatory obligations of your firm are in providing services in Australia and New Zealand and make sure that procedures are implemented to enable you to comply with these.
- Make sure that all staff involved are aware of the new procedures, and receive appropriate training.
- Do not be rushed into giving the go ahead to trade before you feel that all bases have been covered.
- Find out why Compliance was not consulted in the business development/recruitment phase for this activity and devise a way of making sure that you are brought into the loop earlier next time.

Dilemma 34

The FSA conducts a periodic inspection visit of your firm. You are aware that there have been a number of breaches in terms of the provision of key features documentation not being sent and suitability records not being adequate, but you are pleased that this is not identified by the FSA during their review and that the impression they formed of your firm is fairly positive. However, you are not convinced that the favourable light in which they see your firm is correct, given the breaches that you are aware of, and do not know whether you should bring these to the FSA's attention.

Key issue

- Relations with regulators.

Comments and possible solutions

- Deciding whether or not to make a disclosure to the FSA will probably be one of the hardest calls that a Compliance Officer has ever had to make.
- Review the guidance provided by the FSA on what needs to be notified to them and if the situation within your firm meets the FSA notification criteria then you would find it difficult to justify not making a disclosure.
- The fact that an inspection visit has just taken place is to some extent irrelevant: if something needs to be notified to the FSA this will be the case whether or not the FSA has just carried out an inspection.
- If you do notify, you are advised also to explain exactly what remedial action has been taken to rectify the situation that led to the breaches.

Dilemma 35

You have provided training on conduct of business procedures to all of your firm's customer facing employees. This training is obligatory and will count towards each employee's competency assessment under your firm's training and competence regime. During the training sessions, you notice that certain members of senior management spend their time checking messages on their Blackberries and you are not sure that they have actually taken in what is being said. Nevertheless, the staff involved have signed in to show that they have attended your training and so you have the required 'tick in the box'.

Key issues

- Training and competence.
- Approved Persons.

- Fitness and propriety.
- The competent employees rule.

Comments and possible solutions
- Quite apart from setting a bad example to other people in the training session. The manager's behaviour also defeats the purpose of giving the training – you have your tick in the box to provide a training record, but the people concerned are clearly not paying attention and are not learning anything.
- This is especially serious given that senior management are responsible for Compliance and it is important that people in their position know what is required, not only for their own conduct, but also to provide guidance to their teams.
- Pop round to the people's desk afterwards and run through the training with them in person, highlighting the major points of relevance to them and next time, make a no Blackberries or mobile phones rule.

Dilemma 36

You learn that your firm will soon receive a routine inspection visit from your regulator. Some of the staff are nervous, even though you do not think they have done anything wrong and ask you to give them guidance on what they are likely to be asked and how they should respond. You are not sure whether it is right to 'coach' your staff in this way prior to the visit.

Key issue

Relations with regulators.

Comments and possible solutions
- There is a difference between coaching staff (not appropriate) and giving them guidance on what will be expected of them (perfectly acceptable).
- Gather together the staff who are most likely to be selected for interview and explain to them as much about the inspection visit as you know.
- Give them an opportunity to ask questions.
- Provide refresher training in any areas where you think this might be needed.
- However, do not give staff scripts to learn, or anything approaching this; the FSA is likely to see through it and their suspicions will be raised.

Dilemma 37

There has been a significant failing to act in a client's best interest in your Stock Broking department and the person responsible has resigned, even though the firm was considering dismissing him. You need to deregister him as an Approved Person and are not sure what you should note as the reason for leaving.

Key issues
- Approved Persons.
- Fitness and propriety.
- Relations with regulators.

Comments and possible solutions
- You are required to notify the FSA of any matter that might have an impact on the person's fitness and propriety, so the fact that the person has resigned before he can be dismissed is irrelevant – he still has engaged in the relevant behaviour.
- If you think that what the person has done does impact his fitness and propriety (see guidance at APER and FIT in the FSA Handbook) then you should notify the FSA.
- Seek guidance from the HR department, and legal counsel before proceeding as this is a very sensitive area.

Dilemma 38	You have identified a number of Compliance breaches in one of your Back Office departments and on discussing this with the manager involved – who is covered by the training and competence rules as the clients concerned are retail – it becomes clear to you that this person has very poor knowledge of the applicable regulatory requirements. Despite this, his manager has signed him off as competent and you wonder whether this 'competent' status should be removed while he undertakes further training.
Key issues	• Training and competence. • The competent employees rule.
Comments and possible solutions	• Is this person competent in other areas? If not, he should clearly not be performing his role. • If the person is not competent only in relation to regulatory matters, he should receive intensive training and guidance, and should conduct his work under close supervision and review until you are satisfied that relevant requirements are being met. • Think about having the person resit his regulatory exam. • Also provide training to the person who assessed the individual as competent so that she understands what is required in this regard. Point out that if she assesses someone as competent who then goes on to perpetrate major breaches or errors, she could also be implicated. • Check to see whether the same situation applies to other people who she has assessed as competent. • Review the work of the person whose competency you are questioning and see what remedial action is required. • Consider whether any of the breaches identified requires the FSA notification, or customer compensation.
Dilemma 39	A routine monitoring review uncovers that risk warnings are sometimes sent to clients just a few minutes prior to trades being undertaken in the instruments to which the risk warnings relate.
Key issues	• The client's best interest rule. • Suitability and appropriateness. • Risk warnings.
Comments and possible solutions	• If a risk warning is sent only a couple of minutes before a trade then it would be very hard to argue that the client had had enough time to digest its contents and understand the risks involved. • Explain to the staff involved that risk warnings should be sent on time to give the client adequate opportunity to read and digest their contents. Provide training until you are satisfied that the relevant employees understand what is required. • Review the transaction history of the customers concerned – have they been disadvantaged in any way through not having an adequate understanding of the risks involved? Should they receive compensation? Are you now satisfied that they understand the relevant risks?

Dilemma 40

Your retail client advisory team has got into the habit of e-mailing clients with trade recommendations and telling the clients that, unless they say otherwise, the recommended trade will be executed within the next 24 hours. The trading has been successful and no client has complained, but you are not sure that what the team is doing is right.

Key issues

- The client's best interest rule.
- Suitability and appropriateness.
- Permitted activities.

Comments and possible solutions

- This practice would seem to go beyond the advisory service that the clients signed up for and is therefore not appropriate in the circumstances.
- It is more akin to discretionary management so you need to check that your firm has the relevant permission to provide this service, and that the staff have been assessed as competent in this area.
- If the answer is 'no' to either of these questions then you are in a difficult position as this is definitely the sort of thing that the FSA is interested in hearing about.
- Investigate the extent to which client interests have been damaged by the actions of the advisory team as you may need to pay compensation.
- Give serious consideration to reprimanding the staff concerned. You should definitely provide them with training on how far they can and cannot go in the context of an advisory relationship.
- Assuming that your firm is permitted to provide discretionary management services and that the FSA does not request that you cease operations in this area, if the clients are happy with the way things are, make sure that they are now classed as discretionary management customers and send them the required client agreement for this service.

Dilemma 41

During a Compliance monitoring review of your stock broking team you notice that there are frequently delays in allocating trades: some trades are completed in the morning, but the splits are not done until after trading has finished for the day. You ask the stock brokers about this and they explain that they are waiting to see the price at which the stocks close before allocating so that the best and most profitable clients can receive preferential allocations as a reward for their good custom.

Key issues

- The client's best interest rule.
- Aggregation and allocation of orders.

Comments and possible solutions

- Trades should be allocated on the basis of the firm's order allocation policy, which must establish how fair allocation will be achieved.
- It does not seem fair, nor appear to be in the client's best interests, to wait to see which trades do well to allocate these to favoured clients – comparable orders should be executed in accordance with the order in which they were received.
- Provide training to the team concerned and consider whether disciplinary action is merited.
- Check to see which clients have been disadvantaged – you may need to pay compensation.

Dilemma 42	Your Internal Audit team notified you that there have been regular breaches of the investment and borrowing powers of one of the funds managed by your Fund Management team. When you investigate, your findings concur with those of Internal Audit but you also notice that since the breaches began, the fund has in fact been much more successful than it had been for the previous year.
Key issues	• The client's best interest rule. • Suitability and appropriateness. • Investment and borrowing powers.
Comments and possible solutions	• The fund may well have been more profitable by taking on levels of risk that were not acceptable to the investors, who were happy with lower profits in return for security. The fact that profit has been made does not make the breach acceptable. • Monitoring by the fund's trustees or even by its clients is likely to identify the breaches at some stage so it is best to disclose what has happened and take corrective action rather than try to cover it up. • The Fund Management agreement is also likely to contain a provision that requires you to notify clients of any breaches. • Provide guidance to staff and seriously question why this situation arose in the first place. It seems that all is not well in the Fund Management department, if this has been allowed to continue unchecked for some time.

Dilemma 43	Your Human Resources department has recently recruited a temporary receptionist and they are aware that you are currently providing anti-money-laundering training to all staff. The HR manager asks you whether the new temporary receptionist needs to attend the training.
Key issues	• Anti-money-laundering controls. • The competent employees rule.
Comments and possible solutions	• Staff should receive training that is appropriate to their role. • It is unlikely that a temporary receptionist is going to be in a position of identifying a suspicion of money laundering, but not impossible. • Think about preparing a brief guidance sheet that can be given to any temporary staff on joining, advising them of the key requirements on money laundering and that if they have any concerns they should seek the guidance of the MLRO immediately. The guidance sheet could also contain guidance in other relevant areas such as data security and confidentiality. • Of course, if the person stays longer than was initially envisaged, then additional training is likely to be required.

Dilemma 44	Your Operational Risk department has recently installed some expensive new software from a company with which they have a long-term consulting relationship. As a thank you for your firm's custom, the consultants offer to pay for the Head of Operational Risk and his deputy to attend a sporting event in Spain, all expenses paid. The offer is outside what would normally be permitted under your firm's inducements policy.
Key issues	• Inducements. • Conflicts of interest.

Comments and possible solutions	• Is it likely that accepting this gift could have a detrimental effect on a customer, which is the prime area that the inducements rule is concerned with? In this case it seems not.
	• Is there any other reason why the offer should not be accepted – could it be considered unethical or unjust outside the context of the regulatory environment?
	• You firm probably has a procurements policy so you should ensure that acceptance of the gift does not conflict with the requirements of that policy.
	• If everything seems above board, you may feel comfortable saying yes, although you may be happier simply sticking to the letter of your inducements policy and not making any exceptions. If you make an exception here, it could be the beginning of a slippery slope!

Dilemma 45

You have recently started work at a new firm and notice that the Head of Equities has both the Equity Trading and the Equity Research staff reporting to him. You question the appropriateness of these reporting lines.

Key issues

- Conflicts of interest.
- Market abuse/market conduct.
- Chinese walls.

Comments and possible solutions

- This situation is undesirable as it gives rise to the possibility that the manager will be able to time the purchase or sale of equities to benefit from research issued, i.e. buy before the issue of positive research and sell before the issue of negative research.
- In a large firm it should easily be possible to change the reporting lines to strengthen the independence of the Research team but in a small firm with fewer staff, this will be more difficult to achieve but nevertheless still has to be done.
- Indicate your concerns to senior management and push for the two teams to report to different heads and to implement an effective Chinese wall.
- Until such a time as this can be achieved, supervise and continually review the activities of the two departments to ensure that nothing inappropriate is taking place.
- Provide written guidance to the Head of Equities to ensure that he understands the sensitivity of his position, and what he may and may not do. Ask him to acknowledge the receipt of the guidance in writing.

Dilemma 46

You recently approved a personal account trade for one of your firm's Investment Advisers who wished to buy a relatively illiquid stock. A couple of weeks later you are surprised to see more activity in this stock – this time it has been bought by a number of the firm's customers. Just as you go to discuss this coincidence with the original Investment Adviser, he comes to you with a request to sell the stock as he explains it has now gone up in value and he wishes to realize his profits. You are unsure whether you can approve his trade.

Key issues

- Personal account dealing.
- Market abuse/ market conduct.
- Treating customers fairly.

	(Continued)
Comments and possible solutions	• Your concern here is likely to be that the Investment Adviser has manipulated the market, ramping up the value of the share concerned by recommending it to his clients to push up the price pending his disposal of it. • Ask the Investment Adviser the rationale behind his personal trading. • Find out whether he has been responsible for the client trades recently undertaken in the same stock. • Seek independent advice about the recent market for the stock in question. One feasible explanation is that both the Investment Adviser and his client have been responding to the same legitimate news item or announcement about the stock and that the trading is perfectly acceptable. • If you are unable to get comfortable with the Investment Adviser's activities then this is a serious matter as you will be making allegations of market abuse with the attendant requirements to notify the FSA, consider disciplinary action, seek legal advice, etc. • If this is the case, also consider whether clients have been disadvantaged during the ramping-up process.

Dilemma 47	The Corporate Finance team has been approached by two clients, both wishing to secure your firm's services for bids to buy the same target company. The team is unsure whether they can work for two competing clients.
Key issues	• Chinese walls. • Conflicts of interest. • Confidentiality. • Exclusivity.
Comments and possible solutions	• There is no rule that says that your firm cannot work for the two clients, but it is certainly a very tricky situation to manage. • There may, however, be contractual reasons why the firm cannot act for both – check to see if there are any exclusivity clauses. • If you decide to work for both clients then this should be disclosed to both parties to the maximum extent possible without breaching any confidentiality requirements. If either of the clients objects, then you will need to rethink your strategy unless you are able to reassure them about the robustness of the controls that you have implemented to safeguard their interests. • Set up separate deal teams and ensure that very strict and well-monitored segregation and Chinese walls arrangements are in place to keep details of the two competing clients and their bids separate. • Give written guidance to relevant staff about the sensitivities of the situation they are in and the controls that they will need to implement and follow. Require them to acknowledge this guidance in writing.

Dilemma 48	Your corporate finance team is mandated by ABC Company to help them to fend off a hostile takeover. Shortly afterwards, the team is approached by another client who wishes to secure the advisory services of your firm in their bid to take over ABC Company. The team is not sure whether they can accept this mandate and ask for your advice.
Key issues	• Chinese walls. • Conflicts of interest. • Confidentiality.
Comments and possible solutions	• You should ask the first client whether they object to the new mandate as this is in direct conflict with what they have asked your firm to work on for them. • In the extremely unlikely case that they agree you must ensure that very strict and well monitored segregation and Chinese walls arrangements are in place to keep details of the two competing clients and their bids separate. • Give written guidance to relevant staff about the sensitivities of the situation they are in and the controls that they will need to implement and follow. Require them to acknowledge this guidance in writing. • It would be easiest and much less risky to refuse the mandate. Irrespective of the dilemma that exists on a regulatory level, commercially and reputationally the second mandate should be refused.

Dilemma 49	During a review of your Investment Management team's activities you notice that aggregated trades are not always allocated on a pro rata basis: customers placing large orders are sometimes filled completely, to the detriment of customers who have placed smaller orders. You are not sure whether this is acceptable.
Key issues	• The client's best interest rule. • Aggregation and allocation of orders.
Comments and possible solutions	• Check your aggregation and allocation policy: it may be that the allocations were acceptable in the circumstances – perhaps the smaller orders would not have been filled at all if they had not been combined with the larger ones in which case a partial fill may be better than no fill at all. • If so, ensure that the customers have been notified of the policy – they should have been informed that their orders may be subject to aggregation and that this may sometimes work to their disadvantage. • If you cannot justify the allocations, or if the customers have not been informed a general review is clearly in order, and you may have to consider re-allocating affected trades and/or paying customer compensation. • Consider whether to inform the FSA if there have been repeated breaches of the policy, or a repeated failure to inform clients of its terms. • If you have identified breaches, provide detailed staff training to make sure that this situation does not arise again.

Dilemma 50

You notice that there seems to be a correlation between investments purchased on a discretionary basis by your Portfolio Management team and subsequent research reports issued by your Research team. You feel that something is not quite right and think you should investigate further.

Key issues

- Market abuse/market conduct.
- Chinese walls.
- Watch and restricted list.

Comments and possible solutions

- You will probably be concerned that information about future research reports is making its way into the hands of the Portfolio Management team, which could constitute market abuse.
- You should consider what the correlation is. If the pattern is that the research is negative, and then investments are bought after a delay, and that if the research is positive, investments are subsequently sold after a delay, this could amount to price positioning (a form of market abuse). If this is the case, you need to investigate the deal records to see what the rationale was behind each trade. If there has been inappropriate information flow, this is a serious matter – review your controls in this area immediately.
- If the research is bad and the investments are sold, or if the research is good and the investments are bought, it is likely that the Fund Managers are simply reacting to the research as any other client was – check to see that the research was distributed to them at the same time as other clients.
- How have you identified this situation? Was it by chance, or was it through the effective use of your watch and/or restricted lists? If it was a random spot you should seriously consider tightening your controls.
- If you do suspect market abuse, you will need to notify the FSA and enforcement action could ensue – seek legal advice.

Dilemma 51

When reviewing the list of new Corporate Finance mandates you notice one that involves your firm assisting a client with their takeover bid for XYZ Company. You remember that your Fund Management department has recently bought a large holding of XYZ Company shares and you are not sure whether the Corporate Finance mandate is appropriate in these circumstances.

Key issues

- Market abuse/market conduct.
- Chinese walls.

Comments and possible solutions

- As long as you have confidence in your firm's Chinese walls you can allow this mandate to continue – investments in the Fund Management area should not influence Corporate Finance work as the two areas should be independent from one another.
- The Fund Manager buying shares in XYZ is very unlikely to mean that your firm owes that company any duty not to advise a bidder.
- Ensure that your Chinese walls will be able to contain any inside information on XYZ behind the Corporate Finance Chinese wall so that no inside information flows to the Fund Management department (or anywhere else for that matter) as this could influence their trading decisions.
- It may appear suspicious in the market that you bought the shares and then worked for a bidder. Robust controls may be in place but they may do nothing to dispel the appearance of guilt.

Dilemma 52	During a routine review of your Customer Trading desk you notice that there is frequently a delay between a customer placing an order and the order being executed. When you ask why this is, the traders tell you that they have been waiting for the price to move in favour of the client, which, they tell you, is acting in the client's best interests.
Key issues	• The client's best interest rule. • Client order handling. • Best execution.
Comments and possible solutions	• Find out what type of order the clients have placed: perhaps they have asked for their trades to be executed at what the traders consider to be the best achievable price during the day. • From your investigations, assess whether your best execution policy has been complied with. • Determine whether any customers have been disadvantaged – did a delay in execution lead to a higher buy price? If so, where commission is charged on a trade consideration basis there may be an incentive to delay execution until prices have risen as this will increase the commission received. • Evidently this would not be an appropriate practice and you would need to think about compensating relevant clients, disciplining the employees concerned and providing training to other team members.

Dilemma 53	A Fund Manager asks you to approve an arrangement that has been put to him by a well-known brokerage firm whereby in return for free Bloomberg access courtesy of the broker, your Fund Manager agrees to direct all trades through them. You do not think that you should approve this arrangement but are under pressure to do so.
Key issues	• The client's best interest rule. • Best execution. • Inducements. • Conflicts of interest.
Comments and possible solutions	• Firms must not enter into any inducement arrangements that will impair their ability to act in the best interests of their clients, so before signing this agreement you should be very happy that this broker will at all times be able to provide the best possible outcome for your clients. • Unless you are confident that this will be achieved it is unlikely to be appropriate to sign the agreement, irrespective of what your firm is being offered in return.

Dilemma 54	Your firm does not require each personal account trade to be approved on a case by case basis prior to execution, although you do review all employee trades after the event. During one such review you note that a Research Analyst bought shares a couple of days before he issued a positive research report on the issuer. You investigate further and see that the Research Analyst has actually lost money on the trade, but you still feel that his actions were not right.
Key issues	• Personal account dealing. • Watch and restricted list. • Market abuse/market conduct.

(Continued)

Comments and possible solutions	• This may sound like market abuse but before making any judgements you need to determine whether the Analyst had access to sensitive material and was trading on the basis that he thought his research would cause the price of the investment to rise. • If this is the case his behaviour was unacceptable regardless of whether or not he made a profit. • Ask his boss whether he thinks he was behaving properly and ask the employee how he justifies his actions. • If you suspect market abuse this should be reported to the FSA and the employee should be disciplined. • Consider changing your PA dealing policy to require pre-approval on a case by case basis, even if it is restricted to Research Analysts.

Dilemma 55	Your firm's Proprietary Trading team has not been doing well recently. In particular, there is one large position in equities for which the price has fallen considerably since purchase, and which is a cause for concern for senior management. During your routine review of research reports you note that a very favourable piece has been written on the issuer of the shares that are bringing down the performance of the Proprietary Trading team. You are not sure whether you should approve the research for issue.
Key issues	• Market abuse. • Chinese walls. • Conflicts of interest. • Independence of research.
Comments and possible solutions	• The concern here is that the Research team is in league with the Proprietary traders and has issued positive research purely to increase the value of the shares and improve the firm's proprietary position. • Carry out a review to see if you can discover any evidence of inappropriate contact or information flow between Research and Proprietary trading. • Ask the Research team to explain their research rationale to you – it may all be perfectly innocent. • Depending on what you find, this may be market abuse and the FSA will need to be informed. • Alternatively, assuming your Chinese walls are working well, the situation may be perfectly innocent.

Dilemma 56	A Research Analyst comes to you and explains that he has recently been invited to a major sporting event by a company he has not covered for a while. He gets the impression that the company is going to ask him to issue research on them once again and is not sure how this would be viewed under the regulatory system.
Key issues	• Conflicts of interest. • Inducements. • Independence of research.

Comments and possible solutions	• Research Analysts should not accept inducements from persons with a material interest in their research and it would thus be very unwise to accept this sporting invitation. • The danger is that the independence of the Research team's work will be compromised if they feel beholden to the companies they cover – the team should not feel obligated to issue favourable research on the company as a 'thank you' for a gift.

Dilemma 57

Your firm has recently employed a new Head of Research who wants to change remuneration arrangements so that Research Analysts are directly rewarded according to how many trades are attributed to the research they have produced. You are not sure whether this is a good idea.

Key issues

• Conflicts of interest.
• Suitability.
• The client's best interest rule.
• Remuneration policy.

Comments and possible solutions

• This proposed research remuneration strategy creates a considerable conflict of interest as it could incentivize Research Analysts to put undue pressure on the Sales team to advise customers about the stocks they cover in preference to other shares that might be more suitable for them.
• A more independent remuneration strategy is required.

Dilemma 58

You are concerned about the potential for market abuse involving your Sales and Trading team and your Research team: the two teams have always worked very closely together as they tell you that, logically, the Research team needs to know which companies the clients of the Sales team are interested in so that they can produce research to match their interests. You, however, are concerned that discussions between the two teams may lead to impropriety.

Key issues

• Market abuse/market conduct.
• Chinese walls.
• Conflicts of interest.

Comments and possible solutions

• You need to make sure that both teams know where they must draw the line in terms of market and strategy discussions – the Research team must not pass on any price-sensitive information, including news about price-sensitive research that they are about to issue, and they must ensure that the Sales team do not know the content of the research before it is distributed to all recipients.
• Similarly, Sales should not ask for such privileges.
• It is logical for Sales and Research to work together as there is no point in the Research team covering investments in which the customer base is not interested. But there is a big difference between the Head of Sales simply requesting that Research cover a particular stock (acceptable), and him asking Research to let him know what the contents of a research report are before it has been issued (clearly unacceptable).

Dilemma 59

You are revising your personal account dealing policy and it has been suggested that you should not allow employees to carry out PA trades in investments in the sectors they cover due to the risks that they will trade on the basis of inside information. This has not been the firm's approach in the past, and you are not sure whether you should include this restriction in the new policy.

Key issues

- Personal account dealing.
- Market abuse/market conduct.
- Insider lists.
- Watch and restricted lists.

Comments and possible solutions

- Opinion is divided here – some consider that if a trader focuses on the electricity market, for example, he should not be trading electricity stock as the risk of insider dealing is too great.
- Others think that it is far better for that trader to be focused on electricity stocks from a personal perspective as it keeps his mind on his own market and is therefore indirectly beneficial to clients.
- It is up to you to decide what you think is most appropriate for your own firm, but if you do allow traders to carry out PA trades in the sectors they cover, your insider/watch/restricted lists should tell you whether a trader requesting a PA dealing approval has inside information on a particular asset.

Dilemma 60

A member of the Credit department requests permission to do a personal account trade in a share that is currently in your watch list as the Corporate Finance team have a mandate with the issuer to assist them with a takeover bid. You do not think that the Credit department employee has had any involvement with the Corporate Finance mandate but all the same, you are not sure whether you should approve the trade.

Key issues

- Market abuse.
- Chinese walls.
- Watch and resisted list.
- Insider lists.

Comments and possible solutions

- Check your watch and restricted lists to see if the firm has any inside information on the company.
- Also check your insider list to see whether the person requesting to trade has any inside information.
- If you ask the person or his boss whether he has inside information, this might tip them off that some price-sensitive information is about to materialize. It is better to ask the deal team leader whether he has any reason to suspect that the person has any inside information, and how he feels about the trade being permitted.
- Think carefully before you prohibit the trade unless you have a very good reason for doing so as your rejection may notify the employee that significant news is about to be announced in relation to the share.

Dilemma 61	Historically you have only applied voice recording to Sales and Trading staff, and Back Office employees who deal with settlement and payment instructions. However, you have a new chief executive and he questions why the phones of all Front Office staff are not taped; he asks whether there is any regulatory reason why all customer facing staff should not use recorded lines.
Key issues	• Data protection. • Record keeping. • Confidentiality.
Comments and possible solutions	• Voice recording should not be undertaken just for the sake of it – there should be a logical reason why it is required. • Once a conversation is recorded it is important to have the infrastructure in place to support its security and confidentiality so that it does not fall into the wrong hands. • It is likely to be expensive to purchase voice-recording equipment for the rest of the customer facing staff who are not currently using recorded lines. • In addition, remember that recorded conversations could also be used against the firm. • If there is a logical reason for your voice-recording arrangements to be expanded, then it should be done, but only in accordance with relevant legislative and regulatory requirements.

Dilemma 62	As part of a global training and development initiative the head of your firm's Trading division asks you whether it will be possible for members of the international Trading team to rotate between different international offices to give them experience of different working environments, while still keeping their own client base.
Key issues	• Training and competence. • Approved persons. • Permitted activities.
Comments and possible solutions	• Although a good idea, this is likely to be tricky as in most jurisdictions it is not possible for staff simply to fly in one day and start trading without having the correct regulatory licences, qualifications, work permits, etc. • You should investigate the laws in all the relevant jurisdictions to ensure that you do not breach them before sending any staff on a temporary mission overseas. • In the UK, for example, overseas staff are permitted to perform a customer function under the Approved Persons regime without FSA approval if certain conditions are met (i.e. they must spend no more than 30 days in the UK in any one 12-month period and they must be subject to appropriate supervision). • In my experience, even UK residents about to perform a week-long audit on the Isle of Man, despite not working for a firm but inspecting it, need to get a work permit. So you can see, it is not always possible to second guess what these requirements will be. • Train the relevant staff and supervisors on what is and is not permitted, and make sure that your overseas Compliance colleagues do the same in their own jurisdictions.

Dilemma 63	A prospective client is not happy to accept your firm's standard terms of business as set out in the client agreement and asks whether certain of the terms can be varied.
Key issues	• Terms of business/client agreements. • Information about the firm, its services and remuneration.
Comments and possible solutions	• Whether or not you can vary the terms will depend on whether the terms are required by the FSA or any other legal or regulatory authority. • Even if they are not, do you really have the infrastructure to start varying the terms with which you treat your customers? • Are the varied terms requested by the customer workable in practice? Are they likely to be forgotten and breached? • It is far preferable to have standard terms of business instead of having to remember on what basis each individual client does business with you. But if there is no legal or regulatory reason why a particular term has to be included, there is nothing to prevent you from varying terms if you really feel inclined to do so.

Dilemma 64	One of your firm's traders wishes to start working from home one day a week and his manager asks whether there are any regulatory reasons why he should not do this.
Key issues	• Record keeping. • Supervision. • Senior management systems, arrangements and controls.

Comments and possible solutions	• Find out why the person wants to work from home and if you are satisfied with the response, then theoretically this should be possible, but logistically it will be complex, for example
	
	  – do you have the capability to install the trading software in this person's house?
	  – how will his activities be supervised and monitored?
	
	• If you do decide to approve the request you will need to put strict controls in place including
	
	  – out of office trading policy;
	  – requirement for a recorded phone line to be used, just as it would be in the office;
	  – adequate IT support in case the home system goes down; and
	  – adequate IT security measures to ensure that no one else can log on to the firm's computer network using the remote access system.

Dilemma 65	The Sales team is not doing well and their customers are abandoning them for teams who give more successful advice. A junior Sales Executive asks Corporate Finance for some sales ideas based on the mandates that she is working on, hoping to get a chance to react to a forthcoming event before the rest of the market has had a chance to react, thereby bolstering customer confidence.
Key issues	• Market abuse/market conduct. • Chinese walls. • Training and competence. • Supervision.

Comments and possible solutions	• The Sales Executive is asking for 'inside information'. • This is clearly unacceptable behaviour and you should be thinking very seriously about reporting it to the FSA (both in terms of potential market abuse and in relation to the fitness and propriety of the junior Sales Executive) and obtaining legal advice about how to manage what has happened in case of FSA enforcement action. • Carry out a review to see whether it looks as if any inside information has actually been passed to the Sales Executive. If so, you are likely to be in for a full-scale investigation. • Also review the effectiveness of your firm's training and supervision arrangements. Had this Sales Executive received training on market abuse? How were her activities being monitored by her line manager? • Provide guidance to members of both Corporate Finance and the Sales team on the inappropriateness of what has taken place so that it is not repeated.

Dilemma 66	You see on the Facebook profile of one of your colleagues that he is complaining about your firm and how it is 'the most unprofessional place he has ever worked'. You also note that the work history he has listed online does not tally with what is on his CV. He also refers to his activities on a recent trip to Amsterdam that seems to have involved smoking cannabis.
Key issues	• Fitness and propriety. • Disciplinary action.
Comments and possible solutions	• Consider reporting this person to HR – there should be disciplinary procedures to cover an employee publicly denigrating your firm. • In relation to the drugs reference, do you have any other evidence to suggest that the person has smoked cannabis? If so, it could impact the person's fitness and propriety to work in the financial services industry. Also remember that smoking cannabis is legal in Amsterdam – does this affect your response? • Block access to Facebook on the firm's computer systems.

Dilemma 67	You observe in the course of a PA dealing review that one of your Fund Managers is making serious losses on his personal account. Nevertheless he appears to be performing effectively and diligently in his job. You are not sure whether you should be concerned from a regulatory perspective.
Key issues	• Fitness and propriety. • Personal account dealing.
Comments and possible solutions	• The financial situation of an employee is of direct relevance to the FSA's 'Fit and Proper' test. • You need to keep the employee under observation: he may automatically cease to be fit and proper if he becomes insolvent, and moreover the increasing stress on his personal situation may encourage him to greater recklessness and short-termism in his dealings for clients. • He may also start to pay more interest to his own positions than to his clients during the working day. • You should also think about talking to the employee and his line manager about the problem and discussing possible ways of addressing it. • Seek advice from HR as this sort of situation will require a very sensitive approach.

Dilemma 68	A person asks for approval to do a trade she is very excited about, as she says that the CEO of ABC Company, listed in London, is about to leave his wife and run off with his secretary. She thinks the CEO was a liability and that his departure paves the way for new blood. She thinks this will bring about a rapid increase in share price and wants to cash in.
Key issues	• Market abuse/market conduct. • Personal account dealing.

Comments and possible solutions	• Consider the nature of the information that this person has – if it is inside information or relevant information (as defined in the FSA's Code of Market Conduct) she should not be allowed to trade.
	• Factors to consider are
	   – is the information known to the market already?
	   – would you expect the possible departure of the CEO to be reported to the market, and to be price sensitive? (The answer is almost certainly: yes.)
	   – is the information precise, or is it simply speculative?
	   – even if you are comfortable that the trade would not amount to market abuse, it may be viewed badly by the market (especially if ABC Company is a client of yours) and your firm's reputation could be called into question.

Dilemma 69	When reviewing one of the discretionary client portfolios of your Investment Management team you notice that it contains high-yield bonds of a kind that your firm's Proprietary Trading desks are prohibited from taking onto their books due to their extreme riskiness. You question whether it is appropriate for clients to be exposed to instruments that the firm will not hold itself.
Key issues	• Suitability and appropriateness • Client's best interest rule
Comments and possible solutions	Review the client's suitability fact find and the terms of his investment management agreement – perhaps his risk appetite is genuinely greater than the firm's and the bonds in question are perfectly in alignment with it. In this case, there should not be a problem.

Dilemma 70	Your company provides banking services to a major high street retailer. One of your Investment Banking employees by chance enters a prize draw sponsored by the client and wins a holiday in the Seychelles. He asks you whether he is permitted to accept the prize under your gifts and benefits policy.
Key issues	• Client's best interest rule. • Conflicts of interest. • Inducements.
Comments and possible solutions	• It is probably acceptable to allow the employee to take the prize: as long as you are sure that it was a chance win it cannot be considered an inducement, and it is hard to envisage how this, or any other client, might suffer by dint of the employee's good fortune. Check that his line manager is happy with this. • It might also be worth checking the small print of the competition – perhaps your employee is disqualified due to your firm being a service provider to the client.

Dilemma 71	Your retail Sales team is contacted by an individual, purporting to be a prospective customer of your firm, who they suspect is an the FSA 'mystery shopper'. They ask you whether they should treat this person any differently from a 'regular' customer.
Key issues	• Relations with regulators. • Treating customers fairly.
Comments and possible solutions	• In an ideal world your Sales team would be providing such a good service at all times that there should be no question of them having to improve their standards just because they think the regulator may be on the line! • You may therefore be intrigued to hear why the normal treatment served up by the Sales team might not be satisfactory to any customer who might approach them. • You might welcome the possibility of an the FSA mystery shopping exercise as a reminder to the Sales team that the regulator is a very real presence that takes an interest in their activities. • You might also consider that a report from the FSA about any inadequacies in the way they were treated would be useful tool for assessing the team's service standards (as long as it is not so critical that the FSA threatens disciplinary action). • And, if this is the case, should you not anyway be carrying out routine reviews of taped lines to check that the sales team are treating customers fairly?
Dilemma 72	You have programmed an automatic exception report that highlights incidences when best execution does not appear to have been achieved. This has happened several times over the course of the month that the report covers and you are concerned that you may have to compensate customers who have received unfavourable pricing.
Key issues	• Best execution. • Client's best interest rule.
Comments and possible solutions	• Best execution is not simply a matter of pricing so you need to examine all of the execution factors involved, including size of order and any specific instructions given by the client. It may be, for example, that a client's order was so large or small that normal market prices did not apply. • Ask the Account Executive or Trader responsible to justify the pricing that the client has received. Were the executions undertaken in accordance with your firm's best execution policy? • If there does appear to have been a failure to obtain best execution there will be many things to consider including: notifying the FSA, paying compensation, disciplining the staff concerned, and provision of training. • Think about reprogramming your best execution exception report if it is generating too many false positives. • Finally, think about reviewing the best execution exception report more frequently. Is a monthly check adequate?
Dilemma 73	A Research Analyst submits a request to conduct a personal account trade to sell a large holding of shares in ABC Company. You remember that you recently saw a research report issued by this very Analyst in which he was promoting ABC Company shares as a 'buy'. You do not think that he should be trading contrary to his own research.

(Continued)

Key issues	• Research controls. • Conflicts of interest. • Personal account dealing.
Comments and possible solutions	• Research Analysts should not be trading contrary to their research recommendations so you will need to talk to the Analyst about the trade and his research to find out what is going on. • Perhaps he has recently revised his opinion and has subsequently issued a 'sell' recommendation on ABC Company (in which case you should not approve the trade until you are sure that the market has had an opportunity to react to the latest report). • Or perhaps you will find that the Analyst is in serious financial hardship and needs to sell his share portfolio in order to pay his bills. If this is the situation, you may allow the trade if you consider it to be absolutely necessary, but your rationale and approval should be clearly documented. • Also think about the implications that the Analyst's financial circumstances may have on his fitness and propriety (of which financial standing is a core component).

Dilemma 74	One of your Corporate Finance employees is working on an advisory mandate with ABC Company which is suffering from extreme cash flow problems and may be declared bankrupt. A stock exchange announcement is about to be made in this regard and it is likely to cause a significant fall in share value. The Corporate Finance employee is recorded on your insider list as having inside information on ABC Company and he admits to knowing all about their financial difficulties but he comes to you with a request to sell a holding in their shares. He explains that he has a large holding in the shares and that the profit he was going to take from selling them had been earmarked to pay for a life-saving operation for his mother. If he does not sell the shares before their value falls, possibly to zero, he will not be able to pay for his mother's medical treatment.
Key issues	• Market abuse/market conduct. • Personal account dealing. • Insider lists.
Comments and possible solutions	• It is against the law to trade on the basis of inside information and this would appear to be what this Corporate Finance employee wants to do. You are advised against approving his trade request despite the harmful effect it might have on his mother's health. • If it could be demonstrated that the person had made the decision to sell the shares prior to having come into possession of the inside information, then you may have been able to approve the transaction. If the employee is selling his whole investment portfolio you may be more readily able to believe this than if he is simply selling his holding in ABC Company. • Even if you were able to demonstrate that he did not have inside information at the time he made the decision to trade, you may decide not to approve the trade anyway, as it may be perceived negatively by the market. The reputational risk here is considerable.

Part II
Compliance Perspectives

Box 1   Acting on Principle

The longstanding debate about whether we need financial services regulation, or whether the markets should be left to look after themselves, has more or less been won: few people today would support the removal of independent regulatory oversight of the industry. But no sooner is one debate concluded than another begins. If we are at last all agreed on the need for regulation, then what type of regulation do we need?

In the US, a legislative system is the order of the day (although there have been recent mutterings of a possible softening of this approach) whereas in the UK we have been used to working with a rules-based supervisory regime. Times are a-changing, however, and as part of an initiative to improve the way that it operates (to adopt a 'more confident and less mechanistic approach') the FSA is now going down the route of 'More Principles-Based Regulation' (MPBR for short), a process it hopes to have completed by 2010 and which involves scrapping large chunks of our familiar rulebook to leave us to decide for ourselves what constitutes appropriate behaviour. We no longer have the security of a ready-made, the FSA-approved Compliance framework upon which to base our actions.

The idea that high-level principles have a role to play in regulation is not new in the UK. SIB introduced 10 high-level Statements of Principle in 1990, and these were often cited in disciplinary action by SROs such as the SFA. With FSMA we saw the introduction of the FSA's four statutory objectives which, although not presented as principles, certainly serve as such in terms of programming the FSA machine. FSMA also saw the introduction of the seven principles of good regulation that the FSA must comply with, the revised 11 FSA Principles for Businesses and the seven Statements of Principle for Approved Persons. Since 2005 we have also had the government-sponsored Better Regulation Commission which is applicable right across the regulatory spectrum (not just financial services) and has introduced the five Principles of Good Regulation (proportionality, accountability, consistency, transparency and targeting) to do away with unnecessary and burdensome rules, bureaucracy, and administration.

So whereas we have seen that the role of principles in regulation is not new, what has changed is the enthusiasm with which the concept is being embraced by the FSA, with some of the prime examples of the shift towards MPBR being the removal of prescriptive rules in relation to anti-money laundering, training and competence for wholesale business (replaced with the competent employee rule), complaints handling (replaced with the treating complainants fairly rule) and the introduction of the Treating Customers Fairly initiative (TCF – see page 340) constructed around the FSA Principle 6.

Do we in the regulated community think that the move towards MPBR is a good thing? Well, as a concept it certainly has something going for it. With the FSA now focusing on outputs and intentions rather than on whether we comply with a rigid set of requirements (the old chestnut of complying with the letter rather than the spirit of the rules) we will now have the freedom to decide on a firm-by-firm basis how best to achieve compliance. We can choose a system that works for us in the context of our own business activities and move away from any tendency that we might have had to achieve compliance through box ticking rather than looking at what we really want to achieve.

And this has to be a good thing, hasn't it? After all, if the customers are happy, if they are making money and so are we, if there are no complaints and no breaches of legislation, then does it matter how we reach this point as long as we get there? Shouldn't we be applauding the FSA for bestowing such freedoms upon us?

Box 1   (Continued)

In fact, far from being feted for this shift in focus, the FSA has been severely berated and the first moves that have been taken towards MPBR have hardly been popular. This seems to have been a classic case of 'be careful what you wish for as you might just get it!' Our industry moaned about the FSA rules so the FSA decided to take a lot of rules away. But we are still moaning, and although the complaints may have died down somewhat, is this more a sign of resignation rather than approval? After all, how many people do you know who actually supported the FSA's proposal to do away with the Approved Persons regime? Not many I imagine, as borne out by the fact that the plan was quickly abandoned. And how many people do you know (at least in the wholesale arena) who have not been left a little puzzled as to what exactly is expected of them under by TCF? Indeed, only the removal of the FSA's anti-money laundering rules seems to have any widespread support, but is this because we still have the trusted, tried and tested JMLSG Guidance Notes to rely on? It would be difficult to find a more detailed set of 'guidelines' than these.

The main arguments against the change to a principles-based regime can be summarized as follows:

- The FSA has suffered from bad timing. At the very point that it is trying to move away from prescriptive rules, the EU Commission is busy trying to create them. At least under the old rules-based regime, rules were just rules. But now our rules arguably have the force of law as large chunks of them simply consist of EU legal requirements copied straight from the relevant directive. So our new principles-based regime would seem to consist of rules that are actually law, but with limited the FSA 'padding' to help us to understand what is really expected of us.
- Instead of promoting freedom within the markets the move towards principles-based regulation may actually have the reverse effect, stifling innovation because firms fear the consequences of only knowing 'after the event' whether a particular new product or service meets with the FSA approval. This is particularly dangerous for the FSA given that, in exercising its powers, it is required to have regard to the Principles of Good Regulation, one of which is 'the desirability of facilitating innovation in connection with regulated activities'.
- Compliance departments will no longer have a firm foundation of rules on which to base their Compliance framework, so again, we cannot be sure that what we implement will be deemed appropriate – you could have the best regulatory shot in town, but if you don't know where the target is, chances are you will miss. And here it's important to consider the client's best interests rule in COBS 2.1.1. OK, so we have seen the removal of some rules (eg with training and competence for non-retail business). But the client's best interests rule is a 'catch all' anyway, so even if we do something that the FSA does not like in an area where there was no rule to breach, we can still be caught by COBS 2.1.1.
- Another minus for Compliance departments is that it is certainly easier to argue your point if you can hang your case for taking a particular course of action on a specific rule. That way your message is immediately lent more weight than if you simply tell your chief executive that something just doesn't seem quite right in principle, but there is no rule stopping you from doing it. It is hard enough to stop people from pushing the boundaries as it is, but now we are faced with the prospect of the boundaries being removed altogether!

- Further criticisms are based on concerns about how principles-based regulation will link into the FSA's enforcement regime. Will we see cases mounted against people on the basis that their actions do not now appear appropriate, even though there was nothing explicitly preventing them from doing what they did? Quite possibly, as in its new *Enforcement Guide* the FSA says that it will be taking principles into account more for enforcement action. This does not sit too happily with the Human Rights Act or the European Convention on Human Rights, of which Article 7 requires clarity with regard to whether a particular behaviour is legal or not. This being the case, what sort of enforcement regime will we be left with if we throw out our rules? We are still waiting to see a major test case here.

- There is also a concern that the lack of official rules may lead to a loss of consumer confidence, not only because of a fear that the industry could start being perceived as a 'free for all' but also because s.150 of FSMA gives a right of action for a private person who has suffered loss as a result of a rule breach: with fewer rules to breach the possibility of pursuing this route for redress will be restricted.

- Paradoxically, some have put forward the argument that MPBR will lead to there being more requirements to comply with rather than less, and that it basically amounts to 'gold plating via the back door' through the increased use of industry guidance, which is examined further on page 328.

- The lack of a rules-based regulatory regime will also make it more difficult to keep track of relevant requirements as the FSA will now use an entire range of documents to provide us with illustrations of what it believes does and does not meet its high-level principles. So instead of simply looking through our rulebooks, we will also need to keep track of a plethora of other the FSA material, not just as useful background information, but as material that could be used against us in an enforcement or disciplinary case. Things that you may need to keep track of include: guidance on the FSA website, FSA speeches, newsletters (Market Watch, List! etc.), discussion statements, policy documents, Dear CEO Letters. And then, of course, there is all the guidance prepared by the industry.

The absence of fixed rules will require more judgement calls to be made in relation to what does and does not constitute compliant behaviour. The fear is that the concept of compliance will come down to what a particular the FSA employee feels is acceptable on the day it is considered. A boon for those wanting to exercise their hindsight muscles, but for those of us who don't have that luxury the world is set to get tougher.

Does it sound as if I'm a prophet of doom? Not really, in fact I'm happy enough to give MPBR a try: we have had an ample set of rules for a long time now but we've still had our fair share of financial scandals, so perhaps principles will prove preferable.

Box 2   ARROW

ARROW, which stands for 'Advanced Risk Response Operating FrameWork' is the assessment methodology used by the FSA to identify and manage the risks to its four statutory objectives. It is the driving force behind the majority of the FSA's activities and has the key components that you would expect to see in any risk mitigation programme, namely

- *Identification* – what are the risks to the FSA's statutory objectives?
- *Measurement* – how seriously should the FSA take each of these risks? (probability v. impact.)
- *Control* – implementation of risk management arrangements.
- *Assessment* – how successful is the risk management programme that has been implemented?

Risks are identified in a number of ways including contact with firms during the course of the normal supervisory process, contact with consumer groups and specific ARROW risk assessment visits to regulated firms.

The FSA unveiled its new, improved ARROW 2 at the beginning of 2006 which is designed to further refine what it already considers to be a very successful risk mitigation programme. The new version of ARROW was two years in the offing, so we have a right to expect something quite good. The jury still seems to be out.

If you are notified of an impending ARROW review, turn to page 136 for guidance on how to tackle the FSA visits.

Box 3   Basel II and CRD

- The impact of a bank failure is clearly very damaging – consumers and trading partners are unlikely to receive back all or possibly any of the money they are owed. The failure of one bank may have a knock-on effect across the market, leading other participants to experience financial difficulty, which in turn may result in a general loss of market confidence.
- It follows that one of the key priorities of regulators worldwide is to implement a regulatory framework that reduces the risk that a bank for which they are responsible will not be able to meet its liabilities.
- Rules in this area are referred to as capital adequacy rules and, put very simply, are designed to ensure that banks have adequate financial resources to meet the risks they face: for example: Does a bank have enough capital to cover the risk that a number of its loans will not be repaid?
- For some time now, global regulators have come together to set common international standards for capital adequacy. The two key institutions behind this multi-jurisdictional initiative are

  - Basel Committee on Banking Supervision (BCBS)
  - The European Commission.

- The first BCBS capital adequacy framework, referred to as Basel I, has been in place since 1988 but by the later 1990s was widely viewed as outdated. Its new initiative (the *International Convergence of Capital Measurement and Capital Standards – A Revised Framework*, commonly shortened to Basel II) is in the process of implementation and has been incorporated into EU law through the Capital Resources Directive (CRD).
- The CRD was implemented on 1 January 2007 (with an additional one-year transitional phase for some of its more dramatic innovations) and replaces two existing EU directives:

  - The Capital Adequacy Directive
  - The Banking Consolidation Directive.

- The new regime is designed to require or incentivize firms to analyse and quantify the specific risks (credit, market and operational) that they face, and allow them (on certain very stringent conditions) to use these measures to determine their own capital requirements, thereby (hopefully) making it more risk-sensitive. It is based on three Pillars:

  1. *Minimum Capital Requirements* – This Pillar sets the basic capital requirement for each bank. Banks can choose to use a standard or advanced approach to calculate their capital requirements. Those choosing the advanced approach, which will be based on complex internal models developed by the institutions themselves and which will have to be approved by local regulators, will in theory have lower capital requirements. Pillar I adds the concept of 'Operational Risks' to the risk types established by Basel I, ostensibly stripping out operational risks (human, legal, technological, etc.) that banks face away from the general category of credit risk, and imposing a separate capital requirement for them. The new credit and operational risk capital frameworks have caused controversy because the simple approaches they offer are very capital intensive – to

Box 3   (Continued)

encourage international banks (the real target market of the Basel Committee) towards more sophisticated approaches – whereas the latter are out of the reach of the smaller banks and non-banks that Basel has been applied to across the EEA, who may have no significant history of credit or operational losses on which to base a model application. Hence some smaller institutions will face drastic increases in regulatory capital in part because their businesses are *less* prone to credit or operational losses than their larger peers.

2. *Supervisory Review* – This Pillar will be used to determine whether additional capital should be held to address risks not captured under Pillar I. It adds a range of 'qualitative' standards, under which firms must demonstrate that they analyse and understand their own risk profile and organizational integrity and impose quantified or procedural limits, as appropriate, on the risks they run. For instance they must perform their own internal assessments of capital adequacy, which sit alongside the regulatory prescriptions of Pillar I. (Clearly, the more sophisticated the approach taken in Pillar I, the less a firm will have to demonstrate under Pillar II.)

3. *Transparency and Disclosure to the Market* – The final Pillar requires banks to publish certain information about their risk and risk management arrangements. The rationale is that this will permit natural market forces to assess a firm's position and should result in truer measures of risk than statistical measures or credit assessments alone.

• The new capital adequacy requirements have been incorporated into the FSA rules in the Prudential Sourcebooks but with a number of transitional provisions and parallel run phases intended to allow firms to adapt to the new regime, put in place the considerable measurement and control mechanisms that several of the advanced Basel II approaches require, and permit the regulator the time to review and approve the mountain of risk model applications to which these approaches have given rise.

Box 4   Extradition

The threat of extradition is looming ever larger over the UK regulated community thanks to legislative changes in both the EU and US that were introduced into British law though the Extradition Act 2003.

In the EU, the European Arrest Warrant (EAW) was introduced in January 2004 and is designed to facilitate and expedite the extradition of suspects from one EU country to another. Although it was conceived initially as a counter-terrorism measure following the events of 11 September, it is in practice much more far reaching than that and applies to a number of crimes that are of interest to the Compliance Officer and his flock, specifically fraud for example, and money laundering and terrorist financing.

As well as the EAW we have new arrangements involving the US. Like the EAW these were also introduced into UK law through the Extradition Act 2003 and were also initially conceived as part of the fight against terrorism in the post-11 September world, but in reality have a much wider impact. It is now possible for UK citizens to be extradited to the US without the need for prima facie evidence to be presented. This means that the accused do not have the opportunity to defend themselves in a UK court prior to being delivered into the arms of the US justice system.

While the equivalent arrangements to facilitate extradition from the US to the UK have not yet managed to get themselves implemented, the US is showing an increasing enthusiasm for its new extraterritorial powers. Nowhere is this better demonstrated than with the now infamous case of 'the NatWest 3,' three former employees of NatWest that the High Court has allowed to be extradited to the US for alleged crimes relating to Enron.

There are a number of things that are particularly scary about this case: the three accused were themselves responsible for initially *volunteering* information on the case to the FSA which did not decide to pursue a case against them but instead handed the documents it had gathered over to the US authorities. When the case was eventually brought by the US, it was based almost in its entirety on the documents obtained from the FSA, which, despite feeling it does not have a case against the Three, will not support them in the US. And what is more, the Three were in the UK at the time their alleged crimes were supposed to have been committed, the supposed victim (NatWest itself) is also in the UK and does not even consider that any crime has been committed against it!

The clear message we would seem to be able to take from this sorry tale is that if the US is minded to get you . . . it will, as long as there is even the most tenuous link between you and the States. E-mails passing though the US, information posted on a US server, payment instructions flowing via a machine in the US. Be careful out there!

Box 5   Financial Services Action Plan

- The impetus to create a single European financial market began in earnest with the Maastricht Treaty of 1992, which opened the way for economic and monetary unity across the EU.
- By the end of the 1990s there were increasing demands to introduce greater coordination and strategizing in respect of the 'single financial services market' initiative: some measures had already been taken, other were scheduled, but the process was considered by many to be rather haphazard.
- Other drivers for shaking up the single financial services market process included

  - the impending introduction of the euro – it seemed logical for a single currency to go hand in hand with a single market;
  - the recognition that there was no level playing field for corporate capital raising activities in the EU;
  - the desire to provide consumers the same level of protection no matter which EU country they inhabit;
  - an understanding that difficulties companies faced in offering cross-border services was stifling competition;
  - the need to recognize the implications of the internet and e-commerce in relation to the cross-border offering of financial products and services; and
  - a determination to introduce greater stability into the European financial markets by instituting a single, robust prudential framework.

By addressing all of these issues in a strategic fashion it was hoped that Europe as a whole would be in a better position to compete with the US, which is not characterized by the fragmentation of its financial services markets in the way that the EU is.

- The Cardiff European Council of 1998 set the Financial Services Action Plan (the FSAP) wheels in motion when the Financial Services Policy Group was instructed to come up with a plan for injecting some planning, urgency and coordination into the process of harmonizing the various financial services markets in Europe.
- The FSAP was endorsed at the Lisbon European Council of 2000. It detailed 42 measures that were scheduled to be completed by 2005, and the plans were outlined in the European Commission document entitled: 'Financial Services: Building a Framework for Action.' The 42 measures were of four types:

  - directives;
  - regulations;
  - communications; and
  - recommendations

and came under three broad headings:

  - those affecting the wholesale market;
  - those affecting the retail market;
  - those affecting financial services supervision.

- Further impetus was given to the process of creating a single European financial services market in 2000, with the commissioning of the Lamfalussy review (see page 337).

- Most of the 42 measures have now been implemented (at least by the EU itself, although, as will be noted below, progress still needs to be made in relation to transposing the measures into the national law of the individual member states).
- It is too early to determine the success of the FSAP as there is still much to do before it is fully 'bedded down'. A large part of its success will also depend on the achievements of the EU during the next couple of years – and now that the FSAP is almost complete its focus is shifting to

  - ensuring that all measures are appropriately adopted by each member state;
  - evaluating the effectiveness of the FSAP initiative; and, with potentially earth shattering implications for the Compliance professional;
  - exploring the potential for 'better regulation' whatever that might mean to a European bureaucrat.

- Some of the much-publicised problems with the FSAP include

  - *Gold plating* – The tendency for some directives to be 'over-implemented' resulting in a particular member state introducing requirements that go beyond those required by the original directive. This clearly 'un-levels' the playing field. And, depending on which way you look at it, either serves to protect the businesses of the jurisdiction that has done the gold plating, or puts businesses in that jurisdiction at a disadvantage due to excessive regulation.
  - *Under-implementation* – The opposite of gold plating: some states are lagging behind in respect of transposing EU directives into their own law. And in some cases, even where requirements have been adopted locally it has not been done satisfactorily.
  - *Single criminal market* – To what extent has the single market for financial services facilitated criminal activity across the EU? For example, has the FSAP made it easier for cash stolen from your credit card account in London today, to be freely used in Madrid tomorrow? And if it has, have adequate steps been taken to address this?

Box 6   Going Global?

Just in case you or your colleagues need a little convincing about why you need to be familiar with regulation and legislation stemming from overseas jurisdictions when your firm is based in the UK, take a look at the list below showing why Compliance increasingly needs to go global.

- The UK's legislative and regulatory agenda is largely set by the European Union, thanks to the Financial Services Action Plan.
- Some jurisdictions (notably the US) seek to apply their legislation extraterritorially – for example, if you do a US$ trade in breach of OFAC restrictions, then you are likely to be in trouble. Also see Box 4 on page 323 covering US extradition cases.
- If your firm is part of an international group headquartered outside the UK, you may have to take account of requirements emanating in the country in which your parent company is based.
- If your firm undertakes cross-border activities you need to be aware of the requirements that apply in the jurisdictions in which you are active. Applicable requirements may vary depending on how this cross-border activity is undertaken: do you have a physical presence overseas through a branch or representative office, do you undertake 'suitcase banking' with employees periodically travelling overseas with no firm base (other than a hotel room), or is business undertaken purely from the UK with overseas clients being served purely by phone and e-mail, etc.?
- Global firms often operate global teams through matrix management arrangements. You will no doubt want to know whether or not the latest management initiative from London breaches any requirements applying to team members based overseas.
- Global initiatives in financial supervision are becoming a lot more joined up – regulators in one country are no longer shy about chatting to their overseas peers. The FSA is a great fan of international memoranda of understanding and at the last count was in collusion with 27 regulators across 16 different jurisdictions.
- The Basel Committee on Banking Supervision is increasingly setting the tone for all aspects of banking supervision. Principle 9 of its 2005 publication on the Compliance function in banks reads 'Banks should comply with applicable laws and regulations in all jurisdictions in which they conduct business, and the organization and structure of the compliance function and its responsibilities should be consistent with local legal and regulatory requirements.' You can't get much more explicit than that.

So, in an attempt to bring all of the above together, let's try this little brain teaser:

- Your head office is in Australia.
- The Global Compliance function is run from London.
- An employee of a Chinese entity within the group is seconded to a sister company in Italy.
- This employee has travelled to a Singapore branch office for a two-week period.
- During this time, he has travelled extensively in the South East Asia region promoting your firm's equity trading services.
- He has also arranged for marketing material to be distributed into various countries in the region that he has not been able to visit.

- The marketing material relates to US$-denominated products.
- These products are traded on various global exchanges.
- Settlement has been outsourced to India.

Which legislation and regulations apply?
Which regulators are interested?

Answers on a postcard please . . . !

But, of course, there is no ready answer. There is no handy rule that you can turn to for an explanation of how exactly this situation should be regulated and to do things properly you would really need to take account of rules in each jurisdiction mentioned.

Box 7   Industry Guidance

With the swing towards More Principles Based Regulation (MPBR – see page 317) in the UK we have seen a corresponding rise in the importance of industry guidance to assist us in meeting our regulatory obligations. The phenomenon is not new: we have had such material available to us for a long time, with two of the most well-known examples being the JMLSG Guidance Notes and the Banking Code of Conduct. What is new, however, is that the FSA is positively encouraging industry bodies to prepare guidance and is putting a framework in place for 'confirming' it.

Quite apart from the fact that, with the removal of many of the detailed the FSA rules, industry guidance will have an increasingly central role to play in our regulatory architecture, the arguments in favour of this approach are perfectly clear: it is the industry rather than the regulator that is best placed to know which *practical* solutions will be most likely to meet regulatory requirements. And this new more business-friendly approach should enable our industry to be more successful, innovative and efficient, thereby ultimately better able to meet consumer demands.

Undoubtedly, the use of industry guidance in itself is no bad thing, but almost inevitably, many arguments are being put forward against it.

Industry guidance as a concept

The most vehement dissenters are those who are against industry guidance as a concept and believe that its use simply amounts to the FSA shirking its responsibilities and passing the regulatory buck. They maintain that as the FSA is paid to be our regulator it is only natural to expect it to give us guidance on what it wants from us, rather than having us come up with our own ideas via trade associations (isn't this like employing a plumber to watch you fix your own pipes)?

These naysayers argue that trade associations are not regulators; they have not been trained as such and they do not have the regulator's perspective. They also do not have the regulator's funding, time or neutrality, thus we are compromising the independence of the regulatory process by allowing trade bodies to take on certain regulatory functions in respect of the companies that provide their funding, with no governmental accountability to mitigate the risk of conflict to which this situation gives rise.

There is also a concern that overzealous associations will ramp up the 'requirements' in their guidance in order to ensure that it receives the FSA confirmed status. This would involve requiring the firms adhering to it to go beyond regulatory expectations, thus putting them at a competitive disadvantage to other firms across Europe who comply only with the bare bones of MiFID or other relevant directives.

Status of industry guidance

It is important to remember that the guidance issued by trade bodies will not have the same status as the FSA rules and there will be no obligation to comply with it . . . but the FSA has stated that it 'will take it into account when exercising its regulatory functions' and that if there is a breach of such guidance, this may be relevant in an enforcement case. This would appear to confer it with a quasi-regulatory status yet there will be no statutory consultation during which we will have the opportunity to raise concerns (such as impracticality or conflict with other guidance already in existence) and have them addressed.

It is also important to remember that if you tell clients in your terms of business that you will be adhering to a particular piece of guidance, then you had better make sure that you do so, as you could be laying yourself open to civil action by a client if you then you deviate from it.

Impact on industry associations

There have also been concerns that the growing reliance on industry guidance will weaken the position of trade bodies. This may seem counter-intuitive at first but the concern should be taken seriously: at present, trade associations may limit access to their guidance to fee-paying members but now any FSA confirmed guidance must be freely and publicly available. There will thus be less incentive for smaller firms, who do not expect their voice to be heard within the organizations, to become paying members, which will reduce industry association funding right at the very time that their costs will go up due to the additional financial burden of producing guidance material and making staff available to answer queries on it. (Will there be a corresponding fall in FSA fees? This would seem highly improbable.)

We should also remember that trade bodies may be leaving themselves open to being sued by both consumers and regulated firms alike if reliance on their guidance is accused of having led to a regulatory train smash. The FSA of course can rely on its statutory immunity in similar situations. This does not seem fair.

Small firms at a disadvantage

Fears have also been expressed that the growing use of industry guidance will put small firms at a disadvantage as:

- they may be treated as 'lesser partners' within trade bodies, or may simply not be able to afford to join them and so participate in the development of guidance, or receive answers to guidance-related queries;
- there are fewer trade bodies representing the interests of small firms; and
- the trade bodies that do exist for small firms are likely to be less well resourced than others, and therefore not particularly well placed to prepare guidance for their members.

If you work in a sector where there is a dearth of industry guidance you may decide just to write some yourself!

Box 8   L&G v. the FSA – Who are the real winners and losers?

In a 'flagship' case the FSA fined Legal and General (L&G) £1.1m for alleged endowment policy mis-selling between 1997 and 1999. L&G was not happy with this outcome and took the matter to the Financial Services and Markets Tribunal which subsequently (in January 2005) criticized the FSA's enforcement case and slashed the fine to (a mere) £575 000.

L&G can understandably afford to feel smug about this outcome. But should all of us in the regulated community also feel smug? The victory clearly shows that the Tribunal is fully capable of acting independently of the FSA – previously there had been concerns on this point. And it also shows that firms *do* have a leg to stand on when it comes to challenging the FSA's decisions. We should all take comfort, and confidence, from that.

But what else does the case mean? Well, it shows up the FSA in a bad light and as a country that wants to be a leading financial services centre, our regulator has to do better for us than that: if it really had a good case, then why could it not make it stick, and if it did not have a good case, then why did it bring it in the first place? How can the FSA support its statutory objective of combating financial crime if it does not have a successful enforcement process? What deterrent is there for inappropriate behaviour if the message that comes across is that the FSA is badly organized in terms of enforcement and that if you take it on, you may well win?

By embarrassing itself over L&G, the FSA has, from the purely selfish point of view of the Compliance Officer, taken away one of the stoutest sticks that we could wave at our badly behaved colleagues to bring them into line. It was presumably also a contributing factor in the FSA's decision to carry out a full review of its disciplinary procedures and work very hard at putting its house in order. Its work in this area is now complete. Out went large sections of the rulebook that had previously covered disciplinary procedures and enforcement and in came the 'new, improved' *Decision Procedure and Penalties Manual* and the *Enforcement Guide*. Whoever's firm is next in line for one of the FSA's 'showcase' enforcement actions is likely to find that the FSA does not topple quite so easily this time.

Box 9   Markets in Financial Instruments Directive

Within only a few years of surviving N2 (the last great shake up in the UK's regulatory system when FSMA was implemented in November 2001) we found ourselves being dragged kicking and screaming into MiFID with its equally momentous impact on providers of financial services right across Europe. I remember N2 well. Perhaps because of the perceived deficiencies of the regime that it replaced (under the Financial Services Act 1986) I don't recall encountering too much cynicism or complaining about all the work it involved; there was even perhaps a degree of enthusiasm. It was a different story with MiFID. No one (apart perhaps from the IT companies who stood to gain millions from implementing the hefty IT infrastructure to which it has given rise) showed much eagerness to learn the new rules, determine the effect that they would have, or implement a project to roll them out.

I take this to be because, in contrast with N2, few people had been critical of the previous regime and saw MiFID as a dose of medicine that was not really needed. Obviously there had been the odd grumble, but nothing to justify the wholesale rewrite that we saw to many sections of the FSA rulebook. Indeed, on the whole, people seemed to be fairly proud of the UK regulatory regime and refused to agree that it needed to be changed just because some far away lands on the other side of the EU did not have the same regulatory standards as we do. This is at the heart of one of the main criticisms of MiFID from a UK perspective: London is the biggest financial centre in Europe so it is arguably the one that will see the biggest change, and therefore incur the biggest cost. But it is also considered by many to have had an exemplary regulatory regime well before the days of MiFID, meaning that the enormous costs of compliance far outweigh any benefits. Look at the FSA's own figures: in its November 2006 report *The Overall Impact of MiFID* it estimates that regulated firms could benefit by up to £200 million per year (primarily through reduced compliance and transactions costs). In contrast one-off costs for regulated firms are estimated at £877 million to £1.17 billion with additional ongoing costs of £88 million to £117 million per year. You do the maths . . .

Another major criticism of MiFID in the UK is the FSA's 'intelligent copy-out' approach which was prescribed by HM Treasury for the translation with minimal amendment of all EU directives into UK rules, ostensibly to cool the FSA's ardour for 'gold-plating' international standards. Its real effect, unfortunately, is the absence of much needed explanation and context from the new rulebook, and a grating tendency to refer to opaque European legislation for a definition of its terms. This has not led to improvements in the clarity or concision of the FSA's Sourcebooks and has led some to question whether the term 'intelligent copy-out' should be substituted with 'dilatory cop-out'.

But leaving the objections to one side, MiFID's aims are perfectly laudable and include

- strengthening the single European financial services market that was introduced by MiFID's predecessor, the Investment Services Directive of 1993 (the ISD) by making it easier for firms authorized in one jurisdiction to provide services in another;
- increasing the range of products and services covered by Europe's consumer protection and passporting regimes;
- establishing a regulatory framework for order execution no matter what the trading venue (i.e. systematic internalizer, MTF or regulated market);
- introducing stronger conflicts of interest controls; and
- protecting the integrity and increasing the efficiency of the European financial markets.

Box 9   (Continued)

Some of the main changes introduced by MiFID are as follows:

- *Scope* – As well as covering all of the products and services caught by the ISD, MiFID also covers:

Products

- – Commodity derivatives.
- – Certain additional derivatives – commodity, credit and financial contracts for difference.

Services

- Multilateral trading facilities.
- Advice.

- *Passporting* – As well as expanding the passporting regime to cover the products and services described above, MiFID also clarifies some of the uncertainties relating to home and host state regulator responsibilities.

- *Conduct of business* – There were significant rule changes for UK firms in many areas, including

  - – client categorization;
  - – best execution;
  - – suitability and appropriateness;
  - – order and execution related record keeping and transparency;
  - – client assets;
  - – financial promotions; and
  - – transaction reporting (which falls under the 'Supervision' regime).

- *Systems and controls* – Again, there were significant rule changes for UK firms. Some of the areas where the changes were most keenly felt include

  - – Compliance arrangements;
  - – outsourcing;
  - – business continuity; and
  - – IT arrangements.

It is also worth noting that even though substantial changes to the
FSA rules for training and competence and approved persons were introduced on the same day that the UK implemented MiFID, these did not actually stem from any MiFID-related changes.

As a final point it is important to be aware that despite being one of the key drivers behind the UK regulatory regime the scope of MiFID is unfortunately not the same as the scope of the RAO (see Appendix 3). This leads, to a certain extent, to a two-tier regulatory regime with different regulation applicable depending on whether an activity constitutes 'MiFID business' or not.

Box 10   Money Laundering Statistics

Due to its very nature, it is incredibly difficult to measure the exact amount of money laundering that takes place, but some of the figures that have been put forward are as follows:

- Worldwide income from drug-trafficking alone could be as high as £500 billion[1] and estimates for the EU suggest a £131 billion problem.[1]
- As much as 25% of all money in circulation worldwide could be 'dirty' money.[1]
- In Los Angeles over 75% of money circulating in the city has trace of illegal drugs.[1]
- The US Treasury cannot account for half of its $300 billion currency.[1]
- Estimated money laundering flows are reported to be in excess of US$1 trillion being laundered every year by drug dealers, arms traffickers and other criminals.[2]
- Broad estimates put the economic and social costs of serious organised crime, including the costs of combating it, at upwards of £20 billion a year [in the UK].[3]
- Money laundering in the UK can be roughly valued at between £23 to £57 billion.[4]
- The government estimates that the value of assets laundered through the UK regulated sector each year is £15 billion.[5]

---

[1] The CIMA Guide to the proceeds of Crime Act 2002 and the Money Laundering Regulations 2003, *Money Laundering: What Every Accountant Should Know*, 2004.
[2] The KPMG Global Anti Money Laundering Survey 2007: *How Banks are facing up to the Challenge.*
[3] The United Kingdom Threat Assessment of Serious Organised Crime 2006/7, published by SOCA.
[4] The FSA website, October 2007.
[5] From the report *The Financial Challenge to Crime and Terrorism* issued in February 2007 by HM Treasury.

Box 11   Prudential Regulation of Capital Adequacy

Prudential regulation of Capital Adequacy is a part of the FSMA regime that is not dealt with in any detail in this book as it is generally the responsibility of the Finance department rather than the Compliance Officer. Nevertheless, you should not feel that you can ignore the area altogether: you must at least have a basic understanding of it as it is so fundamental to the regulatory system.

The objective of this limb of regulation is to ensure that firms have sufficient capital to meet their obligations and do not take on risks that are out of proportion to their ability to sustain losses. The reasons behind this are two-fold:

- *Investor protection* – If a firm becomes insolvent it may not be able to honour its obligations to customers.
- *Preventing systemic risk* – This occurs when the financial collapse of one firm has a knock-on effect on its creditors, and so on, eventually putting the entire financial system at risk.

In order to prevent these outcomes firms must pass an initial capital adequacy test on becoming authorized and thereafter must meet their capital resources requirements on an ongoing basis. The FSA's overarching requirement, its overall capital adequacy rule, reads as follows: 'A firm must at all times maintain overall financial resources, including capital resources and liquidity resources, which are adequate, both as to amount and quality, to ensure that there is no significant risk that its liabilities cannot be met as they fall due.'

Until the arrival of the Capital Requirements Directive (CRD) in 2006 this was achieved principally by means of prescriptive rules; sophisticated internal risk management was expected of large banks and securities dealers but was not a point of focus for smaller firms. Under CRD, upon which the FSA's prudential regime is based, almost as much emphasis is placed on firms' internal processes for assessing and limiting their risks – market risks associated with investments, counterparty default risk, legal and operational risk and so on – as on externally prescribed capital resources. These still exist, however, and are more complex and capital intensive than ever.

The regulators' capital adequacy measure has two main components: the evaluation of a firm's capital resources on one hand and, on the other, the identification and evaluation of its risk positions.

'Capital resources' are made up of 'permanent' capital: equity share capital, retained earnings, and subordinated (near-permanent) debt. With 'sub debt' excepted, this number will resemble the 'net assets' or shareholder's equity we see on a company's balance sheet, which are important to its financial stability because they are the sum of what, effectively, the company really 'owns', as opposed to what it has acquired through leverage (i.e. by taking on liabilities in order to acquire assets): these are the proprietary resources it can use to meet unforeseen liabilities.

'Risk positions' include all of a firm's market risk and counterparty credit risk positions in its trading book (e.g. long or short equity positions, options, futures, contracts for difference, and so on) and its non-trading or banking book (e.g. loans, long-term repos). These positions are 'risk-weighted' by prescribed percentages according to their type and their riskiness, such that higher-quality investments benefit from a lower weighting than those carrying high risk – e.g. loans to financially regulated counterparties or those with a high credit rating have a lower risk weight than, say, issuers of high-yield bonds. How these risk-weighted amounts are calculated depends on the nature of the position:

- *Market risk* – Exposures to price movements in the firm's trading portfolio, whether across a market, or to the risk of default of individual issuers. There are separate categories for equity and equity equivalent positions, debt instruments such as bonds or interest rate swaps; options and futures.
- *Counterparty credit risk* – Direct credit exposures to borrowers or trading counter-parties attract risk capital calculated under one of a number of methods, ranging from a prescriptive regulatory approach to sophisticated bespoke models.
- *Concentration risk* – Exposures to a certain group of assets (e.g. one equity or debt issuer, or a borrower and its subsidiaries) over certain thresholds attract accelerating capital charges under the two categories above.
- *Interest rate and foreign currency risk* – These have their own treatments, which respond to whether the exposure is in the trading or the banking/non-trading book.
- *Operational risk* – Several methods – from rudimentary to highly sensitive – are available to quantify the risk of losses due to operational risks (see below).

The essential regulatory capital adequacy test is that the sum of the risk-weighted positions calculated in each of these categories must not exceed the capital resources of the firm.

If the firm's group contains a parent bank which is registered in the EEA then its own, and any other affiliates', capital resources and risk positions will be consolidated with those of the bank.

To these tests CRD has added the concept of operational risk (to capture losses due to human error, IT system failure and suchlike), and the requirement that firms perform their own internal capital adequacy assessments tailored to their own activities, and subject their resources and risk positions to stress testing. For many firms this is a significantly greater burden than previously applied, but it follows the sensible premise that firms themselves are, or should be, most familiar with the risks that they run and how these should be identified, measured and restricted.

A well-known example of a firm running into financial difficulty that it should have been able to avoid is that of Northern Rock, the UK mortgage provider, which suffered from the sub prime credit crunch in 2007. Most mortgage firms fund their loans by taking in customer deposits but 'The Rock' followed a different model and funded its mortgage book by borrowing from other institutions. When these institutions became reluctant to lend to Northern Rock, its sources of cash ran dry and it had to accept emergency funding from the Bank of England as lender of last resort. Northern Rock might have avoided this crisis if it had done more to understand its liquidity risks and, one suspects, diversified its means of funding its mortgage portfolio.

Box 12   The Enforcement Process
Getting on the wrong side of the FSA

Most FSA investigations will be resolved without recourse to the formal enforcement process but anyone unfortunate enough to find themselves facing potential disciplinary action will become familiar with the process summarized below:[1]

- *Stage 1*: Investigators appointed. Notice of appointment of investigators sent to the person concerned, at the FSA's discretion.
- *Stage 2*: Investigation scoped out to inform the relevant persons of what it will involve, e.g. how the process will work and the documents and people to which the investigators will require access.
- *Stage 3*: Investigation work undertaken, e.g. review of documents, witness interviews. Following the investigation there will be an internal legal review of the case by the FSA, undertaken by a person who was not part of the investigation team
- *Stage 4*: Preliminary Investigation Report (PIR) provided to the person being investigated. *(You have 28 days to respond but can ask for extra time if you wish.)*
- *Stage 5*: Case brought to the Regulatory Decisions Committee (RDC) if the investigations team think this is merited. The RDC reviews the investigation report which takes account of the response of the person being investigated to the PIR.
- *Stage 6*: If considered appropriate by the RDC, it sends a Warning Notice to the person being investigated detailing any further action that will be taken. *(You have 28 days to respond and can ask for extra time if you wish.)*
- *Stage 7:* If the person concerned makes a representation after receipt of the Warning Notice, the RDC will meet again to consider the information received.
- *Stage 8*: The RDC makes a final decision and, if appropriate, issues a Decision Notice. *(You have 28 days to take the matter to the Financial Services and Markets Tribunal).* However, if the RDC decides that there is no case to answer, a Notice of Discontinuance may be issued.
- *Stage 9*: The FSA publishes a final notice and makes details of the case public.

Note that the investigation may be closed at any time by the FSA

- with the issuance of a private warning;
- through the use of settlement discussions with the person under investigation; or
- by a decision that there are no grounds for enforcement action.

Good luck!

---

[1] Note that the process described here applies to most, but not all, enforcement cases, for example, it does not cover the bringing of criminal prosecutions or civil proceedings.

Box 13   The Lamfalussy Process

- Mindful that their track record on the implementation of initiatives impacting securities law across the EU was considered by many to be fairly woeful, the EU's economic and finance ministers arranged in 2000 for a 'Committee of Wise Men' to come up with a blueprint to ensure that the securities measures within the Financial Services Action Plan (FSAP) would be delivered more efficiently.
- The Committee was chaired by Baron Lamfalussy and the process it devised (which was unveiled in a 2001 report entitled, *The Regulation of Securities Markets*) became known as the Lamfalussy Process. Although initially applying only to securities market activity it was expanded to cover banking and insurance in 2002.
- The Lamfalussy Process involves a four-layer approach to the implementation of EU financial services legislation which is designed to take account of the need to provide for speed, transparency, efficiency, quality, consistency and flexibility during the implementation process. It represents a significant shift from the traditional EU legislative process.
- The four layers of the Lamfalussy Process are as follows:

  - *Level 1* – The European Commission and the European Council agree on the desired 'output' and basic framework of the legislation being considered. Level 1 directives and regulations are pitched at the 'framing principle' level. The detail of the legislation is decided at Level 2.
  - *Level 2* – The European Commission specifies the technical details of the framework agreed at Level 1. This is known as the 'comitology' procedure and the arrangements arrived at will be contained in either directives or regulations. Both are legislative measures, the difference being that directives need to be implemented separately in each member state, whereas regulations apply directly.
  - *Level 3* – Each member state implements the measures taken at Levels 1 and 2 above. Guidelines and best practice standards are issued in order to bring about uniform implementation.
  - *Level 4* – This will involve the European Commission checking member states' compliance with the FSAP measures, with the threat of enforcement action for any that are 'under-performing'.

- Integral to the operation of the Lamfalussy Process is the operation of what are frequently called the Lamfalussy Committees which operate in the areas of banking, securities (including UCITS – see Appendix 5) and insurance and occupational pensions.
- The committees operate at Levels 2 and 3 of the Lamfalussy Process as follows:

  - *Level 2 Committees (advise the Commission, and assist it in adopting implementing measures at Level 1)*

    - The European Banking Committee
    - The European Insurance and Occupational Pensions Committee
    - The European Securities Committee.

  - *Level 3 Committees (advise on measures to be taken at Levels 1 and 2 as well as working on Level 3 implementing measures)*

Box 13   (Continued)

- o The Committee of European Banking Supervisors
- o The Committee of European Insurance and Occupational Pensions Supervisors
- o The Committee of European Securities Regulators.

(An additional committee covering financial conglomerates was established in 2006.)

- It would appear that the Lamfalussy Process has achieved at least a degree of success – for example, the average time taken from proposal to adoption for the Market Abuse Directive, MiFID, the Transparency Directive and the Prospectus Directives, all of which have been through Lamfalussy, is 20 months. By contrast, the corresponding preparation time for the Investment Services Directive was four years, and two and a half years for the Insider Dealing Directive.
- Before we get too excited, a few words of caution are in order. Could the seed of the Lamfalussy Process's downfall also lie in its very success? Does it really serve our purpose as a regulated community to speed directives through the approval process? Does this leave us with adequate time to eliminate enough of the euro-bureaucratic excesses that might be lurking within? And even if it does, do we as Compliance Officers have enough time and resources to fully implement the flood of recent directives? Only time will tell.

Box 14   The Laundering Process

Money laundering is generally considered to take place in three stages:

- *Placement* – This stage normally involves ready cash and takes place when the criminal first places the illegal funds into the financial system. Obviously, the criminal origins of the funds must be hidden or it would not be possible to bank them – for example, cash collected from selling stolen goods could be placed into a bank account ostensibly opened for a mini cab company so that the large cash sums being paid in do not cause suspicion.
- *Layering* – This stage involves moving the deposited funds through a complex web of transactions in order to hide their origins, the point at which they entered the system and their connection with the person who initially made the deposit. One of the most well-known methods used at this stage is to undertake a series of international wire transfers involving jurisdictions and banks with strong bank secrecy legislation and weak anti-money-laundering regimes.
- *Integration* – Integration takes place when the complex layering stage has been completed: the illicit origin of the funds is considered to be sufficiently well hidden for the money to be safely invested in a perfectly legitimate way, without fear of detection. The criminals spend or invest the illegal funds in whichever way they please.

Organized criminals specialize in devising ever more imaginative and intricate ways of disguising their activities. Would you be able to spot the signals if any of these activities were taking place through your firm? Some things to look out for include

- multiple third party payments for which there is not a clear rationale;
- difficulties in identifying the ultimate beneficial owners of an account;
- multiple transactions which do not appear to have any economic benefits; and
- customers based in one country but using a bank account in another, for no clear reason.

Box 15   Treating Customers Fairly

During the past couple of years considerable the FSA and Compliance department time and effort has been spent addressing the Treating Customers Fairly (TCF) initiative. And TCF would appear to be an excellent example of the FSA's principles-based vision for its future regulatory model as it represents a concept, or way of doing business, rather than a particular set of rules and guidance.

The FSA has identified a number of areas in which firms should apply the TCF concept, including

1. Corporate culture.
2. Identification of target markets.
3. Consumer access to information.
4. Suitability of advice.
5. Product performance.
6. Post-sale arrangements.

But there is no such thing as the Treating Customers Fairly Rulebook. This means that in order to address all the above areas appropriately, firms themselves are required to identify and draw upon the relevant strands of the FSA's (and perhaps other bodies') formal rules and guidance and construct an internal TCF regime based on their own priorities and judgements.

Quite clearly, the FSA Principle 6 is relevant: '*A firm must pay due regard to the interests of its customers and treat them fairly.*' This does not supply much meat for firms to get their teeth into, however. The FSA has also established a TCF Consultative Group, has given numerous speeches and has prepared a substantial amount of documentation on the subject, but nothing that is particularly concrete – other than the deadlines (latest target date for firms to be able to demonstrate that they are treating their customers fairly is December 2008). So, whereas we are probably clear that recent problems involving split cap investment trusts, with-profits products or sales practices for payment protection insurance for example – would not get a tick in the TCF box, instances of good practice have not been particularly well highlighted, although there are some examples on the FSA website.

So firms are on their own in terms of defining what TCF means for them, and need to go through the rulebook to pick out what they consider to be the applicable sections:

- The Conduct of Business Sourcebook, for example

  (1) Having a clear charging structure.
  (2) Ensuring that all communication is fair, clear and not misleading.
  (3) Completing fact finds to promote product suitability.

- Senior Management Systems, Arrangements and Controls, for example

  (1) Constructing sound remuneration policies that are not simply based on sales level and volume.
  (2) Preparing adequate management information on TCF and ensuring that it is delivered to the appropriate people.
  (3) Embedding the TCF concept into written policy and procedure documents.

- Training and Competence, for example

  (1) Ensuring that staff understand what TCF means to your firm and their customers.
  (2) Ensuring that staff know how to apply TCF in the context of their own day-to-day activities.

- Dispute resolution: Complaints, for example

  (1) Implementing robust complaints handling procedures that are known to relevant staff; and
  (2) Running systems for analysing complaints data to identity and address any themes that become apparent.

  Think DISP 1: Treating Complainants Fairly.

When considering TCF it is also useful to bear in mind the five main reasons why a (retail) contract may go wrong (as identified in the FSA Occasional Paper 1[1]), and these are

1. The consumer receives bad advice – perhaps because an agency conflict is exploited.
2. The supplying institution becomes insolvent before the contract matures.
3. The contract turns out to be different from the one the consumer was expecting.
4. Fraud and misrepresentation.
5. The financial institution has been incompetent.

Whereas it does not take much to grasp the basic premise that customers should be treated fairly, the lack of clarity from the FSA is causing a lot of head scratching within the firm it regulates. Some of the questions that firms are asking are

- Will it be enough if we identify what we consider to be relevant rules and comply with them, or do we have to go beyond the contents of the FSA's rulebook?
- Which customers fall within the scope of TCF? The TCF programme was initially considered to be very much a retail initiative, but it now seems that it is to be applied more widely. Does TCF cover relationships with eligible counterparties that the FSA does not define as customers? And what about professional clients? These *do* fall within the FSA definition of a 'customer', even if they are large listed corporates, so theoretically TCF applies. But then many of the detailed consumer protection rules (think conduct of business and complaints handling, for example) are not applicable to them. Where do the boundaries lie?
- How will TCF be used in enforcement action going forward? The FSA has said that it will use its enforcement powers in proceedings where it does not consider that customers have been treated fairly and indeed it has been cited in a number of recent cases. This is quite a frightening prospect given the lack of clear rules and boundaries around which firms can construct their businesses in this area.

With all the uncertainties surrounding TCF, there are a few areas in which we do have absolute clarity:

- TCF is a priority issue for the FSA and is here to stay, so we had better make sure that our firms are ready to do what it takes to comply.
- It will play a large part in the ARROW process (see page 320).

Box 15   (Continued)

- Senior management take note – the FSA has parked responsibility for TCF fairly and squarely with you! Note this quote from Clive Briault, the MD of the FSA's Retail Markets division in November 2005: 'What we are trying to achieve is for *senior managers* to put themselves in the place of their customers and to consider very carefully whether they are being treated fairly by the firm. This offers a simple and effective test – a yardstick against which issues can be tested.'

---

[1] April 1999 – *The Economic Rationale for Financial Regulation* by David Llewellyn.

Index

abusive squeeze 156
actuaries' reports 105
Advanced Risk Response Operating Framework
   (ARROW) 320
advisory work 88–98
   areas to query 91–6
   basic questions 89–90
   choosing an option 97–8
   gut reactions 98
   investigations 89–91
   people to question 90–1
   plans of attack 96–8
   regulatory implications 91–6
   remedial action 97
   routine activities 134–5
   standard approach 88–98
aggregation of orders 225–6, 299, 303
agreements
   clients/customers 216–17, 269
   Legal department 269
   regulatory 145–6
   terms 310
allocation of assets 225–6, 299, 303
annual plans 129–30
anti-money-laundering 44, 195–207
   see also money-laundering
   counter-terrorism 207
   dilemmas 284–5, 287, 290–1, 293, 300
   financial sanctions 198
   Front Office 235–6
   KYC 195–7, 200–3
   MLRO reporting 206
   Patriot Act certificate 203–4
   PEPs 204–6
   regulations 11–12
   suspicious activities 199–200
appendices 121–314
   anti-money-laundering 195–207
   Back Office/support departments 253–76
   conundrums 277–314
   Front Office 209–51
   routine activities 121–94
   senior management 253–6
appointed representative reporting 106
appropriateness requirements 223–4, 279,
   298–300, 312
Approved Persons
   customers 271
   dilemmas 292, 296–7, 309
   FSA serious issues 110
   HR department 258
   Internal Audit 264
   Operations department 271–2
   reporting 106
   rules 228–9
   senior management 254
   status withdrawal 116
ARROW (Advanced Risk Response Operating
   Framework) 320
asset management 211
associations, industry 329
attestation activities 130
auditors' reports 105

Back Office and support departments 84–5,
   253–76
   Company Secretariat 262–3
   Finance 261–2
   HR 256–9
   Internal Audit 264–5
   IT department 265–8
   Legal 268–9
   Marketing 259–60
   Operational Risk 269–70
   Operations 271–4
   Tax department 274–5
Baldwin, Tim 114
banking, BCBS 321–2
Banking Code of Conduct 328
Basel Committee on Banking Supervision
   (BCBS), Basel I/II 16–17, 321–2
benchmarking 65

benefits of compliance   31–7
    clients/customers   33, 34
    corporate governance   33
    firm/colleagues   35
    monetary   34
    reputational   34
best execution rule   218–20, 284–5, 305, 313
best interest rule, clients   214–15, 278–82,
    284–5, 289–90, 295, 298–300, 303, 305,
    307, 312–13
board of directors *see* directors
borrowing and investment powers   239, 300
breaches of regulations/rules   109–11,
    115–20, 170–1
business
    investment   5–8
    types under FSMA/MiFID   8–11
    units   56–60

capital adequacy   321–2, 334–5
Capital Requirements Directive (CRD)   321–2,
    334–5
case law   4
cautions, FSA   118
centralized compliance models   20–1
Charters   43–7
    approval   46–7
    changes   47
    contents   43–7
    Contracts   41, 43–7
    day-to-day activities   44
    escalation procedures   46
    legislative environment   72
    maintenance   130
    objectives   44
    performance measurement   46
    powers   45
    reporting to management   46
    responsibilities   43, 45–6
Chinese walls   157–9, 247–8
    dilemmas   278–9, 282, 284–6, 301–4,
       306–8, 310–11
    Internal Audit   265
    IT department   266
    Legal department   269
    Operations department   272
    senior management   254–5
churning   224–5, 280–1
City Code on Takeovers and Mergers (Takeover
    Code)   12, 110
Civil Procedure Rule   114, 1998
clearing houses   70, 135
clients
    agreements   216–17

best interest rule   214–15, 278–82, 284–5,
    289–90, 295, 298–300, 303, 305,
    307, 312–13
    categorization   185–8, 232–3
    communication   230–1
    limit orders   221
    venture capital   187
close links   106, 262
closure of firm   120
colleagues in Compliance   35
common law   4
communicating with clients   230–1
Companies Act 2006   255
Company Secretariat   262–3
compensation   117
competence *see* training and competence
competent employees rule   171, 297–8, 300
competition   13, 66
complaints   108–9, 119, 169
Compliance Charter *see* Charters
Compliance Contract *see* Contracts
Compliance department   24–30, 87–101
    see also departments; routine activities
    advisory work   88–98
    aspects to eliminate   28–9
    bad regimes   28–9
    Charters   43–7
    concept of compliance   16–18
    conundrums   99–101
    costs   37–8
    danger signals   29–30
    good regimes   24–8
    interactions
       firm   26–7
       third parties   27–8
    internal arrangements   25–6
    key activities   87–101
Compliance function   15–40
    areas of knowledge   49–51
    arguments for compliance   30–8
    bad regimes   28–9
    benefits   30–7
    as a concept   16–21
    costs   37–8
    departments   16–18, 24–30
    Front/Back Office   83–5
    good regimes   24–8
    models   20–1
    Officers   17–24
    professional aspects   38–40
Compliance Mission Statement   41–2
Compliance Officers *see* Officers
Compliance risk *see* risk
confidentiality
    Company Secretariat   263
    dilemmas   285–6, 302–3, 309

Front Office   243–4
Internal Audit   264–5
IT department   266
Legal department   268
Marketing department   260
Operational Risk department   270
Operations department   272
senior management   255–6
conflict of interests   146–9
Company Secretariat   263
dilemmas   284–6, 288–90, 294, 300–3,
   305–7, 312, 314
Front Office   246
senior management   255–6
consultation papers   138
consumer needs table   81
Contracts   41–7
Charters   41, 43–7
Mission Statements   41–2
promoting compliance   41–2
controller reporting   106
controls, Front Office   212–51
conundrums   277–314
   see also dilemmas
lack of cooperation   99–101
tactics list   100–1
conventions, UN   11
cooperation, lack of   99–101
corporate finance   187, 211
corporate fund raising   64
corporate governance   33, 263
corporate knowledge   53–61, 180–1
   see also Know Your Customer
business units   56–60
external service providers   60–1
information log   53
operating entities   53–6
corporate restructuring   65
   see also takeovers
corruption   291
   see also fraud
costs   37–8, 68
counter-terrorism   207, 235–6
   see also anti-money-laundering; terrorism
CRD (Capital Requirements Directive)   321–2,
   334–5
culture   122–3
customers
   see also clients; Know Your Customer
agreements   269
compliance benefits   33, 34
documents   82
fair treatment   260, 301–2, 313, 340–2
sales   210–11
trading   210–11

damages, action for   119
danger signals   29–30, 99
data protection   179–80
Company Secretariat   263
dilemmas   285, 309
HR department   257
Internal Audit   265
IT department   266
Legal department   268
Operational Risk department   270
Operations department   272
senior management   255–6
Davidson, Paul ('the Plumber')   114
day-to-day activities, Charters   44
decentralized compliance models   20–1
deception   157
decision-making   97–8
departments
   see also Back Office and support departments;
      Compliance department; Front Office
Finance   261–2
HR/Personnel   256–9
IT   265–8
Legal   268–9
Marketing   259–60
Operational Risk   269–70
Operations   271–4
Tax   274–5
dilemmas   278–314
   see also conundrums
aggregation of orders   299, 303
allocation of assets   299, 303
anti-money-laundering   284–5, 287, 290–1,
   293, 300
appropriateness   279, 298–300, 312
Approved Persons   292, 296–7, 309
best execution   284–5, 305, 313
best interest rule   278–82, 284–5, 289–90,
   295, 298–300, 303, 305, 307, 312–13
borrowing/investment powers   300
Chinese walls   278–9, 282, 284–6, 301–4,
   306–8, 310–11
churning   280–1
client's best interest rule   278–82, 284–5,
   289–90, 295, 298–300, 303, 305,
   307, 312–13
competent employees rule   297–8, 300
confidentiality   285–6, 302–3, 309
conflict of interests   284–6, 288–90, 294,
   300–3, 305–7, 312, 314
corruption   291
data protection   285, 309
disciplinary action   311
exclusivity   286, 302
execution   284–5, 305, 313
external directorships   289

dilemmas (*Continued*)
  fairness to customers   301–2, 313
  fitness/propriety issues   292, 295, 297, 311
  handling orders   305
  inducements   280–1, 289–90, 300–1,
    305–7, 312
  information about firm   310
  insider lists   281–8, 292, 295, 308, 314
  investment/borrowing powers   300
  KYC   280
  market abuse   278–88, 292–3, 295, 301–2,
    304–8, 310–12, 314
  market conduct   278–88, 292–3, 295, 301–2,
    304–8, 310–12, 314
  PA dealing   281–3, 287–8, 292, 301–2, 305–6,
    308, 311–12, 314
  permitted activities   296, 299, 309
  propriety/fitness issues   292, 295, 297, 311
  record-keeping   309–10
  relations with regulators   296–7, 313
  remuneration policies   290, 307
  research   294, 306–7, 314
  restricted lists   282–4, 286, 292, 295,
    304–6, 308
  risk warnings   298
  senior management   295, 310
  suitability   279–81, 298–300, 307, 312
  supervision   310–11
  T&C   295–8, 309–11
  terms of agreements   310
  voice recording   285
  watch lists   282–4, 286, 292, 295, 304–6, 308
Directives, EU   4
directors   253–6
  see also senior management
  Company Secretariat   262
  external   258, 289
disciplinary action
  courses   113–14, 142–3
  dilemmas   311
  FSA   112–14
  Legal department   269
  procedures   142–3
dissemination of information   151
documentation   79, 82, 145–6
drug trafficking   11

EAW (European Arrest Warrant)   323
elective eligible counterparties   187
elective professional clients   186
electronic order book   67
eligible counterparties   186–7
employment contract breaches   120
enforcement   103–20, 336
  see also Financial Services Authority;
    Financial Services and Markets Act

escalation procedures, Charters   46
ethics   122–3
European Arrest Warrant (EAW)   323
European 'mega' exchange   69
European Union (EU)
  EAW   323
  Lamfalussy Process   337–8
  MiFID   17
  UK regulations   4–5
Europe, FSAP   324–5
EU *see* European Union
examples   315–42
  ARROW   320
  BASEL II/CRD   321–2
  capital adequacy   321–2, 334–5
  enforcement   336
  extradition   323
  FSAP   324–5
  global compliance   326–7
  industry guidance   328–9
  L&G *v.* FSA   330
  Lamfalussy Process   337–8
  MiFID   331–2
  money-laundering   333, 339
  principles-based regulations   317–19
  TCF   340–2
exchanges   64–9, 135
  benchmarking   65
  corporate fund raising   64
  corporate restructuring   65
  differentials   66–7
  internet   67–8
  liquidity   64, 69
  market place organization   65
  price discovery   65
  pseudo-exchanges   67–8
  regulations   65–9
  status   67
  strategizing   65
  trading   64
exclusivity   237–8, 286, 302
execution
  dilemmas   284–5, 305, 313
  Front Office   218–21, 226–7
external directors   258, 289
external service providers   60–1
extradition   323

fair treatment of customers   260, 301–2,
    313, 340–2
false transactions   156
fee payments to FSA   140–1
fictitious devices/deception   157
Finance department   261–2
Financial Ombudsman Service (FOS)   108,
    112, 117

financial promotions   108, 167–9, 231–2
financial sanctions   198
Financial Services Action Plan (FSAP)   4, 7,
       324–5
Financial Services Authority (FSA)   104–20
    anti-money-laundering   11
    applicability   5–8
    ARROW   320
    breaches   109–11, 115–20
    business types under FSMA/MiFID   8–11
    clearing houses   70
    Compliance function   17–19
    disciplinary action   112–14
    enforcement   104–20, 336
    exchanges   67
    fee payments   140–1
    Handbook   7, 17
    information gathering   104–9, 111–12
    L&G   330
    liaising with regulators   108, 112, 119
    MiFID   8–11, 331–2
    NatWest   3, 323
    powers above normal   107–8, 111–12
    principles-based regulations   317–19
    regulatory regimes   3, 5–13
    reporting   139–40
    serendipitous information   105, 108–9
    statutory objectives   104
    TCF   340–2
Financial Services and Markets
       Act (FSMA)   2000
    clearing houses   70
    enforcement   103–20
    exchanges   67
    insider dealing   154–5
    key legislation   71
    UK regulations   3, 5–8, 13
Financial Services and Markets Tribunal   113
fines   117–18
fitness and propriety issues   292, 295, 297, 311
flexibility of pseudo-exchanges   68
FOS (Financial Ombudsman Service)   108,
       112, 117
fraud   190
    Front Office   236–7
    Legal department   269
    Tax department   275
Front Office   83–4, 209–51
    aggregation of orders   225–6
    allocation of assets   225–6
    anti-money-laundering   235–6
    appropriateness   223–4
    Approved Persons   228–9
    best execution   218–20
    Chinese walls   247–8
    churning/switching   224–5

clients
    agreements   216–17
    best interest rule   214–15
    categorization   232–3
    communication   230–1
    limit orders   221
confidentiality   243–4
conflicts of interest   246
corporate finance   211
counter-terrorism   235–6
customer sales/trading   210–11
disclaimers to research   241–2
exclusivity   237–8
execution   218–20, 226–7
financial promotions   231–2
fraud prevention   236–7
inducements   229–30
insider lists   247
investment
    banking   211
    and borrowing   239
    committees   238–9
    management   211
issuing research   240–3
key rules/controls   212–51
KYC   233–4
market abuse   248–9
order/execution records   226–7
PA dealing   244–6
permissions   212–13
prompt execution   220–1
providing information   215–16
relations with Compliance   213–14
research   212, 240–3
restricted lists   248
rules   212–51
suitability   222
T&C   227–8
third party research   242–3
voice recording   230
watch lists   248
whistle-blowing   250–1
written policies/procedures   249–50
FSAP (Financial Services Action Plan)   4, 7,
       324–5
FSA see Financial Services Authority
FSMA see Financial Services and Markets Act
fund raising   64

global compliance   326–7
gut reactions   98

Handbook, FSA   7, 17
Human Resources (HR) department   256–9
Human Rights Act 1998   104, 114

improper disclosure 150–1
independence of research 294, 306–7
Independent Complaints Commissioner 113
individual guidance, FSA 115–16
inducements 165–7
    dilemmas 280–1, 289–90, 300–1, 305–7, 312
    Front Office 229–30
    Marketing department 260
industry developments 138
industry guidance 328–9
information
    disclosure 263
    gathering 50, 104–9, 111–12
    given by Front Office 215–16
    insider 150, 154–5
    misuse 151
    senior management 188–9
    terms of business 310
information gathering 50
    FSA 104–9, 111–12
        further powers 107–8, 111–12
        regular channels 104–7
        serendipitous methods 105, 108–9
informative examples see examples
injunctions, FSA 116
inside information 150, 154–5
insider dealing 150, 255
insider lists 159–60
    dilemmas 281–8, 292, 295, 308, 314
    Front Office 247
insolvency orders 117
inspections, FSA 107
integrity 122–3
Internal Audit 264–5
internal relations 128–9
The International Convergence of Capital
        Measurement and Capital Standards - A
        Revised Framework (Basel II) 321–2
International Organization of Securities
        Commission (IOSCO) 17
internet 67–8
interviews, FSA 111
investigations
    advisory work 89–91
    of firms 108
    formal FSA 112
investment
    banking 211
    and borrowing 239, 300
    business 5–8
    committees 238–9
    management 211
IOSCO (International Organization of Securities
        Commission) 17
IT department 265–8

JMLSG Guidance Notes 11, 110, 328
job satisfaction 38–40

knowledge, corporate 53–61
Know Your Customer (KYC) 200–3
    see also customers
    anti-money-laundering 195–7, 200–3
    dilemmas 280
    Front Office 233–4
    introductions
        from third parties 201–2
        to third parties 203
    new relationships 195–7
    reviews 200–1
    third parties completing on
        firm 202
    vetting 11
KYC see Know Your Customer

L&G mis-selling case 113–14
Lamfalussy Process 4, 7, 337–8
language, Charters 43
Legal department 268–9
Legal and General (L&G) 330
legislation 71–7
    categories 71
    overseas jurisdictions 77
    rules mapping 73–7
    UK 4–5
liquidity 64, 69
litigation 169
London Stock Exchange
        (LSE) 69

management
    see also senior management
    investment 211
    risk 72, 256
manual maintenance 123–4
market abuse 149–53
    device manipulation 151
    dilemmas 278–88, 292–3, 295, 301–2,
        304–8, 310–12, 314
    disseminating information 151
    Front Office 248–9
    improper disclosure 150–1
    insider dealing 150
    Marketing department 260
    misleading behaviour 151
    misuse of information 151
    preventative actions 152–3
    senior management 255
    transaction manipulation 151
market conduct 278–88, 292–3, 295, 301–2,
        304–8, 310–12, 314
market confidence 109

marketing
    the close   156
    exchanges   66
Marketing department   259–60
market-making systems   67
market manipulation   156–7
market place organization   65
Markets in Financial Instruments Directive
        (MiFID)   7, 8–11, 331–2
measurement of performance   46, 270
media   34, 108, 114
mediation   114
membership of professional bodies   141
mergers   12
MiFID (Markets in Financial Instruments
        Directive)   7, 8–11, 331–2,
misleading behaviour   151
misleading transactions   156
Mission Statements   41–2
misuse of information   151
mitigation programmes   72
MLRO reporting   206
modifications of rules   105
monetary benefits   34
money-laundering
    see also anti-money-laundering
    Operations department   271
    process   339
    statistics   333
    Tax department   275
    UK regulations   7–8
monitoring activities   191–4
More Principles-Based regulations (MPBR)
        317–19
mystery shopping   107

NASDAQ   69
NatWest 3 extradition case   323
new offices   182
non-regulatory bodies   63
Northern Rock mortgage provider   335
notification requirements   105–7
novation, clearing houses   70

Office of Public Sector Information
        website   72–3
Officers   17–24
    attributes   22–4
    benefits   30–7
    characteristics   22–4
    concept of compliance   18–20
    job satisfaction   38–40
    professional aspects   38–40
    responsibilities   21–2
ombudsman service, FOS   108, 112, 117
Operational Risk department   269–70

Operations department (Back Office)   271–4
opportunity costs   37–8
order and execution records   226–7
orders
    aggregation   225–6, 299, 303
    electronic order book   67
    handling   305
    insolvency   117
    limit   221
    order/execution records   226–7
    prohibition   116–17
    restitution   117
OTC (over the counter) trading   67
outsourcing   182–4
over the counter (OTC) trading   67
overseas jurisdictions   5, 13, 77
ownership concealment   157

painting the tape   156
Panel on Takeovers and Mergers   12
PA (personal account) dealing   162–5, 244–6,
        281–3, 287–8, 292, 301–2, 305–6, 308,
        311–12, 314
Part IV permission   105, 110, 113, 116
passporting   143–5
Patriot Act certificate   203–4
PEPs (politically exposed persons)   204–6
performance measurement   46, 270
permission   105, 110, 113, 116, 212–13
permitted activities   296, 299, 309
per se eligible counterparties   186–7
per se professional clients   186
personal account (PA) dealing   162–5, 244–6,
        281–3, 287–8, 292, 301–2, 305–6,
        308, 311–12, 314
Personnel department   256–9
Pillars, CRD   321–2
plans
    advisory work   96–8
    annual   129–30
    remedial   127–8
policies
    procedures   125–6, 249–50
    remuneration   290, 307
politically exposed persons (PEPs)   204–6
portfolio management   211
powers, Charters   45
price positioning   156–7
pricing, exchanges   65
principles-based regulations   88, 317–19
private warnings   118
procedures and policies   125–6, 249–50
products   79–82
professional aspects of compliance   38–40
professional clients   186
prohibition orders, FSA   116–17

project work   134–5
promotion   41–2, 108, 167–9, 231–2
prompt execution rule   220–1
propriety and fitness issues   292, 295, 297, 311
prosecutions, FSA   118
prudential regulation of capital adequacy   334–5
pseudo-exchanges   67–8
public censure   117
pump and dump, market manipulation   157

RAO   6–7, 10
record-keeping   181
    dilemmas   309–10
    IT department   265
    order/execution records   226–7
regulations
    advisory work   91–6
    agreements   145–6
    anti-money-laundering   11–12
    breaches   109–11, 115–20
    capital adequacy   334–5
    documentation   82
    enforcement   103–20
    exchanges   65–9
    inconsistencies   36–7
    new developments   138–9
    objectives   36
    principles-based   88, 317–19
    reasons for   36–7
    training   126–7
    UK environment   3–11
regulators   36–7, 63–70
    benefits of compliance   34
    clearing houses   70
    exchanges   64–9
    relationship management   135,
        296–7, 313
    visits   136–7
relationship management   135, 213–14,
    296–7, 313
remedial action plans   127–8
remuneration policies   290, 307
reporting
    actuaries' reports   105
    appointed representative   106
    auditors' reports   105
    controllers   106
    FSA   139–40
    MLRO   206
    requirements   105–7
    senior management   46
    skilled persons   112
    suspicious activity   199–200
    systems-based   194
    transactions   107
reputation   34, 120

research
    controls   314
    Front Office   212, 240–3
    independence   294, 306–7
    IT department   267
    Marketing department   260
responsibilities
    Charters   43, 45–6
    Officers   21–2
    operating entities   53–6
    senior management   18–20
restitution orders   117
restricted lists   160–2
    dilemmas   282–4, 286, 292, 295, 304–6, 308
    Front Office   248
retail clients   186
risk
    ARROW   320
    capital adequacy   334–5
    Charters   43
    concepts of compliance   16
    FSA assessment visits   107
    management   72, 256
    Operational Risk department   269–70
    regulatory register   131–4
    warnings   298
routine activities   87–8, 121–94
    advisory work   134–5
    agreements   145–6
    annual plan   129–30
    anti-money-laundering   195–207
    Approved Persons   174–7
    attestation   130
    breaches of rules   170–1
    charter maintenance   130
    Chinese walls   157–9
    client categorization   185–8
    conflicts of interest   146–9
    consultation papers   138
    corporate knowledge   180–1
    culture/ethics/integrity   122–3
    data protection   179–80
    disciplinary procedures   142–3
    documentation   145–6
    fees payment to FSA   140–1
    financial promotions   167–9
    fraud   190
    inducements   165–7
    industry developments   138
    insider dealing   150
    insider lists   159–60
    internal relations   128–9
    keeping up to date   141–2
    litigation   169
    management information   188–9
    manual maintenance   123–4

market abuse   149–53
market manipulation   156–7
membership of professional bodies   141
monitoring activities   191–4
new/non-standard transactions   177–8
new offices   182
new regulations   138–9
outsourcing   182–4
PA dealing   162–5
passporting   143–5
policies/procedures   125–6
project work   134–5
record-keeping   181
regulatory training   126–7
regulatory visits   136–7
relationship management   135
remedial action plans   127–8
reporting to FSA   139–40
restricted lists   160–2
risks register   131–4
rules mapping   138–9
service providers   137–8
supervision of group entities   131
T&C   171–4
voice-recording   178–9
watch lists   160–2
whistle-blowing   184–5
rules
breaches   115–20, 170–1
Front Office   212–51
mapping   73–7, 138–9
waivers/modifications   105
rules mapping   73–7, 138–9
bottom up approach   74–5
high/detailed levels   73–7
sample map   75–7
top down approach   74–5

sales   210–11
sanctions   198
scandals   31–3
scare tactics   103
search and seizure powers, FSA   112
senior management   83, 253–6
Charters   43
decision-making   97–8
dilemmas   295, 310
information flow   188–9
reporting to   46
responsibilities   18–20
TCF   340, 342
serendipitous information   105, 108–9
Serious Organized Crime Agency (SOCA)   267
service providers   60–1, 137–8
services   79–82
settlement   70

skilled person's report   112
small firms   329
SOCA (Serious Organized Crime Agency)   267
status of exchanges   67
statute law   4, 73
stock exchanges see exchanges
suitability requirements
dilemmas   279–81, 298–300, 307, 312
Front Office   222
Tax department   276
supervision issues   131, 310–11
support departments see Back Office and support
departments; departments
suspicious activity reporting   199–200
switching   224–5
systems-based reporting   194

T&C see training and competence
Takeover Code   12, 110
takeovers   12, 65, 110
taxation   82, 274–5
Tax department   274–5
TCF (Treating Customers Fairly)   260, 301–2,
313, 340–2
terrorism   11–12
see also counter-terrorism
trade associations   114, 329
trading   64, 82, 210–11
training and competence (T&C)   171–4
dilemmas   295–8, 309–11
Front Office   227–8
HR department   257
Operations department   272
TCF   341
training, regulatory   126–7
transactions
false/misleading   156
market abuse   151
new/non-standard   177–8
reporting   107
trash and cash, market manipulation   157
Treating Customers Fairly (TCF)   260, 301–2,
313, 340–2

UK see United Kingdom
UK Statute Law Database website   73
unenforceable agreements   119
Unfair Terms Regulations   110
United Kingdom (UK)   3–13
see also Financial Services Authority
anti-money laundering   11–12
enforcement   103–20
extradition   323
FSMA/investment   5–8
legislation   4–5
overseas jurisdictions   5, 13

UK *see* United Kingdom (*Continued*)
  principles-based regulations   317–19
  regulatory inconsistencies   36–7
  regulatory regimes   3–13
  scandals   31–3
  statute law database   73
  takeovers   12
United Nations (UN)   11
UN (United Nations)   9

venture capital   187
visits by regulators   136–7
voice recording   178–9
  dilemmas   285

  Front Office   230
  Operations department   273

waivers of rules   105
wash trades   156
watch lists   160–2
  dilemmas   282–4, 286, 292, 295, 304–6, 308
  Front Office   248
websites   72–3
whistle-blowing   184–5
  Front Office   250–1
  FSA discovery methods   109
  Operations department   274
written policies/procedures   249–50

Compiled by Indexing Specialists (UK) Ltd